Feminist Conversations

Reading
WOMEN
Writing

a series edited by
Shari Benstock and Celeste Schenck

Reading Women Writing is dedicated to furthering international feminist debate. The series publishes books on all aspects of feminist theory and textual practice. *Reading Women Writing* especially welcomes books that address cultures, histories, and experiences beyond first-world academic boundaries. A complete list of titles in the series appears at the end of this book.

Feminist Conversations

FULLER, EMERSON, AND THE PLAY OF READING

Christina Zwarg

Cornell University Press

ITHACA AND LONDON

First published 1995 by Cornell University Press

Printed in the United States of America

♾ The paper in this book meets the minimum requirements
of the American National Standard for Information Sciences—
Permanence of Paper for Printed Library Materials, ANSI Z39.48-1984

Library of Congress Cataloging-in-Publication Data

Zwarg, Christina, 1949–
    Feminist conversations : Fuller, Emerson, and the play of reading / Christina Zwarg.
        p.   cm.
    Includes bibliographical references (p.) and index.
    ISBN 0-8014-2872-6 (hardcover : alk. paper)
    ISBN 0-8014-8110-4 (paper : alk. paper)
    1. Fuller, Margaret, 1810–1850—Political and social views.   2. Emerson, Ralph
Waldo, 1803–1882—Political and social views.   3. Feminism and literature—United
States—History—19th century.   4. Women and literature—United States—History—
19th century.   5. Books and reading—United States—History—19th century.   I. Title.
PS2508.F44Z92   1994
818'.309—dc20   94-32185

For Billy

A timpani of chasms
—deep incisions—
beating through ivory and horn.

Contents

Acknowledgments

Conversations kept arriving and arriving, so many of them, the stuff of public and private intimacies, my own and those of Fuller and Emerson. They would arrive on the page and in the air, sometimes through letters and journals, at other moments through lectures and seminars. The sturdy conversations occurred as readily over the phone, on tape, in memory, and through dream. More fragile ones arose from messages written on paper too dear to be legible, or messages too dear or legible to be written on paper. The writing of this book is a tale rich in duets, many irretrievable, but as many sustained and thriving.

I thank Marjorie Kaufman, Ben Reid, Charlie Trout and Irving Bear for first stirrings. George Monteiro and Mari Jo Buhle offered substantial support at the earliest moments in my thinking about Fuller and Emerson. Reed College and the Vollum family provided crucial funding for summer trips to the Houghton Library at Harvard. I also thank Haverford College for granting time, money, and good fellowship. Sue and Kim Benston extended their care and wisdom in itinerant hours when both were sorely needed. The Mellon Foundation gave me a year at Harvard, where Marjorie Garber's Center for Literary Studies assisted in bringing conceptual shape to the book. Barbara Johnson's Theory seminar that year was particularly helpful and sharing the Harvard scene with Elin Diamond doubly so. Andy Parker gave me a wonderful opportunity to discuss early thoughts on Fuller and the task of the translator with his Amherst students. Over the years many students, but especially those in my Fuller-Emerson seminars at Harvard and Haverford, have enriched my passion for the dream of a common language.

Robert Hudspeth generously tendered manuscript copy of the Fuller letters. He also provided years of unwavering support. David Robinson, Joel Porte, and Martha Banta did the same. I cannot thank Richard Slotkin enough for his part as audience to the Fuller-Emerson story. Many drafts and conversations later, the final tale emerged. I am particularly indebted to him for his many careful readings. Both he and William Galperin have been attentive, challenging, and sympathetic readers of nearly every page of the book as it transformed from lecture to article to chapter. Nearly half of the text appeared previously in articles, and I am grateful to various editors for permission to reprint them here in part or revised form: "Emerson's 'Scene' before the Women: The Feminist Poetics of Paraphernalia," *Social Text* 18 (Winter 1987–88): 129–44; "Emerson as 'Mythologist' in the *Memoirs of Margaret Fuller Ossoli*," *Criticism* 31 (Summer 1989): 213–33; "Feminism in Translation: Margaret Fuller's Tasso," *Studies in Romanticism* 29 (Fall 1990): 463–90; "Womanizing Margaret Fuller: Theorizing a Lover's Discourse," *Cultural Critique* 16 (Fall 1990): 161–91; "Foot-noting the Sublime: Margaret Fuller on Black Hawk's Trail," *American Literary History* 5 (Winter 1993): 616–42; "Reading before Marx: Margaret Fuller and the *New-York Daily Tribune*," in *Readers in History: Nineteenth-Century American Literature and the Contexts of Response*, ed. James L. Machor (Baltimore: Johns Hopkins University Press, 1993), 228–58.

I have been fortunate as well to have the insightful suggestions of Bell Chevigny and Julie Ellison in the last stages of the writing. Joanne Hindman worked meticulously with me on the final edition, and I am truly in her debt.

Along the way, Homer's *Odyssey* and the poetry of Michael Harper sustained me, as did the conversation of Roger Porter, Tina and Bill Vanech, Tim Gould, Arabella Lyon, Jane Caplan, Sid Waldman, Randy Milden, Joe Russo, Bella Brodsky, Wyatt MacGaffey, and Janet Leskawa. I spent many important hours in the garden, talking over the fence with Elizabeth, Armand, Pete, Denys, Joyce, Joe, and Tony. Lion-hearted support came from Leslie Mechanic, Elin Diamond, Robert Lowe, Mitchell Wiggins, and especially from David Sachs, whose ministrations were both phantastic and writerly.

Feminist Conversations was conceived through an exquisite entanglement of family stories, including those of my grandparents—Mildred Byram, Ella Ockelmann, Leopold Zwarg, and Ross Fishburn. Without question, the most musical and beautiful voices belong to my parents, Nancy and Walter.

Perhaps no one knows better than William Galperin how hard it has been to arrive at this moment. The intimate and unique conversation we have been cradling between us for decades enlivens whatever of substance may lie within these pages.

CHRISTINA ZWARG

Philadelphia

Abbreviations and Editions Cited

Margaret Fuller

LMF   *The Letters of Margaret Fuller*, 6 vols. Ed. Robert N. Hudspeth. Ithaca: Cornell University Press, 1983–1995.

MMF   *Memoirs of Margaret Fuller Ossoli*, 2 vols. Ed. R. W. Emerson, W. H. Channing, and J. F. Clarke. Boston: Phillips, Sampson, 1884. Reprint, New York: Burt Franklin, 1972.

WNC   *Woman in the Nineteenth Century*. A facsimile of the 1845 edition, with an introduction by Madeleine B. Stern, textual apparatus by Joel Myerson. Columbia, S.C.: University of South Carolina Press, 1980.

Ralph Waldo Emerson

CW   *The Collected Works of Ralph Waldo Emerson*. 4 vols (to date). Ed. Robert Spiller et al. Cambridge: Belknap Press, Harvard University Press, 1971–.

EL   *The Letters of Ralph Waldo Emerson*, 8 vols. Vols. 1–6 ed. Ralph L. Rusk. Vols. 7–8 ed. Eleanor M. Tilton. New York: Columbia University Press, 1964; 1990, 1991.

JMN   *The Journals and Miscellaneous Notebooks of Ralph Waldo Emerson*, 16 vols. Ed. William Gillman et al. Cambridge: Belknap Press, Harvard University Press, 1960–1982.

W   *The Complete Works of Ralph Waldo Emerson*, 12 vols. Ed. Edward Waldo Emerson. Centenary Edition. Boston: Houghton Mifflin, 1903–1904.

Feminist Conversations

Introduction: Fuller, Emerson, and the Task of Reading

> My prospectus runs thus I believe. History, *languages*, literature.—
> Whatever I please or whatever I think best synonymizing with
> this.
>
> —Margaret Fuller, LMF 1: 276

> History is a vanishing allegory . . . and repeats itself to tedious-
> ness, a thousand & a million times. The *Rape of the Sabines* is per-
> petual, and the fairest Sabine virgins are every day pounced upon
> by rough victorious Romans, masquerading under mere New
> Hampshire & Vermont & Boston names, as Webster, Choate,
> Thayer, Bigelow or other obscurity.
>
> —Ralph Waldo Emerson, JMN 11: 435

Our literary history has deeply denied the conversation between Sarah Margaret Fuller and Ralph Waldo Emerson. Whereas Emerson has
always been at the center of a continuous and extraordinarily diverse
body of scholarship, Fuller, well known and widely read during her
lifetime, has remained nearly lost to the critical world of the twentieth
century. To be sure, the dramatic text of Fuller's life has always generated reader interest; new biographies have appeared with rhythmic reg-
ularity since her death in a shipwreck in 1850. But because her provocative personal narrative, with its cosmopolitan scale and power, has
remained the central focus of scholarly attention, the bulk of her writing
continues to remain veiled in mystery or misreading. This devaluation
of Fuller's work allowed Emerson scholars to depict Fuller as a colorful
but marginal influence despite the intense literary interaction with her
that we find recorded in his journals and letters.[1] Perhaps because femi-

---

[1] Two articles are notable exceptions: Carl F. Strauch, "Hatred's Swift Repulsions: Emer-
son, Margaret Fuller, and Others," *Studies in Romanticism* 7 (Winter 1968): 65–103; and
Henry R. Warfel, "Margaret Fuller and Ralph Waldo Emerson," PMLA 50 (June 1935):
576–94. For an interesting dismissal of the relationship see Julie Ellison, *Delicate Subjects:
Romanticism, Gender, and the Ethics of Understanding* (Ithaca: Cornell University Press, 1990).
See also Dorothy Berkson, "Born and Bred in Different Nations: Margaret Fuller and Ralph
Waldo Emerson" in *Patrons and Protégées: Gender, Friendship, and Writing in Nineteenth-
Century America*, ed. Shirley Marchalonis (New Brunswick: Rutgers University Press,
1988), 3–30; Susan B. Smith, "The Liberal Air of All the Zones: Another View of the
Emerson-Fuller Relationship," CCTE Proceedings 52 (September 1987): 28–35; Marie

nist critics needed to accept this hierarchical conception of their friendship in order to condemn it, they too have been reluctant to explore the
Fuller-Emerson relationship.[2] In a sense, American feminist critics no
less than conventional critics have depended upon two traditions to
make their case: one masculine and self-obsessed and one feminine,
subversive, and polyphonic; one written by men, the other by women;
one paradoxically more traditional in its preference for experimental
form, one paradoxically more radical in its use of traditional sentimental
and novelistic form to further a subversive political agenda. Fuller did
not, of course, write fiction, but instead entered the Emersonian ground
of anticanonical form. And because of the kind of writing that she
produced—translations, criticism, journalism, and history—she vastly
complicates our interpretation both of the feminist tradition in America
and that tradition in general.

I argue in this book that Fuller's significance as a feminist and as a
theorist can be revealed through a serious consideration of her relationship with Emerson; the exquisite entanglement of these two powerful
and distinctive voices produced "conversations" spanning a broader
cultural register than previously understood by those determined to
keep certain intellectual and cultural projects worlds apart.

Rethinking Feminism

Throughout this book I use the word *feminism* provisionally, since it is
a term still very much in embattled conversation with itself. The last
twenty years have witnessed numerous feminist readings in literary
studies, though with the flourishing of feminist criticism disagreements
have developed between those inclined to view feminism as a way to

---

Olesen Urbanski, "The Ambivalence of Ralph Waldo Emerson toward Margaret Fuller,"
Thoreau Journal Quarterly 10 (1978): 26–36; Ann Douglas's chapter on Fuller in her *Feminiza-
tion of American Culture* (New York: Alfred A. Knopf, 1977), 259–88; Jeffrey Steele's chap-
ters on Emerson and Fuller in his *Representation of the Self in the American Renaissance*
(Chapel Hill: University of North Carolina Press, 1987); Eric Cheyfitz, *The Trans-Parent:
Sexual Politics in the Language of Emerson* (Baltimore: Johns Hopkins University Press, 1981);
Erik Ingvar Thurin, *Emerson as Priest of Pan* (Lawrence, Kans.: The Regents Press of Kansas,
1981); and George Sebouhian, "A Dialogue with Death: An Examination of Emerson's
'Friendship,'" *Studies in the American Renaissance*, ed. Joel Myerson (Boston: Twayne, 1990),
219–39.
[2] See, for example, Paula Blanchard's chapter, "Emerson and Alcott," in *Margaret Fuller:
From Transcendentalism to Revolution*, Merloyd Lawrence Book (Reading, Mass.: Addison-
Wesley, 1978), 98–117.

recover a narrative about woman's experience and those focusing on the theoretical assumptions underlying the expression of such experience. Alice Jardine was among the earliest to argue persuasively for a dialogue between the various forms of feminist criticism developing throughout Europe and North America in this period.[3] And with the work of Gayatri Spivak and others, this call for an enlarged view of feminist strategies has broadened to include the challenging discourses of the Third World.[4] As the inevitable tensions and disciplinary tendencies have begun to emerge, some critics have even begun to argue that we are entering a "postfeminist" stage. Although this last seems doubtful, we must still recognize that the current usage of the word *feminism* no longer necessarily enhances our understanding of the deep critical issues implied by the term.

How did writers like Fuller and Emerson address feminist issues without having one word to encompass them? What does it mean for us now to call Fuller a feminist? The answers to these questions will help us to understand the extent to which Emerson's work also participates in a type of feminist (if unnameable) discourse.[5] The range of issues and problems engaged by Fuller and Emerson may return us to ourselves in compelling and productive ways by recovering forms that have been lost to feminism through the very act of naming them. This process of recovery, played out in the conversation between these two literary figures, is central to my project.

Conversation is a term often associated with both Fuller and Emerson, though in separate and distinctive ways. Fuller was well known for her conversational skills; Emerson more than once called her the most gifted conversationalist in America, and accounts of her life invariably emphasize this attribute. Though her friends insisted that Fuller's conversation never found adequate expression in her writing, one cannot survey her career without noticing her incessant theoretical return to the process of conversation. For example, she called her seminars for women "Conversations"; moreover, conversation became central to her larger feminist orientation, particularly the revised theory of pedagogy and reading so vital to her later work. The early stages of her feminism emerge through

---

[3] Alice Jardine, *Gynesis: Configurations of Women and Modernity* (Ithaca: Cornell University Press, 1985). See also Toril Moi, *Sexual/Textual Politics: Feminist Literary Theory* (London: Methuen, 1985).

[4] Gayatri Chakravorty Spivak, *In Other Worlds: Essays in Cultural Politics* (New York: Methuen, 1987).

[5] Alice Rossi argues that the word *feminism* was "rarely used in the mid–nineteenth century and referred simply to the 'quality of females.'" See *The Feminist Papers: From Adams to de Beauvoir*, ed. Alice Rossi (New York: Columbia University Press, 1973), xii.

her selective reading and translation of works by several German authors, most notably Goethe's *Tasso* (where the conversation of women is given an important critical status), Eckermann's *Conversations with Goethe*, and two epistolary novels by Bettina von Arnim, *Goethe's Correspondence with a Child* and *Die Günderode*. Fuller's focus sharpens around the site of rereading—a potential feminist space—and widens through the conversational process elaborated in each. In the same way, conversation informs the development of her two most famous publications, *Summer on the Lakes* and *Woman in the Nineteenth Century*. And, as we shall see, Fuller's conversation with Emerson both heightens and influences this ongoing critical enterprise.

Throughout his career, Emerson also sustained an interest in the concept of conversation, even if in the estimation of his critics that interest is internal to the very structure of his thought. Stanley Cavell, for example, has characterized all of Emerson's writing as a "battle to remain in conversation with itself, answerable to itself."[6] Although some critics have acknowledged Fuller's influence over Emerson's understanding and deployment of conversation, few have discerned the specifically feminist components of that influence. Realizing that Fuller's feminism emerged and developed before the word *feminism* itself, however, we can see how certain attributes of Emerson's work may also depend on a type of philosophical engagement with feminism *before the letter*. His conversations with Fuller are the clue to understanding the various attributes of that engagement.

"Placing" Margaret Fuller

Not surprisingly, a parallel exists between today's confusion over the word *feminism* and the confused sense of Margaret Fuller's value that has emerged in the critical discourse about her. The experience of reading about Fuller can be as unsettling as the experience of reading Melville in his late parodic phase. Readers familiar with *The Confidence-Man* (1857) will remember Goneril as one of Melville's most undecidable characterizations: her features seem to evaporate from every sentence used to speak of her manner and appearance. According to R. W. B. Lewis, the "whole tone, purpose and strategy" of the novel can be found in the sentences describing Goneril, "with their parade of notations and

[6] Stanley Cavell, *The Senses of Walden: An Expanded Edition* (San Francisco: North Point Press, 1981), 134.

counter-notations," together with their "final flurry of phrases that modify, hesitantly contradict, and then utterly cancel one another."[7] As anyone who has reviewed the literature on Fuller can testify, this same
evasive style of writing, bordering on a parody of deconstructive writing, pervades the critical discourse of her work. The question remains:
Why should this be so?

Certainly, in the past twenty years, American feminists have attempted to attribute the harshly critical style—used with equal frequen-
cy in discussions of Fuller's life and writing—to the misogyny of her
narrators. But, like the word *feminism*, the word *misogyny* may be worth
reconsidering, for even the lethal hostility of the misognynistic enterprise cannot veil its core dissatisfaction with the normative image of
woman, a dissatisfaction shared by most feminists. The assumption that
misogyny functions as the primary motive behind the contradictory
image of Fuller reigning in critical work about her, though initially useful and important, finally tends to close down interpretive possibilities.
Using the concept of misogyny without examination is merely another
way to reduce the critical complexities of the moment, particularly the
cultural imperatives at play in the concept. Moreover, such a reading
obscures the fact that even sympathetic accounts of Fuller are marked by
unstable images of her. That women were as capable as men of developing these curious portraits makes the critical problem still more acute.

Fuller was unconventional in nearly every respect: in her appearance,
her manner, her thinking, and in her writing. Every effort to frame her in
conventionality results in a destabilization of that frame. I believe that
she remains largely unread by most feminists today because this odd
instability rings throughout all of the critical and biographical treat-
ments of her. One might argue that the "body image" of Fuller which we
have been given in portraits of her constitutes an allegory for the critical
image deployed on the body of Fuller's work: in both there is a perpetual confusion and absence of certainty. Fuller was not conventionally
beautiful, and descriptions of her are radically contradictory. Julia Ward
Howe's description of Fuller's neck in the early pages of her 1884 biography *Margaret Fuller* (*Marchesa Ossoli*) typifies the treatment she has
received from sympathetic readers. According to Howe, "in moments of
tender or pensive feeling" the curves of Fuller's neck "were like those of
a swan," whereas her movements "under the influence of indigna-

---

[7] R. W. B. Lewis, "Afterword," in his edition of Melville's *Confidence-Man: His Masquer-
ade* (New York: New American Library, 1964), 265. The character of Goneril in Melville's
The Confidence-Man (1857) may well be a critique of the portraits of Fuller that emerged just
after her death in 1850.

tion . . . were more like the swoopings of a bird of prey."[8] Of course, many women in history have suffered from this type of contradictory portrayal. Still, those who have suffered as consistently as Margaret Fuller warrant particular attention.

As the proliferation of biographies shows, Fuller broke with tradition throughout her life.[9] Born in 1810, she was the first child of Timothy Fuller and received from him the rigorous education in languages and history usually restricted to male children. It was not then common for young girls to declaim upon their lessons, yet Fuller expected his daughter to do so daily. The combination of her own natural talents and her father's aggressive support meant that Fuller achieved a high level of proficiency early in her schooling. Although institutions of higher learning were closed to women, she was an accomplished and omnivorous reader, and found herself well placed in the company of Harvard students, some of whom she actually tutored. At the time of her meeting with Emerson in 1836, she had already taught herself German and had become, by Emerson's admission, one of the most advanced readers of German literature in America.

Fuller was unconventional in selecting the languages she learned as well as the works she translated. The rigid hostility toward German literature in New England, particularly the harsh critique of Goethe fashionable in many intellectual circles there, made her translation and defense of Goethe's work an extraordinary act. This same bold use of translation as a form of social intervention continued during her tenure as a journalist for Horace Greeley's *New-York Daily Tribune*, where she translated one of the first notices of Marx and Engels in the United States from a German immigrant newspaper. Indeed, because Marx began to publish in the *Tribune* shortly after her death (and because he initially

---

[8] Julia Ward Howe, *Margaret Fuller (Marchesa Ossoli)*, Famous Women Series (Boston: Roberts Brothers, 1884), 89. Howe is paraphrasing William Henry Channing's description of Fuller; her decision to do so is as problematic as it is interesting.

[9] MMF; Thomas Wentworth Higginson, *Margaret Fuller Ossoli*, American Men of Letters Series (Boston: Houghton Mifflin, 1884); Howe, *Margaret Fuller*; Katherin Anthony, *Margaret Fuller: A Psychological Portrait* (Carby, Pa.: Darby Books, 1920); Margaret Bell, *Margaret Fuller* (New York: Albert & Charles Boni, 1930); Mason Wade, *Margaret Fuller: Whetstone of Genius* (New York: Viking, 1940); Madeleine B. Stern, *The Life of Margaret Fuller* (New York: E. P. Dutton, 1942); Faith Chipperfield, *In Quest of Love: The Life and Death of Margaret Fuller* (New York: Coward-McCann, 1957); Arthur W. Brown, *Margaret Fuller*, United States Author Series (New York: Twayne Publishers, 1964); Joseph Jay Deiss, *The Roman Years of Margaret Fuller* (New York: Thomas Y. Crowell, 1969); Paula B. Blanchard, *Margaret Fuller: From Transcendentalism to Revolution*, Merloyd Lawrence Book (Reading, Mass.: Addison-Wesley, 1978); Margaret Vanderhaar Allen, *The Achievement of Margaret Fuller* (University Park: Penn State University Press, 1979); and Charles Capper, *Margaret Fuller: An American Romantic Life*, Vol. 1, *The Private Years* (New York: Oxford University Press, 1992).

needed the assistance of a translator for this endeavor), it is tempting to imagine the interaction that might have developed between the two, especially given how thoroughly imbricated translation and social issues are in Fuller's work. Her first official publication was a letter to the editor of a newspaper in which she took issue with the methodolgy of the well-known historian George Bancroft. Her later, more mature publications tended to follow the same bold character: all were unhampered by convention and prepared to question the frame through which historical issues are formulated.

This provocative intellectual style no doubt accounts for some of the highly unstable critical judgments that have been made upon Fuller's work. Ladbroke Lionel Day Black understood the unsettling nature of Fuller's work when in 1931 he wrote his book *Some Queer People* and included chapters on Fuller and Poe as two writers who should be placed next to the likes of Benedict Arnold and King William IV.[10] And in 1904 Fuller and Nietzsche were rather intriguingly linked by the oculist George Gould in a study entitled *Biographic Clinics*. Gould's analysis is beautifully skewed by an alternating respect and disdain for the work of both writers. Recognizing that they were each prodigious readers, Gould theorized that the dangerous direction taken in their work as well as the calamitous deaths experienced by both were due to the egregious force of "eyestrain."[11] The bizarre relationship of body and text in Gould's reading generates some wonderful effects: even Fuller's fatal shipwreck at the age of forty is linked to the poor eye care that she received in the early nineteenth century. Gould's charmingly self-serving theme almost allows us to forget the more intriguing impetus behind his thesis: his presumption, however botched by the optic lenses through which he invites us to stare, that we are what we read.

The odd literary history surrounding the works of authors such as Poe, Fuller, and Nietzsche suggests that something embedded in their work interrupts the usual commodification process of literary history which invariably turns the defamiliarizing capacities of a work (and its radical critique of cultural discourse) into something familiar, habitual, traditional.[12] Thus the erratic critical industry around Fuller's work, particularly the extraordinary critical denigration that attends and

[10] *Some Queer People* (London: S. Low, Marston, 1931).

[11] Gould wrote that both Fuller and Nietzsche were gifted "with a power of absorbing knowledge scarcely equaled in the world." George Milbry Gould, *Biographic Clinics*, vol. 2 (Philadelphia: P. Blakiston's Son, 1904), 280.

[12] For an interesting examination of this process see John Frow, *Marxism and Literary History* (Cambridge: Harvard University Press, 1986), especially his chapters "Text and System" and "Limits: The Politics of Reading."

seems to motivate much of it, provides what Shoshana Felman, borrowing from pyschoanalytic discourse, would call a "case history" of literary history.[13]

Fuller was, of course, Poe's contemporary and at times the subject (as opposed to the object) of his work. She functions in the nineteenth century as the "reader" of the men around her, of their "unconscious," to use Lacan's formulation. And in her reading of Emerson (and Emerson's reading of her) we can find our way back to Nietzsche. My interests, however, are less with her reading effect on nineteenth-century writers than with her attempt to reach the broader culture with a revisionary reading procedure. This persistent attempt to provide a radical theory of reading pervades all of her writing and provides the clue to her significance for our understanding of Emerson's development and of the theoretical foundations of feminist criticism today.

Fuller and the Task of Reading

Because Fuller initiates her "feminism" through her reading—which is to say, through the activity of translation and literary criticism, shifting only then to a theory of history as an *act* of reading—she is valuable both to our understanding of American literary history and to the complex history of feminist criticism of which she is a part. The direction of her thinking oddly anticipates the feminist negotiation with the theoretical turns of deconstruction and helps to show how feminists in the United States, who are now turning to this European framework, are in many ways returning to their own theoretical legacy.

Fuller's history also provides a narrative about the conflicting imperatives developing in feminist criticism. The early emphasis on her life tended to support the critical inclination of those critics interested in recovering the "experience" of women, but her writing could not readily be interpreted through the same intellectual frame, in part because of the strong theoretical focus of her work. Thus a reconciliation of her life and work helps to provide a reconciliation of the schism between theoretical and historical concerns in contemporary feminist criticism.

Fuller's intense interest in reading situates her in a discursive field actively identified today as reader response criticism. Even so, Fuller's approach challenges the markers of that discourse in vital ways. Jon-

---

[13] See her interesting discussion of Poe, "Renewing the Practice of Reading, or Freud's Unprecedented Lesson," in her *Jacques Lacan and the Adventure of Insight* (Cambridge: Harvard University Press, 1987), 31.

athan Culler's chapters "Reading as a Woman" and "Stories of Reading" in *On Deconstruction* are most useful here. His reformulation of Shoshana Felman's question "Is it enough to be a woman in order to speak like a woman?" to "Is it enough to be a woman in order to read like a woman?" is answered ambiguously by Fuller.[14] If one can speak firmly about history (and Fuller is aware of some of the difficulties of doing so), one fact of history that Fuller depends on is that women were most often *positioned* as readers of the culture even when they were kept from the literal practices of writing. She refuses to adopt the position of the "resisting reader" as articulated by Judith Fetterley because she believes that such resistance is already an *obligation* of many Western texts. For Fuller, the text of experience and history is one that can be read through an understanding of the enormous gap within the process of reading itself.[15]

That Fuller is perhaps one of the best-known, least-read critics and authors of the nineteenth century is, I argue, the ironic byproduct of her own astute examination of the process of reading that I describe. Her work as editor for the *Dial*, the literary journal of the so-called transcendentalists, is often remarked upon, but few readers have made a serious effort to analyze the work generated there. Her book reviews alone are worth examining for the complex theory of reading that she developed while an editor.[16] Of course, she is best known for an essay that grew out of one of her contributions to the *Dial*, *Woman in the Nineteenth Century*, yet even this document has had a troubled critical career. Traditional literary critics have dismissed it as a "feminist tract," and some early feminist critics have found it unsatisfying in its failure to supply the "foundational" feminist argument they apparently were seeking.[17] Fuller's elaborate accretion of literary allusion in this essay has made

[14] Jonathan Culler, *On Deconstruction: Theory and Criticism after Structuralism* (Ithaca: Cornell University Press, 1982), 49. Shoshana Felman, "Women and Madness: The Critical Phallacy," *Diacritics* 5 (1975): 3.

[15] Judith Fetterley, *The Resisting Reader: A Feminist Approach to American Fiction* (Bloomington: Indiana University Press, 1978). See also Jonathan Culler, *On Deconstruction*, p. 67: "To read is to operate with the hypothesis of a reader, and there is always a gap or division within reading."

[16] One notable exception is the work of Joel Myerson, *The New England Transcendentalists and the "Dial": A History of the Magazine and Its Contributors* (Madison, N.J.: Fairleigh Dickinson University Press, 1980).

[17] An active rebuttal to this position has been made by Marie Urbanski in *Margaret Fuller's "Woman in the Nineteenth Century": A Literary Study of Form and Content, of Sources and Influence* (Westport, Conn.: Greenwood Press, 1980). See also David Robinson, "Margaret Fuller and the Transcendental Ethos: *Woman in the Nineteenth Century*," PMLA 97 (January 1982): 83–98. More recently two readings have defended the theoretical sophistication of *Woman*: Jeffrey Steele, *The Representation of the Self*; and Julie Ellison, *Delicate Subjects*.

some critics fearful that her feminism is too textual in focus and thus too far removed from the bounds of history.

There is also confusion about just what constitutes the Fuller canon. *Summer on the Lakes* is considered her first book even though it was written eleven years after she completed her first book-length translation of Goethe's *Tasso*, the first of at least three important translations she would complete before writing *Summer*. Here again Fuller forces us to relinquish our tidy critical categories: her translations are arguably as original as her work in *Summer*, though to insist upon this comparison is to stay trapped within the somewhat useless idea of originality. Better, I think, to focus on the way in which *Summer* modulates the critical enterprise first initiated in her translation of *Tasso* and developed through her translation of Eckermann's *Conversations with Goethe* and Bettina von Arnim's *Die Günderode*.

As my reading of these translations will show, Fuller's position as a reader is complicated by her gender, though in ways that could not have been predicted for this period. Unlike most American women of the day, Fuller was rigorously trained in a series of classical languages, and this training clearly widened her access to history, if only in the range of historical texts available to her. But it also widened her access to history by setting into motion a transvaluation of the historical itself. For Fuller, the historical became radically enmeshed in the process of reading. Thus, when hired in 1844 to review books and artistic public performances (dramas, concerts, and lectures) for the *Tribune*, she immediately extended the review format to include essays that amounted to her reading of the culture.

Fuller's skill in languages, her tireless reading, her interest in translation and artifacts of high and low culture are precisely the tools that enabled her to develop what is undoubtedly a radical social perspective. Thus, far from anticipating the formalist argument that holds the literary text to be radical because of its destabilizing potential, her writing shows her struggling to reorganize our understanding of the literary by expanding its range. In her work, the focus of the literary becomes not the text alone in isolation, but the text in play with the reader. And her concern, moreover, is with the balance of power within that dialogic structure.

Fuller's engagement with such theoretical issues may help to explain why even books such as Bell Gale Chevigny's important and groundbreaking 1976 collection, *The Woman and the Myth*, ultimately prove unsatisfactory.[18] Chevigny's text anthologizes material written by and

---

[18] Bell Gale Chevigny, *The Woman and the Myth: Margaret Fuller's Life and Writings* (Boston: Northeastern University Press, 1994).

about Fuller in an effort to establish her representative nature: rather than conceiving of Fuller as unique, Chevigny attempts to historicize her by showing the ideological pressures exerting themselves on all women of her class. The problem with Chevigny's approach is not that it once again supplies many conflicting images, but that it too quickly assumes Fuller's diversity of vision to be the consequence of ideological pressure, making the fragmented nature of her image the product of political deformation. Such a position causes Chevigny to devalue her early work, which, she argues, was ultimately marred by this same process of deformation.

Despite the recognition that Fuller felt "herself divided into separate selves," the frame that Chevigny uses to analyze this sense of fragmentation foreshortens her interpretive range. Uneasy with both the contradictory images of Fuller and the paradoxical nature of her early writing career, Chevigny sets out to narrate Fuller's "progress" toward a unified and therefore liberated "identity." By Chevigny's account, Fuller gains this sense of identity after she leaves the ideological constraints of America to travel in Europe, eventually involving herself in the Italian Revolution.[19] Chevigny's reading here depends on two assumptions that have now become problematic for feminists such as Jardine and Spivak; that is, it assumes the possibility of escape from ideology and with it the achievement of an undivided sense of identity. Although this interpretation has the effect of turning Fuller into a revolutionary figure in an old-fashioned sense, among the negative effects of Chevigny's approach is the neutralization of Fuller's actual writing career. Ironically, such an approach places emphasis on the work that we literally cannot read: Fuller's history of the Italian Revolution, which was lost in the very seas that took her life.

It may well be that until recently feminists working in the field of American literature have simply lacked the reading strategies adequate to cope with the kind of instability provoked by Fuller's writing. For we have only now begun to understand the radical instability working its way through the meaning of feminism itself. I believe that these shifting images, tending toward what Chevigny has called "distortion," were motivated as much by Fuller in her time as by her reviewers.[20] The ensemble we call Fuller (her life and her work) reads like an indecipherable text because she participated in its production. This assertion is not quite the same as saying that Fuller willfully produced conflicting images of herself; rather it suggests that throughout her life she actively

[19] Chevigny, *The Woman and the Myth*, p. 22.

[20] Ibid., p. 8. "Given the distorting intensity of the response to Fuller, the unusually poor condition of her papers, and the ambiguity of much of her writing, all interpretations must be partly speculative."

participated in a series of cultural negotiations that constitute the type of resistance—sometimes contradictory in nature—that lends meaning to the word *feminism* today.

Agency and the Subject of Feminism

Fuller's cultural negotiations are vital to the concept of agency as it has been developed by theorists who are trying to find a way to reconcile without affirming the subject of humanist discourse with the decentered subject of poststructuralism. At stake in this struggle is the very possibility of political resistance, a key concern for feminist critics in particular. Jardine and Spivak contend that influential and important critics such as Derrida and Lacan have radically blurred (for better and for worse) the traditional focus of feminist inquiry by challenging the humanist conception of woman's experience. Rather than despairing over the conflict between critics favoring the somewhat older concept of "woman as sexual identity" (or humanist subject) and those who prefer to consider the idea of "woman as process" (under the influence of poststructuralism), however, Jardine and Spivak argue persuasively for a continuous negotiation between these two positions.[21] For Paul Smith this "double strategy" of feminist criticism constitutes a particularly powerful form of political resistance.[22] Smith's reading is a useful one to examine for a moment, since he acknowledges a debt to those feminists who have insisted that some conception of a singular history or subjectivity is necessary for the recovery of agency in political resistance. Accepting this premise, Smith contends that it is still possible to consider the notion of a radically divided subject without losing the significance of the subject's singular history. To accomplish this, Smith invests the Althusserian notion of ideology with a still richer Lacanian complexity.

Louis Althusser is best known for his radical reformulation of the Marxist concept of ideology. By his account, there is no escape from ideological formation, since representation itself, the language through which we think ourselves, is the primary instrument of social reality. In his work, ideology is important to the constitution of the individual; individuals are "interpellated" as subjects in much the same way that an individual might be hailed in the street with the call "Hey, you there." Smith draws upon this idea of interpellation to distinguish between the

---

[21] Jardine, *Gynesis*, p. 41; Spivak, *In Other Worlds*, p. 241.
[22] Paul Smith, *Discerning the Subject* (Minneapolis: University of Minnesota Press, 1988).

subject and agent of ideology: for him the subject is "the term inaccurately used to describe what is actually the series or the conglomeration of positions, subject-positions, provisional and not necessarily indefeasible, into which a person is called momentarily by the discourses of the world that he / she inhabits." By contrast, the agent marks "a form of subjectivity where, by virtue of the contradictions and disturbances in and among [these various] subject-positions, the possibility (indeed, the actuality) of resistance to ideological pressure" is generated.[23] Smith achieves this distinction by returning to the Lacanian idea that "subjectivity is always a product of the symbolic in an instance of discourse." That is, because Lacanian subjectivity is "constructed as a process" and is continuous, it "leaves room for a consideration of subjectivity as contradictory, as structured in divisions and thus as never the solidified effect of discursive or ideological pressures."[24]

Recovering Fuller's Agency

This dispersion of subjectivity which can result in agency can help us to understand how the odd shape of Fuller's life and work demonstrates a particular form of political resistance. Our understanding of Fuller is radically overdetermined by what John Mowitt calls a "conflict of interpellations."[25] For the difficulty that critics encounter in their study of Fuller's career, both personal and critical, is a measure of the complex series of negotiations demanded by her position in the culture. Chevigny's admirable attempt to contend with these negotiations ultimately places too much emphasis on Fuller's political deformation in America. By Chevigny's account, Fuller is the subject of a specific ideological formation. Still, she is not merely the subject of her ideological moment, but also a radicalizing agent of the same. The task of reading these moments of agency in her life and work is the challenge Fuller's writing sets before feminist critics, and indeed all critics, today.

Like some of our contemporary feminists, Fuller consistently adopts a double strategy, one that emerges in many forms, including her interest in translation, her focus on the benefits of conversation, and in her growing fascination with the discourse of the French utopian Charles Fourier. Her choice of literary form—as well as the very form of her literary production—therefore is unconventional. In *The Feminization of*

---

[23] Smith, *Discerning the Subject*, p. xxxv.

[24] Ibid., p. 22.

[25] John Mowitt, "Foreword: The Resistance in Theory," in Paul Smith, *Discerning the Subject*, p. xix.

American Culture Ann Douglas characterized Fuller's "disavowal of fiction" as a powerful recognition of the feminization (and therefore weakening) of that literary form. Yet Douglas's characterization creates a needless polarization: a kind of polemical disturbance in the engendering of genres that would have bewildered Fuller.[26] Fuller's primary literary format is the critique, and her decision not to write fiction is a sign of her pressing desire to engage in a critical discourse about all forms of writing. She enjoyed fiction as much as any other genre; her tastes were remarkably eclectic because of a desire to uncover in writing, her own and that of others, a sense of what we would now call agency—intelligent political resistance to the codes of her culture.

Because Fuller's writing is densely theoretical in orientation, while her subject matter remains rooted in familiar humanistic terms, the result will be something of a disappointment to those who privilege one form over the other. The persistent desire to maintain a tidy narrative about Fuller's "emancipation" in Italy, for example, prevents critics from seeing the radical potential throughout her work. But those more comfortable with the multiplicity of concerns and determinations through which she consistently had to negotiate may see in her career a range and subtlety that anticipate and inform the double strategy of feminist discourse today.

Rethinking Emerson

Fuller's relationship with Emerson is the key to opening to view a primary set of interpellations. Chevigny's resistance to Fuller's early work—for example, the writing produced when she was still very much in contact with Emerson—is also a resistance to Emerson. As such, it reveals how some feminist critics depend on Emerson even when they choose to shun him in the formulation of their literary history. I do not argue either with or against that dependency so much as I deploy and exploit it by subduing the unquestioned assumption that Emerson constitutes the negative or (to use terms affiliated with Emerson) the "fatal" pole of Fuller's early career. Her relationship with Emerson is complex, mutually empowering and interactive. As long as we continue to view her interaction with him suspiciously, we underestimate her ability to do the same. Worse, we devalue the larger role that she plays in his work and in the intellectual debates and trends that develop in conversation with his thinking.

These trends in the Emersonian tradition are not incidental; indeed,

[26] Douglas, *The Feminization of American Culture*, p. 259.

we continue to find ourselves locked into patterns formalized through them. Yet today's theoretical climate suffers precisely because the interpretation of Emerson and writers influenced by him (including, among others, Nietzsche) remains a reading stripped of crucial feminist influences, crucial feminist conversations, within their work.

Because of the Emersonian legacy, in fact, his critics have been far more receptive than Fuller's readers to the strategies developing in the wake of structuralism and poststructuralism. Criticism of Emerson's work divides roughly into two camps—the historical and the linguistic—but scholars of both persuasions agree that his strange and sometimes estranging writing played upon the dense ideological confusion of his time. More than the linguistic critics, then, it is the proponents of the historical Emerson who, ironically, have reinforced an earlier critical tendency in excluding Fuller from the Emerson canon, making it still more difficult to conceptualize the developing feminist trends of his thought.[27] Such historical readings invariably place Emerson's writing in the service of a larger narrative in conjunction with which he often appears trapped by the very ideological fervor he chooses to resist.[28] Two particularly subtle and interesting examples of this type of criticism are the arguments of Carolyn Porter and David Leverenz. Porter calls Emerson "the era's most insightful diagnostician" of the effects of "reification" in the culture. Nevertheless she sees in his work a paradoxical "saturation" of the very ideas he labors to refute. Correctly resisting the earlier tendency to "dehistoricize" Emerson by attempting instead to "reconnoiter the cultural ground on which he fought his battle with alienation," Porter overlooks an equally important "saturation" of his mental environment: the developing discourse of feminism available to him through Fuller and the busy activity of reformers around him who

[27] Two notable exceptions are Jeffrey Steele, *The Representation of the Self*, and Larry Reynolds, *European Revolutions and the American Literary Renaissance* (New Haven: Yale University Press, 1988). Fuller appears briefly in works like Lawrence Buell, *Literary Transcendentalism: Style and Vision in the American Renaissance* (Ithaca: Cornell University Press, 1973); David Robinson, *The Apostle of Culture: Emerson as Preacher and Lecturer* (Philadelphia: University of Pennsylvania Press, 1982); and Joel Porte, *Representative Man: Ralph Waldo Emerson and His Time* (New York: Oxford University Press, 1979).

[28] See, for example, Myra Jehlen, *American Incarnation: The Individual, the Nation, and the Continent* (Cambridge: Harvard University Press, 1986); and Michael Gilmore, *American Romanticism and the Literary Marketplace* (Chicago: University of Chicago Press, 1985). See also Carolyn Porter, *Seeing and Being: The Plight of the Participant Observer in Emerson, James, Adams, and Faulkner* (Middletown, Conn.: Wesleyan University Press, 1981); and David Leverenz, *Manhood and the American Renaissance* (Ithaca: Cornell University Press, 1989). A notable exception is found in the work of Donald Pease, though he too has sometimes argued that Emerson is a man "outside" of time. See his discussion of Emerson's Sublime in "Emerson, Nature, and the Sovereignty of Influence," *Boundary 2* 8 (Spring 1980): 43–74; and in "Sublime Politics," in *The American Sublime*, ed. Mary Arensberg (Albany: State University of New York Press, 1986). See also Donald Pease, *Visionary Compacts: American Renaissance Writings in Cultural Context* (Madison: University of Wisconsin Press, 1987).

were influenced by the French theorist Charles Fourier.[29] Attempting to sustain the same balance in his reading of Emerson, David Leverenz argues that "class and gender relations" superseded "the man-thing relation" in importance. In talking about Emerson's recognition of the dominant and brutal "ideology of manhood," however, Leverenz, like Porter, overlooks both the discourse of Fourier and Fuller's powerful influence, advancing instead the thesis that Emerson labors ultimately (and conservatively) to fashion an abusive "man-making" rhetoric.[30]

A stronger potential for a recovery of a feminist agency in Emerson's work emerges, paradoxically, from the linguistic school of criticism that has developed since 1980. Though critics of this school also tend to ignore Emerson's relationship with Fuller, they pay tribute in various ways to the tension in his writing most susceptible to the type of feminist reading I have been discussing. Not surprisingly, this opportunity develops through a productive ambivalence about deconstruction and poststructuralism on the part of some of his most prominent critics— one that has had the curious effect of establishing his unique role in the formation of deconstruction. Stanley Cavell, for example, has outlined affinities among Emerson, Nietzsche, and Heidegger; in the process, and despite efforts to resist the affiliation, his argument regarding Emerson is necessarily (according to this genealogy) a deconstructive one.[31] Richard Poirier also observes these theoretical tendencies in Emerson's thought, particularly the decentering of the self so prevalent throughout his essays. Yet Poirier also identifies a quality of action in Emerson's thinking which supersedes the terms of deconstruction as they are generally understood.[32] The effort by Poirier and Cavell to situate Emerson both inside and outside the legacy of deconstruction, therefore, shows a

---

[29] Porter, *Seeing and Being*, pp. xxii, xx. Her fascinating argument that Emerson's "disaffection with reformers . . . turns out to represent not an antisocial persuasion, but a profound understanding of the infiltration of human consciousness by the very destructive social forces whose effects the reformers were trying to combat" (p. xx) loses its power when she resists making a reading of the *Second Series*, the volume produced at the height of his thinking about these very issues. As a result, her readings strip Emerson's work of the cultural grounding that she hoped to supply. At the same time, two of the essays upon which she does base her argument—"Circles" and "Fate"—were written with Fuller very much in mind.

[30] Leverenz, "The Politics of Emerson's Man-Making Words," PMLA 101 (January 1986): 54, 39. See also *Manhood and the American Renaissance*.

[31] At the same time, Cavell insists that Emerson's vision can be distinguished from deconstruction by "a certain sociality or congeniality—a circulation . . . given over to the reaction of an other." *This New Yet Unapproachable America: Lectures after Emerson after Wittgenstein* (Albuquerque, N.M.: Living Batch Press, 1989), 23. See also his *In Quest of the Ordinary: Lines of Skepticism and Romanticism* (Chicago: University of Chicago Press, 1988).

[32] Richard Poirier, *The Renewal of Literature: Emersonian Reflections* (New Haven: Yale University Press, 1987). Poirier argues that "at nearly every point [Emerson] knows what he is doing" (p. 148) when he begins to make arguments that have a deconstructive ring. See also Poirier, *Poetry and Pragmatism* (Cambridge: Harvard University Press, 1992).

remarkable affinity with the endeavor of those critics attempting to situate feminism in a poststructuralist frame.

Harold Bloom's earlier advocacy of humanism against the gathering forces of deconstruction has had a similar effect. His theory of influence, with its overt Freudian tenets, opens the way for a consideration of the decentered self in Emerson's work, enabling Eric Cheyfitz, for example, to find an ironic feminist dimension in Bloom's "central man," one formulated through the very tropes of power that Bloom so forcefully delineates.[33] Cheyfitz, not surprisingly, is one of the few critics to take Fuller's relationship with Emerson seriously, which helps to explain his sensitivity to certain feminist strains in Emerson's work. But Cheyfitz is finally too tentative about the feminist issue, perhaps because his approach centers on a rhetorical rather than an historical analysis. Although he describes Fuller as "one of [Emerson's] heroes of Eloquence, perhaps the foremost of those heroes," he does not actively pursue the relationship for its larger impact on Emerson's work.[34] In any case, the recognition of something exorbitant in Emerson's style has recently generated readings that can be said to align with the double strategy of feminist theory in a simultaneous affiliation with humanist and counter-humanist camps.[35] For this reason alone, Emerson's relationship with Fuller can provide us with some productive insights into the complex nature of the feminist conversation developing between them.

The Feminist Poetics of Paraphernalia

Emerson begins his essay "Experience" with a question that is equally appropriate to the "vertigo" of modern feminist critics.[36] "Where do we find ourselves?" he asks, before answering, "in a series of which we do not know the extremes, and believe that it has none." As I show, how-

[33] See Harold Bloom, *The Ringers in the Tower: Studies in Romantic Tradition* (Chicago: University of Chicago Press, 1971); *Figures of Capable Imagination* (New York: Seabury Press, 1976); and *Wallace Stevens: The Poems of Our Climate* (Ithaca: Cornell University Press, 1977). Eric Cheyfitz, *The Trans-Parent: Sexual Politics in the Language of Emerson* (Baltimore: Johns Hopkins University Press, 1981), esp. in chap. 3, n. 30.

[34] Cheyvitz, *The Trans-Parent*, p. 102.

[35] In the same way, Emerson's relationship with Fuller could be said to provide a significant support of the argument made by David Porter about Emerson's literary "change": "Because his prose was heuristic and conversational, a form more of talking than writing, concerned with process instead of meaning, it seemed indeterminate. In reality, it held new power and new perceptions. That liberation into the resources of reality, the self, and language allowed what was previously absent—the mind's infinite activity in a world of matter—to enter the modern consciousness." Porter, *Emerson and Literary Change* (Cambridge: Harvard University Press, 1978), 216.

[36] For an excellent discussion of the "vertigo" of feminist critics see Jardine, *Gynesis*, pp. 13–87.

ever, the association between Emerson and feminist criticism is less arbitrary than it might at first appear. He writes in response to the failing social reform of his day, and the dislocations of "Experience" emerge from his desire to explore the theoretical implications of that failure. Emerson's confusion resembles that of critics attempting to pass empirical feminism through the theoretical turns of deconstruction. Like Emerson, these feminists find themselves precariously situated. Although deconstructionists, following the lead of Jacques Derrida, have put Woman into discourse in order to reverse and ultimately displace the metaphysical tradition, they have done so by describing feminism as the logical "appendix" to the hermeneutic tradition they attack. This distrust of feminism is the legacy of Friedrich Nietzsche, "who made a scene before the women," by openly denouncing the woman's movement.[37] Yet deconstruction also follows Nietzsche's program for reversing the hierarchy between knowledge and life and displacing it by a more balanced interaction of thought with life.[38] If we engender these values as they have been en-gendered throughout history (masculine = knowledge; feminine = life), Nietzsche's transvaluation aligns easily with a feminist orientation. In fact, Gayatri Spivak goes so far as to suggest that the harsh critical reaction to Derrida's work among some literary critics is the product of an unconscious association between feminism and deconstruction, which together pose a threat to the masculine literary tradition.[39]

Because the texts making up the tradition are considerably more confused and contradictory about sexual difference than the dogmatic traditions of interpretation, the alliance between feminism and deconstruction might be said to turn on an unspecified alliance between writing and a writerly way of reading quite distinct from the canons of reading with which we are familiar. Paul de Man's defense of Rousseau's deconstructive insight illustrates how certain literary texts have projected an unrealized feminist poetics closely aligned but not synonymous with the deconstructive power of literary texts.[40]

[37] Interview with Jacques Derrida by Christie V. McDonald, published in "Choreographies," *Diacritics* 12 (Summer 1982): 72, 69.

[38] Friedrich Nietzsche, *Philosophy in the Tragic Age of the Greeks*, trans. M. Cowan (Chicago: Henry Regnery, 1962). See also the description by Gilles Deleuze, "Thought and Life," in his *Nietzsche and Philosophy*, trans. Hugh Tomlinson (New York: Columbia University Press, 1983), 100–101.

[39] Gayatri Spivak, "Love Me, Love My Ombre, Elle," *Diacritics* 14 (Winter 1984): 21.

[40] Paul de Man, "The Rhetoric of Blindness: Jacques Derrida's Reading of Rousseau," *Blindness and Insight: Essays in the Rhetoric of Contemporary Criticism*, 2d ed. (Minneapolis: University of Minnesota Press), 102–41. For an interesting interpretation of the significance that de Man's challenge to Derrida holds for the development of deconstruction in America, see Michael Sprinker's excellent review essay "Deconstruction in America," in *MLN* (Winter 1986): 1226–42.

One could argue, for example, that Plato's *Republic* is constitutive of a feminist poetics, though not in the traditional sense of that term. Here I do not refer to the well-known "feminist" argument that Socrates makes on behalf of women. The discussion of equality between men and women that takes place in Book V merely reinforces the hierarchical agenda of the work. Women are given a kind of equality (they are said to be the same) only after it is established that they are inferior or weaker in degree. Yet because we are able to detect these discrepancies, we can argue that a superior feminist argument has already been initiated, or at the very least figured, by the expulsion of the poet from the *Republic*. For the writer of the first feminist argument must be cast out in order for the truth of the argument to prevail. But to cast the poet outside the text is also to make it possible for the reader to become the poet as the writerly reader of the text. (The truth of the *Republic*—which is its untruth—can be realized only by the reader who perceives this.) The deconstructive moment is therefore generated from within the text (when the poet is expelled), whereas the feminist moment issues from the untraceable text produced by the writerly reader. The difference between the two, in this sense, is a difference of place.

Invariably, this complex sense of place gets lost when deconstruction and feminism collide. The curious double standard that emerges in Derrida's treatment of the home provides but one example. He views the home as a metaphor for metaphor (the "borrowed dwelling") and the site of representation and philosophy.[41] As a man and as a philosopher, Derrida is situated inside the closed structure that he seeks to open. Alice Jardine describes his acknowledgment of this process well: "Given that *ethos* means *heim*, at home, as in Plato's cavern, the point may be not to rush out of the cavern with everyone else, but rather to stay, to render it strange, uncanny—to develop an *ethos unheimlich* by questioning the writing on the walls of the cave itself."[42] As women in the same closed system, feminists also emerge from a place. If, as Derrida argues, we begin the process of deconstruction "wherever we are," then the feminist question of "woman's place" becomes an important deconstructive question as well. When asked by Christie McDonald to define "woman's place," however, Derrida responded:

I believe that I would not describe that place. . . . Do you not fear that having once become committed to the path of this topography, we would

[41] Jacques Derrida, "White Mythology: Metaphor in the Text of Philosophy," *Margins of Philosophy*, trans. Alan Bass (Chicago: University of Chicago Press, 1982), 253. See also Spivak, "Translator's Preface," in Derrida, *Of Grammatology* (Baltimore: Johns Hopkins University Press, 1974), lxxxiii.

[42] Jardine, *Gynesis*, pp. 153–54.

inevitably find ourselves back "at home" or "in the kitchen"? Or under house arrest? . . . Why, for that matter, should one rush into answering a *topological* question? . . . Or an *economical* one (because it all comes back to *l'oikos* as home, *maison*, *chez-soi*—[at home in this sense also means in French within the self], the law of the proper place, etc. in the preoccupation with a woman's place.[43]

Derrida's retreat from the home is a retreat from the same mechanism that enables him and his philosophy. But for women, by contrast, the home is not the site of philosophy but of its banishment. If for men, then, the home has been the site of writing *and* the paraphernalia of the self simultaneously, for women it more often has been the site of reading *as* the paraphernalia of the self. The word *paraphernalia* refers to the goods beyond the dower which are controlled (though not possessed) by the bride. Derrida's hasty retreat from the home in this instance robs Woman of her paraphernalia and thus her agency. For women, the concept of the home as the site of reading generates an area of legibility beyond the written text as it has been controlled (or read) by men, a provisional self beyond the proper. And because there are finally several versions of the home, McDonald might have responded to Derrida in Nietzschean fashion by asking not "what it was" about the home that he wished to escape, but "which [home]."[44]

With this argument in mind, we can say that Derrida has won an audience in the United States (the "borrowed dwelling" for his work) because of the curious affinity between his project and the literature of American culture—a literature alternately condemned and praised for its retreat from patriarchy and the abusive tropes of the home.[45] And this view is ironically reinforced by the fact that the feminist critics who describe American literature as a "masculine wilderness" suspect the

[43] Derrida and McDonald, "Choreographies," p. 68.

[44] The quote is from Gilles Deleuze, *Nietzsche and Philosophy*, pp. 162–63, who emphasizes the significance of Nietzsche's question.

[45] Three very powerful and different approaches to this topic are Leslie Fiedler, *Love and Death in the American Novel* (New York: Stein and Day, 1966); Quentin Anderson, *The Imperial Self: An Essay in American Literature and Cultural History* (New York: Knopf, 1971); and Eric Sundquist, *Home as Found: Authority and Genealogy in Nineteenth-Century American Literature* (Baltimore: Johns Hopkins University Press, 1979). Carolyn Porter characterizes this critical narrative of retreat as a retreat from history favored by critics such as R. W. B. Lewis, Richard Chase, and, with some important modifications, Richard Poirier. See her chapter "American Ahistoricism," in *Seeing and Being*, pp. 3–22. Harry Henderson notes that "to deny history, to hate it, curse it, wish it away—all of these are attitudes toward history." Henderson, *Versions of the Past: The Historical Imagination in American Fiction* (New York: Oxford University Press, 1974), viii. Thus it has been argued that male American writers were engaged in a retreat from history in their retreat from domesticity (what Fiedler calls a "strategy of evasion" [*Love and Death in the American Novel*, p. 76]), but it might also be argued that they were engaged in a nascent feminist revaluation of both.

same of Derrida's theoretical universe.[46] Although the suspicions of these critics are understandable, they are nevertheless misguided because they emerge from an engagement with the traditional reading of American literature. Feminist critics in the field of American literature have accepted with little debate the thesis that traditional American literature is masculine. Although this approach has encouraged the recovery of women writers, it has also initiated the idea that there were two separate traditions.[47] Thus, Hawthorne's famous declamation against the "scribbling women," which enabled generations of critics to label American literature masculine (with all the positive and negative virtues that obtain), can actually help us in revaluing the scene North American writers made before the women of the nineteenth century.[48] Indeed, such scenes are integral to literary productions, as Derrida shows in his discussion of Nietzsche's scene before the feminists of his time.[49] Derrida argues that because Nietzsche's scene is "overdetermined, divided, apparently contradictory," it is integral to the "question of style" and the deconstructive formations of his work.[50] Critics have similarly begun to observe the deconstructive tendencies of American writers, but because it is assumed that "lighting out" has nothing to do with feminism, the feminist vectors of this scene are unfortunately not being followed.[51]

[46] The phrase "masculine wilderness" is quoted in Judith Fetterley, *The Resisting Reader*. The quotation brings the unintended irony of the phrase into play. The distrust of Derrida was more acute when the gap between American and French feminisms was wider (or so perceived) than it is in 1994. For an interesting discussion of the various worlds of feminist criticism see the essays in *Diacritics* 12 (Summer 1982), and *Diacritics* 21 (Summer–Fall 1991). See also Elaine Showalter, "Feminist Criticism in the Wilderness," *Critical Inquiry* 8 (Winter 1981): 179–205.

[47] Nina Baym, *Woman's Fiction: A Guide to Novels by and about Women in America, 1820–1870* (Ithaca: Cornell University Press, 1978); Douglas, *The Feminization of American Culture*; and Mary Kelley, *Private Woman, Public Stage: Literary Domesticity in Nineteenth–Century America* (New York: Oxford University Press, 1984).

See especially Lawrence Buell, *New England Literary Culture: From Revolution Through Renaissance* (London: Cambridge University Press, 1986).

[48] One attempt to consider this interaction has been made by David S. Reynolds in *Beneath the American Renaissance: The Subversive Imagination in the Age of Emerson and Melville* (Cambridge: Harvard University Press, 1989).

Unfortunately, Reynolds greatly diminishes the impact of Fuller and Fourier. His dismissal of Fuller emerges from the oddly prevalent misconception that scholarship on Fuller has kept critics from exploring the writing of other women authors of the time. In fact, only a handful of dedicated scholars have read Fuller, and the critical environment has suffered greatly as a result.

[49] Derrida, *Spurs: Nietzsche's Styles*, trans. Barbara Harlow (Chicago: University of Chicago Press, 1978).

[50] Derrida and McDonald, "Choreographies," p. 69.

[51] Of course, much depends on the critics developing the canon. Poe, hardly canonized in America (yet not forgotten), was valorized by French critics and, therefore, early at the center of a heated theoretical debate. See Barbara Johnson, "The Frame of Reference: Poe,

In fact, the feminist and deconstructive trends that have emerged in the criticism of American literature have much in common, but they rarely seem to meet because both schools tend, like Derrida, to reduce the complexity of the home. The retreat from the home (presumed to be characteristic of the traditional American canon) is now sometimes viewed as a nascent deconstructive impulse, whereas the "painful return" (presumed to be characteristic of the tradition of scribblers) is considered an antithetical feminist response. But if the home was a force common to much of the writing of the period, then the discriminations now separating the field of American literature do not apply. This discrepancy certainly becomes apparent when we return once again to the work of the father of American literature, Ralph Waldo Emerson.

Fathering a Tradition

If Emerson is the father of American literature, he is an unconventional father who does not so much flee from the home as he enters there in an attempt to transvalue it entirely. In this, he is more closely aligned with the "scribblers" of the day than with the other tradition he is said to have spawned. Those critics who discern this gentility in his writing, among them Stanley Cavell, are puzzled by his tendency to feminize his philosophical interests ("playing Dido to his Aeneas").[52] Yet in view of his relationship with Fuller, Emerson's gentility is better understood through the feminist and deconstructive crosscurrents of their work together. Such an approach reunites the hitherto severed traditions of American literature and reveals more about the troubled alliance of feminism and deconstruction as it has developed in today's critical discourse.

Lacan, Derrida," in her *The Critical Difference: Essays in the Contemporary Rhetoric of Reading* (Baltimore: Johns Hopkins University Press, 1980), 110–146. For a feminist commentary on this interaction, see Spivak, "Love Me, Love My Ombre, Elle," *Diacritics* 14 (Winter 1984) 19–36. Louis Renza, "Poe's Secret Autobiography," in *The American Renaissance Reconsidered*, ed. Walter Benn Michaels and Donald E. Pease (Baltimore: Johns Hopkins University Press, 1985), 58–89 gives another turn of the screw to the purloined Poe. As the canon in America was revised to incorporate Poe, the deconstructive nature of the old canon begins to emerge. See John Irwin's *American Hieroglyphics: The Symbol of the Egyptian Hieroglyphics in the American Renaissance* (New Haven: Yale University Press, 1980); Joseph Riddel, "Decentering the Image: The 'Project' of American Poetics," in *Textual Strategies: Perspectives in Post-Structuralist Criticism*, ed. Josué V. Harari (Ithaca: Cornell University Press, 1979), 322–58. See also John Carlos Rowe, *Through the Custom House: Nineteenth-Century American Fiction and Modern Theory* (Baltimore: Johns Hopkins University Press, 1982); and Gregory S. Jay, *America the Scrivener: Deconstruction and the Subject of Literary History* (Ithaca: Cornell University Press, 1990).

[52] Stanley Cavell, "Genteel Responses to Kant? in Emerson's 'Fate' and Coleridge's *Biographia Literaria*," *Raritan* 3 (Fall 1983): 34–61, esp. p. 36.

In examining the Fuller-Emerson conversation, I do not attempt to move our thinking about the two authors from its humanistic frame to a wholly deconstructive frame, though that is sometimes the unspoken motor behind current Emerson criticism—and understandably: Nietzsche's hungry reading of Emerson gives sufficient substantiation to this critical tendency, since his work is crucial to the development of deconstruction. My aim instead is to arrest that critical tendency, or interrupt it, because the degree to which Nietzsche screens out the aspect of Emerson's writing that is his conversation with Fuller is the degree to which deconstruction and feminism have lost a model of conversation between them.

This model of conversation, then, is in some sense the quest at the center of some of the most interesting feminist criticism today: what Gayatri Spivak calls the process of "interruption" and what Naomi Schor calls a "certain insistence on doubling."[53] Both of these critics are speaking, once again, of the effort to reconcile (without affirming) the subject of humanist discourse with the poststructuralist problematization of the subject. Intriguingly, both Fuller and Emerson demonstrate early signs of this tension in their work. Though the humanist concept of the individual holds real power over both of them, a considerable range of flexibility and play also applies to their conceptions of the idea. The individual, and with it the notion of the identity of each person, proves a useful political subvention of their respective concerns for women and their development. And in this sense both writers are willing to take what Spivak has called the "risk of essentialism" in order to protect women from cultural oblivion.[54] Nevertheless, they are not afraid to interrogate all the terms of the humanist lexicon, particularly those terms that had obviously served so well to efface women throughout history.

This tension certainly resides behind the development of Fuller's feminist agency, particularly her interest in reading and its pedagogical effects. From her early translations, and, following them, her first "original" publications—*Summer on the Lakes* and *Woman in the Nineteenth Century*—through her elaborate and cunning editorial work and labor for the *Dial* and the *New-York Daily Tribune*, her feminism continually manifests itself in what she calls the odd "synonymizing" of "history, *languages* [and] literature." I show that reading history becomes the first

[53] I borrow this method of interruption from Gayatri Spivak. See her translation and interpretation of Mahasweta Devi's "Stanadayini" in "A Literary Representation of the Subaltern: A Woman's Text from the Third World," in *In Other Worlds*, p. 241. Naomi Schor, "Dreaming Dissymmetry: Barthes, Foucault, and Sexual Difference," in *Men in Feminism*, ed. Alice Jardine and Paul Smith (New York: Methuen, 1987), 110.

[54] Spivak, "Subaltern Studies: Deconstructing Historiography," in *In Other Worlds*, p. 205.

step in the process of making history, and that language is the inevitable medium for this feminist agency. Throughout her work a kind of double strategy can be found, particularly when we discover the way her interests in translation and conversation are effectively pressed into changing the way Americans read the world around them. These interests, it must be said, are actively promoted and enhanced by Emerson, whose confidence in Fuller supersedes her father's in both balance and insight.

Later I show that Derrida's understanding of translation as a "marriage contract in the form of a seminar" proves useful in demonstrating the complex issues engaged by Fuller's early work in translation.[55] And it may well be that Derrida's interest in translation forms a bridge between deconstruction and feminism that Derrida himself has not yet fully perceived, since translation combines linguistic concerns with an unavoidable historical dynamic.[56] Fuller's early engagement with translation forms an interesting focus for the conversation now being sought between feminism and deconstruction, and it is vital to my argument that her interest in translation develops through her interaction with Emerson. Fuller uses her translations of Goethe's *Tasso* and Bettina von Arnim's *Günderode* as models for the feminist insights on conversation and pedagogy that begin to emerge through her conversation with Emerson.

This tension between a humanist sense of agency and its radical deconstruction can be located in Emerson's work as well, particularly as it comes under Fuller's powerful influence. When Emerson first met Fuller, he was struggling to complete the final section of his famous essay "Nature," and, from that initial interaction, he developed an intimacy with her that continued until her death in 1850, when he had begun to write the essays for *Conduct of Life*. Because the relationship spanned most of his mature career, returning to Fuller's early contact with him helps us to observe the implicitly feminist conversation slowly shaping the critical work of both writers.

Rethinking Fourier

The work of the French utopian Charles Fourier, which gained wide influence in the United States and provoked the interest of both Fuller

---

[55] Jacques Derrida, "Des Tours de Babel," in *Difference in Translation*, ed. Joseph F. Graham (Ithaca: Cornell University Press, 1985), 234.

[56] See the "Roundtable on Translation," in *The Ear of the Other: Texts and Discussions with Jacques Derrida*, ed. Christie McDonald, trans. Peggy Kamuf (Lincoln: University of Nebraska Press, 1985).

and Emerson, can also be said to have enhanced the tension in their thinking between humanism and its radical deconstruction. Fourier is best known for his elaborate and sometimes fanciful critique of Western culture; for him, nothing less than a program of "absolute doubt," and "absolute divergence" from our intellectual heritage would deliver us from the vices plaguing society.[57] At the same time, Fourier made passion, the relation of the sexes, and particularly the woman's role in every facet of life the pivotal issues of his utopian vision. Thus the discourse of Fourier as it developed in North America quickly attached itself to a feminist agenda. Indeed, one could argue that it formed the core around which the emergent feminism of the 1840s and 1850s defined itself.[58]

Fourier's focus was deeply structural: by attacking marriage and the home (or the "isolated household") as the leading metaphors of society, he opened the possibility for rethinking the entire language of social intercourse. Thus, even more than translation, the domestic theories of Fourier forge a wedding of linguistic and historic concerns and, as such, provide a perfect site for a consideration of the feminist poetics of paraphernalia. Deeply concerned with "woman's place," Fourier attempted to conceptualize that site by rethinking the constitution of the individual. According to him, it took an entire phalanstery (1,620 people) to construct one whole person.[59] As I show, Fuller and Emerson find in the discourse of Fourier (a discourse that widened to include their conversation with one another), an opportunity to rethink the metaphors of marriage and the home, not as fixed symbolic resonances, but as fluid allegories for the construction of gender and the individual.

Indeed, because of the popularity of Fourier's theory in America in the early 1840s—a popularity that coincided exactly with Fuller's growing intimacy with Emerson—it is perhaps more accurate to talk about Fuller and Emerson's Fourierism in addressing their thoughts on women.[60] Of course, the utopian world of Fourier has always been the great unspoken topic in our interpretation of the American Renaissance. F. O. Matthiessen, for example, confessed that the book he did not write when he ultimately composed his famous study of the American Renaissance

[57] Quoted in M. C. Spencer, *Charles Fourier* (Boston: Twayne Publishers, 1981), 31.

[58] Support for this argument appears in Dolores Hayden, *The Grand Domestic Revolution: A History of Feminist Designs for American Homes, Neighborhoods, and Cities* (Cambridge: MIT Press, 1981). See also her *Seven American Utopias: The Architecture of Communitarian Socialism, 1790–1975* (Cambridge: MIT Press, 1976); and "Two Utopian Feminists and Their Campaign for Kitchenless Houses," *Signs* 4 (Winter 1978): 274–90.

[59] Nicholas V. Riasanovsky, *The Teaching of Charles Fourier* (Berkeley: University of California Press, 1941), 43.

[60] For an excellent recent analysis of Fourier's importance, see Carl J. Guarneri, *The Utopian Alternative: Fourierism in Nineteenth-Century America* (Ithaca: Cornell University Press, 1991).

was the book that would have had borne the subtitle "In the Age of Fourier."[61] Part of the credit for this critical ambush must go to Fourier himself, for even as his biographer Jonathan Beecher has noted, there is something destabilizing about the body of his work and career.[62] Critics have invariably handled the difficulties of his career by dividing Fourier into the separate, seemingly controllable, roles of prophet and madman. There is the Fourier capable of espousing radical social change, quoted favorably by Marx in "The Holy Family." And there is the Fourier capable of creating fanciful enumerations such as his elaborate "hierarchy of cuckoldom." How can we not be amused by such elaborations? Consider Cuckold No. 20, "The Hastening or Onrushing Cuckold," who "strives to precipitate events. He eagerly shows off his wife in society, encourages her to go to the theater, to be affectionate with friends, to move in fast circles." "This species," Fourier continues, "is comparable to a package sent by fast mail: it arrives speedily at its destination."[63]

Fourier's example is ridiculous but it is arguably at the core of the ridiculous that all three writers—Emerson, Fuller, and Fourier—did their most subversive thinking. It is no accident that Fourier's analogy works by the letter, since his understanding of the ridiculous, like that of Fuller and Emerson, works the odd conduction of meaning and misunderstanding that we associate with the problematic of language itself. Because the silhouette of the ridiculous always threatens to subsume the prophet in Fourier's case, critics have tended to obscure both aspects of his work to avoid that possibility. That our reading of Fuller has also followed this pattern may tell us something about the bond between both thinkers, one that passes through at least two levels of denial in our critical vocabulary. Moreover, the degree to which traces of Fourier and Fuller are both absent from our reading of Emerson is the degree to which the Age of Fourier has been radically normalized, which is to say, repressed.

Yet the recovery of Fourier in the works of these two authors is not easy to do. Quite the contrary. The frustrating aspect of such a task is that the name "Fourier" holds the same wide resonance for Fuller and Emerson that the name "Napoleon" does. The sheer scale of this signifier and the cozy assumption that a trail of ideas are immediately summoned by its utterance means that very little time is actually devoted to an elaboration of what they mean in referring to Fourier.

[61] F. O. Matthiessen, *American Renaissance: Art and Expression in the Age of Emerson and Whitman* (New York: Oxford University Press, 1941), viii.

[62] Jonathan Beecher, *Charles Fourier: The Visionary and His World* (Berkeley: University of California Press, 1986), 3.

[63] See *The Utopian Vision of Charles Fourier*, trans. and ed. Jonathan Beecher and Richard Bienvenu (Columbia: University of Missouri Press, 1971), 183, 186.

Nor is it easy to discover which version of Fourier they were read-ing.[64] Perhaps it was the version of Albert Brisbane, the most visible disciple of Fourier in America and one of the few who had actually met Fourier in Europe and who began upon his return to America to advo-cate Fourier's ideas in the columns of Horace Greeley's *New-York Daily Tribune*. What we might call a radical translator of Fourier, Brisbane attempted to delineate the elaborate plan of Fourier, though he was hampered in his efforts by topics considered far too volatile (or "French" in the then-current euphemism) for American consumption.[65] Bris-bane's censorship often took the verve out of Fourier's vision, emphasiz-ing the mechanical and eliminating the intriguing novelesque shape of

[64] In an 1843 journal (JMN 9: 6), Emerson shows that he was familiar with vol. 5 of the collected Fourier published as *Théorie de l'unité universelle, Oeuvres completes de Ch. Fourier*, 2d ed., 6 vols. (Paris, 1841–45). In her letters, Fuller writes on January 28, 1844, to Orestes Brownson: "Mr. Brisbane offered to lend me a volume of Fourier now in your hands" (LMF 3: 174). Her journal for 1844 shows that she had read Fourier's *Nouveau Monde industriel et sociétaire* (Paris, 1829). Emerson met Brisbane when he was in New York in March 1842, where he may have encountered copies of *The Phalanx*, the magazine pub-lished by Brisbane in New York. Emerson's journals suggest that he was familiar with the *London Phalanx* published by Hugh Doherty (JMN 7: 258; JMN 8: 230), whom Fuller met when she was in England. Emerson's journals also suggest that he was familiar with *Future: Devoted to the Cause of Association and the Reorganization of Society*, edited by Bris-bane and Greeley and published January 30–July 10, 1841 (JMN 8: 216–17). He was also familiar with *The Harbinger* (JMN 9: 464), published between 1845 and 1849. During her stay in New York, Fuller met Park Godwin, editor of *The Harbinger* and author of *A Popular View of the Doctrines of Charles Fourier* (New York: J. S. Redfield, 1844). While in France, she also met Prosper-Victor Considerant, another French advocate of Fourier. Both Emerson and Fuller were well acquainted with William H. Channing, who published two Fourieris-tic periodicals, *The Present* and *Spirit of the Age*.

[65] See Brisbane, *The Social Destiny of Man: Or, Association and the Reorganization of Industry* (Philadelphia: C. F. Stollmeyer, 1840). Brisbane made an effort to distinguish between Fourier's attack on the "isolated household" and the institution of marriage. According to him, "We condemn the system of Isolated households, but not Marriage, which is an institution separate and distinct from our present domestic arrangements. People suppose that the marriage tie could not be maintained in Association, and would be dissolved if it were not confined to the isolated household."

See Brisbane, *Association; or, A Concise Exposition of the Practical Part of Fourier's Social Science* (New York: Greeley & McElrath, 1843), 9; and *Theory of the Functions of the Human Passions, Followed by an Outline View of the Fundamental Principles of Fourier's Theory of Social Science* (New York: Miller, Orton, & Mullian, 1856). Fourier believed that man's passions were the secret to social harmony and that three "distributive" passions needed to func-tion in order for harmony to be achieved: the "Butterfly passion, based on a desire for variety"; the "Cabalist passion, which catered to man's need for intrigue and rivalry"; and the "Composite passion" or the "free, blind enthusiasm engendered when both the spirit and the senses were stimulated" (*The Utopian Vision*, trans. and ed. Beecher and Bienvenu, p. 50). These three Brisbane rather flatly described as the "Separating," "Modulating," and "Combining" faculties of man. In fact, Brisbane's description of Fourier tends to tone down the longer he is in America. His earlier version of the "three directing passions" in 1840, for example, was a little closer to Fourier's original: "the Emulative, Cabalistic, Dissident; the Alternating, Connecting, Changing; and the Composite, Exalting, Concor-dant" (Brisbane, *Social Destiny*, p. 166).

Fourier's theoretical universe. These literary offenses far outweigh Brisbane's other more obvious deviations from Fourier's theory, since the work of Fourier is about nothing, as Roland Barthes tells us, if it is not also about the play of style in the creation of a new way of speaking about things. Fourier, according to Barthes, is a "logothete," the inventor of a new language.[66]

There is little trace of the usual scholarly schizophrenia in Barthes's treatment of Fourier: the radical sexual reforms that prove too controversial for many of his nineteenth-century disciples merge easily in Barthes's reading with the reforms either perceived or imagined to be part of Fourier's scheme—reforms focusing on the "harmonic association" of men and women in their working and social relationships. This effluence of one topic into another is what makes Fourier such an important thinker, according to Barthes, particularly when it fosters a dramatic call for an "absolute deviancy" *from* the "deformation" of civilization and its systems.[67]

In Barthes's reading, Fourier becomes a kind of deconstructor, providing a discourse without an object or a subject. His is a discourse "without subject" because, as Barthes argues, Fourier performs "his enunciatory role . . . in such a manner that we cannot decide whether it is serious or parody." And it is a theory "without an object" because it is not about application in the usual sense of the word. For Barthes this means that it is not about "found[ing] a reality that is incorrectly defined" as exterior to language. For Barthes, rather, Fourier's enterprise is about the substantial reality of language.[68]

Obviously influenced by his poststructuralist orientation, Barthes's reading of Fourier bears an uncanny resemblance to the readings adopted by Emerson and Fuller in the nineteenth century. Both of these authors find Fourier less important for the substance of what he actually said than for the interpretive possibilities opened by his method. For both, the method is one attentive to the complex intersection of social and domestic terms in the construction of the individual subject. Does this convert Emerson and Fuller into proto-deconstructors, or perhaps show Barthes as a lapsed humanist? I would argue for a little of both, though the terms *humanism* and *deconstruction* have themselves begun to resonate as loudly and as problematically as did the name "Fourier" in the nineteenth century.

[66] Roland Barthes, *Sade, Fourier, and Loyola*, trans. Richard Miller (New York: Farrar, Straus and Giroux, 1976), 3.
[67] Ibid., pp. 88, 110.
[68] Ibid., pp. 110, 109.

Emerson's Utterances

Such a thesis might be quite impossible to demonstrate if we did not in fact have Emerson's extensive correspondence with Fuller. These letters comprise one of the most interesting set of documents relating to Emerson's career, supplying ample testimony of Fuller's influence. Even more than his journals, which provide another strong source of information about his relationship with her, his letters provide a narrative of their conversation, which ranged from the intimate to the restrained over the fourteen years of their contact. Indeed, when he first learned that a trunk of letters had washed ashore from the shipwreck in which she died, he panicked, and his anxiety tells us something about the unusual emotional pitch of his letters to her.

Given this emotional heat and narrative thrust, I begin my study by reading Emerson's letters to Fuller. Because the letters are addressed to Fuller, we have the advantage of a text written for a feminist audience. We are rereading a text already given a feminist frame. And because Emerson increasingly comes to rely on this transformation in his audience, studying his letters to Fuller enables us to reconsider the reading habits that we have used in our evaluation of his more traditional work.

Here we might invoke the difference between "utterances" and "sentences" made by Mikhail Bakhtin in his essay "The Problem of Speech Genres." According to Bakhtin, "When one analyzes an individual sentence apart from its context, the traces of addressivity and the influence of the anticipated response . . . are lost . . . because they are foreign to the sentence as a unit of language."[69] In this sense we have been reading Emerson's sentences and ignoring his utterances, particularly those utterances that play into the unexpected turns of Fuller's radical feminism.

The correspondence between Emerson and Fuller also affords us an overview of the whole span of their relationship. Emerson's epistolary exchange with Fuller begins with her arrival shortly after the death of his brother Charles and his frugal accounting of that loss ("I can gather no hint from this terrible experience" [EL 2: 25]), and it ends with Fuller's death, which generates a very different textual reaction. His response to the calamity of her death shows something about what he calls the "essential line of American history" (JMN 11: 258) as it unfolds in his conversation with her and in the events of their relationship, including their heated debate in the fall of 1840 when they attempt to define the

---

[69] Mikhail Bakhtin, *Speech Genres and Other Late Essays*, ed. Caryl Emerson and Michael Holquist (Austin: University of Texas Press, 1986), 99.

meaning of their unusual interaction, a debate about identity exacerbated in compelling ways by the invitation and challenge provided by the Brook Farm community. For the proponent of self-reliance, this act of self-definition is uneasy and unsettling: Fuller's questions are on a continuum with those provoked by the experiment in the "conduct of life" at Brook Farm. (Though not yet officially formulated as a Fourieristic community, the expectations that would make it possible for Brook Farm to become one were already in place.) Thus Emerson's reaction to Fuller easily merges with the discourse of Fourier as it finds expression among his circle of friends over the years.[70] The letters reveal that Fuller learns more readily from this "crisis" than does Emerson, perhaps because she is accustomed to negotiating her way through changing subject positions: her Conversations in Boston are models of the delicate "code-switching" necessary for such negotiations. Indeed, her experience with Emerson encourages her to consider the advantages of such maneuvers, ultimately provoking a type of feminist agency.

Emerson's confusion—so vivid in the narrative of his epistolary exchange with Fuller—generates the subplot for his *First* and *Second Series* of *Essays*, particularly the second, which forms a type of experimental romance, one marked by the Fourieristic dialogue he is having with Fuller. Only her death, in fact, would eventually release him and enable him to accept the negotiations that had previously been so troubling, yielding a criticism that takes on something of Fuller's agency as its own. As I show, this recognition is first made evident in his contribution to the *Memoirs of Margaret Fuller Ossoli*, where he begins to see how Fuller's conversation forms the model for his most satisfying literary strategy. Finally his lecture before the Boston Woman's Rights Convention in 1855 and his essay "Fate" constitute a complex allegory about Fuller's death and his acceptance of key attributes of this feminist agency as his own. Rather than viewing his later work as the product of a slow passage into a false transcendental vision, then, we would do well to view this buoyant work as the product of an emerging feminist poetics.

For Fuller, the conversation mapped out in the letters also has increasingly productive results. Not only does it help her to sharpen her critical method; it also gives impetus to her focus on reading as a form of agency. This interest emerges in her engagement with translation, and

---

[70] For support for this argument see the excellent essay by Richard Francis, "The Ideology of Brook Farm," *Studies in the American Renaissance*, ed. Joel Meyerson (Boston: Twayne Publishers, 1977), 1–48. See also Charles Crowe, *George Ripley: Transcendentalist and Utopian Socialist* (Athens: University of Georgia Press, 1967); and his essay, "Fourierism and the Founding of Brook Farm," in *Boston Public Library Quarterly* 12 (April 1960).

again in her effort to study the structure of her own reading strategies in *Woman in the Nineteenth Century* and *Summer on the Lakes*, where European and Native American discourses clash in a productive moment of encounter. Her conversation with Emerson stimulates her to consider how the success of our engagement with history depends on the linguistic structures through which history finds its expression. Thus her *Tribune* articles generate a lively extension of her effort to formulate a theory of reading that would be productive of significant historical change.

Emerson's epistolary exchange with Fuller forms the focus of my initial chapter because it necessarily shapes the entire course of this book. For throughout I show how Fuller's conversation with Emerson consistently forces both of them to cross difficult thresholds of passion and desire. Watching him contend with these "lords of life" in his interaction with Fuller tells us as much about her and her effort to reconstitute those terms along radical lines as it does about him and his shared conviction that a transvaluation of the terms by which we live is necessary for the successful "conduct of life." This difficult entanglement of life and letters goes to the heart of my project; and it registers the heat at the center of the critical enterprise today.

1

Falling without Speed:
The Feminist Frame of
Emerson's Letters to Fuller

To whom do you think he is writing? For me it is always more
important to know that than to know what is being written; moreover I think it amounts to the same, to the other finally.
                                    —Jacques Derrida, *The Post Card*

Every man is entitled to be measured or characterised by his best
influence.
                                    —Ralph Waldo Emerson, JMN 11: 38

Emerson's letters to Fuller constitute one of the most interesting documents of his career. Even more than his journals, which provide another
strong source of information about his relationship with Fuller, his letters give a unique account of their almost fourteen-year-long "conversation" modulated by tones of intimacy and restraint. Emerson met Fuller
when he was struggling to complete the final section of his famous essay
"Nature" (1836), and their epistolary interaction continues until her untimely death in 1850, when he began to generate essays for *The Conduct
of Life*. Before going to Europe in 1846, Fuller made extended visits to
Concord, where she and Emerson exchanged letters, conversations,
journals, and manuscripts. The letters between the two reveal an extended consideration of the challenge posed by gender and desire. In
effect, Emerson's letters to Fuller provide an intrinsic feminist frame. In
reading through that frame, one begins to see not only how he cherished
her feminist perspective but also how he eventually came to rely on a
feminist reader for his work. Studying the letters to Fuller thus encourages a reconsideration of the critical frames we have used to evaluate
Emerson's more traditional writing.

We see in the flood of words between Fuller and Emerson how gender
took on a wonderfully fluid character in their interaction with one another. Fuller's public and often political orientation was kindled by the
masculine tutelage of her father, as some have averred, and Emerson's
decision to eschew the public role of minister was arguably the result of
the strong feminine strains of his upbringing, particularly those pre-

sented through his relationship with his powerful Aunt Moody.[1] As the younger of the two (by seven years), Fuller was fascinated by a man who would relinquish a platform of power (and a textual one at that) denied her by her sex. Moreover, because of Emerson's active hostility toward authority, he often celebrated a feminine subversion in his work.[2] Even critics who tend to avoid feminist issues often find themselves writing through highly gendered terms to characterize his work. Indeed, as described by Stanley Cavell, the unique epistemological turn of Emerson's thought bears a familiar feminist orientation: "Emerson's most explicit reversal of Kant lies in his picturing of the intellectual hemisphere of knowledge as passive or receptive and the intuitive or institutional hemisphere as active or spontaneous."[3] Emerson's letters to Fuller also reveal how his fascination with the realm of the feminine is sometimes disabling. His protective concern over the potential violence of unlicensed masculinity often produces a sense of textual and social restraint, so that whenever the concept of freedom seems to degenerate into an obsession with virility, he feels compelled to observe the restrictions on femininity and the fate of the female sex. Emerson's caution should hardly be surprising since he became, with Fuller's help, an astute student of social manners. His journals are cluttered with feminist observations such as this one recorded in 1841: "I gave you enough to eat & never beat you: what more can the woman ask? said the Good Husband" (JMN 7: 454). Or another: "Society lives on the system of money and woman comes at money & money's worth through compliment. I should not dare to be woman. . . . What is she not expected to do & suffer for some invitation to strawberries & cream" (JMN 9: 108). Still, Emerson has trouble making the subtle distinction between gender and sex that theorists have begun to make today.[4] By contrast, Fuller's unconventional experience as a woman enabled her to remind Emerson through her complex alignment with masculine activity that one's sex, though seemingly fatal in nature, need not be restrictive in life. Rather presciently, then, Cavell's description of Emerson's reversal of Kant is also a description of the roles Fuller and Emerson occasionally play in

---

[1] For an analysis of Moody's importance, see Evelyn Barish, *Emerson: The Roots of Prophecy* (Princeton: Princeton University Press, 1989).

[2] On this matter, see especially Eric Cheyfitz, *The Trans-Parent: Sexual Politics in the Language of Emerson* (Baltimore: Johns Hopkins University Press, 1981).

[3] Cavell, "Thinking of Emerson," in *The Senses of Walden*, expanded ed. (San Francisco: North Point Press, 1981), 129.

[4] For one of the most complex theoretical investigations into the complications of these terms, see Judith Butler, *Gender Trouble: Feminism and the Subversion of Identity* (New York: Routledge, 1990).

each other's life: he frustrates her with his passive or percipient stance toward the world, and with her intuitive and spontaneous powers, she taunts him for his failure to achieve an active realization of his thought in the text of the world.

Perhaps the most important aspect of Fuller's influence recorded in Emerson's letters is the way she enhances his *desire* to write (as well as his ability to name that desire). Invariably this desire fosters a sense of experiment: "I have read through a second time today the entire contents of the brown paper parcel and startled my mother & my wife when I went into the dining room with the declaration that I wished to live a little while with people who love & hate, who have Muses & Furies, and in a twelvemonth I should write tragedies & romance" (EL 2: 245). There are, to be sure, often two familiar voices crossing the texture of his letters to Fuller: an unself-conscious experimental voice (the voice of freedom) capable of writing "We read Porphyry, and Duc de St. Simon and Napier's Peninsular War & Carlyle's Lectures to pass away the cold & rainy season & wish for letters every day from Margaret Fuller" (EL 2: 395–96), and an embarrassed voice (the voice of fate), capable of offering "You have a right to expect great activity great demonstration & large intellectual contributions from your friends, & tho' you do not say it you receive nothing. as well be related to mutes as to uncommunicating egoists" (EL 2: 342). Luckily, Fuller's frustrated investment in the tension of those voices diminishes after she recognizes the traps of tragedy and seduction set by their dialectical configuration. Through Fuller's strategic work with translation, as I demonstrate in Chapter 2, she begins to realize that the merit of Emerson's style in his letters to her resides not in the reiteration of his familiar dialectical tactic, but in those moments when he moves well beyond its orbit.

It is easy to agree with Fuller's assessment of Emerson's letters. Their seductive urgency humanizes the "man of snow" found in his formal work. He often described the process of writing letters to Fuller as a pleasurable activity because it liberated him from what he called the "canonical dimensions" (EL 2: 98) of his address to other friends, as well as from the formidable restrictions of the lecture platform. Discoursing on "Human Life in Ten Lectures," Emerson jokingly told Fuller at one point, is as laughable as "the Soul of man neatly done up in ten pinboxes" (EL 2: 179). For her part, Fuller believed that many passages in Emerson's letters to her were "finer than anything" he had published (LMF 2: 183). And she was unafraid to tell him so. "Write me a letter quick," she once wrote, "before your pen gets so ethical and dignified that it will turn off nothing but lectures" (LMF 2: 251).

One letter in particular stands out as a kind of intellectual striptease, revealing Emerson at his most rhapsodic. In it, Emerson writes:

> Will you not bring me your charitable aid? If my tongue will wag again, I will read you some verses, which, if you like them, you shall have for the Dial. . . . I will lend you the most capacious ears, I will listen as the Bedoween listens for running water, as Night listens for the earliest bird, as the Ocean bed for the coming Rivers, as the Believer for the Prophet. Do you not hate these racing Days? I must think they charge us Americans foolishly with our national hurry It is Time, it is this foolish world & fantastic constitution of things we live in, that spends with this immoderate celerity & lights both ends of its candle. . . . If our incarnations here could manage to acquire some little increments, if we could play at dice as Hermes did with the moon for intercalary lunations, if instead of this shuttle or rocket speed, we could vegetate along like a good Dragontree . . . think how life would gain in invention & diversity. We could afford then to try experiments & obey all beautiful motions. We could live alone *& if that did not serve,* we could associate. We could enjoy *and* abstain, *and* read *and* burn our books *and* labor *and* dream. But fie on this Half this Untried, this take-it-or-leave-it, this flash-of-lightning life. In my next migration, O Indra! I bespeak an ampler circle, the "vast year of Mizar & Alcor," an orb, a whole! Come, o my friend, with your earliest convenience, I pray you, & let us seize the void betwixt two atoms of air the vacation between two moments of time to decide how we will steer this torrent which is called Today. Instantaneously yours, Waldo E (EL 2: 398–400).

Fuller was quick to discern how Emerson's private writing to her takes on a social dimension that often eluded him in his public performances. Emerson rarely took such care to express the unique value of his audience in his work. Here, however, he recognizes Fuller not only as a valued audience, but also as a necessary one.[5] To be sure, the rhetoric of restraint that Emerson often used to defend himself in public appears in his letter to Fuller. He pretends to object to the "fantastic constitution of things we live in" and its "immoderate celerity." Yet the force of that rhetoric becomes subsumed by the language itself. Hesitation is spent by the speed and acceleration of his writing, which takes on an experimental quality that allows him to obey "all beautiful motions" despite his

---

[5] To be recognized was key for Fuller, who, at the height of their debate about the nature of their relationship, wrote: "I am now full of such sweet certainty, never never more can it be utterly shaken. All things have I given up to the central power, myself, you also; yet, I cannot forbear adding, dear friend, I am now so at home, I know not how again to wander and grope, seeking my place in another Soul. I need to be recognized. After this, I shall be claimed, rather than claim, yet if I speak of facts, it must be as I see them" (LMF 2: 160).

fear of doing so. All his familiar efforts to regulate and control his thought according to certain ethical standards are subverted here by the steady movement of his prose.

The tributes to Fuller's influence which abound throughout Emerson's correspondence often exhibit this same stylistic exorbitance. "I have heard of Niagara that it falls without speed," he wrote to her during her tour of the Midwest. "Whatever [the falls] gave you, you will one day give me, O most bountiful of friends" (EL 3: 178, 179). Because her encounter with the American sublime deepened her appreciation of the need to keep the terms of her feminism provisional, his imaginative characterization of the falls proves doubly apt. "Falling without speed," a phrase that joins the terrific force of flooding water with the paradoxical elegance of slow descent, neatly allegorizes his own elusive desire to deploy agency or power without violence. As I show in Chapter 4, Fuller's strategic use of Fourier to elaborate the terms of her feminism assists Emerson in the elaboration of his own sense of agency. Though recoverable in his essays, his gradual endorsement of the feminism at the core of his own radical thought is charted most visibly in his epistolary exchange with Fuller.

In fact, because Emerson's correspondence with Fuller provides one of the tidiest narratives of his career, we can read his letters to her *as* a text. Distinguishing a set of letters according to the status of their recipient is not a new strategy in literary criticism nor in the study of Emerson. Six separate editions of his letters to various men of distinction have been published, the most notable being the edition of his letters to Thomas Carlyle published one year after Emerson's death.[6] Presumably the curators of Emerson's memory felt that the reputation of his correspondents would serve to enhance his stature as a writer. Certainly the narrative provided by his correspondence with Carlyle neatly established the frame for the developing literary history favoring Emerson as North America's "Central Man." In addition, his growing abolitionism and Carlyle's conservative support of the Confederacy (which became symbolic of the differences between them in the course of their letters to each

<hr>

[6] *The Correspondence of Thomas Carlyle and Ralph Waldo Emerson*, 2 vols., ed. Charles Eliot Norton (Boston: James E. Osgood, 1883). Five separate collections of this nature followed: *A Correspondence between John Sterling and Ralph Waldo Emerson*, ed. Edward Waldo Emerson (Boston, 1897); *Letters from Ralph Waldo Emerson to a Friend*, ed. Norton (Boston, 1899); *Correspondence between Ralph Waldo Emerson and Herman Grimm*, ed. Frederick W. Holls, *Atlantic Monthly* 91 (1903): 467–79; *Records of a Lifelong Friendship, 1807–1882: Ralph Waldo Emerson and William Henry Furness*, ed. H. H. Furness (Boston, 1910); and *Emerson-Clough Letters*, ed. Howard F. Lowry and Ralph L. Rusk (Cleveland: Rowfant Club, 1934). See also *One First Love: The Letters of Ellen Louisa Tucker to Ralph Waldo Emerson*, ed. Edith W. Gregg (Cambridge: Harvard University Press, 1962).

other) helped reinforce the critical need to establish Emerson's preeminence as the author of a distinctly American tradition.

Nevertheless, an unspoken emphasis on sex roles plays a part in these early editions of Emerson's letters: all of the works center around his interaction with other men. By contrast, the publication of his fascinating letters to Fuller would have been too daring an enterprise, in part because of her reputation for radical political activism and her unorthodox marriage (if, indeed, it was one). And if their letters *had* been collected, they likely would have been read as a type of epistolary novel, the usual interpretive frame given to the publication of letters between famous men and women. Such a tendency abets the popularity of *Goethe's Correspondence with a Child* by the German author Bettina von Arnim, a text that becomes an important part of the conversation between Fuller and Emerson.

Fuller herself would be at the center of an epistolarity frame twice: in his biography, Higginson published her letters to Ossoli, and in 1904 a cluster of letters written to James Nathan appeared under the title *Love-Letters of Margaret Fuller*. In Fuller's case, the sex—not the literary status—of her correspondents made these separate texts worthy. Although a determination to situate Fuller within a critical frame "suitable" for a woman motivates these publications, their appearance reflects a matter crucial to the developing forces of feminism in the culture: the discourse of desire.[7] Because Fourier and his theory of passionate attraction prove so central to the theory of feminism that both Fuller and Emerson eventually endorse, the play of desire becomes integral to an elaboration of that theory. Thus the frame produced by this epistolary exchange forms a bridge to my reading of Emerson's published work: it establishes the relationship between his own desire and his growing understanding of the part culture helps to play in the construction of that desire.

From the start, Emerson was enormously troubled by the seductive energy released through his intellectual conversation with Fuller. In a culture where changing roles of women were often articulated in Fourieristic terms, the management of that discourse became a point of concern for American reformers. The fantastic social theory of Charles Fourier was both attractive and dangerous to American intellectuals, particularly since Fourier married apocalyptic and utopian yearnings to the tropes of gender.

---

[7] *Love-Letters of Margaret Fuller: 1845–46* (New York: D. Appleton, 1903). For a reading of *Love-Letters* see my article, "Womanizing Margaret Fuller: Theorizing a Lover's Discourse," *Cultural Critique* 16 (Fall 1990): 161–91; see also Thomas Wentworth Higginson, *Margaret Fuller Ossoli* (Boston: Houghton Mifflin, 1885).

Fourier's philosophy begins with the expression of "absolute doubt" about the intellectual tradition of Western civilization; indeed, he rejects its fundamental faith in rationality as both repressive and unscientific. For Fourier the strongest force in men and women was clearly not their ability to think but rather their ability to experience passion. Fourier's elaboration of this law of passionate attraction is enormously complex, including a scheme of the human psyche which attempts to establish both its material base and its preeminence in social interaction. In his plan, all labor, whether intellectual or physical, will be made attractive when the passions of men and women are given their full range and play. Because desire is relational, however, only by revisioning a person as a communal entity can such a plan be carried out. Fourier's central vehicle for this change in the conception of subjectivity is the phalanstery, a cluster of 1,620 people whose passions are mathematically balanced (or "harmonized") in order to insure their successful expression throughout the community. Significantly, Fourier views women as "pivotal" to the construction of this new model of social interaction because of their peculiar relationship to the rational and passional discourses of Western culture.[8] This perspective issues in a particularly acute critique of the traditional marriage bond and with it the "isolated household." In Fourier's view, the institution of marriage holds the true passions of men and women in disdain, endorsing a hierarchical understanding of the skills of each and insuring a double standard concerning the sexual mores of both. The true source of human power will remain thwarted, and the successful transformation of society into a system of mutual trust, labor, and sharing will remain impossible until women and men are equally free to choose their sexual partners and openly express their desire.

Like Roland Barthes, Emerson knew that an erotic component inflected every aspect of Fourier's vision. Unlike the twentieth-century Barthes, however, the nineteenth-century Emerson worried that this concession to the passions of man would be particularly dangerous for women. Thus we find journal entries in which Emerson writes, "Fourier, in his talk about women, seems one of those salacious old men. . . . In their head, it is the universal rutting season" (JMN 9: 191). Or, "We cannot rectify marriage because it would introduce such carnage into our social relations" (JMN 8: 95). At the same time, however, the journals show an Emerson intrigued by certain aspects of the Fourieristic agenda: "Men have never loved each other. . . . Love which has been

[8] Fourier, "Civilization in Historical Perspective," in *The Utopian Vision of Charles Fourier*, ed. and trans. Jonathan Beecher and Richard Bienvenu (Columbia: University of Missouri Press, 1983), 191.

exclusive shall now be inclusive" (JMN 7: 396, 397). Or, more playfully, "Will they, one of these days, at Fourierville, make (new) boys & girls to order? . . . I want another girl like the one I took yesterday only you can put in a leetle more of the devil" (JMN 10: 359).

Without question, Emerson's relationship with Fuller both confuses and influences his response to Fourier.[9] Emerson is acutely aware that his interaction with Fuller provides an active demonstration of Fourier's critique of the marriage relation: the equality between them and their shared intellectual concerns makes the relationship both stimulating and exemplary of the type of companionship often inhibited by the traditional marriage bond. Moreover, the feminist audience Fuller provides creates an experimental site for Emerson's writing, allowing him to discover the pleasure of the text that he was creating for that audience. The components of Fourier's domestic utopia are everywhere evident in Emerson's relationship with Fuller: a change in the conceptualization of human interaction, bolstered by the change she distributes about her, culminating in a change in the play of passion itself.

"It is always a great refreshment to see a very intelligent person," Emerson wrote to his brother William about Fuller's initial visit to his home in Concord. "It is like being set in a large place. You stretch your limbs & dilate to your utmost size" (EL 2: 32). As Ann Douglas has shown, Emerson later uses this idea in his preface to *Representative Men*, in which he describes the "delicious sense of indeterminate size" stirred by a powerful intellectual presence (W 4: 17).[10] For Douglas, Fuller's invisible influence on a text entitled *Representative Men* proves both disappointing and ironic.[11] I argue that Emerson's refusal to acknowledge Fuller and openly address the complication that gender brings to intellectual discourse signals a double irony. Although frustrating to our understanding of his relationship with Fuller and the other women of his day, such silences in Emerson's work owe much to his early feminist inclinations. In the story that is told in the letters, his trial feminism considerably complicates *our* feminist expectations.

It is hardly surprising that we have misinterpreted some of the ten-

[9] Emerson's response to Fuller proved extraordinary (and it is essential to focus first on Emerson's response, since the traditional feminist reading of the interaction—one I find unsatisfactory—has focused on Fuller's response to Emerson).

[10] That letter describing Fuller's first visit provides an eerie pretext for Emerson's *Representative Men*, since it is clear from the letter that Goethe was a major topic of discussion between them. Subsequent to her visit, as Emerson professed in his letter, he went out and purchased sixteen volumes of Goethe's work, insisting still further in his letter that he needed to think far more about the man. His decision to end *Representative Men* with a chapter on Goethe is a complex tribute to Fuller and the great men she forced Emerson to consider.

[11] Ann Douglas, *The New Republic*, Oct. 8, 1984, 36.

sions at work in Emerson's writing over this issue, especially since our understanding of the management of sexuality and gender throughout history has often been misguided.[12] The codes of sexuality were so firmly drawn by the middle of the nineteenth century that Emerson's image in *Representative Men* ("a man seems to multiply ten times or a thousand times his force . . . elastic as the gas of gunpowder" [W 4: 17]) was unthinkable in polite company as a reference to the erotic component of intellectual discourse between men. But as a reference to the interaction between a man and a woman it was apparently unthinkable in other terms. Emerson's decision to omit references to women at this point could be a compromise between two bad choices: the lethal force of a culture that would see nothing but the erotic component for one type of intellectual relationship and nothing *but* the intellectual component for the other. He boldly exhibited and problematized this bind in his letters to Fuller. Most important for our concerns, his obsession with the growing management and deployment of the discourse of sexuality was a result of his growing sympathy for the plight of women and the limited roles that men and women were forced to assume in their interaction with one another.

Because she was self-conscious about her unique position in culture, Fuller discovered the lineaments of that management much sooner and with greater force than did Emerson. As I show in Chapter 2, her translation of Bettina von Arnim's epistolary novel *Die Günderode* (one of Fuller's earliest publications) reflects her powerful determination to turn the lessons of her correspondence with Emerson to good effect. She likely read his letters as an epistolary novel, in part because she could thereby gain an objective perspective on the significant issues contained within them. The letters show, for example, how she began to tailor her reading of Goethe to reflect the growing and significant influence of Fourier in the United States. Reading the letters as a text, then, allows us to read Emerson as Fuller did, with a cultivated insight into his growing need for the experimental space that writing to her provided.

By framing Emerson's letters to Fuller in this way, we gain access to an important set of issues motivating the work of both writers, particularly the complex interplay that the discourse of Fourier holds for the feminist

---

[12] That sexuality was "carefully confined" to the home for reproductive purposes during Victorian period, the familiar idea that on "the subject of sex, silence became the rule," is the "repressive thesis" that Michel Foucault discredits in *The History of Sexuality* (New York: Random House, 1978), 3. "Western man," he asserts, was instead "drawn for three centuries to the task of telling everything concerning his sex," causing a "constant optimization and an increasing valorization of the discourse on sex; and . . . this carefully analytical discourse was meant to yield multiple effects of displacement, intensification, reorientation, and modification of desire itself" (p. 23).

conversations between them. Emerson knew that he had a unique reader when he wrote to Fuller. Over the course of the correspondence we see that he came to appreciate how her theory of reading made creative use of Fourier's radical socialism. Her letters in turn show how she encouraged Emerson to absorb that theory of reading into his own work.

Most of the correspondence shows Emerson naively basking in the aura of passionate stimulation that Fuller drew from him in his letters to her: "I plunge with eagerness into this pleasant element of affection with its haps & harms. . . . The weal & wo is all Poetic—I float all the time— nor once grazed our old orb. How fine these letters are! I do not know whether they contented or discontented me most They make me a little impatient of my honourable prison—my quarantine of temperament" (EL 2: 239). Fuller is the recipient of a text, then, unlike any Emerson had presented to the public: the style is warm, highly personalized, and often flirtatious, its energy and excitement attributed to an unusual audience. This style also means that she was under considerable pressure to read his letters without being seduced wholly by them: in other words, she was under pressure to realize their best Fourierist potential. As her translations attest, her success in this matter precedes Emerson's by several years. But if, as Emerson often said of himself with regard to Fuller, the "utmost of [his] offense" was the "sluggishness of [his] perception," he was not "a whit behind" her in his "admiration" of this "noble gift" (EL 2: 226).

But what is this tone and quality of Emerson's letters to which I refer? Again, it all seems to revolve around the surprising influence that Fuller exerts over him. At one point he called Fuller "my tutelar Genius" (EL 3: 242), and his letters are strewn throughout with references to his "need" to write her in order to "feel myself again" (EL 3: 19). He tried to handle this surprising influence (the word *surprise* is his own, repeated throughout the correspondence, and inserted, dramatically, in his last letter to her) as if it were the unavoidable product of their difference. And he tends to fall back on this idea of difference. Fuller met Emerson as he was pulling away from the church, renouncing the power of the clergy. At that point, she appeared to be moving in the opposite direction, attempting to gain power by embracing opportunities normally closed to women. But this reading is a superficial account of their difference; if anything their ambitions were synonymous at this point. Both were determined to break from tradition and both tended to define that break in linguistic terms; Emerson rejected the limited tropes of Christianity and Fuller rejected the limited tropes of society. Significantly, both maintained a faith in the subversive powers of the literary text to support their goal. Emerson's initial excitement upon meeting Fuller was related to his immediate recognition that they shared this faith. It represented a bond from which all others could and naturally did develop. The problem came when he had to reconcile their shared aspirations with the grammar of sexual and gender difference as it was managed by the culture.

At the same time, death frames the narrative of their letters in a way that is too compelling to ignore. The death of Emerson's brother Charles two and a half months before Emerson's first meeting with Fuller forms a dramatic opening. A letter to Harriet Martineau sets the scene: speaking of the loss of Charles, "philosopher," "poet," "hero," and "Christian . . . whose conversation made Shakspear more conceivable" to him, Emerson asks the question that will soon be answered by Fuller's arrival: "Even his particular accomplishments, who shall replace to me?" (EL 2: 25). His letters to Fuller show that her obvious accomplishments, apparent to Emerson from the beginning of his interaction, slowly displaced his unnameable grief over the loss of Charles. His excitement proved immediate and steady and was registered in a gradual increase in intimacy and contact between them. Within time, his letters to her began to develop a buoyant experimental voice. This mood continued until Fuller's equally buoyant response, drawn out in the pitch of their pleasurable volleys, finally caused him to retreat into an embarrassed voice, a veritable feminist retreat from the seductive passions stirring both of them. Near the middle of this experience, Emerson's son Waldo died, and Fuller's presence at the scene of his mourning once again soothed and stimulated him. In effect, Waldo's death marks the middle of the text, and it is a moment when Emerson's relationship with Fuller is arguably at its most intimate, contradictory, and powerful.

As I show in later chapters, traces of the power and confusion generated by their interaction are everywhere evident in their respective publications, including Fuller's *Summer on the Lakes* and *Woman in the Nineteenth Century* and Emerson's *Second Series*. Over time, Emerson's experimental voice slowly resurfaced in the letters, but by then Fuller was protective of herself and more attentive to the Fourieristic nature of *his* excitement. When she moved away, first to New York to work for the *Tribune* and then to Europe, their contact began to wane even as the influence of their conversation with one another grew more profound. Fuller's articulation of her theory of reading in the *Tribune* owes as much to her conversation with Emerson as his publication of *Representative Men* pays tribute to his interaction with Fuller. When she became embroiled in the Italian Revolution, he tried to draw her back to America to live near him; that is, he actively wooed her until he learned that she had secretly taken a lover and borne him a son. Emerson's familiar cycle of retreat into an embarrassed voice following this intelligence was inter-rupted by a third calamity, Fuller's death. The work of mourning, now done in her absence, alerted him to the Fourieristic nature of his excite-ment over Fuller (which she had long understood), releasing him from the guilt and sense of infidelity that always threatened his interaction with her. The narrative ends after Fuller's tragic death, with Emerson's letter to Sam Ward in which he considers the importance of writing "some Life of Margaret" (EL 4: 222). He proceeded to write that life in three very different places: his contribution to the *Memoirs of Margaret Fuller Ossoli*, his lecture before the Boston Woman's Rights Convention in 1855, and his essay "Fate" (see Chapters 8 and 9).

In many ways, then, the narrative of the letters provides an outline of the themes that are central to my reading of the texts written by Emer-son and Fuller. If the events of the correspondence merely impose them-selves with the obstinate authority of fact, then the texts produced in response give them a compelling form, and it is this conflation of fact and text that is of interest to us. While the three deaths merely lend a classical literary form to the text of the letters, our reading of at least two familiar facts of Emerson's life—the deaths of his brother and his son—is altered by the pressure that Fuller's death brings to the narrative. When we consider the critical energy spent over his grief for his brother and particularly for his son, it is remarkable how little effort has been made to interpret the work of mourning inspired by Fuller's passing.[13] Reading his letters to Fuller helps us to see how his work of mourning for her enabled him to make productive use of the thwarted passions spinning in endless orbit around the earlier two calamities so familiar to readers of his work. We can, by placing her death in the context of these earlier losses, review the codes informing our traditional reading of his work. By emphasizing the bond of father and son, brother to brother, and minimizing the problematic bond formed in his relationship with Fuller, we have allowed the seemingly natural affiliations of patriarchy to bias our sense of literary influence.[14] Harold Bloom's famous triad of freedom, fate, and power, so much a part of the critical dialogue on Emerson, is arguably a result of this inclination.[15] A consideration of the

[13] See particularly James Cox, "Ralph Waldo Emerson: The Circle of the Eye," in *Emerson: Prophecy, Metamorphosis, and Influence*, ed. David Levin (New York: Columbia University Press, 1975); Sharon Cameron, "Representing Grief: Emerson's Experiences," *Representations* 15 (Summer 1986): 15–41; and Mark Edmundson, "Emerson and the Work of Melancholia," *Raritan* 6 (Spring 1987): 120–36.

[14] This is especially true since efforts to dismiss the relationship as a love relationship were fraught with difficulty; Fuller was considered too "unattractive" to be hailed as Emerson's lover.

[15] Harold Bloom, *Wallace Stevens: The Poems of Our Climate* (Ithaca: Cornell University Press, 1977), 8. See also Stephen Whicher, *Freedom and Fate: An Inner Life of Ralph Waldo Emerson* (Philadelphia: University of Pennsylvania Press, 1953).

alternative narrative of Emerson's letters to Fuller can help us to decipher the codes that until now have limited our reading.

Emerson's special sense of agency or power is more fully developed in this feminist narrative that includes concerns often neglected in the familiar reading of his work (and in the work of philosophers in general). Moreover, the conversational structure of his letters to Fuller assists us in finding those elements in his published work which are in large part a consideration of feminist issues. If *fate*, a term Emerson often affiliates with the feminine form, also becomes a sign for his developing theory of skepticism, Fuller's revision of the feminine to include a feminist poetics causes him to view the power of fate in a new light, as a limit or provisional site of transition toward a renewed sense of power and acceptance.

Emerson adopts a range of rhetorical postures throughout his correspondence with Fuller. To trace the variations in his stance is tantamount to tracing the competing selves or subject positions at play in his writing. The most formidable pattern is the structure of "difference" (this is Emerson's word) between the author of the letters and their reader. Over the years he depends on a variety of binary oppositions to explain that difference. Most of them are familiar terms that appear often throughout his essays, terms such as *freedom* and *fate*, and he casts these binaries in roles in his letters. If, for example, he insists that he is "slow" in his movement, Fuller is "fast"; if he is inclined toward "prose," she exhibits a talent for "conversation"; if he insists upon the imperatives of "solitude," she insists upon "the social"; if he uses too many aphorisms, she uses too few; if he is the advocate of "prudence," she is the champion of "passion"; if he is hailed as "Unit," it is because he is "tormented & impoverished by the dins & combinations which enrich" her, whom he hails as "Polyanthos" (EL 2: 258). In the course of the correspondence—as in his work in general—all of the terms are invariably inverted, with Emerson adopting the very characteristics previously assigned to Fuller, and vice versa. Yet the alternation of these binary terms is of less interest than their inevitable displacement. As the correspondence reveals, Emerson's relationship with Fuller enables him to unsettle himself, to stray "afield of himself" as Foucault has put it, and ask "if one can think differently than one thinks," beyond the limits of one's terms.[16] At base, the letters demonstrate how Fuller encourages Emerson to sail around his binary oppositions into the boundless and uncertain territory beyond. She is the one who finally prompts him to think both through and beyond their differences.

[16] Michel Foucault, *The Use of Pleasure* (New York: Random House, 1985), 8.

We might use Emerson's phrase from *Representative Men*, "summer-saults, spells and resurrections," (W 4: 17) to describe the mood shifts experienced in his interaction with Fuller. The source is appropriate, since, as we have noted earlier, his articulation of the influence of great men is drawn from his own experience with Fuller. The phrase forms a nice revision of the triad of freedom, fate, and power that critics like Stephen Whicher and Harold Bloom have found so useful in their dis-cussion of Emerson's more familiar literary career. Instead of *freedom*, *summersaults* more aptly describes the explosive and passionate nature of Emerson's response to Fuller's mind, tumbling old habits aside and reinforcing his already strong proclivity toward experiment. And as opposed to Whicher's and Bloom's use of *fate* to describe the counter movement that has been noticed in Emerson's work, I believe the word *spells* more properly describes the moments when the flow of his grasp-ing imagination is held in check by fear that the plastic nature of lan-guage and the fluid state it projects for society are too treacherous to be trusted. *Resurrections* neatly describes the moments in the correspon-dence when Fuller is capable of displacing both impulses. Though pow-er is certainly at issue, *resurrections* lends a feminist aura to the force that she draws out in Emerson's writing; power becomes a virtue for Emer-son when it is stripped of its violent effects and Fuller's feminist recep-tion of his work ultimately supplies the key to that paradoxical force, that slow, powerful descent.

Critics have customarily argued that *Nature* is the product of Emer-son's emergence from orthodoxy, and that the death of his brother Charles proved a test of that emergence. Barbara Packer, for example, finds a connection between the ambivalence in "Prospects," the closing chapter of *Nature*, and Emerson's grief. Yet because Fuller visited Emer-son as he was attempting to complete *Nature*, "Prospects" may as well record the unsettling force that she brought into his life.[17] No sooner did Emerson tell Harriet Martineau that he had experienced an irrevocable loss than he was compelled to tell his brother William how he had begun to dilate to his utmost. Indeed, this early letter to William describing his initial encounter with Fuller provides dramatic evidence of her power to "bring to crisis" Emerson's "relation with language" and the "consisten-cy of his tastes."[18] If, as Packer argues, the closing section of *Nature* is where Emerson first demonstrates his awareness of "the representation-

---

[17] "A spirit of so much hilarity and elegancy that he actualized the heroic life to our eyes" (EL 2: 25). See Barbara L. Packer, *Emerson's Fall: A New Interpretation of the Major Essays* (New York: Continuum, 1982), 22–84.

[18] Roland Barthes, *The Pleasure of the Text*, trans. Richard Miller (New York: Hill and Wang, 1975), 14.

al possibilities of stylistic differences," Fuller's arrival is most likely the cause.[19] The same letter describing Emerson's "dilation" in Fuller's presence, the letter disclosing how Goethe was a topic of discussion between them, also reveals his sense of the inevitable chasm or "crack" in his writing (EL 2: 32). Certainly, there is ample evidence to suppose that her entrance upon the scene of his grief serves to make the crack in his thinking all the more vivid.

Part of Emerson's initial excitement upon meeting Fuller has to do with the sheer joy that he experienced from the letters Fuller almost immediately began to write to him. Through them, Emerson discovered a new model of "hilarity and elegancy" (EL 2: 25). Moreover, if in Charles he "found society that indemnified [him] for almost total seclusion from all other[s]" (EL 2: 24–25), in Fuller he found a society that works in reverse. "You certify me of great riches, and these too of many proprietors. good books, good friends, wit, beauty, art, character," he wrote Fuller in an early letter, "certainly society still exists: the cynics, the ravens must be wrong" (EL 2: 76).

Writing to Fuller, Emerson discovered an arena in which to address openly the issue of intellectual embarrassment at the end of *Nature* ("man and woman and their social life" [CW 1: 44]), a form in which to marry his percipience with a spontaneity that excited him. And given the unusual abandon of his letters to her, Fuller saw more than anyone how Emerson's public utterances tended to be polarized, structured by an antithesis of spontaneity and freedom at one extreme, and passivity and fate at another. For Fuller, a continuous and exploratory oscillation between these terms seemed not only possible beyond the utopian sanctum of their exchange, but also necessary and vital as a strategy for social change, particularly when implicit (yet unexamined) assumptions about gender informed the use of those terms. She saw, moreover, how Emerson's increasingly obvious attempt to fix certain terms in his work in the face of the challenge posed by Fourier, particularly those clustering around his understanding of fate, represented a costly retreat into a more traditional skepticism.

We must remember, of course, that we are reading a correspondence, an epistolary conversation, descriptions of which demand that we arrest what is always in motion. Both Emerson and Fuller exhibit moments of expansion and restraint over the course of their interaction, sometimes passing well beyond his or her audience and at other times waiting with patience and care for the other to catch up. Fuller's influence on Emerson must therefore be measured against her own growth and develop-

---

[19] Packer, *Emerson's Fall*, p. 63.

ment over the course of the dialogue. What is certain, however, is that she accepted responsibility for the professed goal of their interaction—the development of a genuine intellectual relationship between a man and a woman—since the cost of failure in the project was more obvious and onerous to her. As a woman, she was the outsider and the one on whom the burden of proof would lie. Nevertheless, the loss that a failure in this endeavor held for Emerson was equally great.

Because Fuller took charge of the correspondence in this way, she was also the one who directed the conversation toward the work that both of them were doing, often to her own advantage. Through their correspondence, she was able to secure her first major publication, her translation of Eckermann's *Conversations with Goethe*, her second major translation. No doubt Emerson supplied her with a series of contacts for her budding professional career. Yet what often goes unnoticed is his eager determination to make those contacts.[20] He recognized something of his own ambition in Fuller and constantly worked to support the opening of a literary space that could include them both. It seems almost inevitable that the *Dial* would grow up between them, since their letters show evidence of the need for such a space. "I should heartily greet any such Journal as would fitly print these Journals of yours, & will gladly contribute my own ink to fill it up" (EL 2: 229), Emerson writes after one exchange of papers between them. The letters also show that the *Dial* did not ultimately satisfy that need, which is hardly surprising, since the important and energizing relationship between author and audience could neither be as controlled nor as responsive in the journal as in their letters to one another. This, at least, was Emerson's belief. Because Fuller eventually saw in their interaction a potential model for social change, she repeatedly asked Emerson to consider the actual nature of their interaction and the possibility of its extension to other realms. The conversational structure was what attracted her; the give-and-take between them resisted the usual hierarchy found in most dialogues between men and women and seemed preferable for the development of new model of social interaction.[21]

[20] Emerson's concern for Fuller's professional success can be said to frame the narrative of his epistolary novel. His last letter to her addresses his desire to help her procure a publisher for her history of the Italian Revolution.

[21] See Fuller's letter dated September 1842: "Yet I deeply wish to keep some record of these days; for if well done, though not as beautiful and grand, yet they would be as significant of the highest New England life in this era, as Plato's marvellous Dialogues were of the life of Attica, in his time. For I do not believe that a life has been ever lived which without effort so nearly approached that of the academic Grove. A conversation in Landor between Sir Philip Sidney and Lord Brooke is in the same style. Nor are ours inferior in quality to that" (LMF 3: 93).

The Challenge

Inevitably, Emerson's celebration of the "approximate ubiquity" (EL 2: 221) that writing to Fuller afforded him led to a crisis between them. He continually thanked her for the kind of influence that she supplied ("Since I have been an exile so long from the social world and a social world is now suddenly thrust on me, I am determined by the help of heaven to suck this orange dry" [EL 2: 332], and told her to write "from any mood" ("I would not lose any ray from this particular house of heaven in which we have lately abode" [EL 2: 328]). But when in the fall of 1840 she took him up on his desire "to be pommelled black & blue with sincere words" (EL 2: 240), she discovered that he was not making an invitation so much as indicating his pleasure at the sense of connectedness (sense of "presence in two places" [EL 2: 142]) that he was experiencing. The idea that Fuller might experience the same pleasure seemed never to occur to him until she wrote asking him to consider the value of their relationship for their work.

The letter written to Emerson in October of 1840 was apparently destroyed. And rather perversely the absence of this letter has caused critics to assume that Fuller was attempting to seduce him.[22] Because he was married and she was not, it seemed natural to assume that she sought to interfere with his traditional marriage. But this absent text cannot be taken as proof of that intention, particularly since the intention is not the issue so much as the text of it: namely, seduction. The textual record left in both the journals and in the letters alters the biographical narrative somewhat, showing how the issue of seduction itself simultaneously became a contaminating and motivating force for both of them, at once polluting the progress of their discourse and, because of Fourier, opening new channels of meaning.

The omission of Fuller's letter is extremely provocative, to be sure, precisely the kind of thing that a novelist might do, since it places a considerable burden on the Emerson character. Did he destroy the letter? If so, why, when so many of *his* letters are so clearly seductive? Was he afraid that we might interpret her letter differently from the way that

---

[22] See Carl F. Strauch, "Hatred's Swift Repulsions: Emerson, Margaret Fuller, and Others," *Studies in Romanticism* 7 (Winter 1968): 65–103. For an assessment of the various positions that have been adopted concerning this moment in their relationship, and a slightly different interpretation, see Dorothy Berkson, "Margaret Fuller and Ralph Waldo Emerson," in *Patrons and Protégées: Gender, Friendship, and Writing in Nineteenth-Century America*, ed. Shirley Marchalonis (New Brunswick: Rutgers University Press, 1988), 6–8. Berkson dismisses the passionate tone of their letters as merely rhetorical in an effort to get away from Strauch's thesis. Yet the discourse of Fourier led inevitably to a consideration of passionate issues, and obviously Fuller and Emerson found themselves invested in them.

he did? Even the biographical texts outside the realm of our epistolary narrative, texts like his journal entries, support the idea that Emerson, not Fuller, repeatedly confused the passion that he felt for her with a limited understanding of seduction.[23] In September 1840, for example, he wrote in his journal: "Can we not trust ourselves? Must we be such coxcombs as to keep watch & ward over our noblest sentiments even, lest they also betray us, & God prove a little too divine? . . . Love which has been exclusive shall now be inclusive. . . . Where there is progress in character, there is no confusion of sentiment, no diffidence of self, but the heart sails ever forward in the direction of the open sea" (JMN 7: 396–97). And later: "You would have me love you. What shall I love? Your body? The supposition disgusts you" (JMN 7: 400).[24] As we see in the same journal pages, this experience with Fuller fostered his radical mood, familiar to readers of "Circles": "I am only an experimenter. Do not, I pray you, set the least value on what I do, or the least discredit on what I do not as if I had settled anything as true or false. I unsettle all things. No facts are to me sacred, none are profane; I simply experiment, an endless seeker, with no past at my back" (JMN 7: 395).

But when Fuller wrote her now missing letter several weeks later, no doubt seduced by Emerson's growing experimental and intimate tone ("You cannot surprise me with your love. Of that surely I was apprised in my own nature & yours" [JMN 7: 395]), Emerson was dumbstruck. He responded by enveloping himself once again in a tapestry of restraint. And he began by comparing himself to his son Waldo:

> I have your frank & noble & affecting letter, and yet I think I could wish it unwritten. . . . I see precisely the double of my state in my little Waldo when in the midst of his dialogue with his hobby horse in the full tide of his eloquence I should ask him if he loves me? — he is mute & stupid. I too have never yet lived a moment, have never yet done a deed. . . . I talk to my hobby & will join you in harnessing & driving him, & recite to you his virtues all day — but ask me what I think of you & me, —& I am put to confusion (EL 2: 352).

Fuller was certainly willing to discourse on Emerson's "hobby" and chose in her letters to do almost nothing else. Indeed, she paid scru-

[23] I thank Joel Porte for a conversation we had in which he expressed the opinion that Emerson was in love with Fuller. Support for this idea can also be found in an essay by George Sebouhian, "A Dialogue with Death: An Examination of Emerson's 'Friendship,'" in *Studies in the American Renaissance, 1989,* ed. Joel Myerson (Boston: Twayne, 1990), 219–39.

[24] The quote continues: "I see no possibility of loving any thing but what now is, & is becoming; your courage, your enterprize, your budding affection, your opening thought, your prayer, I can love,—but what else?"

pulous attention to these matters (at the time they were working on the *Dial* together) almost as if she was self-conscious about the kind of text she was producing in her letters to him. His response to her at this moment proved both disappointing and instructive. Yet once she detached herself from the passion of his letters, something she did almost immediately when she saw his distress ("I am no usurper. . . . If it be found that I have mistaken [the] boundaries [of my inheritance] I will give up" [LMF 2: 159]), she began to see that the spells of restraint in Emerson's work emerged whenever he retreated into this same model of eloquence.

Fuller understood all too well the anomalous nature of her interaction with Emerson; few women were able to develop a correspondence of the kind that she cultivated with him. But she also understood that this good fortune worked two ways: few men had been lucky enough to have a female correspondent like her. She saw how his power developed out of the Fourieristic dimension of their interaction where gender roles were no longer fixed. Thus she balked when he attempted to deflect a discussion of their relationship by describing their interaction as a "robust & total understanding" as in the "relation of brothers who are intimate & perfect friends without having ever spoken of the fact" (EL 2: 352). Whether he was describing a father with his son or a brother in the company of his brother, Emerson responded to the confusion of his interaction with Fuller by creating a paradigm of mute eloquence: a community of isolated, disunited men totally false to the pattern that had developed between them. In his retreat he withdrew from the passionate power literally "engendered" through Fuller's presence as his reader.[25]

According to Stephen Whicher, Emerson "entered a period of comparative unsettlement" in 1840 when "his revolutionary position" (the "positive power" which "was all") became "shaken by the growing realization that negative power, or circumstance, [was] half."[26] The vexing difficulties of his intimate encounter with Fuller easily account for this important shift in his thought. And the nearly simultaneous application of similar questions from George Ripley and others associated with Brook Farm powerfully reinforced the significance of this crisis for him. (The invitation to join Brook Farm followed almost immediately after

[25] It is interesting how careful Emerson was here to strip the erotic component from his description of the intimacy of two men. Emerson was much freer in *Representative Men* in his expression of this erotic dimension, perhaps because he believed he had eliminated the dangerous erotic implications by covering up the heterosexual source of his experience. Ironically, and powerfully, this covering of his relationship with Fuller liberated a form of homosexual expression in him.

[26] Stephen Whicher, *Freedom and Fate*, pp. 94–95.

Fuller's lost letter in October of 1840.[27]) As his letters repeatedly show, Emerson's intimacy with Fuller often inspired his strongest experimental tendencies; yet the keen sense she had given him of the lopsided development of feminine and masculine principles in society makes the Brook Farm project appear too aggressively disruptive. By his own admission, he wanted to experiment with and, if necessary, break open sacrosanct notions, but he did not like the idea that a certain amount of what he considered masculine aggression was necessary to do so. For this reason, he recoiled from the social reform of the day, especially those reforms focusing on the role of women, because he felt that there was an abusive virility at work in that model of experimentation.

For Emerson, it is one thing to break open the Word and liberate it from the false meaning of the church; it is quite another, however, to break meaning from the social contract, particularly the meaning that had become attached to women. He described his response to Brook Farm as a refusal to leave the "present prison" of his domestic situation for prison "a little larger" (JMN 7: 408), and the image of imprisonment will prove central to the growing defensiveness of his theoretical orientation. Through his response to Fuller, Emerson recognized the inadequacy of his domestic arrangement, which in turn showed him the problematic nature of the marriage relation. Yet his fear of the consequences of marriage reform, his belief that masculine desire, unhinged from the responsibilities of the marriage bond, would create "carnage" (JMN 8: 95) (a fear bolstered by his own recognition of the desire he experienced in his Fourieristic interaction with Fuller), led him to turn this critique back on itself, using the concept of marriage to characterize the philosophical restraints of existence. "It is never strange, an unfit marriage," he wrote at one point, "since man is the child of this most impossible marriage, this of the two worlds" (or Kantian duality of freedom and fate [JMN 9: 105]).

Fuller's vulnerability and genius enabled her to see that Emerson's retreat into this ethical restraint represented a false chivalry recuperating the hierarchy between men and women, public and private, author and reader which their personal encounter had been working to dissolve. The experimental space of their letters, reordering public and private, masculine and feminine, and social and domestic modes, was the consequence, she believed, of the unusual status awarded her in the interaction. She occupied a provisional space not yet defined by the culture which produced a number of important insights for both of them. She realized that he was effectively allegorizing social issues from a conser-

[27] JMN 7: 407–8; see also LMF 2: 163.

vative position, and when he used those allegories, as he increasingly did, as a strategy for theorizing, he was inevitably led to theorize about the conservative limits of language itself. Thus, when he employed the concept of marriage to characterize the philosophical restraints of all expression, she challenged him to reverse his procedure and consider the social or lived implications of his thought. "Is it not deeper," she wrote, "and true[r] to live than to think? . . . These chasings up and down the blind alleys of thought neither show the center nor the circumference" (LMF 2: 203). From her perspective, his gathering skepticism was generated by his failure to see that the allegorical field of his theory (increasingly informed by what Barthes would call the "image repertoire" of domestic life[28]), was dependent on inhibiting and unnatural forms. Emerson's use of the field of his domestic life for his theory resembled, as Fuller saw it, his earlier complaint about the misuse of the allegorical potential of Christ by the church: it became a totalizing symbolic system (sacrosanct) rather than a yielding allegorical field (experimental).

Fuller gained a great deal from this interaction: through it she was encouraged to elaborate her own thinking about the forces operating behind gender assignments in the culture. Some of her most interesting work for the *Dial* is the direct result of this encounter (see Chapter 2). Moreover, her insight into these matters grows after her trip to the Midwest, when she was forced to measure her faith in the progressive rhetoric of democracy against the terrible fate of the North American Indians. After her encounter with this violent limit of democracy, her understanding of the ideological productions of society, including her own early understanding of feminism, became still more sophisticated. She was once again assisted in her thinking by Fourier, whose absolute doubt about Western culture caused him to value what he called "transitional" figures of culture, particularly women who are often positioned both inside and outside its hegemonic discourse.

Fuller's reading of Fourier, apparent throughout her writing from *Summer on the Lakes* on, essentially confirms Barthes's later argument that the real value of Fourier's approach revolves around a rejection of a single model or system of reform for the promotion of a systematics. Like Barthes, Fuller wanted to focus on a dialogical transformation of society, one that would proceed through a process of transition or negotiation and play. Although Emerson himself articulated the philosophical importance of transition throughout his writing, he was noticeably uneasy with the terms of transition when applied to the conduct of life,

[28] Barthes, *Roland Barthes*, trans. Richard Howard (New York: Hill and Warg, 1977), 44.

as they are in Fourier's theory. For Fuller the critique of domestic life at the center of Fourier's theory holds value precisely because it conjoins the literal and the figurative by showing the fluidity and interpenetration of our mental and social worlds.

Emerson also recognized this attribute of Fourier's theory, but for personal reasons made apparent in his correspondence with Fuller, he felt the need to maintain some boundaries. Though he seems to have intuited the parallel between his argument for the dissolution of the church (built, as it was, on Christ's tropes, not his principles [CW 1: 81]) and the argument for the dissolution of the traditional marriage bond, he was uncomfortable with it. "Shall I say that I am driven to express my faith by a series of skepticisms? The lover & philanthropist come to me & propose alliance & cooperation: & I am forced to say . . . You blow against the wind" (JMN 9: 229). His 1842 *Dial* essay on Fourier reflects his discomfort, for there he tries to discredit the parallel by inverting it.[29]

Emerson's recourse to a familiar line of reasoning in the essay makes clear the instability of his inversion: earlier, in his Divinity School address, Emerson had complained that in their devotion to church ritual the church fathers had lost the ability to address life (or more specifically, "life passed through the fire of thought"[30]). By the same logic, according to Emerson, Fourier in his elaborate "mechanical sublime" had made a similar error, skipping "no fact but one, namely, Life." Yet his complaint against Fourier actually assumes a paradoxical form. Although he contends that Fourier "makes the mistake" of treating man "as a plastic thing," Emerson's criticism works in the service of a plastic "faculty of life which spawns and scorns system and system makers," one "which makes or supplants a thousand phalanxes and New Harmonies in each pulsation."[31] Emerson's criticism of Fourier and his approach to life draws upon the familiar boundaries between idea and thing, social reality and consciousness, but it also tries to elaborate a conception of reality that would abolish them. He knows well enough that Fourier had attempted to confound those boundaries; but he knows that such confounding has been part of his own enterprise as well. Fourier worries Emerson much more than the earlier church fathers because the radical nature of his own intellectual method is readily reflected in Fourier's work.

This plastic quality is precisely what Barthes locates at the center of Fourier's utopia. Indeed, Emerson's refusal to acknowledge the fluidity

---

[29] "Fourierism and the Socialists," *Dial* 3 (July 1842): 86–96.

[30] *Selections from Ralph Waldo Emerson*, ed. Stephen Whicher (Cambridge, Mass.: Riverside Press, 1957), 109.

[31] Emerson, "Fourierism and the Socialists," *Dial*, p. 88.

of Fourier's theory represents a shock of recognition and is likely a realization of the radical implications of his own thought. Emerson essentially acknowledges the writerly nature of Fourier's plan, the motility of his thought, yet he cannot accept the chaos that seems destined to result from its application.

Thus Emerson feels compelled to make the mistake that Barthes warns us against, the mistake of thinking a reality that is exterior to language, even though it is clear from his own work that he himself finds such a procedure problematic. But his letters to Fuller reveal that he does so in the service of what he took to be a feminist impulse: the consideration of the rights of women and the instrumental way that such reform might be used against them. Thus his early resistance to Fourier in a way is like the resistance to deconstruction adopted by many American feminists in the latter part of the twentieth century.

After her trip to the Midwest, where she experienced an important clash of cultures, Fuller came to rely much more heavily on Fourier. Fuller of course underestimated the way in which her own reading had already initiated a radical transvaluation of key terms in Western culture: much of her focus on Goethe emphasized his interest in the unique space occupied by women, and led naturally to her interest in the feminist epistolary novels produced by Bettina von Arnim. Nevertheless, the theories of Fourier to which she returned after her trip helped to reinforce the most radical aspect of her earlier reading strategies, particularly those that set in motion a trend toward transitional or conversational structures.

Among other things, Fourier assists Fuller's appreciation of the power of the materialist argument later made by Marx that "it is not the consciousness of men that determine their existence, but on the contrary their social existence that determines consciousness."[32] Though she never accepts this structuralist argument as the whole truth of our existence, it enables her to focus on the necessary dynamic residing between consciousness and society. This dynamic is nicely expressed in *Woman in the Nineteenth Century*, where she summarizes the approaches of both Fourier and Goethe: "Fourier says, As the institutions, so the men! All follies are excusable and natural under bad institutions. Goethe thinks, as the Man, so the institutions! There is no excuse for ignorance and folly. A man can grow in any place, if he will" (WNC, 111–12). By praising Goethe, Fuller warns the social reformers of the day that "unready men" (WNC, 112) would cause a feminist reform to fail. Correspondingly, her

---

[32] Fredric Jameson, *The Prison-House of Language* (Princeton: Princeton University Press, 1972), 184.

argument about Fourier allows her to admonish Goethe for his failure to achieve a more active understanding of the power of social structures. ("Ay! but Goethe, bad institutions are prison walls . . . that make [man] stupid, so that he does not will" [WNC, 112].)

Fuller's use of Fourier to supplement her interest in Goethe can be read as a critique of Emerson's position toward reform. And at one level it is. Her reference to "prison walls" is not arbitrary; with it she consciously echoes Emerson's sense of domestic imprisonment. To her there is no more vivid an example of the inhibiting patterns of Emerson's thought than the inhibiting social patterns of men and women.

Yet such a reading proves superficial, particularly since Fuller's own understanding of the relationship between Fourier and Goethe is more subtle, informing the complex theory of reading she later set forth in the *New-York Daily Tribune*. In many important ways, Fuller discovers through Emerson the value of Fourier as a supplement to Goethe. It was Emerson, after all, who found the institution of the church too constricting; his recognition of the power of social structure over thought paved the way for his departure from the church. His subsequent hesitancy to apply this radical argument to the structures under attack by social reformers (where marriage and Woman's role were the central tropes of that reform) never fully negates his early understanding of their power to inform and shape our thought. Fuller reminds Emerson of the contradictory nature of his intellectual response even as she initially draws the largest benefits from those contradictions.

The letters show how the debate between them, opened to view in their intimate crisis of 1840 and allegorized by the challenge set forth by Brook Farm, works beneath and inflames the conflict (or "crack") in Emerson's work. I would add that the name "Fourier" becomes a particularly volatile sign of that conflict and conversation, and Fuller, in turn, becomes the omnipresent embodiment of that sign. The problem with Emerson's use of Fourier is that he continued to situate Fourier in the text of desire, what Barthes calls the "readerly" text, or the familiar text of skepticism. This approach helps to explain the structure of the skeptical argument threading Emerson's famous essays in the *Second Series*. But in Fuller's handling, Fourier's theories are more suited to the "writerly" text, the text of jouissance represented by the experimental side of Emerson's thinking as it begins to develop with her help.

In a way, Emerson has a harder time accepting the radical elements of his thought than Fuller because her life seems to set the stage for experimental expression. His relationship with her reveals to him the liabilities of his traditional marriage where the roles of husband and wife became sacrosanct and unyielding. To reach the freedom that she appears to have achieved in her thinking, he feels that he would first have to make a Fourierist revision of his own life. This is a treacherous idea for him to consider, especially when he finds he has to fight to distinguish the passionate experimentation of his correspondence with Fuller from the experimental passion he is beginning to feel for her. Frightened by this passion, he returns once more to his older model of agency and eloquence: solitary, blocked communication. In fact, this fear of the erotic power of writing undoubtedly explains the restraint that begins to reinfuse his work in general.

Yet Emerson's letters to Fuller show him becoming impatient with this division in his work. "My chapter on the Poet grows very slowly," he told her as he was composing the essay; "it is like the Concord River,— one may sometimes suspect it moves backward" (EL 3: 59). His impatience increased after she finally left the small world of Concord; and when the number of letters passing between them diminished, he became still more aware of his dependency on her. At one point he wrote, "I often suppose myself quite incompetent to do you any justice in these years & think I shall in some hour of power roll up all your letters in cloth of asbestos & shooting across this lunar & solar sphere alight on the star of Lyra . . . [and] meditate your genius until I have computed its orbit & parallax" (EL 3: 62–63). Interestingly, this dependency coincided with his gathering impatience with the intellectual climate of America, for which he blamed himself as much as anyone else.

In 1847 Emerson revealed a readiness to mend his way when he wrote to Fuller of the "comico pathetic experience" he had of reading his lecture on "Eloquence," only to hear from his audience—some of his closest friends—that they found the lecture "old" (EL 3: 377). Emerson attempts to shed this model of agency in *Representative Men*, wherein he begins to examine the implications of Fuller's double advocacy of Fourier and Goethe (see Chapter 7). At the same time he wrote a series of seductive letters to Fuller, beseeching her to meet him in Europe and return to America to live with him in Concord (EL 3:446–48; EL 4: 26–28). But this personal remedy appeared ill conceived when he received news of her "marriage" to Ossoli. He was less shaken, perhaps, by the scandalous overtones of her affair with Ossoli than by the curious familiarity of the bond that she had made; the unequal intellectual status between Fuller and Ossoli closely resembled the hierarchy of his own marriage. Her compromise on this issue forced Emerson to see how he had taken her complaints about the ethical restraints of his work too personally. Her assaults had been on the principle of hierarchy at work in his writing, and nothing more. But his letters show that he was not fully liberated from his spells of restraint until another great calamity: her tragic shipwreck off the coast of Fire Island.

Neither Fuller's body nor Ossoli's were ever recovered. The body of her son, the fruit of their controversial love affair, washed ashore, along with a small trunk filled with love letters exchanged between Fuller and Ossoli. If the trunk of letters symbolized her erotic life exposed to view, it also suggested Emerson's confused passion for her. For this reason, he paused several times over the detail of the trunk of letters. When he mistakenly believed the trunk contained letters from a variety of her correspondents, he projected his anxiety about the discovery of his own letters to her, observing "what a panic would strike all her friends, for it was as if a clever reporter had got underneath a confessional & agreed to report all that transpired there in Wall Street" (JMN 11: 258). In fact, his letters to her were neither lost at sea (representative of the loss of power he most feared upon hearing of her death), nor washed ashore and exposed (placing his writing in an embarrassing context.) Fuller had taken care to leave them with various friends. This amazing, protective, and ennobling gesture (suggesting to him that the letters had a larger context than the private one between them) allowed Emerson time to reconsider his panic ("You look as if you had locked your trunk & lost the key" [JMN 11: 262]) and to assess fairly his method in them as natural and powerfully related to Fuller's "worthy force" (JMN 11: 449).

As will become apparent in later chapters, thinking about Fuller's death enabled Emerson to recover a sense of agency modeled directly from images in his correspondence with her, images that accepted the relational nature of his writing. It was as if he began to accept what he had earlier written to her, that it is only when "relations shall rule" that "realities shall strike sail" (EL 3: 105). He based his new model on an acceptance of the passion of his prose as an experimental communal product. "Dear Margaret, born for my benefactress," he once wrote to her, "your letters are benefits. Whatever comes to me from a friend looks unpayable. It ought not. If the earth draws an apple, the apple draws the earth, and they meet at *their* middle point" (EL 3: 137). In effect, he began to accept and explore Fourierist elements underlying Fuller's feminist theory of reading.

The increasing difficulty with which Emerson found himself writing to Carlyle after Fuller's death would appear, then, to register his gathering Fourierism. Unlike his correspondence with her, his correspondence with Carlyle is a canonical text in literary history. Matthew Arnold bestowed it with especial significance when he proclaimed that Carlyle should only be known for the letters that Emerson drew out of him. But

Emerson's correspondence with Carlyle is perhaps more revealing for the way that it shows a vital shift in Emerson's thinking. The conflict of issues between Carlyle and Emerson is nothing compared to the larger conflict of poetics between them. Emerson himself adverted to the conflict when answering Sam Ward's fears about the projected *Memoir* of Fuller's life. When Ward noted the redoubtable nature of the project, offering that perhaps it could not be done, Emerson countered with the argument that "it must be done," but "tête exaltée, & in the tone of Spiridion, or even of Bettine, with the coolest ignoring of Mr. Willis Mr. Carlyle and Boston & London" (EL 4: 222). Emerson elaborated these terms in the actual *Memoirs* and in his more famous essay "Fate," as we shall see in Chapters 8 and 9. But his reference to Bettina von Arnim reveals the impact Fuller's earlier interest in epistolarity held for both of them in their formative considerations of a feminist agency.

2

Feminism in Translation:
Fuller's *Tasso* and *Günderode*

> The basic error of the translator is that he preserves the state in which his own language happens to be instead of allowing his language to be powerfully affected by the foreign tongue.
> —Walter Benjamin, "The Task of the Translator"

> Translation does not come along in addition, like an accident added to a full substance; rather, it is what the original text demands— and not simply the signatory of the original text but the text itself. If the translation is indebted to the original, . . . it is because already the original is indebted to the coming translation. This means that translation is also the law. There is a dissymmetry here but it's a double dissymmetry, with the result that the woman translator in this case is not simply subordinated, she is not the author's secretary. She is also the one who is loved by the author and on whose basis alone writing is possible. Translation is writing; that is, it is not translation only in the sense of transcription. It is a productive writing called forth by the original text.
> —Jacques Derrida, *The Ear of the Other*

Critics only now turning their attention to the writing produced by Margaret Fuller before *Woman in the Nineteenth Century* continue to overlook her first book-length translations: Goethe's *Torquato Tasso*, Johann Peter Eckermann's *Conversations with Goethe*, and Bettina von Arnim's epistolary novel *Die Günderode*.[1] Presumably the classical understanding of the translator as a neutral agent for the transfer of meaning from one language to the next has kept critics, especially feminist critics, from reviewing Fuller's early translations. With the linguistic turn of recent literary history, however, translation has increasingly become the vehicle through which history, meaning, and language come to crisis. As a result we are better able to ask whether a feminist component to translation exists. Margaret Fuller apparently thought so, though the fact that she could not use the word *feminism* to describe her revisionary model of reading suggests how her early writing can enlarge our understanding

---

[1] Fuller, *Woman in the Nineteenth Century* (New York: Greeley & McElrath, 1845); *Tasso*, trans. Fuller, published posthumously in *Art, Literature, and the Drama*, ed. Arthur B. Fuller (Boston: Brown, Taggard and Chase, 1860); Eckermann, *Conversations with Goethe in the Last Years of His Life, Translated from the German of Eckermann*, trans. Fuller (Boston: Hilliard, Gray, 1839); Arnim, *Günderode*, trans. Fuller (Boston: E. P. Peabody, 1842).

of the way in which feminist issues are often enmeshed and perhaps even articulated through the task of the translator.[2]

Some might think that translation was a process forced upon Fuller because she was writing at a time when women were still discouraged from becoming authors. The conception of translation as a passive activity made it a neutral zone where women could write without asserting their own authority. This was not the case for Fuller. Most women translators were also heir to an aristocratic education, and Fuller's North American birth considerably complicated her entry into the safe world of translation. Because of her nationality, womanhood was not an asset; rather, she had to overcome her womanhood in order to translate. She had to transgress the usual bounds of democratic education in the United States, challenging the very rhetoric of that democracy by gaining access to an equal education in language skills. Because she actually did gain that equality, because her father insisted on giving her a rigorous training in languages equal to any given to an American male child, her relationship to language (both her own and those given to her) assumed a subversive content, a subversion simultaneously influenced by her education and the translation of her gender(s) in the United States afforded by that education.

Thus one of the most important aspects of Fuller's focus from the very start remained her understanding that gender itself depended on a collision of languages, which is another way of saying that a determinate part of our experience imitates the array of divisions issuing from translation. This complex understanding is what makes her early work so difficult and so important in our assessment of her career; it folds within itself a paradigm of translation that will forever characterize and complicate her thinking. This paradigm is equally evident in her later, better-known work, whose complexity will be undetected by readers who rush beyond this early material where the complication of gender first makes its impact and begins to show the range of her thinking about feminism.

Through translation Fuller found a way to begin a translation of women into democratic culture. But in the process, and perhaps because of that process, her feminism was grounded in a linguistic complexity unusual for her time. Her interest in translation enabled her to address the vehicles of cultural assimilation and transmission: the writing, reading, and *making* of history and the pedagogical model at the center of that process.

Moreover, translation became Fuller's way of dealing with the primary intellectual and personal relations in her development. Her father

[2] Alice Rossi argues that the word *feminism* was "rarely used in the mid-nineteenth century and referred simply to the 'quality of females.'" See *The Feminist Papers: From Adams to de Beauvoir*, ed. Alice Rossi (New York: Columbia University Press, 1973), xii.

gave her the gift of languages, and Emerson supported that gift, not only by encouraging her to publish a series of translations, but also through his active and complicated reading of them. Her engagement with translation thus involved something far greater than an engagement with the formal properties of two languages in contact. Through two translations in particular, her translation of Goethe's *Torquato Tasso* and Bettina von Arnim's *Die Günderode*, she wove an elaborate allegory about the feminist lessons she found herself deriving from her conversations with Emerson.

Trained early in Greek and Latin, Fuller later gained command of French, German, and Italian.[3] It is telling that most of her published translations were from German, the one language she taught herself. This fact alone reveals how her acts of translation were never acts of modesty. Still, if she translated from the German because it was her language and not the language of her father or a tutor, she nevertheless surrounded herself with a series of German mentors and tutors, albeit at a safe distance, the most notable being Goethe. Translation enabled Fuller to decanonize her literary fathers without destroying them. Although the Harvard graduates with whom she consorted (some of whom she tutored) often matched her in linguistic skills, few among them shared her interest in and facility with translation's decanonizing potential.[4]

The act of translation in America was often seen as an act of simple importation—bringing yet another treasure or text from the Old World. Fuller often accepted this image of herself as the bearer of civilization to the New World, though even this assumption was complicated by the fact that she was a woman. Translating from the Old World in effect transformed she into an early settler; the cargo she brought was the cargo of "civilization." In so doing, she needed to take on the dress of masculine privilege, since women were more often viewed as the cargo or as texts supercharged with civilizing possibilities rather than the agents of civilization itself.

Because Fuller's dual image as a translator repeated the dual image of herself that she developed through her education, her translations inevitably moved toward twin goals. At one level, she translated in order to "contribute to the dominant position of certain poetics, and to the subsequent canonization of certain authors," yet at another she deployed her

---

[3] J. F. Clarke writes that Fuller was "familiar with the masterpieces of French, Italian and Spanish literature" before he met her, though it is not clear whether Fuller read Spanish. See his chapter "Studies" in MMF 1: 112.

[4] For a discussion of translation's decanonizing potential, see Paul de Man, "Conclusions: Walter Benjamin's 'The Task of the Translator'" in *The Resistance to Theory* (Minneapolis: University of Minnesota Press, 1986), 83.

translations as "instruments of change within the literary system" and hence instruments of change within the larger cultural system of which she was a part. Behind her translations resided a revisionary model of reading, for, as Andre Lefevere reminds us, translations (or "refractions," as he calls them) "are made to influence the way in which readers read a text."[5] Hence Fuller's early interest in translation developed naturally from her desire to elaborate a new pedagogical model for her culture; again and again, the "foreign" or different nature of another language assisted her in her efforts to exhibit the play of difference within her own culture.

The Advantage of Difference

According to classical theories of translation, the translator attempts to normalize the difference between two languages.[6] More recent linguistic theories, however, regard such difference as inevitable or as a system of "difference" internal to every language which makes translation a metaphor for the operation of language itself.[7] Within this play of difference, the *différance* of deconstruction finds its unstable and destabilizing existence as that which temporalizes by deferring and spatializes by differing. This radical linguistic perspective has caused some, like Rodolphe Gasché, to define translation as the "operator of *différance*" because of its tendency to enhance the already unstable structure making language possible.[8] The traditional and more contemporary approaches to translation would seem to be antithetical. Nevertheless, there are moments when the historical or hermeneutic sense of difference between two languages becomes implicated in the poetics of *différance*.[9] In these moments, we find a crossing of feminist and linguistic

[5] Andre Lefevere, "That Structure in the Dialect of Men Interpreted," *Comparative Literature* 6 (1984): 89.

[6] For an excellent bibliography of translation compiled by L. G. Kelly, see "Bibliography of the Translation of Literature," in *Comparative Literature* 6 (1984): 347–372.

[7] See George Steiner, *After Babel: Aspects of Language and Translation* (New York: Oxford University Press, 1975); and de Man, "Conclusions," in *The Resistance to Theory*. Also helpful are Lawrence Venuti, "The Translator's Invisibility," *Criticism* 28 (Spring 1986): 179–212; Andre Lefevere, "That Structure in the Dialect of Men Interpreted"; and Joseph F. Graham, ed., *Difference in Translation* (Ithaca: Cornell University Press, 1985).

[8] See Jacques Derrida, "*Différance*," trans. Alan Bass, *Margins of Philosophy* (Chicago: University of Chicago Press, 1982), and "Roundtable on Translation," in *The Ear of the Other: Texts and Discussions with Jacques Derrida*, ed. Christie McDonald (Lincoln: University of Nebraska Press, 1985), 113.

[9] "It is the domination of beings that *différance* everywhere comes to solicit, in the sense that *sollicitare*, in old Latin, means to shake as a whole, to make tremble in entirety. Therefore it is the determination of Being as presence or as beingness that is interrogated by the thought of *différance*" (Derrida, "*Différance*," p. 21).

concerns, one consisting of a type of double strategy that can help us to understand Fuller's engagement with the advantage of difference issuing from translation.

As we shall see, much depends on the threat inscribed in these conflicting views of translation. A comparison of two essays on translation is useful here. Barbara Johnson's essay, "Taking Fidelity Philosophically," analyzes the issue of translation in the work of Derrida; in "Des Tours de Babel," Derrida provides an interpretation (he calls it a "translation") of Walter Benjamin's essay "The Task of the Translator."[10] Where a sense of crisis attends Johnson's discussion of translation, there is, predictably, none in Derrida's. It is ironic, then, that Johnson, whose understanding of difference has been sophisticated through her translation of Derrida's work, would gravitate toward this notion of crisis and Derrida would not, but it may be that Johnson's essay "conveys a difference from itself which it 'knows' but cannot say."[11] That difference, I argue, concerns her search for a feminist critique in the world of deconstruction. Although Johnson's essay does not purport to have a feminist edge, an implicit feminist position informs her discussion. Without naming it, her discussion enacts a concern for the loss of feminist agency through dissemination.[12] At the same time, Johnson's sense of crisis, born of this feminist inclination, necessarily obscures the covert feminist operation of translation as it is articulated by Derrida. The seeming incompatibilities between feminism and deconstruction (allegorized in the antithetical claims of translation mentioned above) momentarily disturb Johnson, but they become oddly enabling for Derrida, perhaps because his focus is on matters quite apart from these concerns.

Johnson draws a parallel between what she calls the contemporary "crisis in marriage" and the contemporary "crisis in translation." Her alarm over this parallel assumes a traditional feminist form when her discussion of fidelity slips into a discussion of mastery.

> For while both translators and spouses were once bound by contracts to love, honor, and obey, and while both inevitably betray, the current questioning of the possibility and desirability of conscious mastery makes that contract seem deluded and exploitative from the start. But what are the alternatives? Is it possible simply to renounce the meaning of promises or the promise of meaning?[13]

---

[10] Both essays are published in *Difference in Translation*, ed. Joseph F. Graham (Ithaca: Cornell University Press, 1985).

[11] Barbara Johnson, *The Critical Difference: Essays in the Contemporary Rhetoric of Reading* (Baltimore: Johns Hopkins University Press, 1980), 12.

[12] It is significant, of course, that Johnson translates *Dissemination* by Derrida (Chicago: University of Chicago Press, 1981).

[13] Johnson, "Taking Fidelity Philosophically," p. 142.

The argument that "the current questioning of . . . mastery" has jeopardized our understanding of fidelity leads to the suggestive but ultimately misleading idea that the deconstruction of mastery in language also deconstructs the traditional feminist concern for fidelity in marriage. Luckily a considerable distance separates the concepts of fidelity and mastery, which may help to defuse the threat Johnson describes. Unwittingly confusing one symptom of the marriage crisis (infidelity) with a feminist interpretation of its general cause (mastery), Johnson's feminist metaphor for translation (marriage in distress) obscures the positive sense of infidelity that plays itself out in the deconstructive reading of translation.[14] If the translator is found to be "unfaithful" in the court of *différance*, it does not follow that this infidelity is a display of "mastery." Thus the deconstructive questioning of mastery easily assimilates a feminist perspective: the translator's infidelity can also be viewed as a strategy for undoing the traditional mastery of all difference between languages.

The historical and feminist hermenuetic implicit in Johnson's use of the word *mastery* conceives of difference as positive. The effort to reduce the subjectivity of an Other to one's own identity is assumed to be an aggressive and exploitative act. It is odd, then, that the poetics infusing Johnson's argument about translation characterizes *différance* in negative terms, which happens because her feminist sense of crisis overlooks the double strategy implicit in the contemporary theory of translation. In fact, the realization that historical difference must be acknowledged in a kind of radical intersubjectivity indicates that the difference structuring language (and the *différance* that produces it) yields more of an opportunity than a threat. This understanding of translation oddly resembles Derrida's and returns us to Johnson's initial if implicit feminist concerns.[15]

[14] It is a natural progression from that reading into a conceptualization of the translator as a "faithful bigamist with loyalties split between a native language and a foreign tongue" (Ibid., p. 143). Whereas Johnson is careful to make the gender of the bigamist irrelevant, her rendering of the crisis of translation nevertheless depends on the feminist assumption that one agent of the contract is more passive, more generally exploited, than the other. Derrida, on the contrary, would argue that despite the dissymmetry of translation, both agents must be active. "An agreement or obligation or whatever sort—a promise, a marriage, a sacred alliance—can only take place, I would say, in translation, that is, only if it is simultaneously uttered in both my tongue and the others" (*The Ear of the Other*, p. 125). For another feminist reading of Derrida's understanding of translation, see Lori Chamberlain, "Gender and the Metaphorics of Translation," *Signs: Journal of Women in Culture and Society* 13, 3 (1988): 454–72.

[15] Interestingly, the language with which Johnson closes her discussion of the poetics of translation is infused with tragic metaphors of history: "Translation is a bridge that creates of itself the two fields of battle it separates" ("Taking Fidelity Philosophically," p. 148). It is as if history cannot be effaced without reinscribing itself. By the end of her essay, Johnson

In "Des Tours de Babel," Derrida also brings the concept of marriage into his discussion of translation. But if for Johnson the crisis of marriage is identical with the crisis of translation, Derrida momentarily borrows from Heidegger (and "Heideggerian hope") to argue that the concept of marriage is the same as, but not identical with, translation. This notion makes marriage an "ammetaphor" for translation, something that allows us to consider the important differences between both concepts.[16]

In effect, Derrida employs a feminist reading of marriage in order to change our understanding of translation. (His interpretation differs from Johnson's reading, which, following the usual operation of symbolic identity, ossifies the concept of translation.) For Derrida, the concept of marriage is one of fidelity without mastery; and through this essentially feminist "translation" of the concept of marriage, he describes translation as a "marriage contract in the form of a seminar." In other words, without the feminist understanding of difference which both derives from and turns on an historical sense of the term, Derrida could not begin to describe his deconstructive sense of translation. But no one

seems closer to the position of her mentor, Paul de Man, whose vigilant concern for the difference between hermeneutics and poetics finally moved him toward a theory of history.

Certainly, Johnson's argument repeatedly returns us to the question of history. This is made particularly acute when we see how her discussion of Derrida brings to mind the position adopted by a critic whose work on translation strongly resists the deconstructive challenge to hermeneutics—George Steiner. It is as if the concept of translation momentarily serves as a bridge for two antithetical positions. Certainly Steiner's avid interest in the linguistic turn of literary history enables him to agree with Johnson and Derrida that translation is in fact another way to describe discourse, or the operation of language itself. "The schematic model of translation is one in which a message from a source-language passes into a receptor-language via a transformational process. The barrier is the obvious fact that one language differs from the other, that an interpretive transfer, sometimes, albeit misleadingly, described as encoding and decoding, must occur so that the message 'gets through.' Exactly the same model—and this is what is rarely stressed—is operative within a single language. But here the barrier or distance between source and receptor is time" (Steiner, *After Babel*, p. 28). For both Steiner and Derrida, moreover, the work of discourse—"writing" in Derrida's case, "communication" in Steiner's—is the work of translation. The difficulty of translation merely serves as a metaphor for the difficulty of language itself.

[16] For marriage as "ammetaphor" see "Des Tours de Babel," p. 190. The phrase "Heideggerian *hope*" appears in the closing section of Derrida's essay "*Différance*" (p. 27). For Heidegger, "The same never coincides with the equal, not even in the empty indifferent oneness of what is merely identical. The equal or identical always moves toward the absence of difference, so that everything may be reduced to a common denominator. The same, by contrast, is the belonging together of what differs, through a gathering by way of the difference. We can only say 'the same' if we think difference. It is in the carrying out and settling of differences that the gathering nature of sameness comes to light" (*Poetry, Language, Thought*, trans. A. Hofstader [New York: Harper and Row, 1971], 218–19). For the potential limitations of this concept, see the introduction to *Deconstruction in Context: Literature and Philosophy*, ed. Mark C. Taylor (Chicago: University of Chicago Press, 1986), esp. 2–21.

argues for this ironic dependency on traditional concepts more than Derrida does in his own essay *"Différance,"* where perhaps his most succinct statement about translation appears: translation "always must be, a transformation of one language by another."[17]

"A Marriage Contract in the Form of a Seminar"

Derrida's understanding of translation as a "marriage contract in the form of a seminar" can be read as a feminist revisioning of both translation and marriage. And, significantly, the point of intersection for both translation and marriage is the pedagogical forum of the seminar. This is the point, then, at which we return to the concerns of Margaret Fuller.

If, in the classical sense of translation, an incipient sense of its ultimate impossibility holds sway, in the deconstructive reading of translation its inevitability becomes paramount. Margaret Fuller can be said to have embraced both the impossibility and the inevitability of translation. She worked hard to remove the harsh overtones of mastery so worrisome to Johnson, even as she attempted to renew an understanding of the fidelity or kinship between languages.[18] She did this by revisioning translation as a pedagogical enterprise. And, understanding that what we learn can always revise how we learn, she actively revised her own sense of pedagogy in the process.

Behind Fuller's translations there resides a model of pedagogy not unlike Derrida's "marriage contract in the form of a seminar." She attempts to devise a new relationship for student and teacher, English and German, by replacing the play of dialectic (where success is an issue of mastery) with dialogue and conversation (where a new kind of fidelity is the issue.)[19] Translating from German becomes a way to revise the terms of both Germanic and American culture.

Tellingly, it was Fuller's relationship with Emerson—something of a

[17] Derrida, "Des Tours de Babel," pp. 191, 14.

[18] Here I am using Derrida's understanding of kinship in Benjamin's "Task of the Translator": "This process—transforming the original as well as the translation—is the translation contract between the original and the translating text. In this contract it is a question of neither representation nor reproduction nor communication: rather, the contract is destined to assure a survival, not only of a corpus or a text or an author but of languages. Benjamin explains that translation reveals in some way the kinship of languages—a kinship that is not to be conceived in the manner of historical linguistics or on the basis of hypotheses about language families, and so forth. It is a kinship of another order" (*The Ear of the Other*, p. 122).

[19] See Barbara Johnson, "Teaching Ignorance: *L'Ecole des Femmes*," *Yale French Studies* 63 (1982): 165–82.

"marriage" and a "seminar" for both of them—that emboldened her sense of the transforming agency made available through translation. Her attempt to revise the pedagogical model embedded in the highly ritualized activity of translation is most apparent when she turns two of her major translations from German—*Torquato Tasso* by Goethe and Bettina von Arnim's *Die Günderode*—into elaborate allegories of her interaction with Emerson.

Fuller on Goethe

Fuller translated Goethe's *Torquato Tasso* sometime around 1833, several years before her father's death (1835) and before her first meeting with Emerson (1836). In 1833 she was sufficiently immersed in her reading of Goethe and German literature to believe that she might write a critical biography of his life and work. Her decision to translate *Torquato Tasso* emerged quite naturally out of this engagement with Goethe (who had died the year before[20]), though it is too easy to overlook the complex series of impulses that went into her decision to translate this particular drama. *Torquato Tasso* deals forthrightly with the calumnies of literary history and interpretation, and, indeed, Goethe's drama highlights virtually all of the issues emerging in Fuller's writing career: the problematic tangle of mastery, pedagogy, and difference; the conflict and confluence of poetry and history; the marginalization of women; and a theory of interpretation that attempts to reorganize them all.

Torquato Tasso gives an imaginative account of the relationship between the Italian renaissance poet Torquato Tasso, his patron, the Duke of Ferrara, and three important members of the court: the Duke's sister, Leonora D'Este, with whom Tasso was said to have had a complicated emotional bond; Leonora Sanvitale, countess of Scandiano, whose affection for Tasso amplified the play of his emotions; and Antonio Montecatino, the secretary of state with whom Tasso fought for the favor of the Prince. The mystery surrounding Tasso's incarceration by the Duke, the controversy over his amorous ties to several significant women, the rumors of his fiery personality and gathering fits of fear and paranoia were part of the literary history out of which Tasso's work was read in the eighteenth century. Because Tasso was considered a major literary figure during this period, writing about him was a way for Goethe to

[20] When Goethe died on March 22, 1832, Weimar performances of *Torquato Tasso* were suspended for four days. For interesting biographical details, see the introduction to the edition published by John Prudhoe.

project himself onto the horizon of literary history. Moreover, Goethe's classical drama was heavily influenced by his own experience in the courts of Weimar, particularly his complicated interaction with Charlotte von Stein. Since Fuller's translation was itself motivated by a compounding of personal and critical forces, this blend of autobiography and critique naturally appealed to her.[21]

The play is remarkably compact; there are only five characters, two of whom share the same name, Leonora. The doubling of names was not uncommon in Goethe's work, and here the doubling conflates the two female characters of the play: Princess Leonora and Leonora Sanvitale. The double name provides the literal model for the second doubling of names that takes place in the play, the doubling between Tasso the character and Tasso the idea, or the poet as he is represented in the minds of the different characters, including Tasso's own. Because each character in the drama tends to remain locked inside a private and divided discourse, conversation between poet and patron and poet and friend becomes next to impossible. Given this, the pretense of reading and interpreting the work of Tasso outside of the drama is problematized. Thus the play engages the problem of literary history and poetic influence; there is the Tasso of historical reality, as well as the Tasso of literary history. As most acts of interpretation are shown to fail *within* the environment of the drama—the poet's world—our own interpretation of the poetry produced by Tasso is similarly problematized.

In her translation, Fuller highlighted this failure of interpretation by showing wherever possible the denial of difference upon which it depends. When, for example, the two male antagonists, Tasso and Antonio, embrace in the end, she made it clear that it was an embrace of wreckage and confusion developed through Tasso's description of the two Leonoras as identical. (In Fuller's translation, Tasso's previous declamation against Leonora Sanvitale as a "soft siren" gives resonance to his later and similar description of the Princess. In Goethe's version, the word *siren* appeared only in the later scene.) This gathering of identities into lethal oppositions and the circling of desire and pain that it produced—Tasso and siren; poet and philosopher; master and slave—enabled Fuller to translate the play as a demonstration of translation's radical imperative.

Even the decision to title the work *Tasso* (dropping the first name from Goethe's title) shows something of Fuller's active sense of this impera-

---

[21] For Goethe's relationship with von Stein see the introduction to the German edition of *Goethe's "Torquato Tasso"* by E. L. Stahl (Oxford: Basil Blackwell, 1962). This edition is my reference for the German text.

tive. Though never published in her lifetime, the translation circulated among her most important literary friends.[22] It was a virtual pretext for her interaction with Emerson, who began his chapter in the *Memoirs of Margaret Fuller Ossoli* by describing the arrival of her translation to his house two years before she arrived there in person.[23] The drama touched on so many relevant themes discussed among members of the Concord circle that "Tasso" the name became for Fuller and her friends, particularly Emerson, the signal of their own complicated interaction. (Emerson's references to Tasso throughout his essays are always burdened by this complication; see especially "Prudence," CW 2: 137.)

If Goethe's decision to entitle his drama *Torquato Tasso* can be said to reflect a desire to push the drama away from its strong autobiographical reference by imposing the historical man's name over the enterprise, Fuller's decision to name her translation *Tasso* might be said to work the opposite way. Tasso is less the historical man's name than the name of the literary history of the man; Fuller cunningly affiliated herself with the text of literary history through the enabling confusion of this reference. Moreover, when her friends spoke of Tasso, they were not speaking only of the man, the poet of literary history, or of Goethe's construction of the man (and with it, Goethe's own place in that history); they were also referring to Fuller's critical redaction of all three. Such a maneuver has the important effect of highlighting the female figures, already there in Goethe's *Torquato Tasso*. Fuller's translation of *Tasso* frames the drama in such a way that it actively releases the radical if supplementary potential of women. When she uses the name Tasso, she means to highlight not only the poet and her own affiliation with that poet, but also some of the important questions of gender produced by that affiliation.

Although Fuller did not publish the entire translation of *Tasso*, she did publish a fragment of it when she was editing the *Dial*. In 1842 she reviewed a book entitled "Conjectures and Researches concerning the

---

[22] Fuller made several early attempts to get the drama published. She rejected the idea of publishing it anonymously and circulating it as if it were imported from England. An English translation was in fact published in London in 1827 by Charles Des Voeux, Esq., under the heading *J. W. Torquato Tasso, with Other German Poetry* (London: Longman, Rees, Orme, Brown, and Green, 1827). I have found no evidence to suggest that Fuller knew of this translation, either before or after making her own. For a discussion of the way in which Fuller's translation was a "rendering of the spirit rather than the letter" of Goethe's text, see Frederick A. Braun, "Margaret Fuller's Translation and Criticism of Goethe's *Tasso*," *Journal of English and Germanic Philology* 13 (1914): 202–13.

[23] See "Visits to Concord," MMF 2: 201.

Love, Madness, and Imprisonment of Torquato Tasso," and ended by inserting two scenes from her translation.[24] The fact that she inserted this fragment into a book review is a compelling one, showing how interpretation and translation had become interchangeable for her. Certainly the scenes selected for her review provide a useful site with which to open our interpretation.

Fuller published two scenes from the beginning of Act 2, the first of which finds Princess Leonora and Tasso alone together. The Princess encourages the poet to develop relationships with the other members of the court. Tasso's systematic rejection of each person suggested by Leonora (the other three characters in the drama) causes her to discuss the different roles of men and women in the court, as well as her own sense of isolation there and her dependence on Tasso's poetry for her happiness. The second scene is a soliloquy by Tasso in which he interprets Leonora's confession as a sign of his election in her eyes, a sign of her love for him. Unfortunately for Tasso, Leonora's love cannot be construed in the narrow and personal sense that he conceives. The Princess clearly intends that their love not be constrained by Tasso's possessive model of seduction. Yet Tasso has not totally misread Leonora, and this confusion between them supplies one of the most compelling aspects of the drama. Elsewhere the Princess expresses the kind of love for Tasso that Tasso reads out of his interaction with her; but she cannot act on that love, if only because her training has been in the lore of passivity. This passivity and self-denial is shown, furthermore, to be the product of her unusual education in philosophy and rhetoric which allows the drama to confuse the normally prescriptive boundaries of gender and class. For example, the feminine restraint of the Princess has been the product of a traditionally masculine education.

The Princess, we have seen earlier in the drama, has inherited the privilege of her position in the court, and part of that privilege has been her education in "ancient lore and speech," enabling her to "hear when wise men speak" and "understandingly receive those words."[25] This ability, taught to her by her mother, distinguishes her from the other female character of the drama, Leonora Santivale, who claims only to understand the "poet's gentle yet inspiring influence" (1.1.362). The two women have thus experienced two different pedagogical influences.

---

[24] *Dial* 2 (January 1842): 399–407. That Fuller used her review of a book about the historical figure Tasso to publish a section from her translation of Goethe's dramatic reading of the same is itself material for a separate essay, one that examines the complex theory of reading that she begins to develop during her book review career.

[25] Fuller's brother did not give a line count in his publication of Fuller's translation. I therefore refer to the page number from his text. Here the reference is from act 1, scene 1, p. 362; future references will be as follows: 1.1.362.

And because they are women, each is envious of the other's training, even as each is in a position to regard the limitations set upon the other by that training. The Princess is more subtle in her ability to ascribe to the philosopher his ability to "refine upon the simplest, obscure action" (1.1.362), conflating thereby the work of science and philosophy, but she is less able than Leonora to see the feminist hazards of such an observation. To valorize philosophers as the champions of simple, obscure action is to suggest a sensitivity to the simple, obscure lives of women in culture, which, as Leonora realizes, is more properly the poet's achievement.

The difference between the two women is complicated not only by unequal education, but also by their marital status. Sanvitale, already married and a mother, seizes upon the poetry of Tasso and the love lyrics ambiguously addressed to "Leonora" as a vehicle for passing beyond the simple obscurity to which her maternity and marriage condemn her. If she cannot act in the public sphere, as she would like to, she believes that she can seize recognition and "Fame" in "the Fatherland" (3.3.408) through the echoing verses of the poet Tasso. The Princess, by contrast, has resisted marriage and with it the simple obscurity of such a connection, yet her relation to Tasso is burdened by a dangerously conflicted desire to possess and to teach the poet. The desires of both women are shown to be contaminated by the false or dangerous attributes of the world of men as it is controlled by "the Fatherland."

In her recent and remarkable reading of Goethe's *Torquato Tasso*, Avital Ronell finds in the conversation between the two women conflicting "aesthetic and pedagogical positions" soon to emerge in the writing of Kant and Hegel. Ronell argues that the discourse of the two women, detached as the "foreplay" (606) of the drama, demonstrates both their exclusion from the masculine stagings of poetry and philosophy and their deeper implication in the development of a radical feminist reading of both disciplines. Ronell's focus on the two female characters helps us to understand Fuller's earlier fascination with the drama.[26]

At one level, Ronell minimizes the false "identity" of the two Leonoras by matching their differences to Hegel and Kant. But, as might be expected, she encounters some difficulty when she attempts to maintain a strict correspondence between each philosopher and his respective representative in the play. Because the Princess has access to philosophical training unavailable to Sanvitale, she espouses an argument that, according to Ronell "can be understood provisionally in its most

---

[26] Avital Ronell, "Taking It Philosophically: *Torquato Tasso*'s Women as Theorists," *MLN* 100 (April 1985): 599–631, esp. p. 606.

general sense, as the philosophy which exacts full self-realization through experience." For Ronell, this means that the Princess can be identified with a "Hegelian type of pedagogy," one that "restlessly" seeks a "completed discourse." By contrast, Sanvitale's apathy for "the specific, knowledge yielding contents of a discourse" allows her to emphasize poetry and the "intersubjective response it evokes," offering a critique of Hegelian pedagogy by positing a "discourse whose apprehension does not necessarily involve a concept of mastery."[27] But this reading of the two Leonoras actually tends to fix the pedagogical positions of the women in a way not borne out by their later interaction in the play. Eager to show Goethe's simultaneous anticipation and critique of both Kant and Hegel, Ronell tends to freeze the discourse of the drama far more radically than necessary. If anything, the pedagogical positions espoused by Leonora and the Princess undergo a series of important revisions throughout the play, an idea more in keeping with Ronell's sense of the radical position given to the women by the play.

Ronell is particularly interested in the way that Goethe staged a critical drama anticipating Kant's notion of genius as "foreign to philosophy" or as the "talent capable of discovering that which cannot be taught or learned."[28] Here Ronell again locates the issue central to Fuller's own fascination with the drama. Yet arguing that genius should be privileged as a concept making pedagogy unnecessary is different from arguing, as Fuller does, that genius is the embodiment of a difference that cannot be mastered or colonized but instead requires the conversational transaction of translation. Although Goethe wrote his drama in anticipation of Kant, Fuller later translated the same drama in an climate saturated by Kant's ideas. As a result, her rendering of aesthetic and pedagogical issues within the text represents an after-image, if you will, of the issues generated by both Kant and Hegel. She writes beyond Goethe in this sense, anticipating Ronell's reading by emphasizing the "provisional foreignness" of the women in the play in an effort to show the dangerous imperialist implications that became attached to Kant's reading of genius.[29] Her translation extracts from the drama the possibility of a new kind of relationship for men and women in their foreign or different worlds. One might say that she labors to keep Goethe from being assimilated too quickly into what was becoming the reified legacy of Kant and Hegel.

Some of the most interesting moments in the drama, therefore, are when the two Leonoras attempt to explain to one another their different

[27] Ibid., pp. 610, 612.
[28] Ibid., pp. 622, 621.
[29] Ibid., p. 622.

but related views. Their conversations are often allegorical, analyzing the men around them in an effort to interpret the world for each other and to analyze these interpretations. Their conversation goes far, for example, in assessing the breach between Antonio and Tasso, two men working from opposite poles toward the same goal: recognition and value in the court of Alphonso. Both women know well Tasso's desire to be considered useful in the world of court politics; as women, they both know better than Tasso the way his poetry ought to deliver him from simple obscurity. Both women understand as well Antonio's disdain for Tasso's brash and immoderate behavior, particularly the latter's pretense to genius or knowledge untaught—his vain belief that the poet can interpret a world beyond experience. Furthermore, both women know that Antonio's disdain is a defense in the same way that Tasso's response to Antonio is also a defense. Tasso would indeed like nothing more than to be invited into the world or company of men, but in being rejected by Antonio as useless he is forced to argue that his power and its source are foreign to the world. Antonio, for his part, would like nothing more than to be invited into the company of women and tutored by them as he sees Tasso tutored, but because the two Leonoras have little apparent use for Antonio, he accuses Tasso of infantilization in the company of women.

Fuller's decision to publish the prolonged interaction between the Princess and Tasso at the center of the play highlights these various themes, suggesting their centrality to her reading of the play.[30] Through this scene, we are shown odd parallels between the Princess and the poet, which are couched in descriptions of their difference. Both confess to an envy of a world beyond them. Tasso opens by confessing his envy of Antonio's sphere of influence: "With all these glowing, grand, and restless shapes, / Which such a man can charm into his circle, / Submissive to the spells his wisdom frames."[31] This envy is shown to be the inevitable outcome of his early exposure to the lists of knighthood at the Feast of Ferrara's court, where as a young man Tasso "felt [his] littleness" before the "spectacle of worldly splendor" and "shrank abashed." The Princess, for her part, expresses envy for the exposure to this spectacle that Tasso experienced: "How differently did I pass those moments! / Which sowed ambition in thy heart," she begins, describing how instead of fostering ambition, her upbringing imposed the "lore of sufferance" upon her. Gravely ill as a young woman, the Princess was kept

---

[30] Fuller published the first two scenes from act 2 in the *Dial*.

[31] Because Fuller's brother made some revisions in Fuller's manuscript when he published *Tasso*, I cite the *Dial* version whenever possible. The reference for this quote is *Dial*, 2.1.402.

away from the dramatic ritual of courage witnessed by Tasso and instead experienced courage firsthand through her illness: "Before my eyes / Death waved his broad black pinions" (*Dial*, 2.1.403).

In her translation, Fuller observes the curious gender confusion in this mutual envy (the Princess's of the poet, the poet's of the courtier) by keeping Goethe's reference to the mythical figure of Echo. When Tasso shrinks in envy from Antonio's world, he tells the Princess "*my* world sank in the distance / Behind steep rocks,—on which I seemed to fade— / To Echo—to poor shadow of a sound,— / Bodiless— powerless" (*Dial*, 2.1.402). In many nineteenth-century translations, this reference to Echo was often eliminated (including Arthur Fuller's posthumous publication of his sister's translation in 1860).[32] Because German substantives are always capitalized, it was perhaps possible to assume that Goethe intended only to remark on the physical phenomenon. Yet such a reading does considerable damage to this pivotal moment in the text; closing down the classical reference also closes down the many complications of gender imposed on the moment by the classical text of Echo.

Fuller loved Goethe's consistent play with classical figures and through the permutations of the myth understood how Tasso's humiliation before Antonio is a humiliation that he unconsciously affiliates with women, thus engendering his own narcissism as feminine. The humiliation of the Princess, by contrast, is one that she unconsciously affiliates with the heroic activity of men. The chamber in which she battled death was one where "not an *echo* of this gayety / Could penetrate" (*Dial*, 2.1.403; my emphasis). Upon meeting the Princess as she emerged from her death chamber, the poet remembers having recognized in her a way to "turn aside" from his unworthy ambition toward the spectacle of power. Simultaneously, the Princess found in the poet a vague new "lease of Life" a passage beyond the "lore of sufferance" inscribed by

---

[32] Goethe's text reads:
>   Doch ach, je mehr ich horchte, mehr und mehr
>   Versank ich vor mir selbst, ich fürchtete
>   Wie Echo an den Felsen zu verschwinden,
>   Ein Widerhall, ein Nichts mich zu verlieren (2.1.797–800).

Arthur Fuller changed his sister's translation to:
>   For as I gazed, *my* world sank in the distance
>   Behind steep rocks, on which I seemed to fade
>   To echo—to poor shadow of a sound—
>   Bodiless—powerless (2.1.380).

Another nineteenth-century translation (by Des Voeux) reads the following way:
>   Yet, ah! the more I heard, the more and more
>   I sank before myself, and fear'd to die
>   Like echo on the crags away, and be
>   A mere reverberation, lost in nought (2.2.49–50).

her stoic battle with illness. Both recognized in the other a better teacher than the one imposed upon them by the echoing chambers of culture and experience (*Dial*, 2.1.403).

In the course of the drama we see how neither can sustain the promise of this pedagogical discovery. Tasso continually falls back into his feminine envy of the political sphere, one hopelessly conflated with narcissism; the Princess lapses too often into her masculine speeches of renunciation, wedded as they are to the law of the court, the walls of propriety and morality, and contaminated by the language of possession and control. As the scene opens, in fact, both Tasso and the Princess reveal their vulnerabilities quite openly as they unconsciously exchange accounts of their difference.

These gender formations trap the two characters in a familiar binary opposition; that they seem to have exchanged male and female longings does not in any way release them from the restrictive gender codifications of their society. Indeed, both of them tend to remain trapped within a series of binary oppositions that keep them from breaking the very codes they most abhor. The prevalence of this binary system means that desire itself gets circumscribed by blinding oppositions.

Fuller was particularly attentive to these traps, as her translation decisions show. The most prominent example of her decision to highlight this double bind appears in two small but significant changes that she makes at the end of both scenes. After an important discussion about the Golden Age (to which we will return), the Princess is provoked by Tasso into declaring her dissatisfaction with her suitors; Tasso (mis)interprets this as a sign of his favor, which it is, but in a complicated way. When pressed by Tasso to consider her loneliness and dependence upon him, the Princess, in a series of rhetorical inversions, lapses into thoughts of possession and control. Thinking about the influence of his poetry, the Princess tells Tasso:

> Thy poem's highest praise
> Is that it leads us on and on; we listen,
> We think we understand,—nor can we blame
> That which we understand,—and thus become thy captives.
>
> (*Dial*, 2.1.406)

Fuller emphasizes the way possession and control are recuperated by selecting the word *captive*, modifying by making stronger the effect of the translation: "and win us over" ("und so gewinnt uns dieses Lied zuletzt"). Pushing the meaning beyond simple seduction, she insists upon reading this type of seduction along the hierarchical axis of power and control. This is most pronounced in the equally significant change that she makes in Tasso's response, where she places the word *slave* into his soliloquy.[33]

The words *slave* and *captive* were explosive terms for Fuller's American audience, informed by resonances of race and colonialism: white women were the primary subjects in captivity narratives, and black men were central to abolitionist tracts about slavery. Whereas the two words bind these seemingly divergent narratives together in ways that exceed this discussion, they work, in any case, to emphasize the perils of the dialectic at work between the Princess and the poet: both pretend to be different if not opposites, yet both find themselves trapped in a larger dialectic of control.

On Lordship and Bondage

Fuller's insertion of the words *captive* and *slave* can be said to provide a feminist gloss to Hegel's treatment of Lordship and Bondage in the *Phenomenology of Spirit* (1807). It is possible she had heard something about this aspect of Hegel's thought from her friend Frederick Henry Hedge, whose command of German and interest in philosophy made him a particularly useful contact.[34] But it is more likely that her analysis emerges from her own feminist sense of the problem, particularly since her translation emphasizes the traps rather than the benefits of dialectical thinking. Fuller's concern, as we have observed, had been the Lordship / Bondage relationship in its other manifestations, most notably the hierarchies separating teacher and student, man and woman, and philosopher and poet, or even the hierarchy in translation. This insertion of slave and captive into the end of these two scenes provides a social legend for the tragic movement of the drama. Leonora's sense of herself as the poet's captive misleads Tasso by reversing the ultimate structure of their relationship: in the court of the Prince, Tasso is Leonora's captive. But Leonora's dependency also signals the play of Hegel's dialectic since it reveals how Leonora's relationship with Tasso is one of a "dependent consciousness," limiting her "enjoyment" of his "labor." And Tasso's description of himself as slave to Leonora quickly fosters his

[33] Fuller translates "Ja, fordre was du willst, denn ich bin dein!" (2.2.1154) as "Whate'er / Thou wilt, ask of thy slave" (*Dial*, 2.2.407).

[34] Hedge eventually became a professor of German at Harvard. Fuller gave her translation of *Tasso* to him to read before anyone else. See Rene Wellek, "The Minor Transcendentalists and German Philosophy," *The New England Quarterly* 15 (December 1942): 652–80.

own fatal sense of an "independent consciousness," the fatal uniqueness that triggers the clash of forces in the court of Ferrara.

Fuller also emphasizes the hierarchical oppositions in the scene between Leonora Sanvitale and Tasso, where the latter angrily denounces Antonio for failing to acknowledge his "natural gift." Fuller heightens the meaning of Goethe's text by using the word *gift*, particularly since it resonates with her earlier insertion of the word in Tasso's soliloquy; there Tasso interprets the captivity of the Princess as a "free gift" (*Dial*, 2.1.407) and is otherwise allowed by Fuller to make a connection between his poetic genius and his interaction with the Princess. The reader can instantly see, however, that when Tasso loses sight of that "free gift," he loses his poetic genius as well. That is, once his gifts are assumed to be natural and not something actively given to him, Tasso begins to conceive of gifts (and of himself) in imperial terms. And once he adopts that frame of mind, everything becomes colonized, including the Princess, whom he hopes will feel an "o'ermastering passion for him." (4.3.422) In the same vein, he feels an "o'ermastering" hatred for Antonio:

> Man must have in his narrow being
> The double impulses of love and hatred.
> Are they not day and night? sleeping and waking?
> And I must hate this man—must have the pleasure
> Still worse and worse to think of him.
>
> (4.2.419)

This binary sway of captive and slave, love and hate, day and night considerably reduces the alternative possibilities momentarily surfacing in the text, moments in which the dialectical thrust of those terms is otherwise displaced. Not surprisingly, one of the most important of these moments comes in the first scene of act 2 when Tasso and the Princess discuss the Golden Age. Here Tasso enters into a nostalgic yearning for the age of "blissful freedom" (*Dial*, 2.1.404), while the Princess reproves Tasso, noting that his view is both naive and self-serving. "Most like 't was then as now, / United noble hearts *make* golden days, / Interpret to each other the world's beauty" (*Dial*, 2.1.405). When Tasso attentively follows his teacher by suggesting that a "synod of the wise and good" should "decide on what *is* meet" the Princess adds that it should be a "synod of good *women*" since "propriety" and "morality" were their "defence" (*Dial*, 2.1.405).

As always, the Princess cannot long maintain the radical possibilities of her theory; her argument for the "interpreting community" of women soon lapses into a conservative defense of "decorum" and "propriety" since "lawlessness," as she says, is her "foe" (*Dial*, 2.1.405).[35]

But in this moment when the interpreting community of women is invoked, we glimpse the pedagogical model with which Fuller was experimenting. It was no accident, in fact, that her publication of this fragment of *Tasso* appeared in the same issue of the *Dial* in which she included her article about Bettina von Arnim's *Die Günderode*, an epistolary novel composed of letters exchanged between two women that Fuller was translating.[36]

Fuller's double promotion of *Die Günderode* and this fragment from *Tasso*, however, was not prescriptive; she did not want interpreting communities to be restricted to a single gender. By 1842 she had experimented with a variety of such communities, which included her conversations with Emerson and her own Conversations in Boston, where women assembled to discuss and reproduce their early education with one another.[37] Fuller's experience in Boston proved sufficiently ambiguous: she began her classes in the belief that the only difference between the education of men and women was that women were never asked to use their training in life, but she soon came to understand that difference in education was itself the issue, that men and women experienced the pedagogical process in ways that served to reinforce the differences that would prevail in life.

Fuller's reform, and her sense of the best pedagogical model for that reform, emerged from her relationship with Emerson and the interpretive community between them. Her classical education made her interaction with him more equal than the average interaction of men and women in America, something akin to the equality she found in the interaction between Arnim and Günderode. Yet, in the manner of Tasso and Princess Leonora, her conversation with Emerson was also troubled by an outworn dynamic of seduction. Her experience with Emerson

[35] Fuller's concept of the "interpreting community" would be antithetical to the concept of the "interpretive community" as it has been espoused by Stanley Fish. Fuller depends more heavily on a concept of revisability, one operating through a dialogic system, whereas Fish depends more on a sense of conformity and "shared values." See Fish, *Is There a Text in This Class? The Authority of Interpretive Communities* (Cambridge: Harvard University Press, 1980).

[36] Fuller's article appeared in January of 1842, and her translation of *Die Günderode* appeared two months later, in March. "Bettine Brentano and Her Friend Günderode," *Dial* 2 (January 1842): 313–57.

[37] Fuller began her Conversations in November of 1839 and repeated them yearly through the early part of 1844. For an excellent reading of her procedure there see Julie Ellison, "Performing Interpretation," *Delicate Subjects: Romanticism, Gender, and the Ethics of Understanding* (Ithaca: Cornell University Press, 1990), 217–60.

thus spurred the conflicting imperatives that made her simultaneous publication of fragments from *Günderode* and *Tasso* necessary.

Fuller on Emerson

Emerson's relationship with Fuller was extremely important to her during the first part of her career. It was Emerson who encouraged and enabled her to publish her translation of Eckermann's *Conversations with Goethe* (her first book-length publication), and it was Emerson who heightened her ambition to write a critical biography of Goethe.[38] He gave support to her for projects that would momentarily turn him into her student, perhaps the most overlooked aspect of his early interaction with Fuller. As we saw in Chapter 1, his letters give ample testimony to this complication. And Fuller found in Emerson the nearly perfect student, if only because *student* is a provisional term. His response to each new lesson forced her to reestablish her position vis-à-vis the German texts adopted for her own pedagogical pursuits.

Emerson's enthusiasm for Fuller's intellectual capacity paved the way for her publication of Eckermann's *Conversations*, yet his sense of her intellectual power also enabled him to use Eckermann's text to caution her regarding the larger Goethe project: "Cannot a biography of this minutely faithful sort be written without self-destruction?" (EL 2: 64). But Fuller's publishing decisions reveal that she was sharp enough to interpret his response to Eckermann less as a warning than as a projection of his own struggle with Goethe, a struggle that she had in fact initiated.

Emerson was clearly more disturbed, for example, by Eckermann's book about Goethe than he was by Bettina von Arnim's epistolary novel entitled *Goethe's Correspondence with a Child*, a work based on Arnim's correspondence with Goethe.[39] His letters to Fuller describe the two works in antithetical terms: he thought Eckermann self-effacing, but Arnim appeared to be a "sublime original" (EL 2: 236). Because Fuller was a woman ambitious enough to write a critical work on Goethe, she responded quite differently. She admired Eckermann for providing a domestic view of Goethe, the kind of table talk that Goethe alone would

[38] *Conversations with Goethe, in the Last Years of His Life, Translated from the German of Eckermann*, vol. 4 of *Specimens of Foreign Standard Literature*, ed. George Ripley (Boston: Hilliard, Gray, 1939).

[39] First published in Germany as *Goethe's Briefwechsel mit einem Kinde* (Berlin: F. Dummler, 1835). Arnim did her own English translation, as *Goethe's Correspondence with a Child*; the first American edition from the London edition was published by D. Bixby (Lowell, Mass., 1841).

not supply.[40] She also may have enjoyed the way that Eckermann's text destabilized Goethe's authority. Scholars to this day have a difficult time distinguishing the words of Goethe from Eckermann, and Fuller found this kind of confusion fascinating.[41] Certainly, though, she took the occasion to separate herself from Eckermann, and her separation was based on a dissatisfaction with his secondary role: "We are jealous for minds which we see in this state of subordination. . . . Rare as independence is, we cannot but ask it from all who live in the light of genius."[42] Yet because she was a woman, her separation carried less threat for her than it did for Emerson.

A more difficult separation colored her response to Arnim's *Correspondence*. Fuller's relationship to Goethe was closer to Arnim's than to Eckermann's. Like Arnim, she was much younger than Goethe, and like Arnim, she had chosen Goethe as a vehicle for her own entry into literary history. She greatly admired Arnim's style and capacity to engage Goethe; like Emerson, she believed that "Bettine's" work could be characterized as a conversation with Goethe (as opposed to the monologue of Eckermann's work where Goethe tended to prevail).[43] Remarkably, the 1841 publication of Arnim's English translation of *Correspondence* made Fuller's ten years of agitation and argument on behalf of German literature seem almost irrelevant. Arnim's novel was an instant success, as popular as much of the women's fiction of the day. Fuller was initially pleased with the reception, noting that in this instance the "vulgar" was "not the same with the mob."[44] Still, she could not escape the fear that the reaction to Arnim's novel had less to do with the expanding critical faculties of the American audience than with the authority of seduction at the center of its reading. In a letter to her friend, William H. Channing, she expressed her astonishment over the reception of the book, attributing its popularity to the fact that "men wish [to be] loved by Bettine . . . [whereas] girls wish to write down the thoughts that come, and see if just such a book does not grow up" (LMF 2: 172). She was in fact repulsed by what she took to be Goethe's condescending tone in the text. "There is an air as of an elderly guardian flirting cautiously with a giddy inexperienced ward . . . willing to make a tool of

---

[40] See Fuller, "Translator's Preface," in *Conversations with Goethe*.

[41] See Avital Ronell, *Dictations: On Haunted Writing* (Bloomington: Indiana University Press, 186), part 2.

[42] Fuller, "Translator's Preface," in *Conversations with Goethe*, p. ix.

[43] For Fuller's thoughts about the monologue of Goethe in Eckermann, see ibid., p. viii. For her thoughts about Arnim and Goethe, see her *Dial* essay "Bettine Brentano and Her Friend Günderode," esp. pp. 314–17: "She has followed like a slave where she might as a pupil," p. 316.

[44] "Bettine Brentano and Her Friend Günderode," p. 313.

this fresh, fervent being."[45] She felt, moreover, that there was something undignified in Arnim's description of herself as a child when in fact she had been in her early twenties. For Fuller, Arnim's interaction with Goethe in *Correspondence with a Child* lapsed into the dialectic of captive and slave that she had critiqued through her translation of *Tasso*. The hierarchy between Arnim and Goethe remained too clearly defined for Fuller, and it provided even less of a model for her projected critical biography of Goethe than did Eckermann's *Conversations*.

Emerson, for his part, responded more favorably to Arnim's *Conversations* but not because he admired the hierarchy between the man and woman that Fuller found unsatisfactory. Rather, he responded to Arnim because, as a man, he could appreciate the subversive nature of Bettine's posture toward Goethe, a posture more in keeping with his own competitive inclination.[46]

In puzzling out Emerson's response—and her own—to these two German texts, Fuller began to see how both she and Emerson were struggling with conflicting theories of literary influence. When she began to express doubts about her ability to write her projected critical biography of Goethe, Emerson penned a letter of encouragement that may in some way have been responsible for her decision to shift the focus of her Goethe project. Writing to lend support, he told her:

> On our beginnings seems somehow our self possession to depend a good deal, as happens so often in music. A great undertaking we allow ourselves to magnify, until it daunts & chills us and the child kills its own father. So let us say; self possession is all; our author, our hero, shall follow as he may. I know that not possibly can you write a bad book a dull page, if you only indulge yourself and take up your work somewhat proudly. . . . It seems too so very high a compliment to pay to any man, to make him our avowed subject, that the soul inclines to remunerate itself by a double self trust, by loftier & gayer sallies of joy & adventure, yes & I think by some wicked twitting & whipping the good hero himself, as often as occasion is, by way of certifying ourselves that he still keeps his place there & we ours here, and that we have not abated a jot of our supremacy over all the passengers through nature. *They* must all be passengers whosoever & howsoever they be, & *I* the inmate & landlord, though I were the youngest & least of the race. On these conditions, no subject is dangerous: all subjects are equivalent (EL 2: 197–98).

[45] Ibid., p. 316. The full quote is: "There is an air as of an elderly guardian flirting cautiously with a giddy, inexperienced ward, or a Father Confessor, who, instead of through the holy office raising and purifying the thoughts of the devotee, uses it to gratify his curiosity."

[46] Emerson's response to Bettina von Arnim appears vividly in his correspondence to Fuller, and later in his repeated references to her throughout his essays. See especially EL 2: 210.

The agonistic model, while clearly pragmatic (and playfully summoned here by Emerson), was one Fuller would not use. For this view of literary history repeats rather than inquires, encouraging a mastery that she sought to destroy in her own relationship to the text of literary history. Emerson gave her this advice as a sign of his confidence in her, a granting, as it were, of masculine privilege. But the playful tone also reveals his unspoken need to distance himself from this model.

Luckily, Fuller's self-possession was even greater than Emerson had imagined, though it had in fact emerged from her extraordinary interaction with him. His argument is almost a parody of Tasso's reaction to Antonio and an oddly inverted version of Fuller's reading of Arnim's *Correspondence*. Neither model of influence would suffice for Fuller. Her decision to delay, postpone, put off her work on Goethe was marked by a need to clear a better space from which to articulate her relationship to Goethe and literary history. This she would accomplish by translating Arnim's *Die Günderode* and publishing an article on *Günderode* in the same issue of the *Dial* containing her essay on *Tasso*. By denouncing Arnim's *Correspondence* as undignified ("The aim is to meet as nymph and Apollo, but with sudden change the elderly prime minister and the sentimental maiden are beheld instead"[47]) and introducing Arnim's earlier correspondence with Caroline Günderode (to which Fuller gives the title *Günderode* in her own translation) as a far superior text, she found a way to engage in a metatranslation of the issues so important to her in *Tasso*.

Fuller argued in her *Dial* essay that *Die Günderode*, an epistolary novel about the early exchange of letters between Bettina and another writer, the canoness Günderode, was superior to Arnim's *Correspondence* because the two women were closer than Bettine and Goethe in both age and social standing. The two women resembled the two Leonoras of Goethe's *Torquato Tasso*: Günderode, the eldest, was like the Princess, trained in philosophy and history; and Bettina, like Leonora, had been educated through the fine arts. Between them they create a kind of interpretive community, each teaching the other from her own particular training. In publishing the article introducing the Arnim work in the same edition of the *Dial* into which she slipped her translation of the two scenes from *Tasso*, Fuller paid a complicated tribute to the relationship between the Leonoras by contrasting it to the relationship with Arnim in which Goethe was more immediately involved.

In fact, Fuller's favorite model of pedagogy appears in a conversation

---

[47] "Bettine Brentano and Her Friend Günderode," p. 322.

between the two Leonoras of Goethe's drama. When told of Leonora's plan to take Tasso from the court of Ferrara, the Princess resists mildly, but not before she describes her happiest moments with Tasso.

> How sweet the anticipation
> Of passing with him the calm evening hours,
> With every conversation still increasing
> The desire to know each other more completely,
> And each new day bringing new harmony
> To our accordant souls! . . . We rudderless
> Sailed, joyous-carolling, on the sea of Time.
>
> (3.2.406)

The description of the "rudderless" interaction between Tasso and the Princess is a literal translation here, and Goethe's decision to use the term *rudderless* ("ohne Ruder hin," 3.2.1877) was arguably the aspect Fuller most admired about the drama. It contains the condition for the interpreting community which she sought, suggesting a suspension of mastery and control between men and women.

Interestingly, however, in the ardently heterosexual world of the nineteenth century, this rudderless drive could only appear safe and productive as a model of interaction between a man and a woman when it was framed by the retrospective gaze of two women separated from the interaction. The term *rudderless* is thus not to be applied to the interaction of the Princess and the poet alone, since without the frame of the two women analyzing or "translating" it, it would be charged with dangerous connotations of unbridled desire. Nor is the term *rudderless* applied to the interaction between the two women, for such a term would imply a powerlessness already evident by their marginalization in the court of Ferrara. Only by this double frame, in suspension between two different worlds, could a community of women articulate an ideal model of pedagogy. For *this double frame is also the double frame of the translator,* through which uneasy and sometimes conflicting strategies can be wed. As such, the frame of the translator opens a wonderful site for feminist concerns, where, as we have already seen, seemingly irreconcilable issues may be summoned to conversation and critique. Fuller repeated this double frame when she published her *Tasso* fragments along with her essay on Arnim's *Günderode*. Together they were meant to show how the virtues of the relationship between Arnim and Günderode could have applicability to men and women alike.

In *Tasso*, predictably, this double suspension must be initiated by

women. This imperative is especially evident in the conversation between the two men in Goethe's drama which cannot find the virtues of
rudderless interaction. When, in the end, Tasso explains his relationship
with the Princess to Antonio, his terms are relentlessly hierarchical. And
Antonio, who makes valiant efforts to cool the harsh misogynistic rhetoric that Tasso summons (at one point Tasso calls the Princess a "siren," a
lethal "echo" of his earlier analysis of Leonora[48]), nevertheless reinscribes the code of interpretation that enables Tasso to use this kind of
language. Antonio tells the poet to "Be a man / Collect thyself, and all
may yet be well" (5.5.448). After several turns, the poet accepts this
advice, embracing Antonio with the admission:

> The rudder breaks; the trembling skiff gives way,
> And rocks beneath my feet. With both my arms
> I clasp thee. Stir not. Here is all my hope.
> The mariner thus clings to that rude rock
> Which wrecked his friends, his fortune and his home.
>
> (5.5.449)

Interestingly, Fuller emphasized the connection between the Princess
and Tasso by using the word *rudder* instead of *helm*, (*Steuer*) which has
been a more literal translation of Goethe's text. With this doubling, she
clearly demonstrates the radical difference between the Princess and the
poet. In effect, she shows how, in their separate communities, the two
exemplify good and bad models of translation. The first, as exemplified
in the interaction between two women, is a model where unthought and
untried possibilities are allowed to hover. The second, as shown in the
conversation between Tasso and Antonio, is an older model of translation and influence modeled on imperial gestures of mastery and control.

For Tasso, this moment of rudderlessness is the consequence of a
botched interaction with the Princess and not its goal. It is a moment of
shipwreck and ruin, rather than a moment of "joyous-carolling," a moment when the issue of mastery becomes reinscribed into a text of tragedy. Thus the real tragedy of the drama is that Tasso will continue to
read women as sirens, reinforcing the tragic dimension to pedagogy and
interaction which is his final support.

---

[48] Fuller makes this echo possible by adding the word *siren* to Tasso's earlier commentary on Leonora. The original reads "Leonore Sanvitale, / Die zarte Freundin! Ha, dich
kenn' ich nun!" (4.3.2490–91). Fuller translates it as "Leonora Sanvitale—the soft siren. / I
know her now" (4.3.423). Tasso calls the Princess a "siren" at the end of the drama
(5.5.446).

Fuller on Bettina von Arnim

Perhaps the most intriguing aspect of Fuller's translation of *Tasso* is the part it played in displacing her original determination to write a critical biography of Goethe. Critics have offered numerous theories about her failure to write that biography. Yet together with her translation of Eckermann's *Conversations* and Bettina von Arnim's *Günderode*, *Tasso* completes a kind of critical biography of Goethe, one that we have not been able to read because we have been looking for the wrong kind of text.

Indeed, by the time that Fuller was in a position to publish her translation of *Tasso* in its entirety, she chose to publish only the two first scenes from act 2. This decision emerged out of a growing impatience with the rigid and unforgiving nature of the American idiom. Cultural restrictions on the American poet seemed so great that even Emerson, who, through Fuller's help, could read and enjoy Goethe and Arnim, would not quite find the practical application of their works for the country. Emerson could argue forcefully, as he did in a letter to Fuller, that Arnim was the "only formidable test that was applied to Goethe's genius" (EL 2: 210), which observation distinguished him from the average American reader, who, as Fuller expressed it, read Bettina von Arnim's *Correspondence with a Child* as a tantalizing novel of seduction. Yet although Emerson could concede Arnim's power in her interaction with Goethe and even outline what might be called her deconstructive gestures toward Goethe's work, he could not apply it to his own relationship with Fuller, at least not until after her untimely death, when he returned to "Bettine" for help in writing the *Memoirs*.[49]

Though fully aware of Fuller's power to influence his thought, Emerson played Tasso to her Princess while she was alive, haunted by false threats of seduction and captivity. This sense of seduction was enhanced, as we have seen, by the fact that feminism and the discourse of Fourier had become enmeshed in Emerson's mind. Confused by his own expectations, he both repressed and sublimated the desire set in motion by the intense intellectual stimulation he was experiencing through his interaction with Fuller. The result, as Fuller knew, was everywhere apparent in the tension of his *Essays, First* and *Second Series*, often the site of his tragic perceptions.

---

[49] "Here was genius purer than his own, and if without the constructive talent on which he valued himself yet he could not have disguised from himself the fact that she scorned it on the whole" (EL 2: 210).

Fuller could easily see how her influence over Emerson was being acknowledged allegorically through his praise for Bettina von Arnim. When pressed, however, he would not translate that allegory, at least not when pressed in a personal way. His admitted model of literary influence remained agonistic, like the model of interaction (and translation) between Tasso and Antonio, crossed with images of mastery and tragedy, or by silence and defeat.

Through her intense intellectual interaction with Emerson, Fuller saw a different model of pedagogy developing between them, more like the positive "rudderless" moments of interpretive freedom described by the Princess to Leonora. Recognizing the need for the female frame in order to translate that interaction for her American audience, she printed her article on *Günderode* as a gloss for her relationship with Emerson, itself an allegory for the model of literary influence and pedagogy that she was attempting to describe for herself and her American readers. Thus one could argue that her editorial control of the 1842 issue of the *Dial* (one of her last editions—she resigned her job as editor two months later) became her ultimate act of translation, a grafting of the complexities of Arnim and Goethe onto her own relationship with Emerson, all in the service of a usable model of feminist conversation.

For Fuller, the model of seduction at the center of the correspondence between the two relatively obscure women in *Günderode* was a better model for American readers to explore because the gender shift displaced the hierarchical power at work in Arnim's epistolary novel about Goethe. The text of seduction between the women was a process related to a mutual development of consciousness rather than the activation of a powerful and potentially tragic hierarchy. Translating *Günderode* was much like separating the interaction between the Princess and Leonora in Goethe's *Tasso* from the rest of the play, focusing on what critic Avital Ronell has called the "foreplay" of the drama. When "the women are on the sidelines, next to the work; they are engaged," writes Ronell, "in their own words, in a *Nebengeschaft* and play within a kind of transcendent exteriority which touches, plays with, introduces the work, the poet and his poem."[50] In this sense, Fuller's decision to translate *Günderode* registered a gathering interest in the production of literary texts by women and constituted the first stage of her argument (later developed in *Woman in the Nineteenth Century*) that women, not men, would lead the way in the development of a new critical mode.[51] Because, as it has

[50] Ronell, "Taking It Philosophically," p. 606.
[51] "The Time is come when Eurydice is to call for an Orpheus, rather than Orpheus for Eurydice" (WNC: 13).

been argued, the works of American "scribbling women" were also designed to subvert the traditional seduction theme, her preference for *Günderode* helps to align her with a mode of literary production which is wrongly seen as antithetical to her feminist poetics.

But the uniqueness of Fuller's perspective lies not in her preference for women writers but in the way she establishes a causal link between the condition of society and the productions of the literary mind. By her account, "men buckler one another against the million" because "they have still more the air of brothers in arms than of fellow students" and tend to produce texts that participate in that strife. For this reason she argued that the relationship of Günderode and Arnim was more poetic than that of Goethe and Arnim. Unlike *Goethe's Correspondence with a Child*, where, as Fuller argued, the reader was encouraged to consider the two worlds of Goethe and Arnim as separate spheres of entitlement (public vs. private, masculine and imperial vs. feminine and sentimental), the correspondence between the two German women encouraged its readers to see how "the pure products of public and private are on a par." Importantly, however, Fuller believes that this balance is only possible when the arbitrary barriers of gender are confused, as in her own experience with Emerson. Understanding the need to frame, or translate, this experience for him and the rest of her American readers, she essentially refigures it in the discussion of *Günderode*, observing the "high state of Culture in Germany" which "presented to the thoughts of . . . women themes of poesy and philosophy as readily, as to the English and American girl come the choice of a dress."[52]

Thus Fuller's 1842 *Dial* issue did not register a turn from her relationship with Emerson so much as an enhancement of that relationship in allegorical form. Moreover, the preference for the text of *Günderode* did not register a change in her evaluation of *Tasso* so much as her understanding of the complexities surrounding the reception of Goethe's work in the United States. In many ways, her displeasure over the Goethe depicted in the first Arnim novel was displaced anger over the conditions that a decade earlier had made it impossible for her to publish her full translation of *Tasso* in America. And because she had read Goethe's drama as a complex staging of the feminist questions posed by Arnim's work, her translation of *Tasso* was oddly prophetic, not only of the work by Arnim that she would come to admire, but of the complex interplay between all three works—*Tasso*, *Goethe's Correspondence with a Child*, and *Günderode*—and her developing interaction with Emerson.

[52] "Bettine Brentano and Her Friend Günerode," pp. 319, 321, 320.

Rethinking Suicide

The stunning events of Arnim's actual correspondence with Günderode, ending as they did with the latter's suicide, both enriched and
limited the value that *Die Günderode* held for Fuller as a translator's
frame. Arnim's relationship with Günderode came to an abrupt end
before Arnim's relationship with Goethe began. After Günderode's
death, Arnim wrote letters first to Goethe's mother and then to Goethe
himself. Fuller notes in her *Dial* essay that the *Correspondence* contains
the tragedy of Günderode. But this tragedy extends well beyond the
narrative of Günderode's suicide in the section of the *Correspondence*
addressed to Goethe's mother; rather, it involves the connection between Günderode's death and the initiation of Arnim's lengthy interaction with Goethe. In effect, Fuller's resistance to Arnim's *Correspondence*
was a resistance to the power of that text to name and, in effect, dismiss
the death of Günderode by calling it "tragic."

Timothy Reiss has argued that by "grasp[ing] and enclos[ing]" a certain "absence of significance," tragedy "fulfills the role of making a new
class of discourse possible," marking the " 'hole' in the passage from one
dominant discourse to another." As Reiss shows, however, this radical
potential of tragedy also "runs the risk . . . of being deflected toward
goals that are not its own . . . [and] confirming . . . established forms of
knowledge and truth." By Reiss's account, "to say something is 'tragic' is
[also] a means of recuperating a situation that would otherwise remain
unaccountable, of relating it to the known."[53] The narrative of Günderode's suicide within the first section of *Goethe's Correspondence with a
Child* had the latter effect for Fuller. Once identified as tragic in the
context of Arnim's interaction with Goethe, Günderode's suicide became enclosed in the larger narrative of Arnim's seduction. As Fuller
makes clear in her *Dial* essay, she found this interpretation an intolerable
recuperation of Günderode's death as well as a gross misrepresentation
of Günderode's place in Arnim's life. Her translation of Arnim's *Günderode* was therefore her effort to critique that very process of recuperation.

Certainly by the time Fuller wrote her article on *Günderode*, she was
far less interested in the radical if dangerous promise of tragedy as a
genre than she had been a decade before when she had attempted to
write a few tragedies of her own. Furthermore, recalling her efforts to
translate the nature of her interaction with Emerson to the American

---

[53] Timothy Reiss, *Tragedy and Truth* (New Haven: Yale University Press, 1980), 284,
300, 11.

public, her use of *Günderode* also helped her to clarify her position toward his internalization of Tasso's tragic sense of pedagogy and interaction. Her argument in support of *Günderode* allowed her to explain her developing sense of a Fourieristic interaction—what we might otherwise call her feminist agency—where the motors of seduction, once dependent upon a form of appropriation, a dialectic of loss and gain, absence and presence, had been reordered. Seduction emanating from disparate and uncertain sources—such as the seduction of her correspondence with Emerson—had instead begun to promise a new choreography of values, a movement generating form and value all at once. Not surprisingly, this new seduction depended on a complete confusion and ultimate displacement of familiar gender roles as well as some traditional genre considerations.

In attempting to work through this, Fuller adopted what Derrida has called a "double register" for her thinking. Her desire to overturn the traditional concepts of history, including the devastating effects of gender, enveloped as they sometimes were in tragic overtones, was matched by her desire to "mark the interval" with a new model of seduction so that "the interval [could] not be reappropriated."[54] Fuller found herself attempting to transvalue the rendering of masculine and feminine ways of vivifying Tasso's tragic sense. This meant finding a text that not only would reverse these gender distinctions, but would be able to "mark the interval" from the original terms through displacement. Her translation of *Die Günderode* provided her with that text. In the ardently heterosexual world of nineteenth-century North America, Günderode provided a model of interaction where seduction can be

[54] Jacques Derrida, "Positions: Interview with Jean-Louis Houdebine and Guy Scarpetta," *Positions*, trans. Alan Bass (Chicago: University of Chicago Press, 1981), 68. Derrida draws upon Nietzsche to overturn and displace the tenets of Western metaphysics. Yet Derrida cannot avoid falling into Nietzsche's tragic figurations as they apply to gender. Though Woman emerges as the figure of displacement for Derrida, his use of Woman has a tendency to hover within the first stage of the deconstructive project, reversing the hierarchical status given to Man/Woman in Western thought. Locked in this stage, the concept of Woman that Derrida uses can sometimes recuperate terms he means to displace, as in the citation from Nietzsche that he makes in *Spurs*, where the important issue of suicide emerges: "Would a woman be able to captivate us (or, as people say, to 'fetter' us) whom we did not credit with knowing how to employ the dagger . . . skilfully *against* us under certain circumstances? Or against herself; which in a certain case might be the severest revenge?" (*Spurs: Nietzsche's Styles* [Chicago: University of Chicago Press, 1978], 53).

It is interesting to see Derrida's allusions to Bettina in *The Post Card*, where he writes, "Ah Bettina, my love and it will be even worse if I publish your letters under my name, signing in your place. Listen Bettina, do what you want, I will restore everything to you, *j'accepte* everything, from you I will receive my last breath. I have no right to the history that we have told each other" (*The Post Card: From Socrates to Freud and Beyond*, trans. Alan Bass [Chicago: University of Chicago Press, 1987], 231).

safe.[55] The two women bring to each other radially different discourses, yet their interaction achieves something of the "rudderless" effect described by the Princess in *Tasso*. At the same time, however, the relationship provides a gloss on the way that gender can circumscribe such interactions when it is allowed to reassert itself: whenever, for example, Günderode lapses into the paradoxical polarity of her "masculine" and "feminine" training. These lapses were, as Fuller read them, the source of Günderode's suicidal tendencies.

Caroline Günderode was eight or ten years older than Bettina and a canoness. She therefore adopted the part of educator and advocate for the traditional representations of history and philosophy, even as she was the first to concede that the educational process was in a constant state of flux between the two women. Though far less generous and supportive of Arnim's imaginative flights than Goethe had been, Günderode also proved a sterner taskmaster, consistently challenging Bettina to take her tutoring more seriously. In her *Dial* essay, Fuller criticized Goethe's tolerance by calling it "manly" condescension and praised Günderode's occasional resistance to Arnim's flighty genius as a more dignified approach. Günderode was critical, but she was gentle in her reproaches. Fuller admired Günderode for this and often found herself performing the same role for her American sisters and students.

The vital give-and-take between the two women is perhaps most apparent in Günderode's description of Bettina's chamber. Because the image produced by Günderode in this exchange also tells a great deal about the hazards of Günderode's experimental approach, Fuller quotes the passage in her *Dial* essay:

> In thy chamber it looked like the shore where a fleet lies wrecked. Schlosser wanted two great folios that he lent you now three months ago from the city library which you have never read. Homer lay open on the ground, and thy canary-bird had not spared it. Thy fairly designed map of the voyages of Odysseus lay near, as well as the shell box with all the Sepia saucers and shells of colors; they have made a brown spot on thy pretty straw carpet. . . . In thy box where are sowed oats and I know not what else, all has grown up together; I think there are many weeds but, as I cannot be sure, I have not ventured to pull any thing up. Of books I have found on the floor Ossian,—Sacontala,—the Frankfort Chronicle, the second volume of Hemsterhuis which I took home with me because I have the first already: in Hemsterhuis lay the accompanying philosophical essay, which I pray thee present me . . . as thy dislike of philosophy makes thee esteem them so lightly I should like to keep together these studies against thy will, perhaps

[55] See Carroll Smith-Rosenberg, "The Female World of Love and Ritual: Relations between Women in Nineteenth-Century America," *Signs* 1 (Autumn 1975): 1–29.

in time they will become interesting to thee. . . . From under the bed Liesbet swept out Charles the Twelfth, the Bible, and also a glove which belongs not to the hand of a lady, in which was a French poem; this glove seems to have lain under thy pillow. . . . I saw two letters among many written papers, the seals were unbroken. . . . I left them on the table. All is now in tolerable order so that thou mayst diligently and comfortably continue thy studies."[56]

If the disarray of Bettina's chamber amuses and disturbs Günderode, Bettina nevertheless retains a certain power over Günderode because she is fearless before the chaos of the room. A serious internal conflict generates Günderode's attempt to tidy the chamber: by her own description she is at once the reproving masculine tutor and the subservient feminine domestic and Günderode admires Bettina's resistance to both roles. Like the Princess in Tasso, Günderode's feminine constraint is the ironic by-product of a masculine education. Indeed, Günderode's statement of envy over Bettina's "Careless away over the plains where thou seest no path dug before thee by the boldest pioneer" appropriately prefaces this critique of Bettina's room.[57] It is this "careless away" that enables Bettina to grow impatient with the closed representations of the philosophers and historians that she is advised to study, providing a valuable counterbalance to Günderode's despair over her necessary exclusion from those representations.

Arnim's response to Günderode in these moments also parallels Fuller's response to Emerson, whose occasional despair bordered on the tragic. For Fuller, Emerson's intellectual "suicide"—which is to say, his tendency to slide from a tragic perception into a limited skepticism—could be averted by an acceptance of the issues that he explored through his interaction with her, including the absorption of a type of Fourierism or feminist agency for his thought. The parallel was clearly on Fuller's mind, as we see in a letter dated 1841 to William Channing in which she wrote enthusiastically about *Die Günderode* and at the same time registered her famous complaint about Emerson's brooding approach.

Read these side by side with Waldo's paragraphs, and say is it not deeper and true to live than to think. . . . It seems to me that these childish stammerings of imperfect feeling intimate all, while these chasings up and down the blind alleys of thought neither show the centre nor the circumference. Yet his is noble speech. I love to reprove myself by it (LMF 2: 203).[58]

[56] Fuller, "Bettine Brentano and Her Friend Günderode," pp. 347–48.
[57] Ibid., p. 347.
[58] Fuller wrote "I prefer [*Die Günderode*] to the correspondence with Goethe. The two girls are equal natures, and both in earnest" (LMF 2: 202).

Fuller's letter is similar to the one written by Bettina in her struggle against one of Günderode's dark moments:

> But now thou sayest, we will trifle,—because thou wouldst remain untouched; because thou findest no community, and yet thou believest that there is somewhere a height where the air blows pure, and a longed for shower rains down upon the soul, making it freer and stronger. But certainly this is not in philosophy. . . . Imagine to thyself a philosopher, living quite alone on an island, where it should be beautiful as only spring can be. . . . Dost thou believe that he would take such flights as those which I cannot constrain with thee? I believe he would take a bite from a beautiful apple, rather than make dry wooden scaffoldings for his own edification. . . . The Philosopher combines, and transposes, and considers, and writes the processes of thought, not to understand himself, that is not the object of this expense, but to let others know how high he has climbed. He does not wish to impart his wisdom to his low-stationed companions, but only the hocus-pocus of his superlatively excellent machine.[59]

It may well be that the momentary parallel between Günderode and Emerson helped Fuller to see how Günderode's despair had less to do with her sex than with the resistance of the philosophic mind to the offerings of an intelligence unconditioned by tradition. Fuller intuited that it was not the broken heart that caused Günderode to kill herself, but the cold heartless blade of the two disciplines she revered. In translating Bettina's correspondence with Günderode, therefore, Fuller attempted to deal with two pressing issues: she gave counsel to men struggling with tradition by giving women a vital place in the definition of that struggle. The positive model of seduction between the two women which provided this lesson was not based on a simple tension between genders (this would have been a model of appropriation, one susceptible to a tragic interpretation); rather, the seductive movement of thought between them developed around a displacement of the hierarchy of gender.

There is a paradox to this seduction, however, and it resides in the fact that its movement away from gender depends first on a total immersion in the ideology of gender, a severance or amputation not unlike the severance of the two women in Goethe's *Tasso* from the rest of the play. Thus was Günderode trapped. Her respect for and capacity to enter the intellectual tradition also heightened her sense of exclusion when the fact of gender reemerged; as a woman she found no better text to write for herself than a tragic one. This trap is clear from the last letter to

---

[59] Fuller, "Brettine Brentano and Her Friend Günderode," p. 332.

Bettina that she wrote and which Fuller quotes at the end of her *Dial* essay. There Günderode returns again and again to the limitations imposed on women.

> All men are against thee, the whole world wilt thou feel and experience only through the contradiction in thy soul, there is no other possible way for thee to comprehend it. . . . The actual world has presented itself to thee as a deformed monster, but it did not terrify thee; thou hast at once set thy foot upon it, and although it whirls beneath thee and forever moves itself, thou lettest thyself be borne by it, without ever in thought dreaming the possibility that thou couldst for a moment be at one with it. . . .
>
> If I wished briefly to express thy character I would prophesy that hadst thou been a boy, thou wouldst have become a hero, but as thou art a girl I interpret all these dispositions as furnishing materials for a future life, preparation for an energetic character which perhaps in a living active time will be born. . . . We are now in the time of ebb.[60]

By contrast, Arnim's position outside the disciplines allows her to perceive and challenge the moments when tradition becomes too exclusive and unyielding.

Nevertheless, Fuller believed that this position could be maintained *only* within the boundaries of Arnim's interaction with someone like Günderode. When Günderode's sense of exclusion forces her to yield up her own "history" in suicide, Bettina loses the vital traditional frame that gives her resistance to history and philosophy its potency. By contrast, Goethe's response appeared to encourage both Arnim's frivolous nature and, retroactively, as it were, her friend's suicide.

Whereas Günderode's sense of exclusion forced her in the end to yield up her own history, Arnim's resistance to history actually enabled her to rewrite her own. Fuller's investment in the lives of both women caused her to overlook the crucial fact that Arnim inverted the chronological order of the two correspondences by publishing *Die Günderode* (1840) after *Goethe's Correspondence with a Child* (1835). Indeed, Arnim effectively anticipated Fuller by supplying her own revisionary reading of the *Correspondence with a Child*.[61] Fuller's blindness to the history of the two publications may have resulted from her perilous identification with the paradoxical histories of Arnim and Günderode. She clearly

---

[60] Ibid., pp. 354–55.

[61] Indeed, there are even moments within the text of *Goethe's Correspondence* when Bettina disrupts the hierarchy upon which the narrative seems to depend. She is unafraid, for example, to tell Goethe that he is "a coquettish, elegant writer, but . . . a cruel man" (p. 208), or to declare that she is "better and more amiable than the whole female assemblage in [his] novels" (p. 311).

oscillated in her identification with the two women and, as we have seen, that oscillation was necessary for the model of critical discourse with which she was experimenting. She valued Günderode's connection with Arnim because she needed the discipline of philosophy and history. Without it, her "chamber" reverted to an ineffectual place, one marked as feminine. At the same time, she valued Arnim's ability to challenge Günderode's tragic interpretation of those disciplines, particularly since Günderode's tragic sense was shared by men deeply immersed in the tradition. Nevertheless, Günderode's death suggested the terrible forces conspiring against a woman armed with a tragic sense of pedagogy and interaction. Without Günderode, Bettina seemed still more vulnerable to Fuller, since the stripping away of philosophical and historical inquiry that occurred with Günderode's death appeared to have left Bettina with little more than a fictive power over both.

To be sure, Fuller acknowledged how Bettina's celebration of "phantasy" enabled her to escape the narrowness of tradition. Because critics of Bettina's work sometimes challenged the authenticity of her letters, Fuller discounted such objections by arguing that "it is the highest attainment of man to be able to tell the truth, and more hardly achieved by the chronicler than the Phantast."[62] But if Arnim won an interpretive victory over the fact of Günderode's suicide and her own romantic interaction with Goethe by reversing the history of the two correspondences and placing *Die Günderode* last, that victory was not sufficiently clear for Fuller. Reordering the cold historical fact of Günderode's suicide represented a modest revision of the past but scarcely insured control over the future. Somewhere in the interim between her *Dial* essay and the publication of her own translation of the first section of *Günderode*, Fuller began to feel that to continue to identify with Bettina von Arnim without Günderode was to identify with a compromised control over the text of history, one that Fuller sought to reverse.

Fuller's involvement with Arnim ended prematurely when the plans for completion of the translation fell through, with economic constraints, no doubt, playing a part in this decision.[63] By providing only the early section of the correspondence for her American reader, however, she did keep the necessary but perilous balance between the two correspondents in play. She typically ended her segment of the translation with a letter from Bettina that mocked the limits of philosophy and history even as it sustained an engagement with them. The choice of this letter

[62] Fuller, "Bettine Brentano and Her Friend Günderode," p. 352.
[63] The translation was completed years later, after Fuller's death, by Minna Wesselhoeft and was entitled *Correspondence of Fraulein Günderode and Bettina von Arnim* (Boston: T. O. H. P. Burham, 1861).

seems deliberate, as if Fuller knew that this would supply the formal ending for her English-speaking reader.

> Thy Schelling's—philosophy is to me, indeed, a pit; it makes me giddy to look down and see where I might break my neck, trying to find my way through the dark gulf, yet for thy love I would creep through on all fours. And the Lunenburgh heath of the past, which . . . thou sayst . . . I need all . . . to make me reflect, to know myself; I will not contradict thee! Couldst thou but discern the mischievous, terrific ghosts that follow me in this history-desert. . . . When the tutor opens his mouth, I look into it as an impenetrable gulf which spews forth the mammoth-bones of the past and all sorts of fossil-stuff. . . .
>
> To-day has the past been spewed out . . . the Assyrian empire founded by Asser shortly after the foundation of the Babylonian empire; the word founded always distracts my attention. . . . It reminds me of the battles that these holy captains had to wage with the devil, and then I think of all nations, who were fighting, horned and cloven-footed, spitting fire and breathing out pestilential vapor, which the past blows over me. . . . Meanwhile Ninus, the conqueror, has whisked over from central Asia, built Ninevah, the capital of Assyria, is dead, his war- and building-loving wife, Semiramis, has yet a bit of Babylon left to build, and makes brilliant campaigns; all that was lost through the convent and wood demons, together with holy founders of orders. Through artifices and questions, however, I get from the teacher that nothing further came to pass. Over the story of Semiramis has the past let grow such thick mould, that only through the blue eye of immortality her name looks out, else knew we quite nothing. . . . If thou dost put it in the furnace with the old papers thou wilt destroy for me some very hard won past.
>
> Write of the Tale[64]

The last line of Bettina's letter ("Write of the Tale") beseeches Günderode to reconcile her favorite disciplines with Bettina's love of writing. Not long before her death, Günderode had promised to write a fairy tale for Bettina during one of her solitary walks along the Rhine. According to the narrative that we are given in *Correspondence*, however, every time that Günderode attempted the project, it would trail into an unhappy ending: "It is become so mournful, that I cannot read it; I dare not hear any more about it, and cannot write any more to it, it makes me ill."[65] By ending her translation as she does, Fuller shifts the interaction between Bettina and Günderode away from the suicide that formed its true clo-

---

[64] *Günderode*, p. 103–6.

[65] *Goethe's Correspondence with a Child*, p. 60. Too depressed to sustain her buoyant promise to Bettina, Günderode substituted a narrative about a "visitation" from her deceased sister who had beckoned her to commit suicide.

sure and toward the literary dynamic that had sustained it so well. Bettina's imperative tone turns the reader into a surrogate Günderode: the invited tale marks the hope opened to view by this exquisite entanglement of voices.[66]

In the end, Goethe and Arnim gave Fuller a way to translate her father's extraordinary gift to her—his gift of a classical education. Timothy Fuller's gesture was unusual in democratic America, and his daughter was eager to show the advantages of that bequest. This gift, after all, enabled her to have an intimate and productive relationship with Emerson. But Goethe and Arnim also gave her a way to show how easily such a gift could be appropriated by the rigid structures of privilege and tradition which had commonly educated its women. Women traditionally receiving the gift of a classical education were inevitably, like the Princess and Günderode, restrained by the very structures of nobility affording that gift. Moreover, given her interaction with Emerson, this restraint was clearly not restricted to women and could explain the restraint felt by men as well. As Fuller well understood, somewhere within those structures, momentary resistances were created, resistances not unlike those encoded in the paradoxical rhetoric of American democracy and dramatized in the work of none other than Goethe himself. Translation for Fuller thus became a vehicle for expanding and developing the space of that resistance. By bringing into conversation two cultural subsets, and refusing to force them into imperial conquests of the other, by allowing translation itself to become the model for the rudderless interaction where both mastery and a sense of the tragic are displaced, the issue for her became one of anticipation, growth, and a search for "joyous-carolling."

[66] We know that one reader in particular took Bettina's challenge to heart: Emily Dickinson, whose reading of Fuller's translation of Arnim "helped to shape [her] private mythology of self as well as to set the terms for the poses she assumed in her correspondence with Higginson, Susan Dickinson and the unknown lover of the Master letters" (Barton Levi St. Armand, "Veiled Ladies: Dickinson, Bettina, and Transcendental Mediumship," *Studies in the American Renaissance*, ed. Joel Myerson [Boston: Twayne, 1988], 1–51). I thank Barton St. Armand for showing me an earlier version of his essay and calling my attention to Dickinson's interest in Fuller's Arnim.

3

Footnoting the Sublime:
Fuller on Black Hawk's Trail

> I seem in the bosom of all possibility & have never tried but one or
> two trivial experiments. . . . I have heard of Niagara that it falls
> without speed. . . . Whatever they gave you, you will one day give
> me, O most bountiful of friends.
> —Ralph Waldo Emerson to Margaret Fuller, EL 3: 178–79

After publishing her translation of Bettina von Arnim's *Günderode* in
1842, Margaret Fuller grew frustrated by the limited power of her translations to inspire new thinking about pedagogy and gender. Convinced
that more direct methods were necessary to encourage people to consider gender constraints in the culture, she wrote "The Great Lawsuit" for
the *Dial* in 1843, beginning to outline there what she would elaborate a
year later when she revised her essay and published it under the title
Woman in the Nineteenth Century. In each version, she deliberately
framed her argument around the idea of Woman and the significance of
her position in culture. But an important experience for Fuller separates
the first draft of the essay from the second, one that can help us to
appreciate her revisions: a summer tour of Niagara and the Great Lakes
region. She finished "The Great Lawsuit" just days before she left, determined at the time to go away "quite free" (she told Emerson) without
fear of being "followed by proof sheets to Niagara" (MFL 3: 123). Still, if
she thought that the journey would help her escape the engrossing
theoretical issues she had left behind, she was quite mistaken. Her summer tour resulted in the publication of *Summer on the Lakes* in 1844, a
work that openly explores the delimiting method of reading and interpretation which most Americans and Europeans took to the rim of Western culture.[1] Once again, the problems of pedagogy, translation, and
difference were central to her experience. In particular, she wrestled
with the failure of interpretation underlying the widespread perception
that the Native American was doomed to a tragic fate. At the same time,
writing *Summer on the Lakes* helped her to see how her developing
feminist theory was itself sometimes limited by the cultural frame from

[1] *Summer on the Lakes, in 1843*, intro. by Susan Belasco Smith (Urbana: University of
Illinois Press, 1991). Future citations will be parenthetical textual references with the short
title, *Summer*.

which she wrote. As a result, she found herself drawn more and more toward the feminist strategies emerging from Fourier's radical critique of Western culture.

In one very real sense, Fuller's previous work in translation had prepared her for the trip. The double frame of the translator had made her attentive to interpretive possibilities opened to view by shifting cultural frames, lending her something of an anthropologist's sensitivity to the dynamic of culture contact. She had, after all, deployed the relationship of two European women, Günderode and Bettina von Arnim, as a model for rethinking the codes of pedagogy and interaction in American relationships. When she realized how the tragic account of Günderode's suicide had destroyed the efficacy of that model, obscuring the radicalizing tendencies of her relationship with Bettina, Fuller glimpsed the greater challenge still waiting before her. For if the discourse of the tragic had ultimately obscured the radicalizing tendencies of Arnim's relationship with Günderode, a similar dynamic was at work in the interpretation regarding the tragic fate of Native Americans.

In 1830 the federal government had inaugurated its Indian Removal Policy, and by 1843 most of the Native Americans east of the Mississippi had been defrauded and displaced. The tribes who managed to survive were forced to settle west of the river, in territory already inhabited by different Native American cultures.[2] Customarily, supporters of the policy claimed that Indian cultures needed "protection" by being separated from Anglo-American culture, though the harsher realities of racial intolerance and greed for land underlay the removal. When in 1838 the eastern Cherokees were forcibly marched from their Georgia homeland to new territory in the West despite their efforts at assimilation and petitions for citizenship, it became clear that those attempting to establish a viable interaction between Anglo- and Native American cultures would probably fail. The defeatist idea that the Indian as a type was vanishing from the landscape began to gather force, even in the minds of those most sympathetic to Native American cultures.[3]

When Fuller arrived in the Midwest in 1843, the Great Emigration of white settlers along the Oregon Trail was just underway, and traveling

[2] According to Michael Paul Rogin, "From 1820 to 1844 one hundred thousand Indians were removed from their homes and transported west of the Mississippi. One-quarter to one-third of these died or were killed in the process." See the chapter "Liberal Society and the Indian Question" in his *Ronald Reagan, the Movie, and Other Episodes in Political Demonology* (Berkeley: University of California Press, 1987).

[3] Brian W. Dippie, *The Vanishing American: White Attitudes and U.S. Indian Policy* (Middletown, Conn.: Wesleyan University Press, 1982); Roy Harvey Pearce, *Savagism and Civilization: A Study of the Indian and the American Mind* (Berkeley: University of California Press, 1988).

to Niagara Falls, Chicago, and the territory of Wisconsin was no longer a journey to the frontier. She could see that she was passing over well-traveled roads. Yet the presence of many defeated and displaced Native Americans throughout the landscape prompted her to consider the dangerous narrative through which their fate was being read.

Fuller's exposure to the Indian crisis sharpened her understanding of the forces at play in cultural discourse, particularly the dominance of one frame of reference over others. The model of translation she had been attempting to avoid in her own work—the model whereby the differences between languages are overcome or mastered rather than explored and put to use—clearly had become the model of cultural contact on the American border.[4]

Reading the Sublime

Like many travelers of her day, Fuller assumed that the tour through Niagara Falls would give her an opportunity to have a firsthand encounter with the American sublime.[5] The disappointment on this score—including her realization that her experience there was not firsthand at all but overcoded in a number of distressing ways—provides insight into the conflict between Native and Anglo-American culture around

[4] See Eric Cheyfitz, *The Poetics of Imperialism* (New York: Oxford University Press, 1991). See also his essay "Literally White, Figuratively Red: The Frontier of Translation in the Pioneers," in *James Fenimore Cooper: New Critical Essays*," ed. Robert Clark (Ottowa: Barnes and Noble, 1985), 55–95. It is no accident that translation becomes an important issue at the close of Cooper's *Last of the Mohicans*; see Richard Slotkin, Introduction, *The Last of the Mohicans* (New York: Penguin, 1986), xxxvi. See also his account in *The Fatal Environment: The Myth of the Frontier in the Age of Industrialization, 1800–1890* (New York: Atheneum, 1985), 88–98.

[5] Kant wrote that the sublime heightened our sense of the "*use* we can make of our intuitions of nature so that we can feel a purposiveness within ourselves entirely independent of nature" (Immanuel Kant, *Critique of Judgment*, trans. Werner S. Pluhar [Indianapolis: Hackett Publishing Company, 1987], bk. 2: 100). In her chapter on her visit to the falls, Fuller observes this dangerous sense of utility—though she momentarily represses its implication for the Native American population—when she tells of a man who "walked close up to the fall, and after looking at it a moment, with an air as if thinking how he could appropriate it to his own use . . . spat into it" (*Summer*, p. 5). For more on the sublime see Thomas Weiskel, *The Romantic Sublime: Studies in the Psychology of Transcendence* (Baltimore: Johns Hopkins University Press, 1976), 4; and Donald Pease, "Sublime Politics," in *The American Sublime*, ed. Mary Arensberg (Albany: State University of New York Press, 1986), 21–49. For the easy affiliation between the sublime landscape and the construction of the Native American, see David Levin's account of George Bancroft in *History as Romantic Art: Bancroft, Prescott, Motley, and Parkman* (Stanford: Stanford University Press, 1959). Fuller appears to have read the first three volumes (covering the French and Indian Wars) of Bancroft's *History of the United States from the Discovery of the Continent* (Boston,1834–39); see MFL 1: 313.

which develops the primary intellectual crisis of her tour.[6] Fuller's rendering of her visit to Niagara appears to be a deliberate frustration of the Kantian dynamic that had become standard in nineteenth-century accounts of the sublime: "the feeling of a momentary inhibition of the vital forces followed immediately by an outpouring of them that is all the stronger."[7] As she tells it, she appears to have experienced the blockage usually affiliated with Kant's mathematical sublime as she stood before the natural might of the falls, but little of the compensatory pleasure that Kant predicted would emerge from such a challenge: she did not recover a sense of "unlimited" ability in the presence of the falls.[8] Instead, when she stood by the falls, she found herself imagining an "identity" between the "mood of nature in which these waters were poured down with such absorbing force" and "that in which the Indian was shaped on the same soil" (*Summer*, p. 4). According to Fuller, this association led her to a disturbing fantasy: "For continually upon my mind came, unsought and unwelcome, images, such as never haunted it before, of naked savages stealing behind me with uplifted tomahawks; again and again this illusion recurred, and even after I had thought it over, and tried to shake it off, I could not help starting and looking behind me" (*Summer*, p. 4). Her hallucination bears a remarkable resemblance to the famous rendering of "The Death of Jane McCrea" by John Vanderlyn. His 1804 painting depicted the captive Jane McCrea kneeling with upraised arms beneath the assault of two powerful Native Americans, each wielding tomahawks. (One of the assailants is preparing to scalp her by pulling on her hair.)[9] Vanderlyn's painting, according to Richard Drinnon, "set the pattern for an endless series of pictorial indictments" of the Native Americans.[10] Unhappy with the images of the violent Indian and

---

[6] For a different reading of Fuller's response see Elizabeth McKinsey, "'To woo the mighty meaning of the scene'—Transcendence, Psychology, and Art," in her *Niagara Falls: Icon of the American Sublime* (New York: Cambridge University Press, 1985), 215–28.

[7] Kant, *Critique* 2: 98. For the part that Coleridge played in this view of the sublime, see Raimonda Modiano's *Coleridge and the Concept of Nature* (Tallahassee: Florida State University Press, 1985), 101–37.

[8] By Kant's account, "The feeling of the sublime consists in its being a feeling, accompanying an object, of displeasure about our aesthetic power of judging, yet of a displeasure that we present at the same time as purposive. What makes this possible is that the subject's own inability uncovers in him the consciousness of an unlimited ability which is also his, and that the mind can judge this ability aesthetically only by the inability" (*Critique* 2: 116).

[9] I thank Richard Slotkin for pointing this similarity out to me. See also Lee Clark Mitchell, *Witnesses to a Vanishing America: The Nineteenth-Century Response* (Princeton: Princeton University Press, 1981), 107; and Ellwood Parry, *The Image of the Indian and the Black Man in American Art, 1590–1900* (New York: George Braziller, 1974).

[10] Richard Drinnon, *Facing West: The Metaphysics of Indian-Hating and Empire-Building* (Minneapolis: University of Minnesota Press, 1980), 101.

vulnerable maiden projected by her fantasy, Fuller tried to think them away. Her determination to avoid melodrama and sentimentality in her account meant that she needed to find a way to displace the authority that this fantasy and others like it held for her at the beginning of her trip.

Fuller's fantasy strangely allegorizes the anxiety she had expressed in the *Dial* essay over the crisis between Bettina von Arnim and Günderode.[11] If Bettina was aligned in Fuller's mind with Nature, and Günderode with Representation, then the allegory imagines the relationship of Art and Nature as destructive: when the savage or unruly quality of Bettina's mind takes control, she all too readily slips into the role of Indian, raising her tomahawk over the head of Günderode. Fuller's goal in her translation of *Günderode* had been, of course, to interrupt and displace that formulation (and its tragic overtones) by finding a way to balance without effacing the different qualities of each. Here, on the border of North American culture, the binary trap of nature / representation could recur with still more force. Yet in the very way that Fuller oscillates between Bettina and Günderode, the image that she conjures at the foot of the falls draws simultaneously on the fact that women were often identified *with* the forces of nature.[12] What the image reveals in fact is the manner in which women and Native Americans are both trapped by a tendency in Western thought to appropriate by opposition. If the concept of the savage Indian threatening "civilized" woman was used to read Native American cultures, that image was no less effective an allegory for the opposition that would keep women outside the usual play of representation. In relinquishing the beautiful for the sublime, women were thought to challenge civilization as well, threatening with their uplifted tomahawks to castrate the whole symbolic order.

In her rendering of the sublime, then, Fuller chooses to emphasize the moment in her experience when she felt a crisis in her "standard of sensibility."[13] And by transforming the moment of crisis into an allegory involving issues of gender and race, Fuller sets the stage for an analysis of those standards. This means that the recovery of her powers will occur only if she can make effective use of the "epistemological gaps" opened to view by the terms of her anxiety.[14] The rejection of the "standard of sensibility" operating behind her allegory at the foot of the falls

[11] "Bettine Brentano and Her Friend Günderode," *Dial* 2 (January 1842): 313–57.

[12] According to Michael Rogin, "Jacksonians' personifications of their enemies— whether effeminate aristocrats or the devouring, 'monster-hydra' bank—exhibited fear of domination by women" (*Ronald Reagan, the Movie*, p. 150).

[13] Kant, *Critique*, p. 115.

[14] Bruce Clark cited in Mary Arensberg, "Introduction: The American Sublime," in *The American Sublime*, p. 4.

therefore marks the central labor of her account. Her success in this labor is uneven, yet her struggle enriches *Summer on the Lakes* in ways that prove productive for her later writing. As I shall show in Chapter 4, her discussions with Emerson about the French utopian Charles Fourier play a key role in this struggle.

By opening with the account of Niagara Falls, Fuller found an economical way to establish how inadequately her reading had prepared her for her experience at the rim of Western culture. As Thomas Weiskel has suggested, the Romantic sublime supplied "a remarkably successful way to read, offering formulas which preserved the authority of the past within the ramified structures of dualism."[15] Her insertion of the unpleasant dualism of sentimental maiden and savage Native American into the formula of the sublime revealed the very protocols of reading she had brought *with her* to the falls and which her readers undoubtedly had brought with them to her text. Though she initially admits to her "stupidity in feeling most moved in the wrong place" (*Summer*, p. 8), this feeling eventually becomes a virtue in the text.[16] Thus she makes clear the largely unsatisfying nature of her experience at the falls; indeed, only when she broke away and stood by the rapids stretching well beyond the cataract did she experience something of the unpresentable that she had been seeking all along.

Footnoting the Sublime

Initially, *Summer on the Lakes* appears to work within the accepted genre of travel literature by simply mapping Fuller's passage around the landscape. Through provocative descriptions of natural and domestic scenes, she weaves a tale about her journey, sometimes even inserting letters and poems from her friends that supply alternative responses to her experience. Yet a series of digressions—constituting well over half of the volume—alters by exaggerating the familiar pattern of the travel narrative. She interrupts her account of the journey with mock Socratic dialogues and suggestive stories, including one autobiographical fiction about her schoolgirl days. Nearly a third of the work is a lengthy description of her reading during her trip and later, as she was composing the narrative. In effect, she presents her reader with a saturation of textuality, making the activities of travel and reading synonymous. Thus

[15] Weiskel, *The Romantic Sublime*, p. 4.

[16] Here again Fuller may be responding to Kant's argument that "we say that someone has no *feeling* if he remains unmoved in the presence of something we judge sublime" (*Critique*, p. 125), particularly since Kant means by this that one must lack moral feeling.

travel becomes a deep structure for the text, an internal metaphor for the changing movement of her perspective. To read her travel narrative is to experience layered movement between one terrain of meaning and another, often without preparation. By disrupting reader expectation and making difficulty and dislocation *desiderata* in the experience of reading, *Summer on the Lakes* marshals its various and shifting frames of interpretation in a special type of agency.[17]

Fuller's first sentence in *Summer on the Lakes* oddly prepares the reader for the changes that she will bring upon the discourse of the sublime: "Since you are to share with me such foot-notes as may be made on the pages of my life during this summer's wanderings, I should not be quite silent as to this magnificent prologue to the, as yet, unknown drama" (*Summer*, p. 3). She manages in this twisting opening sentence to turn her experience of the sublime into what is fittingly both a "magnificent prologue" and a "foot-note."[18] As we know from her reading of *Tasso*, neither the prologue nor the footnote was a mean form of expression for her. As a woman writing and publishing her first extended "original" work, she might have been expected to write from the secondary position of the footnote. Yet by inviting her reader to join her in this supplementary position, she subtly changes the relationship of margin and center. Throughout her narrative, the secondary function usually taken by the footnote finds expression instead in the primary flow of the text. No real footnotes adorn her pages, for she has moved them all to the center of her narrative, and everything that she tells is invariably a reference to some previously read text. Hardly casual, the reference to footnotes at this crucial juncture suggests the degree to which textual support will be highlighted in her narrative.

At the same time, the reference to footnotes provides a punning acknowledgment of Fuller's role as pathfinder for her reader. This task assumes a complicated character throughout her narrative, one deeply implicated in the conflict of cultures to which she is exposed and which exposes her in turn. Though she acknowledges her position as a member

[17] For a compelling study of *Summer* as a Romantic fragment, one that encourages the reader to participate in the "process of its making," see Stephen Adams's essay, " 'That Tidiness We Always Look For in Woman': Fuller's *Summer on the Lakes* and Romantic Aesthetics," *Studies in the American Renaissance 1987*, ed. Joel Myerson (Boston: Twayne Publishers, 1988), 247–64. See also Susan Belasco Smith, "*Summer on the Lakes*: Margaret Fuller and the British," *Resources for American Literary Study* 17, no. 2 (1991): 192–207.

[18] When the word *sublime* reappears in her narrative, it assumes a very different aspect, as in her sardonic account of the "sublime" indifference of a certain peddler (p. 31) and in her discussion of the limited virtue of a "sublime prudence" (p. 81). Finally the discourse of the sublime seems to disappear altogether, displaced by her developing interest in the diminutive, the small, those things as "unmarked, as mysterious, and as important . . . as the infusoria to the natural" (p. 31).

of the offending race ("We stepped not like the Indian, with some humble offering . . . but to get" [*Summer*, p. 18]), she attempts throughout to adopt a more than casual awareness of the dangerous implications of this position.[19] In one instance, for example, the people with whom she is traveling find themselves in trouble when they follow a white man's "short cut" (*Summer*, p. 31) and make their way out only after recovering traces of Black Hawk's trail. But, as Fuller also makes clear, following Black Hawk's trail is extremely dangerous, since it has become a trail of annihilation.[20]

Fuller also brought with her a useful predilection for interrogating the most stable and comfortable cultural myths. Indeed, determined to displace the image she summoned at the foot of the falls, she pursues two intertwined narrative ambitions in *Summer on the Lakes*: a change in the attitude toward Native Americans and a change in the attitude toward women in general. These ambitions serve each other, though often in problematic and compelling ways.

Fuller's understanding that, to be met fairly, a Native American culture needed to be comprehended by its own standards and terms, a theme she reiterates throughout her narrative, emboldens her confidence in the idea that women needed to be measured by a standard of their own, despite their participation in the larger culture oppressing them.[21] Thinking about the Native American crisis ultimately strengthens her feminism by forcing her to encounter the problematic grounding

[19] Even here, Fuller creates a complex place for herself. Consider the passage preceding her statement that she "went not to give, but to get, to rifle the wood of flowers for the service of the fire-ship" (p. 19): "On this most beautiful beach of smooth white pebbles, interspersed with agates and cornelians, for those who know how to find them, we stepped, not like the Indian, with some humble offering, which, if no better than an arrowhead or a little parched corn, would, he judged, please the Manitou, who looks only at the spirit in which it is offered. Our visit was so far for a religious purpose that one of our party went to inquire the fate of some Unitarian tracts left among the woodcutters a year or two before. But the old Manitou, though, daunted like his children by the approach of the fire-ships which he probably considered demons of a new dynasty, he had suffered his woods to be felled to feed their pride, had been less patient of an encroachment, which did not to him seem so authorized by the law of the strongest, and had scattered those leaves as carelessly as the others of that year" (pp. 18–19).

[20] Black Hawk and members of his tribe were brutally attacked in 1832 when they attempted a peaceful return to their burial grounds. Drinnon, *Facing West*, pp. 198–99.

[21] The most vivid demonstration of this position occurs toward the close of her chapter on her reading about Native American culture, where she writes, "The Indian, brandishing the scalps of his friends and wife, drinking their blood and eating their hearts, is by him viewed as a fiend, though, at a distant day, he will no doubt be considered as having acted the Roman or Carthaginian part of heroic and patriotic self-defence, according to the standard of right and motives prescribed by his religious faith and education. Looked at by his own standards, he is virtuous when he most injures his enemy, and the white, if he be really the superior in enlargement of thought, ought to cast aside his inherited prejudices enough to see this,—to look on him in pity and brotherly good-will, and do all he can to mitigate the doom of those who survive his past injuries" (p. 144).

of any feminist argument. At the same time, however, the treacherous alignment of feminism with the discourse of progress, which she initially felt compelled to endorse, occasionally mars her understanding of Native American culture.

Rethinking Captivity

Annette Kolodny has described *Summer on the Lakes* as a type of "captivity narrative," and she is right, though for reasons that go beyond Fuller's recognition that the pioneer men had taken their wives, sometimes against their wills, into rough and unfamiliar territory.[22] Fuller also understands the subversive potential of the captivity situation: a captive might find herself strangely liberated by the sudden shift in cultural relationships and expectations. Certainly Fuller hopes for a transformation of the traditional female role in the new environment of the frontier. And she draws on the conflict of standards in the Anglo-Indian encounter when she observes how the daughters "have a great deal to war with in the habits of thought acquired by their mothers from their own early life. Everywhere the fatal spirit of imitation, of reference to European standards, penetrates, and threatens to blight whatever of original growth might adorn the soil" (*Summer*, p. 39). She advocates an education more suited to the environment, one open to unexpected possibilities and offering women a bolder and more productive way of life. That her description of the "war" between the young women and their mothers borrows, however modestly, from the language also framing the battle between Native and Anglo-American cultures proves equally significant, particularly as preference is given to the former.

After observing the potential for change in the woman's role that appears to present itself on the frontier, Fuller asks her reader to consider more thoroughly the dangers to which young women everywhere are exposed in the early stages of their development. She interrupts her travelogue with a mock autobiography, ostensibly an account of a woman named Mariana, whom she claims to have known in boarding school. The Mariana digression establishes a theme she will explore throughout her narrative: the dynamic interplay of political subversion and containment. Like Black Hawk's trail, which in her narrative represents a new and better way of traversing the world even as it remains laden with danger and defeat, Mariana's brilliant and electrical personality—her Otherness—both held out promise of a new and powerful role for her

[22] Annette Kolodny, "Margaret Fuller: Recovering Our Mother's Garden," in *The Land Before Her: Fantasy and Experience of the American Frontiers, 1630–1860* (Chapel Hill: University of North Carolina Press, 1984), 123.

and kept her from "play[ing] her part" first among her schoolmates and later in her marriage. She emphasizes the "provoking non-conformist" (*Summer*, p. 53) quality of the young girl, which made her relationship with her fellow students difficult, sometimes punishingly so. Mariana's strange personality so provokes the other young girls that they play a humiliating prank on her for which Mariana retaliates in kind. Discovered, Mariana loses something of her "wild fire"; in fact, "the terrible crisis, which [Mariana] so early passed through, probably prevented the world from hearing much of her" (*Summer*, p. 58). In this sense, Mariana's powerfully subversive energies are exposed as a prelude to their containment. Recognizing this danger highlights the hazards associated with any type of cultural critique.

Instead of living up to her potential, Mariana has the misfortune to fall in love and marry a young man who can neither appreciate nor help to develop her intellectual qualities. Fuller explains how this lover "became the kind, but preoccupied husband," and "Mariana, the solitary and wretched wife" (*Summer*, p. 60) until, one day, broken and depressed by this uneven relationship, Mariana dies.

The Mariana digression then remains pointedly focused on the forces of culture overwhelmingly set against Mariana's development, particularly the lure of a "golden marriage" (*Summer*, p. 62), often held as the central event of a woman's life. Fuller complains that "such women as Mariana are often lost, unless they meet some man of sufficiently great soul to prize them" (*Summer*, p. 64). Recognizing that "such men come not so often as once an age," she insists that "their presence should not be absolutely needed to sustain life" (*Summer*, p. 64). But she does not end with this radical dismissal of marriage. Instead, she seizes the opportunity to critique the prevailing concept of Man, sustaining an illusion that marriage could still be acceptable by ending her long digression with the question, "When will this country have such a man?" (*Summer*, p. 64) She answers with a list of necessary attributes:

No thin Idealist, no coarse Realist, but a man whose eye reads the heavens while his feet step firmly on the ground, and his hands are strong and dexterous for the use of human implements. A man religious, virtuous and sagacious; a man of universal sympathies, but self-possessed; a man who knows the region of emotion, though he is not its slave; a man to whom this world is no mere spectacle, or fleeting shadow, but a great solemn game to be played with good heed, for its stakes are of eternal value, yet who, if his own play be true, heeds not what he loses by the falsehood of others. A man who hives from the past, yet knows that its honey can but moderately avail him; whose comprehensive eye scans the present, neither infatuated by its golden lures, nor chilled by its many ventures; who possesses prescience, as the wise man must, but not so far to be driven mad to-day by the gift which discerns to-morrow (*Summer*, p. 64).

Significantly, Fuller's description of this man forms an amalgam of the qualities later valorized in her discussion of civilized and savage cultures, an amalgamation combining the "sentiment and thoughtfulness of the one, with the boldness, personal resource, and fortitude of the other" (*Summer*, p. 136). Moreover, by making Mariana the daughter of a Spanish Creole, she introjects by highlighting her racial character so as to provoke an association between Marianna's subversive potential and the Otherness of the Midwest. Mariana's early power, the way she captivates her schoolmates with her "love of wild dances and sudden song, her freaks of passion and of wit" (*Summer*, p. 51), entails a strangeness that Fuller also sees in the alien cultures around her there. The portrayal of the semiautobiographical Mariana in such terms suggests that Fuller's exposure to Native American culture may have influenced her developing understanding of the standards by which she had been measured as a child. The ambition to develop a more sympathetic and comprehensive understanding of the Native American cultures supported an equally powerful desire to rethink the condition of women across cultural differences.

That Fuller's feminist critique drew direct support from her encounter with the Native Americans becomes clearer in her discussions of the role of women. In her effort to read all that she could about Native American cultures, she turned to women writers, maintaining that "the observations of women upon the position of woman are always more valuable than those of men" (*Summer*, p. 110). She found that the three women upon whose writings she had depended—Anne Grant, Anna Brownell Jameson, and Jane Schoolcraft—had conflicting opinions about the status of women in Native American marriages.[23] Though she includes a

[23] Anne Grant, *Memoirs of an American Lady with Sketches of Manners and Scenes in America as They Existed Previous to the Revolution* (1809; rpt. New York: Dodd, Mead, 1901); Mrs. Anna Brownell Jameson, *Winter Studies and Summer Rambles in Canada*, 2 vols. (New York: Wiley and Putnam, 1839). Jane Schoolcraft was the Ojibwa wife of Henry Rowe Schoolcraft, author of *Algic Researches* (1839), which Fuller read during her trip, though her understanding of Schoolcraft is drawn from Jameson's account, and fortunately, since Henry Schoolcraft maintained a Eurocentric bias. For more on this bias see Mitchell, *Witnesses to a Vanishing America*, pp. 168–71. Fuller bemoans the premature death of Jane Schoolcraft, saying that through her death "was lost a mine of poesy, to which few had access, and from which Mrs. Jameson would have known how to coin a series of medals for the history of this ancient people. We might have known in clear outline, as now we shall not, the growths of religion and philosophy, under the influences of this climate and scenery, from such suggestions as nature and the teachings of the inward mind presented" (*Summer*, p. 124). For more on Schoolcraft see Charles S. and Stellanora Osborne, *Schoolcraft—Longfellow—Hiawatha* (Lancaster, Pa.: Jacques Cattell Press, 1942).

section of Jane Schoolcraft's argument that the position of the Native American woman "is higher and freer than that of the white woman," she tends to agree with Anne Grant that the position of the Indian wife is "inferior" to that of her husband (*Summer*, p. 109).[24] Intriguingly, however, she also agrees with Schoolcraft that the two cultures could provide a useful comparison:

> It is also evident that, as Mrs. Schoolcraft says, the women have great power at home. It can never be otherwise, men being dependent upon them for the comfort of their lives. Just so among ourselves, wives who are neither esteemed nor loved by their husbands, have great power over their conduct by the friction of every day, and over the formation of their opinions by the daily opportunities so close a relation affords of perverting testimony and instilling doubts. But these sentiments should not come in brief flashes, but burn as a steady flame, then there would be more women worthy to inspire them. This power is good for nothing, unless the woman be wise to use it aright. Has the Indian, has the white woman, as noble a feeling of life and its uses, as religious a self-respect, as worthy a field of thought and action, as man? If not, the white woman, the Indian woman, occupies an inferior position to that of man. It is not so much a question of power, as of privilege (*Summer*, pp. 112–13).

In this brief review of Native American women Fuller articulates forcefully what she had argued only tentatively concerning women of her own culture. Her distinction between "power" and "privilege" is her way of defining the larger cultural forces that contain the power that might otherwise provide a strong feminist critique.

Fatal Conflicts: The Vanishing American

Fuller's narrative develops a troubling conflict between her faith in the limitless opportunities that might open for women and her sense of the deadly limit that had already been imposed upon Native Americans. Witnessing the many white women traveling west with their families, she focused on the way they could improve their situation. She seemed to gather confidence in the efficacy of a certain type of feminist critique

---

[24] Fuller writes, "Mrs. Schoolcraft had maintained to a friend [Mrs. Jameson] that they were in fact as nearly on a par with their husbands as the white woman with hers" (*Summer*, p. 108). Fuller actually changes Schoolcraft's argument, which was that the Indian woman was held in higher esteem in her culture than the white woman was in hers. That Schoolcraft was a Native American, married to Henry Schoolcraft, makes her point of view all the more intriguing, though Fuller felt that her position was too one-sided.

as she saw how their fatal imitation of European standards could easily be altered to suit their new environment. She was becoming more convinced, in other words, that there was nothing fatal in the construction of a woman's role: nothing, that is, resembling the unhappy condition of the Native Americans in the Midwest. Indeed, she found it much more difficult to refute the fatal construction of the Native American. Torn by guilt and a certain sense of helplessness, particularly in conjunction with her developing feminism, her witness to the crisis of the Native Americans sometimes caused her to endorse the discourse of the vanishing American which, historians remind us, became a deadly excuse for the aggressive expansion of European culture.[25]

Surprisingly, Fuller succumbs throughout her narrative to the argument that the Native Americans were fated as a race to perish. But her interpretation was influenced by the poor state of the available literature. For the most part, she made wonderful use of what material there was, often reading against the grain by observing how the biases of white culture pervaded the texts. Fuller found this bias particularly true of James Adair, who "with all his sympathy for the Indian, mixes quite unconsciously some white man's view of the most decided sort" (*Summer*, p. 131).[26] Unfortunately, however, the argument for the inevitable extinction of Native Americans permeated the many works she read, including George Catlin's *Letters and Notes on the Manners, Customs, and Condition of the North American Indian* (1841), a text she came to depend on rather heavily.[27]

A painter and fledgling ethnographer, Catlin devoted himself to constructing a gallery of Native American images to correct the narrow,

[25] For the vanishing American see Dippie, *The Vanishing American*; Bernard W. Sheehan, *Seeds of Extinction: Jeffersonian Philanthropy and the American Indian* (Chapel Hill: University of North Carolina Press, 1973); Robert A. Trennert, Jr., *Alternative to Extinction: Federal Indian Policy and the Beginnings of the Reservation System, 1846–51* (Philadelphia: Temple University Press, 1975); Levin, "The Infidel: Vanishing Races," in *History as Romantic Art*, pp. 126–32; Robert Berkhofer, Jr., *The White Man's Indian: Images of the American Indian from Columbus to the Present* (New York: Alfred A. Knopf, 1978), 88–89; and Richard Slotkin, *Regeneration through Violence: The Mythology of the American Frontier, 1600–1860* (Middletown, Conn.: Wesleyan University Press, 1973), 357–68.

[26] Fuller refers to James Adair's *History of the American Indians*, published in London in 1775; see *Adair's History of the American Indians*, ed. Samuel Cole Williams (Johnson City, Tenn.: Watauga Press, 1930). Adair was a strong proponent of the theory that the North American Indians were derived from the Lost Tribes of Israel. See the introduction by Williams for a list of others who actively supported this view. See also Slotkin, *Regeneration through Violence*, pp. 360–63.

[27] Fuller nevertheless registers the fact that she had heard from reliable sources that Catlin was "not to be depended upon for the accuracy of his facts, and indeed . . . he sometimes yields to the temptation of making out a story" (*Summer*, p. 20).

sentimental, and frequently hostile image of the Native American in Anglo-American culture.[28] Fuller's resort to Catlin—whom she describes as the best author writing on the subject—reflected her determination to displace the troubling image that haunted her at the foot of the falls. From Catlin, she no doubt developed her thoughts about an ethnographic museum of Native American culture.[29] Yet Catlin, she found, reinforced the idea that contact with the white man had contaminated Native American cultures. She noted many signs of the negative impact of white culture on Native American populations that she encountered, and the idea that Native American could not *endure* contact with the whites (which was the idea behind the Indian Removal Policy) caused many, including Catlin, to assume that the Native American cultures would soon become extinct.[30]

Still, Fuller's endorsement of the rhetoric of the vanishing American did not emerge from such a belief.[31] She reminds her reader how one

[28] See Mitchell's chapter "George Catlin's Mission" in *Witnesses to the Vanishing America*, pp. 93–109. According to Mitchell, "Catlin was the first to teach his countrymen to observe their western landscape and to examine the people who lived there" by providing images that would counteract the sentimental rendering of Vanderlyn's painting. See also Dippie's chapter "The Anatomy of the Vanishing American" in *The Vanishing American*, pp. 12–31.

[29] Although he was unsuccessful in his lifetime, Catlin attempted to sell his collection of Indian portraits and other cultural artifacts to the Federal government. It is also likely that Thomas L. McKenney and James Hall's *Indian Tribes of North America, 1836–44* encouraged Fuller to argue that a "national institute" be established for "all the remains of the Indians,—all that has been preserved by official intercourse at Washington, Catlin's collection, and a picture gallery as complete as can be made, with a collection of skulls from all parts of the country. To this should be joined the scanty library that exists on the subject" (*Summer*, p. 233). For a description of McKenney's "charnel house" in the old War Department Building in Washington where he stored the bones he had been collecting over the years, see Drinnon, *Facing West*, pp. 191–215 and 165–90.

[30] Fuller's confusion was abetted by descriptions of the warrior Red Jacket, who had "steadily opposed the introduction of white religion, or manners, among the Indians. He believed that for them to break down the barriers was to perish. On many occasions he had expressed this with all the force of his eloquence. He told the preachers, 'if the Great Spirit had meant your religion for the red man, he would have given it to them. What they (the missionaries) tell us, we do not understand; and the light they ask for us, makes the straight and plain path trod by our fathers dark and dreary'"(*Summer*, p. 140). Later in the narrative, she refers again to the Chippewa who had endorsed the idea that "the difference between the white man and the red man [was] this: 'the white man no sooner came here, than he thought of preparing the way for his posterity; the red man never thought of this'" (*Summer*, p. 154). She adds at this point, "I was assured this was exactly his phrase; and it defines the true difference. We get the better because we do 'Look before and after.' But, from the same cause, we 'Pine for what is not.' The red man, when happy, was thoroughly happy; when good, was simply good. He needed the medal, to let him know that he was good" (*Summer*, p. 154).

[31] By way of making an argument against Catlin's belief that contact with the white man inevitably led to corruption, Fuller observes "the French Catholics, at least, did not harm them, nor disturb their minds merely to corrupt them. The French they loved. But the stern Presbyterian, with his dogmas and his task-work, the city circle and the college, with their

experiment that would have proved the contrary—the plan of the Cherokee to govern themselves and live within the state of Georgia—was thwarted by the "barbarous selfishness" (*Summer*, p. 144) of American settlers. It was rather the glaring inadequacies of her own culture that tempered her view. (This mood sometimes permeated her feminism as well. Her fatal account of Mariana's life provides a narrative of what might be called the vanishing American woman.) Furthermore, her effort not simply to oppose the American and European settlers from whom she almost immediately felt estranged meant that she occasionally adopted their perspective toward the Native Americans. She observes that she did not want to "distrust or defame" with "stupid narrowness" (*Summer*, p. 18) all that she would find in the West. This effort to be impartial forced her to sympathize with the struggles and attitudes of the Anglo-American settlers, so much so that upon hearing a Chippewa give support to the idea that a certain "superiority" (described as the tendency of the Anglo-American to think about the future) was "on the side of the white man" (*Summer*, p. 123), she could do little more than agree with him.[32]

Fuller's sympathies, though, were also strongly divided. Moments of controlled anger fill her account when she observes, for example, the

---

niggard concessions and unfeeling stare, have never tried the experiment. It has not been tried. Our people and our government have sinned alike against the first-born of the soil, and if they are the fated agents of a new era, they have done nothing—have invoked no god to keep them sinless while they do the hest of fate" (*Summer*, p. 114). She later takes pleasure in observing a Native American woman who had been working for years on a steamer running between Mackinaw and Sault St. Marie and who had "preserved after so many years of contact with all kinds of people" a "perfectly national manner" (*Summer*, p. 146).

[32] Perhaps the most unconsidered comment made by Fuller is found in a poem about Governor Everett's reception of a deputation of the Sacs and Foxes in 1837, which she inserts in her narrative. Although the overall emphasis of the poem is to praise Everett for attempting to "throw [himself] into the character or position of the Indian" (*Summer*, p. 119)—a point Fuller reiterates throughout her work—the poem nevertheless endorses the idea that the Indians are an "unimproving race" in the following stanza:

We take our turn, and the Philosopher
Sees through the clouds a hand which cannot err,
An unimproving race, with all their graces
And all their vices, must resign their places;
And Human Culture rolls its onward flood
Over the broad plains steeped in Indian blood.
Such thoughts steady our faith; yet there will rise
Some natural tears into the calmest eyes—
Which gaze where forest princes haughty go,
Made for a gaping crowd a raree show. (*Summer*, p. 117)

The bulk of Fuller's narrative works against this sentiment, at moments becoming quite heated about the cruelty of the "Human Culture roll[ing] its onward flood." Yet her belief that feminism was a sign of advancing "Human Culture" finally bars her from openly rejecting this tenet of the discourse of the vanishing American.

"stern Presbyterian, with his dogmas and his task-work, . . . niggard concessions and unfeeling stare." On such occasions, she thought the Native Americans would be served better by "their own dog-feasts and bloody rites than such mockery of that other faith." She continues, "Yes! slave-drivers and Indian traders are called Christians, and the Indian is to be deemed less like the Son of Mary than they! Wonderful is the deceit of man's heart!" (*Summer*, p. 114).

Nor is it surprising in light of these outbursts that Fuller's narrative presentation often undermines her pronouncements regarding the fate of the Native American. Fuller's first allusion to the discourse of the vanishing American provides a vivid example of these tensions. Admiring the location of a white dwelling in Rock River, Illinois, she compares it to the sensitive habitats of Native American settlement she had observed during her visit. With this favorable point of comparison between one group of settlers and those from whom they had taken the land, she feels at liberty to complain about the "rude way in which objects around [dwellings] were treated" in most of the white settlements that she had seen, adding that in "twenty, perhaps ten, years" such settlers would "obliterate the natural expression of the country" (*Summer*, p. 29). She adds,

> This is inevitable, fatal; we must not complain, but look forward to a good result. Still, in travelling through this country, I could not but be struck with the force of a symbol. Wherever the hog comes, the rattlesnake disappears; the omnivorous traveller, safe in its stupidity, willingly and easily makes a meal of the most dangerous of reptiles, and one whom the Indian looks on with a mystic eye. Even so the white settler pursues the Indian (*Summer*, p. 29).

If white settlers must have a "victor[y] in the chase" (*Summer*, p. 29), it is scarcely a victory Fuller supports.

An even stronger hesitancy marks a later section where Fuller recalls the reaction of one of her hosts who had expressed indignation upon observing the return of a Native American to an old burial site. "What feelings must consume their heart at such moments!" she writes of the Indians, adding, "I scarcely see how they can forbear to shoot the white man where he stands" (*Summer*, p. 71). Choosing such a moment to note that "the power of fate is with the white man, and the Indian feels it" (*Summer*, p. 71) lends only ambiguous support to this idea, particularly when she then returns to the opinion of her host. Apparently, this man claims that he once "fixed [his] eye steadily" on a Native American in order to keep him from drinking. When he relinquished his bottle and became "quite obedient, even servile," the man interpreted this response as a sign that the Native American "could not resist the look of a white man." That such docile behavior proves the host's moral superiority is immediately questioned by Fuller's additional observation: "This gentleman, though in other respects of most kindly and liberal heart, showed the aversion that the white man soon learns to feel for the Indian on whom he encroaches, the aversion of the injurer for him he has degraded" (*Summer*, p. 72).

In this account, as in so many others, Fuller's position about the fate of the Native American is rapidly subsumed by a graphic analysis of the terrible agents of that fate. Not only does she reveal her disgust over this man's resentment over the fact that in returning to their burial grounds, the Native Americans would drive away the host's hunting game ("OUR game—just heavens"[*Summer*, p. 72]), but she also critiques his claims as a sportsman by observing the highly coded gender references in one of the hunting stories he tells. The host describes his prey displaying some antlers:

> The first was a magnificent fellow; but then I saw coming one, the prettiest, the most graceful I ever beheld—there was something so soft and beseeching in its look. I chose him at once; took aim, and shot him dead. You see the antlers are not very large; it was young, but the prettiest creature" (*Summer*, p. 72).

Significantly, when Fuller's focus on racial issues becomes affiliated with questions of gender, productive tensions in her text occur. Here, her earlier assertion that the Native American is fated to pass from the earth is subsumed by her focus on the prejudicial and insensitive posture of the white man who is not surprisingly the most aggressive proponent of that thesis. By ironic allusion to what she calls the "true spirit of the sportsman, or, perhaps I might say of Man" (*Summer*, p. 72) she shifts the entire frame of reference, moving from an account of the inevitable dominance of one people over another to an account of the acts of dominance inherent in an equally fatal view of gender. Because she has already mounted an argument against such a fatal reading of gender in her thesis about the education of young women on the prairie (among other places), an implicit critique of the fatal interpretation of Native Americans pervades the account.

Rethinking Fate: Emerson and Fourier

An irony infuses Fuller's decision to cast Native Americans in a fatalistic light, an irony registered at the level of composition. She appears to recognize the problematic nature of her argument as she composes it, for she immerses herself not only in the works of Catlin, Adair, and McKenney while writing *Summer on the Lakes*, but also in the theories of Charles Fourier.[33] Indeed, references to Fourier begin to appear carrying a double value throughout *Summer on the Lakes*. They support Fuller's concern for a change in the condition of women, fostering her belief that gender itself was not a fatal category; but they also provoke a larger inquiry into the unresolved racial dilemma in her work.

Though Fuller does not directly refer to Fourier's position on Native American culture, the various allusions to his work in *Summer on the Lakes* indicate that she probably read the third volume of *Théorie de l'unité universelle*, where many of his thoughts on "savage" life appear.[34] Fourier's juxtaposed critiques of "savage" and "civilized" cultures undoubtedly would have intrigued Fuller.[35] Certainly his influence is evident in her argument that man "loses in harmony of being what he gains in height and extension; the civilized man is a larger mind, but a more imperfect nature than the savage" (*Summer*, p. 136). It is certainly no accident that Fourier assumes a rather prominent position at the end of *Summer on the Lakes*: several passengers on the boat heading eastward to Buffalo discuss Fourier, and Fuller expresses the hope that they would return west one day to try "the great experiment of voluntary association" (*Summer*, p. 155).[36]

---

[33] Fuller's 1844 journal shows that she read Fourier's *Nouveau Monde industriel et sociétaire* (Paris: Dossange and Mongie, 1829) in September (MFL 3: 175). She also wrote to Orestes Brownson in January to request a volume of Albert Brisbane's work on Fourier. Robert Hudspeth suggests that the volume may have been *Association: or a Concise Exposition of the Practical Part of Fourier's Social Science* (New York: Greeley and McElrath, 1843).

[34] When Fuller adverts to Fourier, she refers to his transformation of Franz Mesmer's theory of mesmerism and hypnotic states, which appears in the third volume of *Théorie de l'unité universelle*, 2d ed., 4 vols. (Paris, 1841–43).

[35] For Fourier, the "savage men" possessed "seven natural rights" that had been lost in civilization: "the right to hunt, to fish, to gather food, to pasture animals, to steal from strangers, to form alliances with his fellows, to be free from worry" (*The Utopian Vision of Charles Fourier*, trans. and ed. Jonathan Beecher and Richard Bienvenu [Columbia: University of Missouri Press, 1971], 138). Fourier particularly admired this last right and praised the way that the savage man "enjoy[ed] his carefree life and [did] not concern himself with the future" (*Utopian Vision*, p. 143). Fourier did not advocate a return to the savage state, however; he felt that the cause of social harmony would be promoted only if the savage man were offered the type of "attractive productive work" that could be carried out in a "passionate series" (*Utopian Vision*, p. 142). Fourier was also quick to observe that women did not share an equal footing in savage culture (*Utopian Vision*, p. 143).

[36] When Fourier wrote about "savages," as he called them, he tended to promote the savage way of life over the civilized way of doing things by arguing that savage men could enjoy social and physical freedoms lost to civilized men. This assertion does not mean that Fourier fell back on the idea of the noble savage in his analysis. Indeed, his belief that Indian women held an inferior position in their culture gave credence to Fuller's position on this issue.

Thinking about Fourier inevitably returned Fuller to her conversations with Emerson, who also plays an interesting role in the composition of *Summer on the Lakes*. At one point in her text, she attempts to reconcile herself to the terrible fate of the Native American by arguing that it resulted from the "inevitable" collapse of ethical integrity at a collective level. She concludes,

> I have not wished to write sentimentally about the Indians, however moved by the thought of their wrongs and speedy extinction. I know that the Europeans who took possession of this country, felt themselves justified by their superior civilization and religious ideas. Had they been truly civilized or Christianized the conflicts which sprang from the collision of the two races, might have been avoided; but this cannot be expected in movements made by masses of men. The mass has never yet been humanized, though the age may develop a human thought (*Summer*, p. 143).

Emerson, of course, had adopted the same type of rhetoric (setting the individual against the crowd) in his resistance to Fourier and to all that Fourier had come to represent for his American followers. Because Fourier had argued that association among men would form the only basis for a legitimate social critique, his doctrine gave support to those American reformers intent upon wresting a realm of freedom from the realm of fate. Throughout her text, Fuller's growing interest in Fourier signals a productive disagreement with Emerson on the question of agency and social change.

Fuller's first and perhaps most important allusions to Fourier in *Summer on the Lakes* occur in her account of a German book she had been reading while staying in Milwaukee. The book she discusses, *The Seeress of Prevorst*, concerns the clairvoyant experiences of a young German woman, and her digression seems motivated by the cult of mesmerism just gaining popularity as a mode of parlor entertainment in America.[37] She prefaces her discussion by deliberately staging a dialogue "between

---

[37] Justinus Kerner, *Die Seherin von Prevorst, Eroffnungen uber das innere Leben des Menschen und uber das Hereinragen einer Geisterwelt in die Unsere* (Stuttgart, 1829). An English translation was made in 1845. On Mesmerism see Robert C. Fuller, *Mesmerism and the American Cure of Souls* (Philadelphia: University of Pennsylvania Press, 1982); Frank Podmore, *Modern Spiritualism: A History and Criticism* (New York: Charles Scribner's Sons, 1902). For its later manifestations, see Howard Kerr, *Mediums, and Spirit-Rappers, and Roaring Radicals: Spiritualism in American Literature, 1850–1900* (Urbana: University of Illinois Press, 1972).

Fuller's brother chose to omit this section when he published a posthumous edition of *Summer* in 1856—a policy followed by Perry Miller and Mason Wade in their twentieth-century editions of Fuller's work. See *Margaret Fuller: American Romantic*, ed. Perry Miller (Ithaca: Cornell University Press, 1963); and *The Writings of Margaret Fuller*, ed. Mason Wade (New York: Viking, 1941).

several persons" and herself about "clairvoyance" (*Summer*, p. 78), revealing a larger goal. Her first allusion to Fourier occurs here, and with it she argues for mesmerism as social critique. A private allusion to Emerson in this section suggests that her *Seeress of Prevorst* digression renewed her debate with him on issues of agency and social change so crucial to her explorations of gender and race in *Summer on the Lakes*.

When Fuller chose to write about her trip to the Midwest, she knowingly invited an examination of the conflict between her perspective and that of the men and women living on the frontier, as well as the conflict between Anglo-American and Native American cultures. Her decision to address those issues by giving an account of a German clairvoyant, glossed through the thinking of a French theorist, was not arbitrary or idiosyncratic, as some have averred, but a recognition of the complexity of her task. Both Fourier and Kerner represented unorthodox Western thinkers; by reading Kerner's narrative through Fourier, Fuller turned Kerner's narrative into a position paper on social critique as well. By using the digression as a gloss for her visit to the Midwest, and her conversation with Emerson, she addressed both the explicit feminist and implicit racial concerns she had earlier enjoined her reader to consider.

Fourier on Mesmerism: Aromal States

Fourier's adaptations of the theory of mesmerism to social critique underlies Fuller's preface to her discussion of the *Seeress of Prevorst*. The cult of mesmerism developed in late eighteenth-century Europe through the work of Franz Mesmer, who theorized that a fine magnetic fluid permeated all bodies in the universe. Mesmer established quite a following when he emigrated from Germany to Paris in 1778 and began healing physical and mental infirmities by polarizing magnetic fluids, bringing patients to crisis through magnets and mesmeric trances designed to remove obstacles in bodily channels and revive circulation of the vital magnetic fluids.[38] Like Bergasse, one of Mesmer's many French followers, Fourier applied the concept of a universal fluid—which he called "aroma"—to culture itself. In Fourier's vision, the production of a crisis or an "aromal state" could lead to social harmony; death itself was such a crisis, a transition state "hav[ing] little to do with the orthodox Christian view of the afterlife." Believing that our souls "experience a series of rebirths and transmigrations" formed "by the element we call

[38] See Robert Darnton, *Mesmerism and the End of Enlightenment in France* (Cambridge: Harvard University Press, 1968), 142–46.

Aroma," Fourier theorized that a productive cultural critique depended on such transitional moments.[39]

Through her account of the *Seeress of Prevorst*, Fuller's interest in the aromal state endorses what Fourier elsewhere called "transitions or ambiguous types."[40] Her use of Kerner's narrative makes it clear that she agreed with Fourier that unusual personalities, like unusual states of mind, would become "eminently favorable to the development of social virtues."[41]

In the preface to her discussion of Kerner's book, Fuller stages a dialogue between Free Hope and three other allegorical figures: Good Sense, Old Church, and Self-Poise. She explains that Free Hope represents her position. A reader of Emerson's letters to her can recognize Emerson as Self-Poise, since Fuller quotes verbatim from one of his letters in developing that position.[42] The arguments between the three characters address the efficacy of social reform.[43] In response to Good Sense—who adopts a pragmatic position toward the study of anything extraordinary—Free Hope summons Fourier: "The mind, roused powerfully by this existence, stretches of itself into what the French sage calls the 'aromal state.' From the hope thus gleaned it forms the hypothesis, under whose banner it collects facts" (*Summer*, p. 79). When Free Hope goes on to elaborate on the interpretive possibilities that might result, Old Church registers intense dissatisfaction, insisting that men and women should not transgress "boundaries" given to them by God. Fuller as Free Hope answers back that she would prefer to acknowledge "no limit, set up by man's opinion, to the capacities of man" (*Summer*, p. 80).

Implicit in this debate is Fuller's contradiction of the fatal view of social change to which her discussion of Native Americans had led her. As the debate continues, moreover, she alludes to Emerson, presenting a parody of his political position in the persona of Self-Poise, whose skepticism inspires a conservative response. "Our deep ignorance is a chasm that we can only fill up by degrees," according to Self-Poise, who adds that "a sublime prudence" is a "better part of wisdom . . . amid the manifold infatuations and illusions of this world" (*Summer*, p. 81). Given

[39] M. C. Spencer, *Charles Fourier* (Boston: Twayne Publishers, 1981), 101, 103.

[40] Fuller encountered this idea when she read *Nouveau Monde industriel et sociétaire* in September. Passage quoted is from *Utopian Vision*, p. 267.

[41] Here Fourier meant to include somnambulists as well as those who had an "ambiguous gender" (*Utopian Vision*, p. 267).

[42] One can only surmise Emerson's bemusement when he found his own words so displayed. It likely matched Fuller's response when she saw the use to which he put his conversations with her in the *Second Series*.

[43] Fuller's linking of mesmerism and social reform, drawn as it was from Fourier, anticipates the affiliation that will continue in the United States for several decades. See John Humphrey Noyes, *History of American Socialisms* (Philadelphia: Lippincott, 1870).

the value of the sublime in the opening chapter, the coupling of the word *sublime* with *prudence* is particularly provocative in its denial of agency. "Sublime prudence" suggests a resistance to crisis, or to the power of social critique, effectively militating against all that Fuller had set out to accomplish with her narrative. To complete her playful parody of Self-Poise, she quotes directly from one of Emerson's letters, where he alludes to the extravagant excesses of both mesmerism and the theories of Fourier: "I think it is part of our lesson to give a formal consent to what is farcical, and to pick up our living & our virtue amidst what is so ridiculous, hardly deigning a smile, and certainly not vexed."[44] Her inclusion of this particular section from his letter reveals that her engagement with Kerner's book had less to do with mesmerism as a fad than with the way Mesmerism was being transformed by Fourier into a type of social critique. Her decision to incoporate Emerson as a counterpoint to her position allowed her to problematize the fatalistic argument developing elsewhere in her narrative. Interestingly, her defense of "lyric inspirations" and "just such a field in which to wander vagrant" (*Summer*, p. 81) provides another source for Emerson's later description of inspiration in *Representative Men*. "The mind, roused powerfully by this existence" and "stretch[ing] of itself into" the "aromal state" (*Summer*, p. 79) is precisely the condition Emerson describes in his "Uses of Great Men."

Fuller's actual account of *Die Seherin von Prevorst* works on several competing levels at once, though the feminist impulse is the most readily apparent. As described by Kerner, the Seeress of Prevorst was a young German woman, Frederica Hauffe, who responded to the difficult experiences of her life with prophetic dreams. Fuller reads these prophetic moments as possible feminist strategies, as ways of transcending the narrow constraints of Hauffe's life as the daughter of a German gamekeeper. Betrothed by her family to a man she presumably does not wish to marry, Hauffe's mystical trances form a type of self-protective

---

[44] In Emerson's letter, this statement is preceded with the thought that "Fourier & Miller, & Dr Buchanan will not heal us of our deep wound, any more than Spurzheim and the Flying Man, to whom they have succeeded" (EL 3: 246). He writes in response to Fuller's amusing account of the mesmerist who had been given one of his poems to "read" through magnetic channels. Apparently the clairvoyant described the author of the poem as both "holy, true, and brave" (LMF 3: 177)—and flawed. When pressed to describe the poet's fault, the medium said, "It is not a fault, it is a defect—it is underdevelopment; it puts me in mind of a circle with a dent." When asked to elaborate still further, the medium added, "If he could sympathize with himself, he could with every one." Fuller found the medium's final statement on Emerson a "most refined expression of the truth, whether obtained by clairvoyance or any other means" (MFL 3: 178). See Fuller's equally amusing account of the discussion that she had with Sarah Clarke and Caroline Sturgis about the possibility of getting Emerson to attend an evening with a mesmerist (MFL 3: 181).

strategy, sometimes effective, sometimes not. Kerner, Hauffe's doctor, writes with an air of scientific legitimacy.[45] Plagued by visions and prophetic dreams, the young German woman is hostage to a sensitive nature. Nevertheless, Kerner's case history forms a type of captivity narrative that differs from other such narratives (e.g., Cotton Mather's account of Mercy Short and Freud's later account of Dora) in his sympathetic reading of Hauffe's symptoms. Fuller clearly admires the unusual nature of the "relation between physician and clairvoyant" (*Summer*, p. 94), and quotes at length from his work. She read in Kerner's description of Hauffe's condition ("detained at the moment of dissolution, betwixt life and death" [*Summer*, p. 91]) Fourier's transitional or aromal state." Accordingly, she views Kerner as a man unafraid to support transition as a potential site of critique. His work, moreover, provided her with a language through which to criticize sages like Emerson "who will not believe, because, in their mental isolation, they are incapable of feeling these facts" (*Summer*, p. 102).

Fuller's digression enables her both to pursue a feminist critique of culture and to show how disparate cultural practices, when brought together, can provide insight into the limits of cultural standards. For this reason, she emphasizes the *strangeness* of Kerner's book as she introduces it to her narrative about Wisconsin, emphasizing the "strong contrast" (*Summer*, p. 77) it made with life around her. It is no coincidence, in fact, that her digression on the Seeress of Prevorst occurs in her chapter on the territory of Wisconsin, since, as she tells her reader with her opening sentence, Wisconsin was itself in a "transition state" (*Summer*, p. 75). Fuller appears most interested in linking the narrative about the Seeress with the potential agency derived from the condition of transition itself.

Dangerous Allegories

The Kerner digression and the account of Frederica Hauffe become allegories for the extended argument of *Summer on the Lakes*: the encounter of Native American and European cultures. According to Fuller, Hauffe's liminal state provides her with a feminist strategy to escape the strict patriarchal forces of her culture. At the same time, however, Hauffe's mental state incapacitates her by thwarting her interaction with the world. Thus, in Fuller's analysis of her condition, Hauffe goes from

45 For a longer account of Kerner's position, see Frank Podmore's *Modern Spiritualism: A History and Criticism*, 2 vols. (New York: Charles Scribner's Sons, 1902), 1: 99–100.

being a transitional type—representative of one who could live on the border between two orders—to being a representative of Western culture *in extremis*, because her brain was "too much excited on some one side" (*Summer*, p. 99). In her effort to define the problematic nature of Hauffe's condition, Fuller selects terms enriched by the value they held in the larger racial narrative of which they formed a part.

With her digression on the Seeress of Prevorst, Fuller demonstrates the way a certain type of feminist critique or resistance can obscure a larger cultural critique. If, to change the nature of Woman's role in culture, one had to resort to the very excess that had been responsible for still another cultural wrong—in this case the demise of Native American cultures—then the site of critique needed to be reexamined. The highly charged allegorical value of Fuller's terms are unmistakable: "We would rather minds should foresee less and see more surely . . . and the brain be the governor and interpreter, rather than the destroyer, of the animal life" (*Summer*, p. 99). In other words, she uses the cliches of racial difference, which established white culture as prophetic and Native American cultures as harmonious with nature and "animal life," to show Hauffe's feminism to be complicit with the larger limits of Western civilization.[46]

Double Strategies

In her effort to deal with this troubling set of insights, Fuller began to emphasize the need for a double strategy, one that would allow her to shift her frames of reference to observe the various contradictions at work in any serious cultural critique. For this reason she observes both the virtues of Kerner's account of Hauffe's mesmeric trances and the abuses to which such activity could be put (and indeed had been put in the United States.) Like Fourier, she wants to believe in the power that "uncommon characters will always exert in breaking down the barriers custom has erected round them" (*Summer*, p. 112) and fills her narrative with accounts of unusual men and women of several cultures. Yet, as her most vivid examples show—including the tale of Black Hawk and her long digressions on Mariana and Frederica Hauffe—such subversive

[46] Perhaps influenced in her thinking by Fourier, Fuller believed that man "loses in harmony of being what he gains in height and extension; the civilized man is a larger mind, but a more imperfect nature than the savage." Accordingly, she valued the people who appeared to "combine some of the good qualities of both . . . the sentiment and thoughtfulness of the one, with the boldness, personal resource, and fortitude of the other" (*Summer*, p. 136).

power is also subject to containment. The site from which productive critique can emerge can easily become the site of political deformation or annihilation.

Once again, emphasizing shifts in frames of reference became Fuller's best strategy. She closes the chapter containing her account of the Seeress of Prevorst with the observation that one should cultivate "the gift of reading the dreams dreamed by men of . . . various birth, various history, various mind" (*Summer*, p. 102). As if to demonstrate, she follows with a chapter devoted to Native American cultures. A transitional passage at the beginning of that section, where she describes a memorable walk along a beach by an Native American encampment, highlights her strategy. Listening to the shrieks of Native Americans excited by rockets being set off over the water, she observes that her "sensations" were both "dismal" and "pleasant" (*Summer*, p. 105). This description shows the distance she has come from her earlier response to the sublime. Although acknowledging that her dread arose from the perspective of an Anglo-American woman responding to the alien sounds of excited Native Americans, she neither dwells on it nor allows it to ruin the positive feelings she also experiences. Observing the "pleasure" derived from "everything that breaks in upon . . . routine" (*Summer*, p. 105), Fuller also focuses on the pleasure provoked by her sense of alienation.

This interest in the pleasure of "everything strange" (*Summer*, p. 105) prompts Fuller to make an analysis of Native American women and culture, sometimes to advance her feminist perspective and at other moments to consider the standard of the Native American culture itself. The difficult conflicts generated by this type of analysis, some of which we have already addressed, are neatly allegorized in the Native American tale entitled "Muckwa, Or the Bear," which she records toward the end of the chapter. She tells her reader that the story demonstrates a complex understanding of the ethics of hunting. Given her earlier account of her Anglo-American host and his insensitivity both as a hunter and as a man, the tale supplies an interesting rebuttal of his perspective, and thus a rebuttal of the larger cultural perspective of which he (and even Fuller herself, in her tragic mode) form a part.

The story concerns a Native American named Muckwa who is given a friendly reception after he accidentally wanders into a tribe of bears. Invited to marry one of the she-bears and live in harmony among them, Muckwa promises to give up hunting. Two children are born to the marriage, one in the form of a Native American and one in the form of a bear. One day after his wife goes away to gather nuts for the family, Muckwa finds himself bored and decides to return to hunting; in the process, he unknowingly kills his sister-in-law. When his crime is discovered, his wife manages to divert her father's anger. But as they begin to prepare for their winter hibernation, a new set of Native American hunters arrive and Muckwa's wife tells her husband to return to his tribe, explaining that the " 'Indian and the bear cannot live in the same lodge, for the Master of Life has appointed for them different habitations' " (*Summer*, p. 126). (Fuller puts these words in quotation, as if to distance herself from them.) Muckwa reluctantly returns with his Native American son to his own people, but never again hunts a she-bear for fear of killing his wife.

Fuller tells her reader that she admires the story for the "*savoir faire*, the nonchalance, the Vivian Greyism of Indian life" (*Summer*, p. 126).[47] And she calls the tale an apt expression of "unequal relations" (*Summer*, p. 127), a phrase that cannot but reverberate for her reader. Is she referring to the unequal relation between the two children, who are given uneven care by Muckwa and the she-bear? Or does she mean the unequal relation between husband and wife, where the woman does all the labor and the husband merely seeks pleasure and distraction? Or is this tale simply an allegory of the interaction between Native and Anglo Americans? Fuller likely had all of these uneven relationships in mind, all the more in that the tale seems to endorse the fatalistic perspective at work in the discourse of the vanishing American. Yet she rejects this fatalism by implying that social harmony (between children, between husband and wife, between cultures) could have been established if only the "Master of Life" had been "consulted" (*Summer*, p. 127).

Among the binary oppositions in "Muckwa, Or the Bear," no ambiguous or transitional types afford insight into qualities shared by bear and Native American cultures. In her own way, Fuller strains to establish this transitional space by drawing a parallel between this tale and the European story of the "little boy visiting a bear house and holding intercourse with them on terms as free as Muckwa did." The similarity of these tales suggests to Fuller that "the child of Norman-Saxon blood, no less than the Indian, finds some pulse of the Orson in his veins" (*Summer*, p. 127).[48] Her fleeting support of the concept of amalgamation

[47] Fuller may well have borrowed this emphasis on the "savoir faire, the nonchalance" of Indian life from Fourier, who tended to emphasize the "insouciance" of their existence. See Nicholas V. Riasanovsky, *The Teaching of Charles Fourier* (Berkeley: University of California Press, 1969), 144. For a sense of what Fuller describes with the phrase "Vivien Greyism" see her brief review of D'Israeli in "Story-Books for the Hot Weather," in *Life Without and Life Within; or Reviews, Narratives, Essays, and Poems by Margaret Fuller Ossoli*, ed. Arthur B. Fuller (Boston: Brown, Taggard and Chase, 1859), 143–48.

[48] If Fuller refers to "Goldilocks and the Three Bears," she has forgotten some significant aspects of the tale, not only that the interloper was a girl but also that certain negative attributes could be assigned to her aggressive entry into the home of the bears. Fuller's lapse in memory reveals her determination to establish a positive sense of culture contact.

at the close of her chapter manifests the same desire to lay a framework for some sort of peaceful exchange between cultures. Yet amalgamation of this sort appears to be only a theoretical possibility. Bowing to the authority of those whose experience with Native Americans is greater than hers (notably Catlin), she is persuaded that "those of mixed blood fade early" by "los[ing] what is best in either type" (*Summer*, p. 120). Counterexamples appear throughout her text, suggesting her hope that the best attributes of both cultures might one day be combined. She finds something of this balance in the character of Alexander Henry and the account of his relationship with Wawatam, a distinguished chief of the Mackinaw.[49] The same hope is expressed when at the close of her Mariana digression she describes the man needed for America's future in terms borrowed from both cultures.

Most tellingly, Fuller feels that she has herself been cheated of the opportunity to glimpse the possibility of such a mutual sharing between the cultures. And for this reason, she greatly regrets the cancellation of a planned canoe trip "whose daily adventure, with the camping out at night beneath the stars would have given an interlude of such value to [her] existence" (*Summer*, p. 148). Significantly, a feeling of powerlessness infuses her expression of regret: "It did not depend on me; it never has, whether such things shall be done or not" (*Summer*, p. 148). But she does have the power of her narrative at hand, and it is no accident that she ends her book with an account of her ride over rapids in a canoe with two Native American men. Fuller and her Indian guides do not really communicate; no great process of cultural translation has been discovered, save that she is now aware that they have negotiated the treacherous water together, never feeling the "terror and delight" she had been prepared by her reading to expect. Instead she experiences "the buoyant pleasure of being carried so lightly through this surf amid the breakers" (*Summer*, p. 150). And it is notable, finally, that this pleasure—which derives from a deliberate confusion of cultural expectation—is also shared, for as she observes, the men spoke to one another in a tone of "pleasant excitement" as they guided the canoe amid the "jagged rocks" (*Summer*, p. 150). As such, her account offers a momentary suspension of the fatal argument. With this image, moreover, she seals her escape from the hermeneutic of the sublime earlier formulated in her fantasy at Niagara; she's gone from the falls to the rapids, from the sublime to its fluid displacement.

In the interplay of race and gender throughout the narrative, a con-

---

[49] Fuller tells her reader that she would have included Henry's account of cannibalism if she had had the space. She likely piqued Thoreau's interest in Henry with this comment (*Summer*, p. 242).

cern for gender remains primary; Fuller's long digressions tend almost always to carry explicit feminist meaning, whereas their complicated racial tensions remain more implicit and contradictory. Nevertheless, if her hope for feminism mandates that she accept the progressive rhetoric that nurtured the discourse of the vanishing American, she often does so reluctantly. If anything, her own tendency toward a fatal construction of her autobiography serves to reinforce her fatal view of the Native American crisis. It would take more time before she could develop the confidence that she needed to discredit the theory that the Native American cultures were fated to perish. Yet, given the high critical value that she placed on the activity of reading in *Summer on the Lakes*, her call for a thorough record of Native American history and legend situates her thinking on these matters well beyond the dominant cultural bias of her time. More important, her sense that negotiations between different protocols of reading could generate a type of critical agency—a sense oddly strengthened through her reading of Emerson and Fourier—became the hard-won insight of her tour. Thinking about the Native American crisis ultimately strengthens her feminism by forcing her to encounter the problematic grounding of any feminist argument. Thus *Summer on the Lakes* provides an important pretext for our understanding of her complex feminist argument in *Woman in the Nineteenth Century*.

4

Fuller, Fourier, and the Romance
of the *Second Series*

A good deal of character in our abused age. The rights of woman, the antislavery,—temperance,—peace,—health,—and money movements; female speakers, mobs, & martyrs, the paradoxes,
the antagonism of old & new, the anomalous church, the daring
mysticism & the plain prose, the uneasy relation of domestics, the
struggling toward better household arrangements—all indicate
life at the heart not yet justly organized at the surface.
                                          —Ralph Waldo Emerson, JMN 7: 6

March, Gypsies and militia captains, paddies and Chinese, all
manner of cunning and pragmatical men and a few fine women, a
strange world made up of such oddities, the only beings that belong to the horizon being the fine women.
                                          —Emerson, JMN 8: 345

Fuller's trip to the Midwest forced her to consider the value of skepticism as a tool for redefining the terms of her feminism. Her original
assumptions about the role of women in Western culture came into
question when she saw how some of those assumptions carried violent
and destructive meaning for the lives of many Native Americans. Her
interest in the work of Charles Fourier and his "absolute doubt" became
still more intense as a result. As Fourier did, so did Fuller begin to
emphasize woman's precarious relationship to culture: strangely marginalized, often situated at once inside and outside its ideological formations, Woman occupied a unique site from which to offer a critique of
culture, even though the terms of that critique would always be viewed
as provisional. Rather than despairing over this unstable foundation for
her feminism, Fuller found it increasingly helpful to imagine how the
terms of a feminist agency might be continually reevaluated, especially
since the tendency to fix certain terms had resulted in such devastating
results.

Fuller's transitional thinking anticipates the feminist strategy developing among some theorists today, particularly those interested in negotiating between the "absolute doubt" of deconstruction and the pragmatic and historic imperative of a feminist agency. Paul Smith's analysis
of this "double strategy" of feminist theory describes some of the tensions at work in Fuller's approach:

> The effect of feminism's double-play is demonstrably to have broken down the old habit of *presuming* the "subject" as the fixed guarantor of a given epistemological formation, as well as to have cast doubt on the adequacy of the poststructuralist shibboleth of the decentered "subject." . . . [T]he human agent can be dis-cerned from the "subject" . . . at the point where the contradictions between different ideas and positions of the "subject" are recognized and privileged; that is, at the point where the negativity contained in and by social discourses and systems is once again allowed the right to work.[1]

After her visit to the Midwest, Fuller increasingly acknowledged how the humanist conception of the individual underwriting many of her feminist ideas needed reexamination. At the same time, she remained steadfast in her insistence that certain pragmatic issues concerning women could only be addressed through a recognition of the roles the culture had continually asked them to perform. Working with these conflicting imperatives, she began to see the advantage of bringing unresolvable discourses together so that contradictions could be "recognized and privileged" as material through which unthought and unexplored ideas might emerge.

Fuller's conversation with Emerson advanced her thinking about these matters. Despite the tendency of both authors to exaggerate their differences during this period, the record of their private conversation with one another reveals some striking parallels in their thinking. Whereas both authors waivered between a hope for what Emerson calls "new and unattempted performances" (CW 3: 162) and a skepticism about the validity of the assumptions upon which such performances might be based, Fuller's explicit feminist motivation made it easier for her to see the advantage of exacerbating, rather than resolving, the tension between those imperatives. Her growing confidence in the efficacy of a certain type of unsolvability, already clear in the methods employed throughout *Summer on the Lakes*, becomes still more evident in *Woman in the Nineteenth Century*. Thus her engagement with Emerson's simultaneous repulsion over and attraction to the leading aspects of Fourier's theory helped her to refine her growing dependency on this type of double strategy in her feminism. Her response, in turn, prompted him to consider how his own skeptical position could work to inform a type of feminist agency. Indeed, *Essays: Second Series* reveals the intense conflict he was experiencing between the imperatives of social

---

[1] Paul Smith, *Discerning the Subject* (Minneapolis: University of Minnesota Press, 1988), 151.

reform and his developing skepticism about the assumptions upon which an idea of agency or social reform might be based.

Although Emerson's developing skepticism and his complex resistance to social reform have been identified as two thematic strains in the criticism of the *Second Series*, the feminist issues working to inform and ultimately transform both have not been understood. Certainly no one has observed how his thoughts about Fourier permeated his thinking during this period. If we compare the *Second Series* to the conversation with Fuller recorded in his letters and journals, we can see the extent to which the feminist issues both implicit and explicit in the Fourieristic doctrines then flourishing throughout New England informed Emerson's language. Thus it is useful to turn to *Second Series* before considering *Woman in the Nineteenth Century*. The relationship between the two texts is a powerful example of the mutual influence of these writers. It is no accident that his famous essay "Experience"—thought by many to be his work of mourning for his son Waldo and the site of his most powerful statement on skepticism—ends with a peroration on social reform.[2] In fact, the essay's delicate but paradoxical resolution ("the true romance which the world exists to realize, will be the transformation of genius into practical power" [CW 3: 49]) can be read as his effort to address by holding in suspension the wildly divergent strategies generated through his conversation with Fuller.

In his 1876 history of the 1840s and 1850s, O. B. Frothingham identified the "agitation" on behalf of women as the "definitive" reform of the period.[3] The centrality of the "woman question" has become lost in subsequent literary and historical accounts, but we know from Emerson's journals that the feminist issue held significant symbolic value for the entire range of reforms sweeping his part of the country. Few of the obvious and practical feminist issues being discussed in 1844 made their way into the *Second Series*, yet Emerson makes specific mention of the political agitation for women in the essay "Manners" in a passage that derives, as it turns out, from a long and rather extraordinary journal entry on Fuller (CW 3: 88).[4] Though ignored or deemed irrelevant in modern assessments, his specific reference to this movement would have held considerable meaning for his contemporary reader. Certainly

---

[2] For a stunning reading of the essay's elegiac form see Sharon Cameron, "Representing Grief: Emerson's 'Experience,'" *Representations* 15 (Summer 1986): 15–41.

[3] Octavious Brooks Frothingham, *Transcendentalism in New England: A History* (1876; rpt. Philadelphia: University of Pennsylvania Press, 1972), 175–81.

[4] The journal entry on Fuller is JMN 8: 368–69, to which we will return.

one of those readers, Nathaniel Hawthorne, understood its value: his *Blithedale Romance* provides the most vivid example of how Fourier and the agitation on the part of women became a symbolic register for the decade. Indeed, Hawthorne's tale forms a polemical refashioning of many of the issues central to *Second Series*.

Still, to regard the direct mention of "Woman's Rights" (CW 3: 88) in Emerson's essay as proof of his interest in feminism enacts the very "transformation of genius into practical power" (CW 3: 49) that he actually problematizes there. Moreover, through this very problematization traces of his involvement with Fuller and her developing sense of feminist agency are most evident. Fuller was herself only beginning to recognize the complexities of defining a feminist agency, and Emerson's determination to do the same should not draw our contempt or suspicion, as it has for critics who assume that he could not break his man-centered perspective; in fact, his uneasiness looks considerably more alluring when we consider the range of issues at hand in the project of defining a feminist perspective for the conduct of life. That his struggle sometimes proved frustrating for Fuller does not make it any less important. His amazing ability to anticipate the philosophical complexity of certain issues proves a powerful stimulus for the production of her most overtly feminist work. Still, what is true of most of her less explicit feminist writing can also be said of his writing during this period: both tend toward the double strategy characteristic of feminist theory today.

It has long been commonplace to observe the skeptical strain surfacing in Emerson's *Second Series*. More recently readers have elaborated on the linguistic turn of that skepticism.[5] In developing the rich theoretical power of Emerson's skepticism in that work, critics have successfully displaced an earlier view of him as the naive and imperial proponent of individualism. Indeed, a striking feature of this criticism is the tendency toward the paradoxical claim that his work anticipates while superseding the terms of deconstruction. Stanley Cavell likens the philosophical sophistication of Emerson's desire to "take unsolvability to the heart of his thinking" to that of Nietzsche, Wittgenstein, and Heidegger (all of whom Emerson anticipates), and Richard Poirier argues that Emerson's

---

[5] See especially Y. A. Yoder, *Emerson and the Orphic Poet in America* (Berkeley: University of California Press, 1978); B. L. Packer, *Emerson's Fall: A New Interpretation of the Major Essays* (Continuum: New York, 1982); Julie Ellison, *Emerson's Romantic Style* (Princeton: Princeton University Press, 1984); Evan Carton, *The Rhetoric of American Romance: Dialectic and Identity in Emerson, Dickinson, Poe, and Hawthorne* (Baltimore: Johns Hopkins University Press, 1985); and John Michael, *Emerson and Skepticism: The Cipher of the World* (Baltimore: Johns Hopkins University Press, 1988).

"special form of . . . skepticism" precedes and exceeds the formations of both modernism and deconstruction.[6]

Stanley Cavell marks Emerson's difference from Derrida according to what he calls a "certain sociality or congeniality" in his thinking: a "circulation which in turn must be given over to the reaction of an other" that "seems . . . distrusted" in deconstruction. Richard Poirier sees the parallel between Emerson's work and deconstruction in the form of his understanding of the lubricity of language as well as in his critique of humanism. Yet for Poirier it is important that "this very same temporariness is instigated and perpetuated by the human will."[7] The concepts, then, that Cavell and Poirier use to distinguish Emerson's vision from a deconstructive approach are the very concerns displayed by feminist theorists in their own negotiation with the tenets of deconstruction. Both of these critics observe a tension in Emerson's writing that matches the competing imperatives at work in the double strategy of feminist theory, where a provisional sense of human agency is maintained even in the face of a radical inquiry into the very terms and positions enabling that agency. That Emerson begins to exhibit this tension in his own work is no doubt the result of his keen philosophical inquiry into language and the problem of identity; that he slowly came to trust in the process is arguably the result of his conversations with Fuller over Fourier and social reform. As we have already seen, Fuller's developing interest in Fourier reflected her growing belief that a feminist agency would require a complex double strategy of this type.

Although less concerned than Cavell or Poirier with showing Emerson's difference from deconstruction, Evan Carton helps us see how the involvement with "romance" in the *Second Series* submitted Emerson to a double strategy not unlike the strategy inadvertently invoked in the interpretations of Poirier and Cavell. According to Carton, romance is "a specific and urgent kind of rhetorical performance, a self-consciously dialectical enactment of critical and philosophical concerns about the

[6] Stanley Cavell, *This New Yet Unapproachable America: Lectures after Emerson after Wittgenstein* (Albuquerque, N.M.: Living Batch Press, 1989), 79; and Richard Poirier, *The Renewal of Literature: Emersonian Reflections* (New Haven: Yale University Press, 1988), 16. Poirier, though, would insist that Emerson's skepticism did not suddenly emerge in the *Second Series*. He argues that Emerson always saw language as an "imposition" that "human power could only sporadically resist" through "continuous acts of troping, syntactical shiftings," and "rhetorical fracturings" (p. 33). John Michael affiliates Emerson's skepticism with a Lacanian understanding of the "problem of the Other" in *Emerson and Skepticism*. Given Michael's approach, it is unfortunate that he did not discuss "Experience" in his work.

[7] Cavell, *This New Yet Unapproachable America*, p. 23; Poirier, *The Renewal of Literature*, p. 16.

relation of words to things and the nature of the self." For Carton, this "strategy of self-parody by which . . . writers convert limitation into power" also anticipates deconstructive concerns.[8]:

> The writers of romance both dream of a revelatory, world-interpreting art, a full presence that they cannot approach (except, emptily, through free imaginative and verbal play), and approach an art of freeplay that they cannot affirm (except by sacrificing the dream of presence and relegating themselves to solitary confinement in a prison house of language). . . . Such literature, then, shares the predicament of criticism in its assumption of a quest, its ironic investment in an object (whether world or text) which by its nature it cannot realize. Like contemporary criticism, too, romance can only exist by at once confronting the explosion of its "reassuring foundation" and resisting the utter collapse of signification toward which this deconstructive confrontation tends. To resolve the tension . . . is not to achieve the dream of presence or the freedom of play but to be doubly alienated.[9]

One could easily argue that Carton's image of the mechanism of romance—"at once confronting the explosion of its 'reassuring foundation' and resisting the utter collapse of signification toward which this deconstructive confrontation ends"—again provides a strong parallel to the double strategy of feminist theory. From a feminist perspective, however, alienation and isolation are not the only possible readings of the situation that obtains in the double bind described by Carton. After *Summer on the Lakes*, as we saw in Chapter 3, Fuller began to realize that this same uneasy negotiation was the plight of woman in a phallocentric world, her "paraphernalia" and thus the potential site of a complex agency for both men and women. The *Second Series* shows Emerson struggling to comprehend the power of Fuller's perspective on this issue, and the figure of romance functions throughout the volume as a sign of that struggle.

Romance is itself a reiterated trope throughout the *Second Series*. Aside from the use of it in "Experience," it appears in "Nature" where Emerson discusses the "blue zenith" where "romance and reality meet" (CW 3: 100); it is also summoned in "Character" when "those relations to the best men . . . reckoned the romances of youth, become, in the progress of character, the most solid enjoyment" (CW 3: 65); it appears in "Manners" where Emerson writes "there must be romance of character, or the most fastidious exclusion of impertinences will not avail" (CW 3: 86); and it surfaces again in "New England Reformers" when he insists "the

---

[8] Carton, *The Rhetoric of American Romance*, p. 1.
[9] Ibid., p. 12.

life of man is the true romance, which, when it is valiantly conducted, will yield the imagination a higher joy than any fiction" (CW 3: 167). With this reiteration, it is not surprising that romance is an implicit goal in the other essays as well: in "The Poet" romance is the reconciliation of man's division between reception and expression; in "Nominalist and Realist" romance describes the universal in a world of the partial; in the essay "Politics" it assumes the form of a "government of love" (CW 3: 126) in the same way that it is the "majesty of love" in "Gifts" (CW 3: 96). Significantly, a tension between an active and passive reading of romance develops throughout the volume. If the idea of romance expressed in "Nature" lies behind its later articulation as the "life of man . . . valiantly conducted," its formulation in "Character" also shapes its paradoxical expression in "Experience." "The Poet," by contrast, who would "abdicate a duplex and manifold life" (CW 3: 24) appears in a type of limbo between the two.

It is tempting to argue that Emerson's *Second Series* forms a type of experimental romance or radical pretext for Hawthorne's *Blithedale Romance*. Indeed, it is uncanny how many of the same issues appear in both works. In each, Fourier is the catalyst and Fuller is the shaping figure of the debate between the "Poet" and the "New England Reformers." But what distinguishes Emerson's romance is the way it exhibits an internal struggle to exchange the poet's sense of isolation and alienation for another sense of the "Beautiful Necessity" (W 4: 48–49) of relation, or what Cavell calls "congeniality," and Poirier has called "action." In other words, whereas *The Blithedale Romance* might be said to distort Fuller's reading of Fourier, *Essays: Second Series* struggles to cast off that distortion in order to achieve her alternative way of viewing skepticism itself.

Experimenting with Margaret

A powerful journal entry entitled "Margaret" recorded by Emerson in 1843 (some of which finds its way into the essay "Manners") reveals just how powerful Fuller's influence had become. The character of Margaret as it is described constitutes an extraordinary, perhaps utopian, model of agency. The oddly assertive, almost tendentious, language with which Emerson describes her marks a strong contrast to the style most familiar to his readers. Quoting the passage in its entirety, in fact, reveals the contrast well, for he rarely sustains such a positive sense of power in his writing. Here, Margaret embodies remarkable and unequivocal power.

A pure & purifying mind, selfpurifying also, full of faith in men, & inspiring it. Unable to find any companion great enough to receive the rich effusions of her thought, so that her riches are still unknown & seem unknowable. It is a great joy to find that we have underrated our friend, that he or she is far more excellent than we had thought. All natures seem poor beside one so rich, which pours a stream of amber over all objects clean & unclean that lie in its path, and makes that comely & presentable which was mean in itself. We are taught by her plenty how lifeless & outward we were, what poor Laplanders burrowing under the snows of prudence & pendantry. Beside her friendship, other friendships seem trade, and by the firmness with which she treads her upward path, all mortals are convinced that another road exists than that which their feet know. The wonderful generosity of her sentiments pours a contempt on books & writing at the very time when one asks how shall this fiery picture be kept in its glow & variety for other eyes. She excels other intellectual persons in this, that her sentiments are more blended with her life; so the expression of them has greater steadiness & greater clearness. I have never known any example of such steady progress from stage to stage of thought & of character. An inspirer of courage, the secret friend of all nobleness, the patient waiter for the realization of character, forgiver of injuries, gracefully waiving aside folly, & elevating lowness,—in her presence all were apprised of their fettered estate & longed for liberation, of ugliness & longed for their beauty; of meanness, & panted for grandeur.

Her growth is visible. All the persons whom we know, have reached their height, or else their growth is so nearly at the same rate as ours, that it is imperceptible, but this child inspires always more faith in her. She rose before me at times into heroical & godlike regions, and I could remember no superior women, but thought of Ceres, Minerva, Proserpine, and the august ideal forms of the Foreworld. She said that no man gave such invitation to her mind as to tempt her to a full expression; that she felt a power to enrich her thought with such wealth & variety of embellishment as would no doubt be tedious to such as she conversed with. And there is no form that does seem to wait her beck,—dramatic, lyric, epic, passionate, pictorial, humourous.

She has great sincerity, force, & fluency as a writer, yet her powers of speech throw her writing into the shade. What method, what exquisite judgment, as well as energy, in the selection of her words, what character & wisdom they convey! You cannot predict her opinion. She sympathizes so fast with all forms of life, that she talks never narrowly or hostilely nor betrays, like all the rest, under a thin garb of new words, the old droning castiron opinions or notions of many years standing. What richness of experience, what newness of dress, and fast as Olympus to her principle. And a silver eloquence, which inmost Polymnia taught. Meantime, all the pathos of sentiment and riches of literature & of invention and this march of character threatening to arrive presently at the shores & plunge into the sea of Buddhism & mystic trances, consists with a boundless fun & drollery, with light satire, & the most entertaining conversation in America.

> Her experience contains, I know, golden moments, which, if they could be fitly narrated, would stand equally beside any histories of magnanimity which the world contains; and whilst Dante's "Nuova Vita" is almost unique in the literature of sentiment, I have called the imperfect record she gave me of two of her days, "Nuovissima Vita" (JMN 8: 368–69).

Although Emerson's admiration for Fuller is boldly and clearly recorded here, we know that he could as easily retreat from this type of description. In fact, the Margaret passage is most usefully viewed as an experiment in a plain style, a trial in the articulation of agency. Her power emerged for him in the way that "her sentiments [were] more blended with her life" than "other intellectual persons," so that "the expression of them ha[d] greater steadiness & greater clearness." Rarely would he be so forthright in his voicing of power: Fuller is, without any doubt, "an inspirer of courage, the secret friend of all nobleness, the patient waiter for the realization of character," and the "forgiver of injuries." More strikingly, she is the author of inspiration, for "in her presence all were apprised of their fettered estate & longed for liberation, of ugliness & longed for their beauty; of meanness, & panted for grandeur." Though he would remain uneasy with this style, it points to her obvious value in his intellectual world. He chooses not to return to this passage in his essay "The Poet," though it is obvious that he returns again and again to much of its sentiment there. His paragraph describing the liberating attributes of poets—"they are free, and they make free" (CW 3: 18)— seems to draw its faith from the Margaret passage.

> That also is the best success in conversation, the magic of liberty, which puts the world, like a ball, in our hands. How cheap even the liberty then seems; how mean to study, when an emotion communicates to the intellect the power to sap and upheave nature: how great the perspective! nations, times, systems, enter and disappear, like threads in tapestry of large figure and many colors; dream delivers us to dream, and, while the drunkenness lasts, we will sell our bed, our philosophy, our religion, in our opulence (CW 3: 19).

Since there was "no form that [did] seem to wait her beck,—dramatic, lyric, epic, passionate, pictorial, humourous," Emerson eagerly sought the opportunity to read some of the essays of the *Second Series* to Fuller when she visited his household in July 1844.[10] We know from his correspondence at the time that he was anxiously seeking the essay that would bring his *Second Series* to a close. Apparently he had been told by

---

[10] In June Emerson anticipated Fuller's usefulness by writing: "Soon you are coming hither—did you not say so? and I shall try your good nature and aid my sense of proportion by reading to you" (EL 3: 252–53).

his printers in Boston that the manuscript (consisting of eight essays) he had delivered to them "was not large enough for the shape" he had wanted.[11] Because he was experimenting with the idea of romance and its meaning throughout the volume, closure was a problem he had been having all along, "ending his endless chapters," (EL 3: 252) as he told Fuller. Thus the incomplete nature of the volume took on symbolic resonance for him, symbolizing the conceptual difficulties of the entire work. Fuller's part in those difficulties made her a logical audience for the text. Yet for the same reason, his recitation, which apparently took place in their favorite spot in Sleepy Hollow, did not make his editorial decision any easier (LMF 3: 207–9).

Emerson had two essays from which to select an ending: his lecture that same year in Amory Hall and his impending address in August on the emancipation of the British West Indies, which was to be given in Concord. He decided on the former, perhaps because the shifting tones of "New England Reformers" (as the piece was finally called) bore a greater resemblance to the rhetorical maneuvers of the earlier chapters. This reasoning, at least, is how the editors of the most recent edition of *Second Series* have justified its inclusion.[12] The address on the emancipation, by contrast, contained some of Emerson's most unequivocal writing, addressing the slavery issue with uncompromising anger.[13] Yet it is also clear that he did his best to disown the choice that he made. We know, for example, that he would not allow "New England Reformers" to be listed as "Essay 9" in the table of contents. Instead it assumed the status of "Lecture," thus forming a kind of appendix at the close of the volume. While reflecting an understandable resolve to resist extraneous publication imperatives, his subtle editorial tactic also discloses his anxiety about the design and argument of the volume.

Because the issue of agency was bound up with Emerson's use of the word romance, it can be argued that "New England Reformers" provides a thematic closure for the collection, ending as it did with the statement: "The life of man is the *true romance*, which, when it is valiantly conducted, will yield the imagination a higher joy than any fiction" (CW 3: 167, emphasis mine). His denial of that lecture's place in the volume, his refusal to give it the status of a ninth essay, however, suggests his uneasiness with the resolution of the issue of agency (or ro-

[11] See copy of his letter to Caroline Sturgis, July 20, 1844, in EL 7: 605–6, and "Historical Introduction," CW 3: xxix.

[12] "Historical Introduction," CW 3: xxx.

[13] See Maurice Gonnaud, *An Uneasy Solitude: Individual and Society in the Work of Ralph Waldo Emerson*, trans. Lawrence Rosenwald (Princeton: Princeton University Press, 1987), for an assessment of the importance of this essay for Emerson's work. "Address: Emancipation in the British West Indies," W 11: 97–47.

mance) as "the life of man . . . valiantly conducted." The more forceful
valorization of the "blessed necessity . . . always driving" (CW 2: 147)
men and women toward political reform in his emancipation address
amply contested the adequacy of this formulation (even as it established
a precedent for his valorization of the "Beautiful Necessity" at the end of
"Fate" in the *Conduct of Life*) by introducing a paradoxical tension in the
elaboration of agency.

Of course, Emerson's decision not to close the volume with his Concord address on emancipation could be read as a sign that he was
equally uncomfortable with the political agency formulated in that address. But although any straightforward description of "the conduct of
life"—as he came to describe what I am calling agency—always made
him uncomfortable, he apparently thought enough of the address to
have it published in pamphlet form and reprinted in Horace Greeley's
New-York Daily Tribune (CW 3: xxx), the paper for which Fuller began to
write at the end of 1844. The simultaneous publication of *Second Series*
and the address creates a wonderful tension, then, between fragment
and whole. For while "New England Reformers" supplies an uneasy
appendix to *Second Series*, the Concord address on emancipation supplies what might be called its true appendix, putting into question the
formal argument about agency attempted by the equivocal inclusion of
"New England Reformers" into the *Series*.

Fuller's busy publication schedule at the time no doubt affected her
response to Emerson's quandary.[14] Following her work on *Summer on
the Lakes*, (which had recently been published with Emerson's assistance), she was preparing to enlarge and develop her "Great Lawsuit"
for publication in book form, and she appears to have taken the occasion
of his confusion to restate her opinion that he was creating limits for
himself that might be reinterpreted as opportunities. We see this particularly in a letter that she wrote regarding his composition of the Concord address on emancipation and the power of his pen to provide
adequate expression for the abolitionist cause. Through some good-
natured teasing, she suggested that his fear that he could not assume the
role of poet was based on a system of expectation that was not only
unrealistic but also blind to its exclusive and highly gendered sense of

---

[14] Particularly since his writing appeared far more polished than she found necessary
for her own purposes: "You are intellect, I am life. My flowers and stones however shabby
interest me, because they stand for a great deal to me, and would, I feel, have a hiero-
glyphical interest to those of like nature with me. Were I Greek and an artist I would polish
my marbles as you do, as it is, I shall be content whenever I am in a state of unimpeded
energy and can sing at the top of my voice, I don't care what. Whatever is truly felt has
some precious meaning" (LMF 3: 209).

agency. She gave him two parables, the first with a pointed feminist message:

> I always thought the saddest position in the world must be that of some regal dame to whom husband, court, kingdom, world, look in vain for an heir! She is only supposed to eat breathe, move, think, nay! love, for the sake of this future blessing. The book of her life is only permitted for the sake of its appendix. Meanwhile she, perhaps, persists in living on as if her life by itself were of any consequence, is the mother of no Prince or has even the impertinence to encumber the kingdom with a parcel of Princesses, girls who must be "weel-tochered" to make them of any value (LMF 3: 213).

The second parable concerned the burden of cultural expectation, this time focusing on men:

> But what is this pathos compared to that perceptible in the situation of a Jove, under the masculine obligations of all-sufficinyness, who rubs his forehead in vain to induce the Minerva-bearing headache! Alas! his brain remains tranquil, his fancy daughterless! Nature keeps on feeding him and putting him to sleep as if she thought the oak was of any consequence, whether it bear the miseltoe or not! (LMF 3: 213).

We know that Fuller was responding here to Emerson's immediate concern over his emancipation address, but her two parables also reflect an understanding of his general dissatisfaction with the *Second Series*.[15] A genuine sympathy can be detected in her notion of the "masculine obligations of all-sufficinyness." It is also clear, however, that an implicit critique supersedes that sympathy. (Fuller was likely mocking Emerson's notion of "self-sufficinyness" in "Character": "The Fact which character wears to me is self-sufficingness. . . . Character is centrality, the impossibility of being displaced or overset" [CW 3: 58].) Fuller's disingenuous comparison between the two situations could not have been lost on Emerson, particularly since he knew of her impending plans to finish *Woman in the Nineteenth Century*. The feminist parable shows his anxiety as disproportionate to the anxiety of others, her own

---

[15] His immediate solution was local: he altered his routine by refusing his evening walk with Fuller. Her response: "Did you notice that, when you refused to go to walk and declared the dark aspect of your mental fortunes, the clouds that had been hanging lightly full of silver lustre, grew dark too, bent heavily, and soon began to weep It was as miraculous a coincidence as many that have showed the servitude of Nature to Saint or Prophet! In this instance, I fear me, it bodes no good to the hapless Africans (not Afrites!) let me see how many millions, who will be none the better for your silver tongue!" (LMF 3: 213).

included. (It is no accident that she would elaborate on this idea in *Woman*.) Moreover, the prospect that one's book would be "permitted" only for the sake of its appendix made subtle reference to his anxiety about the resolution of the *Second Series*. A cunning act of translation, her decision to employ this metaphor in her parable subtly forced him to witness a feminist argument from inside his own publication experience. Nor is it an accident that what is absent in the second parable about Jove is in abundance in the first; Jove's "daughterless" "fancy," his vain attempt to "induce the Minerva-bearing headache" is oddly compensated for by the "parcel of Princesses" who "encumber the kingdom" of the first narrative. The uneven demands of culture connect the two parables even as the transparency of this inequity supplies a critique.

Fuller's letter also contained two poems. The first warned that Emerson would never assume the role of "lyricist" or "orator" (terms of esteemed value, given his description of the poet as a "liberating god"), if he did not alter his course and choose another vessel or "shell" for his work.[16] In case he could not see how her feminist parable offered a new site for his work, she supplies still another poem that essentially rebuts his tendency toward isolation, his belief that he could not leave his home, or "prison" (JMN 7: 408), for a larger social arena so as to pursue the experiment of social reform. Over the years she had begun to observe how his professed need for privacy and isolation grew especially strong when the conversation turned to the role of women and the issue of marriage reform which, thanks to Fourier and his followers, had become central in debates about social reform. As their correspondence showed us, her own relationship with him was overcoded with symbolic resonances so that the more he found himself engaged by his conversation with her (that is, the more it promised to test if not enact

[16]   Gentle River
                    stealing on so slowly ever
                    from reeds that grow thy bank along
                    easy would flow the pastoral song
                        But the shell
                    Which may be strong for lyric swell
                        Or trumpet spire for oratory
                        Seek these mid the Tritons hoary,
                    Where an incalculable wave
                    Wrecks the warship tall and brave,
                    Rushes up a mile-long strand
                    Hails the stars, and spurns the land
                    Pushes back the noblest River
                    Seeking in vain its love forever,
                        There mightst thou find a shell
                    Fit to be strung for strains of Delphian swell. (LMF 3: 213–14).

Fourier's theory on thwarted passion), the more he saw reason to with-draw from it.

Accordingly, her second poem provides an amusing explanation for the inspirational lapses provoking his conservative if not skeptical turn. "But, Waldo," she wrote, "how can you expect the Muse to come to you. She hovers near. I have seen her many times" (LMF 3: 214). The poem involves an argument between a Poet and his Muse. The position of the Muse supplies a thinly veiled allegory for Fuller's repeated visits to Concord, and the response of the Poet parodies Emerson in one of his most defensive moods. Moreover, it recalls the sense of isolation with which his essay "The Poet" closes.

> Earth and Fire, hell and heaven,
> Hate and love, black and white,
> Life and death, dark and bright,
>   All are One
>   One alone
> All else is seeming
> I who think am nought
> But the One a-dreaming
> To and fro its thought:
> All is well,
> For all is one;
> The fluid spell
> is the cold stone;
> However voluble
> All life is soluble
> Into my thought;
> And that is nought,
> But self-discovering
> self-recovering
> Of the One
> One Alone.

(LMF 3:215)

This speech of the Poet echoes Tasso's embittered speech about An-tonio in the Goethe drama Fuller translated, for the Poet's argument refigures the binary trap of Tasso's isolating vision.[17] Like Tasso, the Poet has closed himself off from an important relationship. Moreover, just as Tasso resists the "rudderless" movement between individuals offered by the Princess, so the Poet rebuffs the gentle promptings of his Muse who is offering much of the same. Fuller knew that in his essay

---

[17] "Man must have in his narrow being / The double impulses of love and hatred. / Are they not day and night? sleeping and waking?" (*Tasso*, trans. Fuller, *Art, Literature, and the Drama*, ed. Arthur B. Fuller [Boston: Brown, Taggard and Chase, 1860], 419).

"Prudence" (*First Series*), Emerson had bemoaned the conflict between Tasso and Antonio in Goethe's drama.[18] His analysis of the crisis was flawed, however, by his sense that Tasso's error resulted from "self-indulgence" and a love of "pleasures of the sense" (CW 2: 137) rather than self-pity and a misguided sense of self-sufficiency. His initial and valuable insight into the "true tragedy" of Tasso (his realization of the false nature of Tasso's interaction with those around him) became mortgaged to a larger fear of passion and "indulgence." (For Emerson the words *impulse* and *indulgence* became synonymous with Fourier's theory of social reform because of his critique of marriage.[19]) Fuller's gathering frustration with Emerson had to do with the sway of this "negative Prudence" (CW 2: 131), a frustration he often shared.

We know from the reduction in the number of letters passing between them that Fuller's trip to New York drew her into a variety of new interests. But Emerson's journals suggest that her physical departure and even the withdrawal of her correspondence as she became involved with James Nathan did little to reduce the part she played in his mental struggle. How then are we to imagine Emerson responding to her playful yet stinging letter? The stark power of his Concord address on emancipation (delivered two weeks after receiving Fuller's letter) and his editorial decision not to give "New England Reformers" essay status provide a clue.[20] One could argue that her letter struck a nerve in him, recalling him to the debate vital to his *Second Series* as it carried over from his conversation with her: the tension in his thinking between a profound skepticism and a desire for agency and social reform.

Marriage as the Pivotal Issue

From Emerson's journals we see that marriage was an issue uniting many of his concerns at the time of the composition of the *Second Series*. Marriage—at the center of Fourier's critique and also an important site from which feminist issues were drawn—remained the social unit or

[18] "It does not seem to me so genuine grief when some tyrannous Richard III oppresses and slays a score of innocent persons, as when Antonio and Tasso, both apparently right, wrong each other" (CW 2: 137).

[19] Emerson later called the Brook Farm community "an expression in plain prose & actuality of the theory of impulse" (JMN 8: 377).

[20] There is no direct letter or response. We know that by August 30, 1844, Emerson was writing to Fuller, "Pity me, O wise & kindest friend, but I can write you nothing of that I should. This proof-correction bewilders my brain with its concentration on nothings and the impracticability & tough unalterableness of sentences which must not stand as they are demonstrates past a doubt the inherent vice of my writing" (EL 3: 259).

pivot structuring all other forms of interaction in society. According to Fourier, marriage represented everything that was wrong in the prevailing conception of society: it demeaned women through its patriarchal structure, and it thwarted the desire of both partners to seek a variety of relationships.[21] As Frothingham made clear in his history of the period, the issue of marriage, particularly as it pertained to women and their role in marriage, assumed totemic power among those reformers under Fourier's sway.

Fuller knew from her many conversations with Emerson that his resistance to the reform movement in general tended to revolve around the issue of marriage.[22] He repeatedly attempted to resist the cluster of issues engaged by marriage reform by resorting to a type of binary logic, in this case theorizing the problems away as "empirical" (JMN 8: 34). This strategy enabled him to contend that "the griefs incident to every earthly marriage are less" because "a strong mind . . . has the resource of the all-creating, all obliterating spirit; retreating on its grand essence the nearest persons become pictures merely. The Universe is his bride" (JMN 8: 34). But Emerson well understood the problem with this simple division between empirical and ideal worlds. And he knew, too, that this conception of marriage left him open to the very melancholy and isolation that Fuller gently ridiculed in her letter.

In fact, Fuller was more successful in getting Emerson to consider the ramifications of marriage reform than he would admit. His journal entries reveal his constant return to the issue as a possible source of power for his personal situation as a writer.[23] Yet, as we have seen, her effort to persuade him to explore the issue of marriage reform was not personal,

[21] See *The Utopian Vision of Charles Fourier: Selected Texts on Work, Love, and Passionate Attraction*, trans. and ed. Jonathan Beecher and Richard Bienvenu (Columbia: University of Missouri Press, 1983), 169–88. See also M. C. Spencer, *Charles Fourier* (Boston: Twayne Publishers, 1981), 56–59.

[22] Fuller appears to have had an ongoing conversation about marriage with Emerson. One letter in October 1842 hints at her effort to change his formulation: "I do not know whether it is owing to this feeling of your mind being too near me that I have not yet been able to finish the ragged rhymes I meant for you. I got along well enough till the point of division came, where I wanted to show that the permanent marriage cannot interfere with the soul's destiny, when lo! this future which has seemed so clear, vanished and left me without a word, yet unconvinced of your way of thinking. There lies the paper, and I expect the hour may yet come when I can make out my case" (LMF 3: 96).

[23] "Saccarappe . . . has a great defect of character and joins a great genius to extreme folly . . . if his genius had led him into love, & he had formed a high connexion, as at one time he might, his genius would have gained a reinforcement thereby, that would have carried the day, but he let his folly instead of his wisdom marry him, he courted a mere girl, and his greatness was indefinitely postponed. In two or three stories I could hint a large part of my biography" (JMN 8: 84).

nor did she want him to view it that way; her concern was with the larger issue of social relations reflected by its terms. Her own theoretical approach to feminism had been formulated through these terms, as well as her developing interest in Fourierism. Because her interaction with Emerson offered the experimental space often described as an alternative to marriage by its critics, his continual return to—and his abstraction from—this relationship in his writing reflects a growing commitment to what I call a feminist valuation of his own terms, particularly the terms of his skepticism.

Certainly, Emerson's record of a dream late in 1840 suggests something of the power that the concept held as a symbolic register for him.

> A droll dream last night, whereat I ghastly laughed. A congregation assembled, like some of our late Conventions, to debate the Institution of Marriage; & grave & alarming objections stated *on all hands* to the usage; when one speaker at last rose & began to reply to the arguments, but suddenly . . . *extended his hand* & turned on the audience the spout of an engine which was copiously supplied from within the wall with water & whisking it vigorously about . . . up, down, right, & left he drove all the company in crowds hither & thither & out of the house. Whilst I stood watching astonished & amused at the malice & vigor of the orator, I saw the spout lengthened by a supply of hose behind, & the man suddenly brought it round a corner & drenched me as I gazed. I woke up relieved to find myself quite dry, and well convinced that the Institution of Marriage was safe for tonight (JMN 7: 544, emphases mine).

Emerson's ambiguous position toward the discussion is manifest in the tensions recorded by his description of the dream. He initially separates himself from the angry orator by confessing to laugh at the vigorous and malicious reply he makes to the reformers, yet he also separates himself from the reformers by his silent, observant status "round a corner." At the same time, the sheepish relief he registers upon waking aligns him with the implied *cause* of the orator. In the process, we have the fragmented figure of romance described by Carton: Emerson confronts the collapse of his "reassuring foundation"[24] by attending the meeting, but he resists its utter collapse through his complicity with the restive orator. The opponent of the discussion about marriage manifests the most overt passion—as the spewing of the water from the hose makes clear—suggesting that his objection to such a discussion develops from a simmering sexuality too dangerous to yield to the experimental fervor of

---

[24] Evan Carton, *The Rhetoric of American Romance*, p. 12.

the conventioneers, whose talk no doubt was under the sway of Fourier. We know from his journal that Emerson often objected to the hazards of sexual arousal permitted by Fourier's theory, calling it too dangerous.[25]

But what are we to make of the fact that the image of the dream's alienated orator oddly prefigures Emerson's discussion in "The Poet" of "these throbs and heart-beatings in the orator, at the door of the assembly, to the end, namely that thought may be ejaculated as Logos, or Word" (CW 3: 23)? Or of its affinity to the portrait of the frustrated and alienated poet he counsels in the same essay: "Doubt not, O poet, but persist. Say, 'It is in me, and shall out.' Stand there, baulked and dumb, stuttering and stammering, hissed and hooted, stand and strive, until, at last, rage draw out of thee that *dream*-power which every night shows thee is thine own" (CW 3: 23)? His highly charged sexual imagery in both is unmistakable: the "wet dream" becomes a symbol of the power that is simultaneously feared and desired.

The Value of Polemic

To be sure, the association between the image in "The Poet" and Emerson's dream is odd. The dream performs what might be called a flirtation with a polemical response, whereas "The Poet" presumes to protect and isolate the poet from polemic. Yet the rage that figures in this image of the poet and the renunciations that serve to make him the most isolated figure in the *Second Series*, the one who "abdicates a duplex and manifold life" (CW 3: 24), suggest a conceptualization of "The Poet" in polemical terms, placing writing and desire at the center of the dilemma. In this way, the figure of the ejaculating orator in the dream becomes a potent register for the issues in conflict in *Second Series*, making the journal entry a colorful allegory for the divided position that Emerson assumes toward the issue of agency throughout *Second Series*: a figure for the skeptic and the poet, at once, the orator of his dream both attracts and repulses him.

The importance of the dream to the volume—its status as a pivot for the issues there engaged—becomes clearer and more compelling when we remember that Emerson returns in "New England Reformers" to the symbolic value of marriage reform, noting that the institution of marriage has been attacked by reformers as "the fountain of social evils" (CW 3: 150). His wavering suggestion that "no society can ever be so

[25] Emerson often replied to the "secret doctrines of Fourier," at one point writing, "I thought no man could be trusted with it; the formation of new alliances is so delicious to the imagination that St. Paul and St. John would be riotous" (JMN 9: 50).

large as one man" (CW 3: 155) recalls the position of the orator of his dream, but fails to exemplify his power, thus revealing the failure of "one man" to "chant our own times and social circumstance" (CW 3: 21). The voice in "New England Reformers" is ultimately not the impassioned voice of the skeptic/poet. If anything, the voice Emerson sought was the voice he sometimes found in his letters to Fuller. If *that* voice is to be found anywhere, it is dispersed in moments throughout the essays framed by both "The Poet" and "New England Reformers." The periodic emergence of this voice represents an effort to reconcile by elaborate negotiation the demands of the passionate, ejaculating fellow with the complex terms of agency emerging in his conversation with Fuller. It represents an effort to transvalue skepticism toward a positive historical end, and to do so by an immersion in the issues generated by the social reform of the day, particularly those clustering around the notion of marriage and gender. Such a voice, then, is especially evident in the essays "Experience," "Character," and "Manners."

"Let Us Treat the Men and Women Well"

Recent important readings of the essay "Experience" have focused on the connection between Emerson's grief for his son Waldo and his engagement with skepticism. Sharon Cameron, for example, has forcefully shown how Waldo became introjected into the argument of the essay, enabling Emerson to elaborate an ambiguous theory of power that resists the traditional model of mourning. According to Cameron, his essay subverts the idea of mourning as a "task carried through," and instead presents the elegiac as a form converting the "dissociation attached to death" into the dissociation facilitating power.[26] Taking his lead from Cameron (as well as Barbara Packer's earlier discussion of Emerson's response to the death of his brother Charles), Stanley Cavell reminds us that Emerson was "awfully adept at incorporating and denying (shall we say transcending) the deaths (of wife, of brother, of son)" in his work. For Cavell this introjection produced what amounts to the larger philosophical task of Emerson's essay: the "transfiguring of founding as finding, of grounding as lasting" and "the stepwise overcoming of skepticism . . . by the process of nearing as indirection."[27]

[26] Cameron borrows Derrida's notion of the "Cryptic text" in his elaboration of Maria Torok and Nicolas Abraham's distinction between the "introjected" and "incorporated" object, where one is secret and one is readable. See Cameron, "Representing Grief," p. 40, nn. 10 and 11.

[27] Cavell, *This New Yet Unapproachable America*, pp. 85, 116, 117. See also Packer, *Emerson's Fall*.

There is much in both readings that I endorse, particularly since each in its own way supports the idea that "Experience" is about an acceptance of the transitional ground of critique. To arrive at their positions, Cavell and Cameron take seriously what previous critics have tended to dismiss or to find bewildering: the famous line at the beginning of the essay, "I grieve that grief can teach me nothing" (CW 3: 29) Yet their conviction that Emerson somehow meant what he said here leaves them oddly confounded by the issue of reform as it appears at the close of the essay. For here, as they construe it, he no longer means what he says; his allusion to the "transformation of genius into practical power" (CW 3: 49) becomes for Cameron a precipitous and unwarranted description of the theory of power painstakingly formulated in the earlier sections of the essay. Cavell is more readily persuaded that the essay "accepts the question" through which the issue of reform is most forcefully introduced ("Why not realize your world?" [CW 3: 48]), yet he, too, argues that "putting the philosophical intellect into practice remains a question for philosophy." According to Cavell, Emerson's introduction of the question "Why not realize your world?" signals a recognition that his strongest philosophical labor continues to elude his audience. Thus Emerson "reject[s] the inquiry philosophically" and "repl[ies] polemically."[28]

Cameron dismisses Emerson's statement about the "transformation of genius into practical power" by accepting his earlier admission that he had been forced to respond polemically to the reformers, whereas Cavell does the same by dismissing Emerson's polemic as philosophical at base. But the irruption of polemic is both more problematic and productive than both Cameron and Cavell construe, since, as we saw in his dream about the convention, it signals a significant tension involving the complex of ideas at work in his discussions with Fuller about Fourier and agency. I do not suggest that the essay does not engage mourning; rather, I contend that dismissing the issue of social reform reduces our understanding of the truly radical ideas motivating Emerson's transvaluation of skepticism and power. In fact, it is interesting to consider how his logic of elegiac (described by Cameron as resisting the logic of dialectic and conflict usually found in Emerson's work) borrows its power from the double strategy of feminism. Fuller's advice in her letter to him about the emancipation address would seem to reveal her own sense that the foundation of a feminist critique would have to accept a provisional status because it would inevitably need to define itself through

---

[28] Cavell, *This New Yet Unapproachable America*, pp. 95, 113. Cavell writes, "Our philosophical experience now, finding ourselves here, necessitates taking up philosophically the question of practice" (p. 95).

the terms of the culture it hoped to change. This paradoxical situation, from which no escape seemed possible, was not the source of defeat, but rather the "blessed necessity" making real change possible. Emerson's unfolding recognition of this strategy for turning skepticism into a type of agency accounts for the thematic development of the essay from grief to reform and may even help explain his patience with his imagined audience at the close of the essay, which Cavell finds confusing.[29] Emerson's self-professed polemic encapsulates a struggle vital to the volume and to the remainder of his work.

Fuller and the Work of Mourning

Although the death of Waldo may be the first cause behind the argument of "Experience," Fuller's position in the development of the essay emerges from her role as interlocutor to Emerson's grief. She had already proven the efficacy of her friendship in helping him to pass through the terrible work of mourning after Charles's death. And if, according to Cameron, the entire essay is an active displacement of Waldo's loss, we must, nevertheless, consider the substance of that displacement, the material through which Emerson moved in his examination of grief. The image repertoire upon which he drew to think through the experience of grief was culled from the landscape of social relations, the terrain of his conversation with Fuller, including the discourse of Fourier.

Cavell's effort to elaborate the affinities in the essay between Emerson and Heidegger opens to view the earlier, more turbulent influence of Fourier. According to Cavell, like Heidegger, Emerson concerned himself with two important aspects of our human condition: the quality of clutching as a way of thinking, the quality of "grasping something," in order to synthesize, and "clutching's opposite which would be the most handsome part of our condition," the quality of "attraction" or being "drawn to things."[30] Cavell gathers this insight from the essay's well-known passage, "I take this evanescence and lubricity of all objects, which lets them slip through our fingers when we clutch hardest, to be the most unhandsome part of our condition" (CW 3: 29). In acknowledging the "autoerotic force projected" in the passage, however (and admit-

---

[29] Cavell finds himself "abashed before Emerson's forbearance: 'Patience, patience.' Even if said mostly to himself, the words are to be announced, say as part of the struggle against a perfect irony, recognizing that cynicism and disillusion are in a democracy politically devastating passions" (*This New Yet Unapproachable America*, p. 113).

[30] Ibid., pp. 86, 87.

ting that such a focus would be absent in Heidegger), Cavell points to an earlier and more pertinent affinity between Emerson's thinking and Fourier's theory of "passionate attraction." In Fourier's thinking, "passionate attraction" is "the impulse, given to us by nature prior to any reflection" and the source of our hope.[31] Through a recovery of those attractions, Fourier insists, our social prejudices could be resisted and overturned. Though Emerson wanted to posit a theory of attraction as the "handsome" part of our condition, (what some might consider the true site of disinterested engagement), the American advocates of Fourier's theory of attraction made him fearful that this approach could also veil a clutching or grasping method. His dream about the orator neatly allegorizes this tension. Cavell is right in asserting the tension between clutching and attraction in Emerson's thinking, and I would further assert that Fourier's challenge shaped that tension by constantly turning Emerson's intellectual struggle into a struggle with desire and its construction.

In the same way, Emerson's intimacy with Fuller also generated unexpected difficulties. The very relationship he was using to work through his grief was also the relationship posing a threat to the marriage that had given him his child.[32] The centrality of passion and marriage reform as it became textured in their discussion makes it easier to understand how a polemical voice could emerge at the close of "Experience." Emerson's effort to approach the topic of grief must be understood to have involved these complex intellectual and emotional negotiations.

The importance of Fuller's role as interlocutor for Emerson's grief and his essay "Experience" can be surmised from a letter he wrote to her on the second anniversary of Waldo's death. The letter itself forms a crude outline for the thematic development of the essay, moving from the issue of grief to a more general theory of loss, including the "impossibility of perfect explication" and a struggle with hope. The struggle becomes articulated through the language of reform early on where "affirmations are tacit & secular" and capable of generating "a hollow & canting sound."

> Thou steadfast loving wise & dear friend, I am always astonished at thy faith & truth—I cannot tell whether they be more divine or human. How have you adopted the life of your poor friend and the lives that are dear to

---

[31] Ibid., p. 86. Fourier, *Oeuvres Completes*, vol. 6, *Le Nouveau Monde industriel et sociétaire*, quoted in Spencer, *Charles Fourier*, p. 39.

[32] Emerson had compared himself to Waldo in his letter that asked Fuller to retreat from too close an examination of their relationship, merely compounding the already overdetermined symbolic resonance of Waldo's life for Emerson.

him, so easily, & with a love at once connate & prophetic, which delights & admonishes me at the same time. I am glad of guardian angels, but life is a treasure of soberer worth under the fanning of their wings. . . . I have had no experiences no progress to put me into better intelligence with my calamity than when it was new. . . . —But the inarticulateness of the Supreme Power how can we insatiate hearers perceivers & thinkers ever reconcile ourselves unto? . . . Does the Power labour, as men do, with the impossibility of perfect explication, that always the hurt is of one kind & the compensation of another. . . . Yet flames forever the holy light for all eyes, & the nature of things against all appearances & specialties whatever assures us of eternal benefit. But these affirmations are tacit & secular. if spoken, they have a hollow & canting sound; And thus all our being, dear friend, is evermore adjourned. Patience & Patience & Patience! (EL 3: 235–39).

The invocation to "Patience & Patience" repeats the language that Emerson will adopt at the end of "Experience," suggesting that the polemical moment does indeed draw from his conversation with Fuller, migrating by turns from the discourse of grief to the discourse of reform. The way that this transformation occurred is still more evident in a journal entry that recalls this letter and elaborates on it.

> I wrote to Margaret Fuller that I had no experiences nor progress to reconcile me to the calamity whose anniversary returned the second time last Saturday. The senses have a right to their method as well as the mind; there should be harmony in facts as well as in truths. Yet these ugly breaks happen there, which the continuity of theory does not compensate. The amends are of a different kind from the mischief. . . . But the astonishment of life is the absence of any appearance of reconciliation between the theory & practice of life. Our sanity, our genius, the prized reality, the law, is apprehended now & then for a serene & profound moment amidst the hubbub of cares & works which have no direct bearing on it; is then lost for months or years, & again found for an interval, to be lost again. If we compute it in time, we may in fifty or seventy years . . . have half a dozen such happy & noble hours (JMN 9: 65).[33]

Here Emerson's grief becomes articulated in terms that explicitly recall larger thematic developments of "Experience," including the way in which "the pith of each man's genius contracts itself to a few hours" (CW 3: 28) and the "absence of any appearance of reconciliation between the theory & practice of life." The first alludes to the unique spatial and temporal concerns of the essay, with its fixation on the "middle" (and

---

[33] Emerson drew from later passages in this entry for his essays on "Montaigne" and "Nominalist and Realist."

dissociated) state emphasized by Cameron in her essay ("Where do we find ourselves? In a series of which we do not know the extremes, and believe that it has none" [CW 3: 27]).[34] The second returns us, of course, to the issue of romance, since for Emerson it is through the "true romance" that the "transformation of genius into practical power" will occur. Even more tellingly, it returns us to Fourier, the most potent symbol of that transformation.

At the height of Emerson's grief, just two short months after Waldo's death, he first encountered Albert Brisbane in New York. The ardency with which Brisbane then pressed Fourier on Emerson may help to explain why the discourse of Fourier became the medium for his work of mourning. He knew well from his dealings with Brisbane that the reconciliation of theory and practice had been promoted as Fourier's central goal by his American proponents. Indeed, he closed an 1842 *Dial* article on Fourier by quoting a question from Brisbane that arguably installs him as Emerson's imagined audience at the end of "Experience": "What is more futile than barren philosophical speculation, that leads to no great practical results?"[35]

That Emerson was thinking about the discourse of Fourier at the close of "Experience" is also suggested by his coupling of Fourier, "romance," and social agency in an 1843 journal entry: "Fourier carries a whole French revolution in his head, & much more. . . . It is very entertaining, the most entertaining of French romances & will suggest vast & numerous possibilities of reform to the coldest & least sanguine" (JMN 9: 8). Rather intriguingly, the repetition put into play to emphasize the phrase "most entertaining" recalls Emerson's use of the same phrase in the Margaret passage from his journal. There, we recall, he describes Fuller as someone who combines "all the pathos of sentiment and riches of literature & of invention" with "a boundless fun & drollery, . . . light satire, & the *most entertaining conversation in America*" (JMN 8: 369, emphasis mine). Indeed, the affiliation between the discourse of Fourier and the power of his conversation with Fuller continually marks the terms of his mourning in "Experience."[36]

The discourse of Fourier was not simply an afterthought, but a perva-

[34] Cameron, "Representing Grief," p. 23.

[35] In his *Dial* essay "Fourierism and the Socialists," Emerson includes a short article by Brisbane entitled "Means of Effecting a Final Reconciliation between Religion and Science" (*Dial* 3 [July 1842]: 90).

[36] The same journal page where Emerson first writes the line with which he closes "Experience" also includes this suggestive passage: "Your abstaining to confess your own trials do not impose on me, or persuade me that you do not feel the ridicule of life. When I think of ridiculous men so aspiring, & nourished by so mean arts, I do not except you" (JMN 9: 53).

sive influence in the essay, as we see in a journal entry that contains a first draft of "lords of life," the poem at the beginning of "Experience." Here Emerson writes more charitably about Fourier and his theory of the twelve passions.

> Fourier said, Man exists to gratify his twelve passions: and he proposes to remove the barriers which false philosophy & religion & prudence have built against indulgence. Some of the old heroic legislators proposed to open public brothels as safety-valves to defend virtuous women from the occasional extravagances of desire in violent persons. . . . Fourier . . . has a sacred Legion and an order called sacred, of Chastity, Virgins & bachelors; a lower order of husband and wife; a lower of free companions & harlots. In having that higher order he gives all up. For the vulgar world not yet emancipated from prejudice replies to his invitation, Well, I will select only that part from your system, and leave out the sty to those who like it. I have observed that indulgence always effeminates. I have organs also & delight in pleasure, but I have experience also that this pleasure is the bait of a trap (JMN 9: 115).

No direct relation between the "lords of life" and Fourier's twelve passions exists, but we do find an affiliation in the growing tension between the ideological (or fatal) constructions through which our subjectivity is forged and the potential for some form of agency through which resistance can be established. Emerson's playful critique of the prevailing code of sexual behavior (specifically a critique of the prohibition on masturbation said to make men effeminate) is experimental and tentative.[37] Nevertheless, it shows a continued fascination with the issues opened to consideration by the prevailing social theory of Fourier and a desire to reconceive our "unhandsome" condition. The realization of this need was Fuller's greatest aspiration for Emerson, combining by turns the efficacy of desire with that of writing.

"Voices Deaf to Each Other's Words"

Cameron asks an interesting question in her reading of "Experience": "Why are there frequently two voices in an Emerson essay? Why two voices that seem deaf to each other's words? In an essay like 'Experience' are claims voiced, repudiated, and differently iterated so that the self that can say words and the self that can hear them may be brought

---

[37] G. J. Barker-Benfield, *The Horrors of the Half-Known Life: Male Attitudes toward Women in Nineteenth-Century America* (New York: Harper Colophon Books, 1976).

into relation and implicitly reconciled with each other?"[38] Rather than directly answer this question, she responds by arguing that the logic of "Experience" is neither one of synthesis nor conflict, but one of elegy, which represents a new figuration of the power of dissociation. But in returning her argument to this idea of dissociation, she slights something of the power of her own question. For "Experience" can be said, in light of Fuller's role, to have been built around the problem of "voices . . . deaf to each other's words." If we were to substitute the word *subject* for the word *self* in Cameron's question, Emerson's essay suddenly becomes one that explores the shifting subject positions accruing from various claims "voiced, repudiated, and differently iterated." And though reconciliation in the sense that Cameron perceives it—as psychological integration—may *not* be the goal of her essay, the expressed desire to bring uneasy terms into relation certainly is. When Emerson writes that the "consciousness in each man is a sliding scale, which identifies him now with the First Cause, and now with the flesh of his body" (CW 3: 42), he is articulating his gathering sense of the shifting subject positions through which one negotiates in life.

For this reason, I argue, Emerson formulates the structure of the essay around a crude opposition between himself and Fuller. We see this, for example, when he writes, "I compared notes with one of my friends who expects everything of the universe, and is disappointed when anything is less than the best, and I found that I begin at the other extreme, expecting nothing, and am always full of thanks for moderate goods" (CW 3: 36). We know that Fuller supplied the model for his "friend" from a journal entry in which he wrote that she was "a person who according to her own account of herself, expects everything for herself from the universe" (JMN 8: 131). Emerson's oppositional stance, however, radically falsifies both Fuller's position and the play of his relationship with her. By constructing this conflict within the larger oppositional frame of "intellectual tasting" versus "muscular activity," (CW 3: 34) he appears to endorse the traditional split between ideal and empirical worlds. Yet, as Cameron herself argues, the essay works at every turn to resist this binary logic. It does so, continually, by questioning the easy formulation of opposition suggested by the description of his friend. What happens in the essay happened in Emerson's correspondence with Fuller: voices continually exchange subject positions, allowing her position to become attractive to him when earlier he finds it repulsive. At stake, then, is not the integrity of the self, but its fluidity. "The individual is always mistaken. He designed many things, and drew in other per-

---

[38] Cameron, "Representing Grief," p. 17.

sons as coadjutors, quarreled with some or all, blundered much, and something is done; all are a little advanced, but the individual is always mistaken. It turns out somewhat new, and very unlike what he promised himself" (CW 3: 40). The movement of the essay is toward what Emerson calls "tendency" as well as the unsettling but, according to Cavell, radical idea that "to finish the moment, to find the journey's end in every step of the road, to live the greatest number of good hours, is wisdom" (CW 3: 35); and it is a movement against an oppositional structure that continually strives to assert itself. To resist this structure, one must move through a succession of positions. This succession happens most vividly in his willingness to assume and play out some of the ideas that came to him in conversation with Fuller, adopting her thoughts as readily as his own, even when they first appear to bear no relation to one another. To advocate tendency, as he knew, was essentially to echo Fuller, who during the summer after Waldo's death told Emerson that "she felt herself amidst Tendencies: did not regret life, nor accuse the imperfection of her own or their performance whilst these strong native Tendencies so appeared" (JMN 8: 196).

Thus the earlier dream about the orator, which allows Emerson to shift his perspective from orator to auditor to audience, establishes a paradigm for the shifting positions endorsed by the *Second Series*. Moreover, the repressed subject matter of the dream is, as I have suggested, the discourse of Fourier, and that same discourse slowly begins to emerge in *Second Series* and most acutely in "Experience." Emerson's argument that "Temperament is the iron wire on which the beads are strung" (CW 3: 30), for example, can be seen as an incorporation, if not an introjection, of Fourier's understanding of the power of the twelve passions through which man negotiates. The same could be said of his argument about another "lord of life," namely, succession. Fourier's argument about the need for variety is played out in Emerson's statement that "Our love of the real draws us to permanence, but health of body consists in circulation, and sanity of mind in variety or facility of association" (CW 3: 32). Even the idea of the phalanx, convened to "complete" each member of Fourier's New Harmony, finds its way into Emerson's articulation of power when he writes:

> Of course, it needs the whole society, to give the symmetry we seek. The parti-colored wheel must revolve very fast to appear white. Something is learned too by conversing with so much folly and defect. . . . Like a bird which alights nowhere, but hops perpetually from bough to bough, is the Power which abides in no man and in no woman, but for a moment speaks from this one, and for another moment from that one (CW 3: 34).

Fourier found little to lament in these facts, whereas, in the context of this essay at least, Emerson articulates these insights with considerable reservation and regret. It is just after this vision of power that he asks the question "what help from these fineries or pedantries? What help from thought?" (CW 3: 34). In so doing, he reasserts the opposition of mental and social worlds which the earlier part of the essay attempted to displace. And the question that must be asked is Why?

One explanation may be that the humanistic opposition between empiricism and idealism is a familiar framework through which most of our intellectual habits are established, despite Emerson's struggle with that framework and its reification of subjective and objective worlds. The gradual attempt, then, to move beyond this familiar opposition is also thwarted by the most radical moment of Fourier's argument: his critique of marriage. Emerson's concern over the "dangerous" aspect of Fourier's proposal drew him back into a polemical defense of his position on marriage. But, as we might surmise from his dream, that defense was already under siege, in part because Fuller was helping him to acknowledge the authority of the feminist component of Fourier's critique. Thus, as if internalizing the *social* difficulties of the marriage bond in that critique without acknowledging them specifically, he writes in "Experience" that

> Marriage (in what is called the spiritual world) is impossible, because of the inequality between every subject and every object. . . . Never can love make consciousness and ascription equal in force. There will be the same gulf between every me and thee, as between the original and the picture. The universe is the bride of the soul. All private sympathy is partial. Two human beings are like globes, which can touch only in a point, and whilst they remain in contact, all other points of each of the spheres are inert; their turn must also come (CW 3: 44).

This passage marks an interesting variation on the passage about marriage quoted earlier, where Emerson remained focused on the difference between empirical and spiritual marriage. Whereas in the earlier passage he defended marriage in the ideal world as a possibility, now he views it as an impossibility. The change seems to reflect an acceptance of the Fourieristic critique of the inequality of the marriage bond. Indeed, the rotating image of human contact draws directly from Fourier's description of the shifting needs of individuals. Nevertheless, even with this new focus, Emerson still manages to maintain a platonic frame for his thinking, reinstating the familiar opposition between the real and ideal worlds. Indeed, this confusion of traditional philosophical concepts with the discourse of Fourier results in a familiar skepticism about the gulf between what he calls "consciousness" and "ascription." The sense that there remains a gulf between the consciousness of the poet and his ascription is the source of the skeptical strain surfacing throughout his discussion in "The Poet." And this skeptical position becomes reinvigorated at the end of "Experience," when he feels the need to respond polemically to the question "Why not realize your world?"

The very fact that Emerson articulates his skepticism through an account of the impossibility of marriage is suggestive, however, because it reveals how the discourse of Fourier continued to shape his skeptical position. More significantly, his decision to call attention to the polemical nature of his argument in the closing section of "Experience" can be interpreted as a sign of his desire to break from this oppositional structure and its mood of alienation. This desire is made particularly clear when he frames his position by writing that "hankering after an overt or practical effect seems to me an apostasy" (CW 3: 48). By summoning the word *apostasy*—used earlier by members of the church community against his own position—he acknowledges a kinship with the very audience he wishes to renounce. As in his dream, the legibility of his polemical stance registers both his alienation from the issue at hand and his desire to resolve it. Moreover, when he elaborates his dilemma by writing, "I know that the world I converse with in the city and in the farms is not the world I *think*" (CW 3: 48), he establishes the frame that will enable him to move beyond it.[39] For by introducing the concept of conversation, he summons the structure central to his interaction with Fuller, the same structure that afforded a release from the logic of opposition by allowing seemingly oppositional positions to be set in relation to one another.

At issue for Emerson in the discrepancy between thinking and conversing (or "consciousness" and "ascription") was the efficacy of writing, the efficacy of the poet/skeptic. His fear was that his poet could only work in isolation and was therefore doomed to alienation.[40] And

[39] Indeed, by writing, "I observe that difference, and shall observe it. One day, I shall know the value and law of this discrepancy" (CW 3: 48), he hints at its significance for him.

[40] A journal entry reinforces another, related gulf between writing and conversation. "You come into this company meanly. How so? We have come for the love of seeing each other & of conversing together. You have come to give us things which are written already in your note-books. . . . The best of our talk is invented here, and we go hence greater than we came by so much life as we have awakened in each other; but you, when your . . . quiver is emptied, must sit dumb & careful the rest of the evening. Every thing you say makes you poorer (you are burning up your ships:) and every thing we say makes us richer: you go home when the company breaks up forlorn (indeed): we go home (without thought on ourselves,) full of happiness to pleasant dreams" (JMN 8: 130). For

although isolation and alienation appear as one important mood in "Experience," another equally important mood surfaces when he writes, "far be from me the despair which prejudges the law by a paltry empiricism" (CW 3: 48). Hence his statement "never mind the ridicule" (the pragmatic response with which he associated Fourier and his followers[41]), and the final and gloriously ambiguous statement about the "true romance which the world exists to realize" (CW 3: 49). This mood change owes to a gradual recognition on Emerson's part, made vivid through his conversations with Fuller, that there was another perspective from which to view his intellectual dilemma. Thus his statement "the true romance which the world exists to realize, will be the transformation of genius into practical power" can be read as an attempt to embody something of Fuller's double strategy: a sustained faith in the efficacy of agency ("the transformation of genius into practical power"), despite the seeming collapse of the categories making a conceptualization of that agency possible.

What is enacted in "Experience," then, is an attempt at translation, a meeting of two opposite and still unapproachable discourses. The very mood productive of skepticism, a sense of the "unhandsome" condition of our lives, suddenly contains the possibility of transformation, though not by dialectical means. "Experience" promotes a type of double strategy similar to the procedure that was beginning to inform Fuller's thinking. Thus, when Emerson invokes "Fortune, Minerva, Muse," he hints at Fuller's place in his development of this positive sense that "the new statement will comprise the skepticisms, as well as the faiths of society, and out of unbeliefs a creed shall be formed" (CW 3: 43). In fact, from a conversation with her he developed his idea that "Power keeps quite another road than the turnpikes of choice and will, namely, the subterra-

Fuller, however, this strict opposition between writing and conversation was false, particularly since Emerson's best conversation with her emerged in his letters, parts of which often found their way into his lectures and essays. In its very dependence on language, writing *was* social, but he would only become persuaded of this when he saw the way his interaction with Fuller often challenged the familiar distinction between the written and the spoken word, just as it challenged other familiar oppositions. Certainly he had been impressed with her famous Boston Conversations. There her willingness to negotiate everything—a willingness to explore a series of discourse strategies—in effect actualized the type of "writing" that Barthes attributed to Fourier's vision: it opened a sight for power and agency (see Chapter 1). This method Fuller drew out in Emerson's letters to her, and it slowly became encoded in the very rhetorical shiftings for which Emerson is so well known.

[41] In a letter to Fuller on April 11, 1844, Emerson wrote, "But Fourier & Miller & Dr. Buchanan will not heal us of our deep wound, any more than Spurzheim and the Flying Man, to whom they have succeeded. I think it is part of our lesson to give a form of consent to what is farcical, and to pick up our living & our virtue amidst what is so ridiculous, hardly deigning a smile, and certainly not vexed" (EL 3: 246).

nean and invisible tunnels and channels of life" (CW 3: 39).[42] And it is this sense of power that enables him to summon the figure of Romance in the end to address the pressing challenge of "practical life."

Both Cameron and Cavell identify attributes of this radical move in Emerson's essay, yet both feel compelled to restrict the social implications of his theory. Cameron's resistance to the last line of the essay results from a rare interpretive lapse on her part: she reads the closing words about that "transformation of genius into practical power" as if they were not radically qualified, as Carton reminds us, by the first words in the sentence: "the true romance which the world exists to realize."[43] The theory of Power that Cameron sees emerging throughout the essay is thus actually reiterated in its closing section. That it finds its articulation through a polemical confrontation with the discourse of social reform is not irrelevant. The power at issue, after all, and the issue toward which Emerson's skepticism is transforming, is feminism in its nascent stages.

"In Conversation, in Calamity, He Finds New Materials"

This transformation toward feminism is also evident in the serial development of the various topics in the volume of the *Second Series*. One could argue that the volume is assembled on the principle of a phalanx, since no single essay can adequately express the issue at hand, just as no single person or marriage, according to Fourier, could fulfill the power of man. And again, Fuller provides the vehicle through which Emerson approaches this material, even as her appearance is always restricted to the strange translations from letters and journal entries as they make their way into these more formal works.

The essay "Character" can be seen as Emerson's effort to *contain* the polemical issue at work in his volume. His formulation for this containment lies in his description of the "expectation which outran performance" (CW 3: 53). With this description, presumably, he attempts to describe a power superseding ordinary political action and to define a true model of agency or "disinterest." He must, however, show how positive moral power resided within an individual whose outward appearance gave no sign of power. Thus in the context of "Character" his confidence in the "reserved force which acts directly by presence, and without means" (CW 3: 53) also appears to have been drawn from a

---

[42] For their conversation, see JMN 7: 512.
[43] Cameron, "Representing Grief," p. 35; Carton, *The Rhetoric of American Romance*, p. 4.

defensive and skeptical position, or a position from which he could argue that "it is disgraceful to fly to events for confirmation of our truth and worth" (CW 3: 58). Certainly, this way of thinking bears a strong resemblance to his surmise after his conversation with Fuller that there were "subterranean,—or say rather, these supersensuous channels of communication" (JMN 7: 512).

> One fact the fine conversations of the last week . . . revealed to me not without a certain shudder of joy—that I must thank what I am & not what I do for the love my friends bear me. I, conscious all the time of the *short coming of my hands*, haunted ever with a sense of beauty which makes all I do & say pitiful to me, & the occasion of perpetual apologies expect . . . to disgust those whom I admire, and now suddenly it comes out that they have been loving me all this time, *not thinking of my hands or my words*, but only of that love of something more beautiful than the world, which, it seems, being in my heart, overflowed through my eyes or the ones of my speech (JMN 7: 512, emphasis mine).

In the context of "Experience" Emerson's focus on subterranean power attempts to displace the familiar oppositions of the ideal and empirical worlds, whereas in "Character" the emphasis on subterranean power is more often working in the service of a polemic. The emphasis on hands in his original statement is revealing. As the passage on our "unhandsome" condition makes clear, finding a way to participate in the character of the age without succumbing to a crude and instrumental self-interest remains his primary goal. The concept of Character provides a momentary compromise; it establishes a defense of the isolated, albeit poised, individual unwilling to "soil [his] white hands by any compliances" (CW 3: 67).

This defensive strain (the same strain that he identified as his "negative" [CW 2: 131] prudence), supports Emerson's opposition between the "uncivil, unavailable man" (CW 3: 59) and the mob or crowd of convention and conventionality. Yet as the essay begins and ends with this polarity more or less intact, the larger elaboration of the concept of Character throughout the essay works to dismantle this formulation. It does so by posing a thesis about attraction or "strict relations of amity" (CW 3: 64). For in this it effectively defies the previous claim in "Experience" about "the inequality of every subject and every object" (CW 3: 44). And once again his relationship with Fuller supplies the most potent model for this disruption of the oppositional.

It is fascinating to see how Emerson arrives at his argument for "joyful intercourse" (CW 3: 64). It develops through a passage revealing an important tension in his initial elaboration of character.

I surrender at discretion. How death-cold is literary genius before this fire of life! These are the touches that reanimate my heavy soul, and give it eyes to pierce the dark of nature. I find, where I thought myself poor, there was I most rich. Thence comes a new intellectual exaltation, to be again rebuked by some new exhibition of character. *Strange alternation of attraction and repulsion!* Character repudiates intellect, yet excites it; and character passes into thought, is published so, and then is ashamed before new flashes of moral worth (CW 3: 61, emphasis mine).[44]

The attentive reader will notice a paraphrase of the "fiery" enrichment that Emerson attempted to describe in his earlier Margaret passage.[45] Yet his style has become considerably more complicated here, and the complication is shaped by a figure of alternation. This alternation may well return us once again to one of his polarities, but it escapes the mood of skepticism and isolation which usually results by his insistence on alternation as a continuous process embodying transition and resisting synthesis. Intriguingly, his concern for the *movement* and interaction of thought and character parallels his perception of the "strange alternation of attraction and repulsion" in his interaction with Fuller.[46] This parallel inevitably leads him to move beyond the presentation of character as it is enclosed in one individual, and to explore the dynamic of character in personal intercourse, presumably in an attempt to build a model of disinterestedness and agency. "What is so excellent as strict

[44] Emerson takes this passage from a journal entry that includes the passage "I feel how deathcold are all literary efforts by the side of this living child" (JMN 8: 5). His substitution of the passage "before this fire of life" suggests that he conflated his earlier response (perhaps to Waldo) with his later response to Fuller. His very next journal entry is interesting in this regard, suggesting that thoughts of his interaction with her were never far from this passage. "I value my welfare too much to pay you any longer the compliment of attentions. I shall not draw the thinnest veil over my defects, but if you are here, you shall see me as I am. You will then see that though I am full of tenderness, and born with as large hunger to love & to be loved as any man can be, yet its demonstrations are not active & bold, but are passive and tenacious. My love has no flood and ebb, but is always there under my silence, under displeasure, under cold, arid, and even weak behavior" (JMN 8: 6).

[45] "The wonderful generosity of her sentiments pours a contempt on books & writing at the very time . . . when one asks how shall this fiery picture be kept in its glow & variety for other eyes. . . . I have never known any example of such growth,—steady progress from stage to stage of thought & of character" (JMN 8: 368–69).

[46] "I would that I could, I know afar off that I cannot give the lights & shades, the hopes & outlooks that come to me in *these strange, cold-warm, attractive repelling conversations with Margaret*, whom I always admire, most revere when I nearest see, and sometimes love, yet whom I freeze, and who freezes me to silence, when we seem to promise to come nearest. Yet perhaps my old motto holds true here also 'And the more falls I get, move faster on.'"(JMN 8: 109, emphasis mine). Fuller was visiting Emerson's household when he was writing in his journal, "Ah if there were not always a new fact! if I could put any dependence in your word of love! but now whilst it still rings in my ear & sweetens the springs of life we are both changed, wiser, sadder, I dare not ask if you love me still" (JMN 8: 108).

relations of amity, when they spring from this deep root? The sufficient reply to the skeptic, who doubts the power and the furniture of man, is that possibility of joyful intercourse with persons, which makes the faith and practice of all reasonable men" (CW 3: 64). This use of the "possibility" of friendship as "sufficient reply to the skeptic" marks an important turn in the essay and an advancement of Emerson's exploration in "Experience," where the possibility of isolation and alienation remain not only in his discussion of marriage but also in the polemic at the end. Even the description of the skeptic as one who doubts "the power and the furniture of man" indicates just how the terms are shifting: "furniture" draws our attention to the necessary accessories of life forming the basis for the "faith and practice" of men. But gone is the assumption made earlier in "Character" that "there is nothing real or useful that is not a seat of war" (CW 3: 59). Instead of contention as the central trope, we encounter "the power to swell the moment from the resources of the heart" (CW 3: 66), which returns us to the concept of attraction in Fourieristic discourse.[47]

The development of this possibility is, of course, tentative at best in "Character," as the reemergence of the image of isolation at the close reveals. Moreover, at the height of this discussion, Emerson restrains himself by describing this relationship as one between "two virtuous men" (CW 3: 64), simultaneously avoiding the complications of heterosexual and homoerotic bonds and erasing what amounts to a genealogy of this idea.[48] Yet his effort to establish a truly disinterested bond also enables him to surrender to discretion and explore the possibility of both insofar as his description of "love in the sexes" as "the first symbol" leaves open the question of "Those relations to the best men" (CW 3: 65).[49]

---

[47] This same power will prove central to "Politics."

[48] Emerson's restraint is evident in his editing of the earlier reference to gender in a passage intended to show how friends "gravitate to each other, and cannot otherwise":

> When each the other shall avoid,
> Shall each by each be most enjoyed. (CW 3: 65)

From his journal we see that he omitted these lines:

> Is it not enough I am
> The husband of that holy dame
> Married in the eternal mind
> And plighted by the laws of kind
> [Then] God said (I felt the while new flame)
> I join you by the love of the same
> Now part this pair who can
> When each the other shall avoid,
> Shall each by each be most enjoyed. (JMN 8: 474)

[49] His model for such relationships was drawn from the desire stimulated in his interaction with Fuller—his desire to "make an experiment of [her] efficacy"—but that fact does

Margaret as Minerva

The tension in "Character" pervades the *Second Series*, and the same tension registers in Emerson's early dream about the angry orator. Fuller's unique role as arbiter of this tension is perhaps best demonstrated in his parable about Minerva at the close of "Manners." Rather suggestively, the connection between Minerva and Fuller, or the discourse of feminism, is adumbrated earlier in the essay when he draws from his Margaret passage (with its comparison to Minerva) to lend support to the "new chivalry on behalf of Woman's Rights":

> A certain awkward consciousness of inferiority in the men, may give rise to the new chivalry in behalf of Woman's Rights. Certainly, let her be as much better placed in the laws and in social forms, as the most zealous reformer can ask, but I confide so entirely in her inspiring and musical nature, that I believe only herself can show us how she shall be served. The wonderful generosity of her sentiments raises her at times into heroical and godlike regions, and verifies the pictures of Minerva, Juno, or Polymnia; and by the firmness with which she treads her upward path, she convinces the coarsest calculators that another road exists, than that which their feet know (CW 3: 88).

The direct mention of feminism is not arbitrary but significant, if we understand the role both Fourier and Fuller played in the creation of the argument of the *Second Series*. But the implied association between feminism and a theory of reading suggested by Emerson's return to Minerva at the close of the essay is more provocative.[50] In the parable borrowed from Silenus with which he ends the essay, Emerson seems to respond to Fuller's letter that contained the two radically different readings of his

---

not displace either possibility. Indeed, her "unsettled rank in the universe" may have provoked certain homoerotic memories in Emerson (JMN 8: 131). See Gay Wilson Allen's account of Emerson's relationship with Martin Gay at Harvard, *Waldo Emerson: A Biography* (New York: Viking, 1981), 53. According to Allen, "this schoolboy infatuation" that showed Emerson "bordering on homosexuality" was "a forerunner of Emerson's later theorizing on love and friendship." I thank Richard Poirier for reminding me of this association.

[50] Evan Carton finds the essay "Manners" exemplary of Emerson's "self-parodic mode" (*The Rhetoric of American Romance*, p. 121). According to Carton, "The essay does not seek to report but to constitute, and Emerson concludes by acknowledging its performative character and implying that a very great deal depends upon such performances" (p. 123). Thus, again, it is through the figure of Minerva that "the world of surface, disguise and indeterminacy dooms language to implication, and by the same stroke, frees it to exercise power" (p. 122). I agree with this reading, though again would reinvest Minerva with the feminist character so clearly indicated by Emerson's mention of her in his discussion of the woman's rights movement.

despair over the efficacy of his emancipation address. Like Fuller, he provides two distinct readings of a similar situation, one embodied in the character of Jove and the other figured by the mythological character of Minerva. In the face of the totalizing skepticism of Jove, who views the experiment of the world as a failure, Minerva argues in support of the "indeterminate aspect" (CW 3: 90) of its population: "If you called them bad, they would appear so; if you called them good, they would appear so; and there was no one person or action among them, which would not puzzle her owl, much more all Olympus, to know whether it was fundamentally bad or good" (CW 3: 90). Minerva and Jove stand, then, as the potential readers of the volume and as arbiters of its meaning. It is just as possible to adopt Jove's alienated skepticism as to follow Minerva in her willingness to "take unsolvability to the heart" of one's thinking.[51] Although most criticism has effectively followed Jove, I argue that Emerson finally adopts Minerva's method by ending his volume with "New England Reformers" and calling it a "lecture." For in this way he leaves open the possibility of a broader interpretation of his "true romance," putting the hard terms of his skepticism about the "unhandsome" condition of man at the service of a feminist quest for agency and change.

[51] Cavell, *This New Yet Unapproachable America*, p. 79.

5

Fuller's Scene before the Women: *Woman in the Nineteenth Century*

Power ceases in the instant of repose; it resides in the moment of transition from a past to a new state, in the shooting of the gulf, in the darting to an aim.
—Ralph Waldo Emerson, "Self-Reliance," CW 2: 40

Anomalous facts, as the never quite obsolete rumors of magic and demonology, and the new allegations of phrenologists and neurologists, are of ideal use. They are good indications. . . . For these abnormal insights of the adepts, ought to be normal, and things of course.
—Ralph Waldo Emerson, "Nominalist and Realist," CW 3: 138

Necessity is not a fact but an interpretation.
—Nietzsche, *The Will to Power*

In August of 1844, after hearing Emerson's emancipation address, Fuller began revising "The Great Lawsuit" for publication as *Woman in the Nineteenth Century*, a task she did not complete until November, after she had reread his published version of the *Second Series* (LMF 3: 240–41). Earlier she had been somewhat amused by his struggle with the closing chapters. But by November her amusement became chastened by the difficulties of her own projected revisions. In retrospect, her teasing letter to Emerson reflects some of her gathering anxiety about the work still before her.

I always thought the saddest position in the world must be that of some regal dame to whom husband, court, kingdom, world, look in vain for an heir! She is only supposed to eat breathe, move, think, nay! love, for the sake of this future blessing. The book of her life is only permitted for the sake of its appendix. Meanwhile she, perhaps, persists in living on as if her life by itself were of any consequence, is the mother of no Prince or has even the impertinence to encumber the kingdom with a parcel of Princesses, girls who must be "weel-tochered" to make them of any value (LMF 3: 213).

Of course, Fuller's vivid description of the constraints on the queen echoes one of the central themes of "The Great Lawsuit": the burden of family expectations on women.[1] But the decision to use the metaphor of book and appendix to describe the queen's situation betrays some new anxieties generated by her return to the essay on women.[2] Although Fuller likely did not think her book on women would be tolerated *for* its appendix (or what we might call its "legitimizing text"), clearly she felt the need to supplement her argument in this more traditional way. Almost too predictably, the lengthy appendix and other interpretive apparatus (such as the preface) that made up a large part of the revisions provide us with some insight into the conflicting imperatives she considered as she composed her final draft.

In fact, both the preface and appendix reveal that Fuller's experience in the Midwest made her return to "The Great Lawsuit" more difficult. The difficulty lay in the recognition that some of the assumptions and interpretive models she had used to build her feminist argument in "Lawsuit" were directly challenged by the terrible fate of the Native American. Her faith in the "great moral law" (L: 8) of Anglo-American culture, as well as the progressive view of history, wavered when she saw how both could support the annihilation of cultures resisting those perspectives. As a result, she returned to the essay with a healthy skepticism about the assumptions underlying its argument, including her decision to discuss the fate of women by drawing from various texts of Western culture.

Fortunately, Fuller's instinctive decision to use Fourier's critique of Western culture in *Summer on the Lakes* served her even more strongly as she returned to "Lawsuit." Fourier deliberately made Woman the center of his focus. Indeed, his approach makes him a precursor to the long list of contemporary European critics who have theorized that the concept of Woman provides a type of reading strategy for exposing the gaps and limitations of Western culture.[3] Fourier himself never articulated his position on women as a reading strategy of course, yet his approach readily lends itself to this type of analysis. When Fuller discovered that many of her previous assumptions in "Lawsuit" already employed a

---

[1] Hence her insistence that the female characters in Goethe's *Wilhelm Meister's Apprenticeship* be thought of as "unrelated" even though they were always seen "in relations." See "The Great Lawsuit: Man versus Men. Woman versus Women," *The Dial* (July 1843): 46. Future references to this essay will be designated by the abbreviation L and the page number.

[2] We know that Fuller's anxiety took a physical form because she told her friend Georgiana Bruce that she suffered from a series of headaches when she first began her revisions in August (LMF 3: 236).

[3] Alice Jardine shows how the concept of Woman became "a metaphor of reading and topography of writing for confronting the breakdown of the paternal metaphor" in critics like Derrida, Lacan, and Deleuze in her *Gynesis: Configurations of Woman and Modernity* (Ithaca: Cornell University Press, 1985), 34.

useful skepticism about Western culture because she, too, had made the center of her inquiry the idea of Woman, she began to see how Fourier might be used to establish just such a strategy.

For this reason, Fuller did not attempt to rewrite her entire argument; indeed, thinking through Fourier's peculiar emphasis on the position of Woman in culture, particularly his understanding of Woman's transitional state, made her more aware of the efficacy of certain critical tendencies with which she had been experimenting before her trip to the West, including her earlier interest in translation and her focus on conversation. Her dependence in "Lawsuit" and *Woman* on a series of conversational sketches reflects how conversation had established itself as one of her primary interpretive tools. Julie Ellison has astutely observed how from a very early age Fuller "regard[ed] the self as the locus of conversation among the many languages of the mind."[4] That is, she always tended to view the world through a complex double consciousness and was comfortable with a dynamic interplay of forces exhibited in the conversational structure. Her early translations, where the conversational exchange of languages entailed a shift in perspective as well as pedagogical principles, simply reinforced her sense that conversation was an important mode of interpretation.

Fuller most explicitly articulated the association between conversation and feminist agency when in 1840 she established her seminars for women and called them Conversations. Her hope was to engage women in a series of conversations in order to give them a stronger sense of their own skills and to exercise their minds so as to oppose the otherwise restrictive intellectual role prescribed for them by the culture.[5] Thus her seminars for women are worth considering here, since through them she

[4] Julie Ellison, *Delicate Subjects: Romanticism, Gender, and the Ethics of Understanding* (Ithaca: Cornell University Press, 1990), 223.

[5] See Fuller's letter to Sophia Ripley explaining her goals. LMF 2: 86–89. Because she deliberately excluded certain volatile social issues from her discussions, notably abolitionism, she was roundly criticized by some who found her "classroom" too esoteric to have had any significant impact on the social ills of the day. Harriet Martineau, who never attended one of the Conversations, gave the most scathing and limited interpretation of Fuller's activity when she wrote that "Margaret Fuller and her adult pupils sat 'gorgeously dressed,' talking about Mars and Venus, Plato and Goethe, fancying themselves the elect of the earth," while "the liberties of the republic were running out as fast as they could." Bell Gale Chevigny, *The Woman and the Myth: Margaret Fuller's Life and Writings* (Old Westbury, N.Y.: The Feminist Press, 1976), 229. Though Chevigny finds Martineau's response uncompromising (attributing its severity to Martineau's displeasure with Fuller's earlier critique of her *Society in America*), she agrees that the Conversations were limited by the transcendental themes that she adopted for her class to consider. Chevigny's frustration with this period of Fuller's life is well documented and reflected in her decision to delete sections of *Woman in the Nineteenth Century* in her anthology of Fuller's work. See Chevigny's introduction to this section for a description of Fuller's conversations (pp. 210–15).

began to enact a strategy that would serve her in her early publishing career as a translator and critic and still more powerfully after her encounter with the limits of the progressive rhetoric of Western culture.[6]

Unfortunately we have few actual records of Fuller's Conversations. Yet from the most thorough record available, the notes taken in 1841 by a young woman named Caroline Dall, we can see that the meetings were also formed through a kind of sociolinguistic understanding of conversation.[7] Fuller intuited that "social variability" was an inherent part of linguistic systems and that conversational exchanges were important in "maintaining the subtle boundaries of power, status, . . . [and] role" in culture.[8] Thus, one goal in her Conversations was to help women disrupt those subtle boundaries.

Because Caroline Dall was a young girl, her notes from the experience form an odd filter through which to grasp the structure of one of these Conversations. Apparently Dall's father had trained her to attend lectures and report on them without the assistance of notes, and this early experience enabled her to adopt a keen recorder's sense.[9] But significant gaps occur in her manuscript because, as she explains, she does not record anything that she does not understand. Fortunately, she cannot always know what she does not understand and she therefore reports more than she might have otherwise. A few unshielded moments in particular reveal that she does not always catch the various discourse strategies as Fuller signals them to her.

In her account, Dall clearly dislikes the interference of the men in the seminar; the normal procedure of the Conversations was to exclude

[6] Recently the strategic value of the subject matter in Fuller's Conversations has drawn some positive critical response. Jeffrey Steele views her focus on mythological figures throughout the Conversations as her way of developing "a body of female archetypes" in order to show how "female personality was a fabrication," and therefore subject to change. Jeffrey Steele, *The Representation of the Self in the American Renaissance* (Chapel Hill: University of North Carolina Press, 1987), 106, 104. In another subtle reading, Julie Ellison elaborates on the "heterogeneity of Fuller's idealistic discourse," finding in the pattern of the Conversations a model for a feminist "ethic of interpretation" that both resists "the hyperrational arrogance of masculine analysis" and the "fantasies of her own centrality which reduce others to appreciative spectatorship." By Ellison's account, Fuller encouraged her students to participate in a revised model of interpretation by performing the role of interpreter before them and occupying "simultaneously the positions of the object and agent of desire, and the roles of lover, analyst, and victim" (*Delicate Subjects*, p. 217).

[7] Caroline Dall, *Margaret Fuller and Her Friends* (Boston: Roberts Brothers, 1897; reprint 1985). For more on Dall's text see Joel Myerson, "Caroline Dall's Reminiscences of Margaret Fuller," *Harvard Library Bulletin* 22 (1974): 414–28, and "Mrs. Dall Edits Miss Fuller: The Story of Margaret and Her Friends," *Papers of the Bibliographical Society of America* 72 (1978): 187–200.

[8] John Gumperz, *Discourse Strategies* (Cambridge: Cambridge University Press, 1982), 6.

[9] See Helen R. Deese, "Alcott's Conversations on the Transcendentalists: The Record of Caroline Dall," *American Literature* 60 (March 1988): 20.

men, but for ten special evening sessions in 1841, men such as Emerson, Henry Hedge, George Ripley, William Story, and Charles Wheeler were invited to attend. Rather intriguingly, these are the sessions recorded by Dall; her records therefore form a register of her own confused ambition by implicitly privileging those meetings with men in attendance. The arrival of the men meant that Fuller's task became more difficult; the speech community was no doubt fractured into a curious range, making her conversational cues sufficiently diverse. One suspects that although she could not have anticipated the impact of the men on the women in the conversation, she hoped that their arrival would encourage the women to see that there was a subtle but important alternation of conversational style at work. She apparently did not intend to encourage women to assume the discourse strategies adopted by the men so much as she wanted the women to be aware of those strategies and in the process to become more cognizant of the speech repertoire shared by women.

One moment in the third evening session on March 19, 1841, is particularly revealing of the complex method adopted by Fuller.[10] She began with a reminder that the group had had a tendency to wander from the subject in their conversations, and she did so in a provocative manner: by wandering herself from the purported subject of the evening—a discussion of the contrast between "Genius" and "Productive Energy" as they were embodied in the mythological figures of Apollo and Ceres.

Fuller wandered from her topic by reciting a Novalis tale from his *Feminine Soul*. The tale involves two children, Eros and Fable, at play in a room also occupied by a man and a woman, History and Sophia. Sophia tests the truth value of words written upon a page; when she dips the pages of History into a vase of water, they emerge blank, impugning his honesty. When she repeats the test with Fable's writing, however, the pages remain clear. Dismissed from the room by the outraged figure of

---

[10] Here Fuller engages in a type of code switching, technically defined as a rhetorical strategy of bilinguals that involves the alternation of languages in one passage of conversation. According to sociolinguist Gumperz, "The alternation most frequently takes the form of two subsequent sentences, as when a speaker uses a second language either to reiterate his message or to reply to someone else's statement" (*Discourse Strategies*, p. 59). When speaking of Fuller's code switching, however, I do not mean to imply that she was making a literal shift to another language (though this was a method she used with great facility). Rather, I suggest that she sought to acknowledge the variety of speech communities *within* one language. This approach conforms in a more general way with the description of code switching provided by Gumperz, which reveals "an awareness that [one's] mode of behavior is only one of several possible modes, that style of communication affects the interpretation of what a speaker intends to communicate and that there are others with different communicative conventions and standards of evaluation that must not only be taken into account but that can also be imitated or mimicked for special communicative effect" (*Discourse Strategies*, p. 65).

History, Fable falls under the sway of the three Fates. History advises the Fates to give Fable the task of catching Tarantulas. But Fable gains the assistance of Eros and uses a lyre to enlist the Tarantulas in a victorious struggle against the Fates. In the end, a new dynasty of Eros and Fable is inaugurated.

According to Dall, "Margaret said that in the story . . . she had set us an example of wandering from the subject, but she hoped to some purpose. She hoped no one would have need to call upon little Fable's body-guard of Tarantulas."[11] Dall's concern with this opening gambit was that Fuller had already wandered too far from the topic of the evening. But Fuller's retelling of the tale actually works against Dall's literal reading, offering a wonderful account of the prohibitions of narration and their curious gender inflections. Here History and the Fates conspire against Fable by enforcing a wandering style that Fable in turn uses strategically. Fuller's claim that she hoped no one would need to call upon Fable's "body-guard of Tarantulas" falls back upon itself, since she has done precisely that in anticipating the variety of conversational restraints that would emerge during the evening. Her introduction of the Novalis story disturbs a formulaic expectation: the men joining the seminar might anticipate that women's "chatter" would wander from the subject. Here Fuller's use of the tale by Novalis—a tale by a man intended to explain the phenomenon of the "feminine soul"— simultaneously supports and rereads the formula to demonstrate the political advantages that might accrue from Fable's method. Fuller's use of the story is a radical double strategy, one that enables the attentive listener to acknowledge the complex ideological grid through which conversation can and must proceed.

Although we have only these fragmented records of Fuller's experience in her seminars, they help in some way to explain the unusual compositional strategies already at work in "The Great Lawsuit." Fuller's shifting position on issues, what Julie Ellison calls her "'Both/and' policies,"[12] her tendency to seek the support of Fable as often as History for her arguments, as well as her decision to make strategic use of conversational sketches, all show that she calls upon a developing sense of the complex ideological negotiations necessary for the creation of some type of feminist agency. After her visit to the Midwest, she began to see how the same type of negotiation could be useful for the development of a general social critique. Thus, although her views about Western culture were unsettled by her trip to the Midwest, her earlier faith in

---

[11] Dall, *Margaret Fuller*, p. 63.
[12] Ellison, *Delicate Subjects*, p. 271.

the efficacy of shifting frames of reference, whether through the devices of translation, conversation, or a simple shift of perspective, was subtly reinforced.[13]

Women and Their Fatal Conquests

In her revision of the *Dial* essay, Fuller began to encounter problems with some of her earlier definitions of feminist agency. Often "Lawsuit" had focused on the nature of Woman's dependence for her identity on her relationships with men. Fuller made clear that this dependence stripped women of their ability to exert some "free agency" (L: 12) in their lives. One remedy to this problem lay in the familiar rhetoric of an unfolding destiny or progress toward freedom and equality. Given the same liberty as men, the theory went, there would be a greater likelihood of feminist agency. Yet, after viewing the conflict of European and Native American cultures, Fuller began to recognize the xenophobic aspect that often accompanied the discourse of democracy and progress.[14] This discourse, with its emphasis on equality, also urged the elimination of difference. It was therefore a discourse of fatalism, prescribing the inevitable silencing of those voices not in unison with the dominant ideological position of the culture.

The tensions in Fuller's thinking about these matters are most strikingly revealed in *Woman in the Nineteenth Century*, where she refers to the Indian translator, Malinche, who aided Cortés during the conquest of Mexico. Her discussion of this woman appears just after her reference to Queen Elizabeth of England and Queen Isabella of Spain. In "Lawsuit" she had argued that the two queens "expressed the beginning of the new state, while they forwarded its progress" (L: 24). In her revisions she sustains that argument amid her growing awareness that

[13] Again we have no way of knowing how accurate Dall's descriptions of Fuller's Conversations were. Yet they do suggest that Fuller continued to adopt a Eurocentric position toward religion. Though in the opening of one session she asks her audience to "denationalize" themselves in order to appreciate the Greek myths they were discussing (Dall, *Margaret Fuller*, p. 28), in the same session she dismisses an attempt by William White to elevate the "North American Indian's worship of the Manitou" over "Greek worship." White admired the way that "the Indian ascribed to his Manitou no passion that had degraded humanity" (*Margaret Fuller*, p. 31). According to Dall, Fuller countered with the idea that "the Indian propitiated his God by vile deeds, by ignoble treacheries and revenge" (*Margaret Fuller*, p. 31). As her work in *Summer* makes clear, she changes this position when she finds herself viewing the Indian cultures for the first time.

[14] See her interesting appendix on Spinoza, where she draws from his treatise on democracy in order to show how a man "of the largest intellect, of unsurpassed reasoning powers" (WNC: 174–75), could support an exclusionary politics.

both women had ruled over the "invasion of America."[15] To her discussion of Elizabeth she adds a lengthy paragraph describing many of the queen's most unattractive characteristics, exposing her behavior as the product of "the conduct and wishes of man in general" (WNC: 52). Thus, even as Fuller attempts to deploy Elizabeth as an example of historical power, she acknowledges the constraints through which such power becomes defined. Elizabeth now emerges as a woman radically restrained by the "spirit of the time," who was "taught by adversity" to "put on her virtues as armor" (WNC: 52, 53). Isabella receives similar treatment: "We may accept as an omen for ourselves, that it was Isabella who furnished Columbus with the means of coming hither. This land must pay back its debt to woman, without whose aid it would not have been brought into alliance with the civilized world" (WNC: 53). There is no doubt, of course, that Fuller intends to praise Isabella as a powerful and visionary ruler. Yet coming as it does after the problematic description of Elizabeth, the assertion of Isabella's power (and the notable absence of an equally detailed description) leaves open the possibility that she too might be subject to a rather different interpretation. We may accept her as an "omen for ourselves," provided we understand that omens can portend ill as well as good. When Fuller adds that the "land must pay back its debt to woman, without whose aid it would not have been brought into alliance with the civilized world," her perspective is strangely outside the civilized frame even as it enjoins it. And as the perspective changes, so the nature of the debt she describes changes, as we see when she adds her reference to Malinche. The Indian translator brought about a similar alliance between civilized and Indian cultures, but because she did so, she was known in Indian lore as a traitor.

The decision to turn to Malinche considerably problematizes the valorization of Isabella even if the perspective of the Native Americans is never wholly achieved.

> A graceful and meaning figure is that introduced to us by Mr. Prescott, in the Conquest of Mexico, in the Indian girl Marina, who accompanied Cortes, and was his interpreter in all the various difficulties of his career. She stood at his side, on the walls of the besieged palace, to plead with her enraged countrymen. By her name he was known in New Spain, and, after the conquest, her gentle intercession was often of avail to the conquered. The poem of the Future may be read in some features of the story of "Malinche" (WNC: 53).

[15] Francis Jennings, *The Invasion of America: Indians, Colonialism, and the Cant of Conquest* (Chapel Hill: University of North Carolina Press, 1975).

The fact that Fuller has chosen at this moment to highlight both gender and race (race being invisible to a white audience if color is absent), demonstrates the gathering nuances of her thinking. Her argument that the "poem of the Future may be read in . . . the story of 'Malinche'" indicates how far she had wandered from the focus of her initial examples. Her acknowledgment of Malinche's extraordinary concern for both Cortés and her "enraged countrymen" reveals that her story would of necessity combine an examination of the many conflicting imperatives of racial and gender-based issues.

Certainly the reading of Malinche as traitor oversimplifies her experience, as contemporary feminists have begun to argue.[16] Chicana feminists now ask the more difficult question summoned by Fuller's interest in this woman: What was her role as a cultural mediator? As a female translator, Malinche must have held particular appeal for Fuller. By turning to the figure of a translator to address the idea of progress at work in her earlier draft, Fuller enacts a radical textual turn that she repeats throughout *Woman*. That is, her theoretical inclination is always toward the complex double strategy that translation embodies. In many ways, her text continually enacts this kind of turn, rather than engaging in a more conclusive analysis. That is, the text repeatedly encounters the tie between feminism and the racism of European-American culture.

Thus, without being thematized as such, the idea of conquest becomes a concept that brings together the disparate fates of Native Americans and women for Fuller. And in this way the revised version of "The Great Lawsuit" attempts to address the lethal fatality that made democracy and equality dependent or conditional on the subordination and conquest of those who reveal themselves to be strange or Other. When Fuller advises her female readers, "Do not rejoice in conquests" (WNC: 127), she is not only admonishing them to avoid the self-flattery of flirtation, but also counseling them against the larger political discourse of conquest. The closing lines of her new preface show how pervasive her concern with conquest had become. After explaining her decision to change her title and soliciting a "sincere and patient attention" from her readers, she expresses the hope that "truth, unpolluted by prejudice, vanity, or selfishness" will be considered the "only valuable conquest for us all!" (WNC: vi). In other words, she opens her revised text with a plea for the transvaluation of conquest itself.

---

[16] Fuller probably had not read the accounts that contradicted historian William Prescott's obvious bias toward Cortés. See also Cherríe Moraga, "From a Long Line of Vendidas: Chicanas and Feminism," in *Feminist Studies/Critical Studies*, ed. Teresa de Lauretis (Bloomington: Indiana University Press, 1986), 174.

Unfortunately *Woman* never fully achieves that goal. Indeed, Fuller does not always see her way beyond the tangle of concerns which she invites with her rather eclectic approach in the work. Sometimes her feminism only obscures a deeper cultural bias at work in her thinking.[17] Yet at other times the determination to sustain her interest in women invites an examination of the very assumptions underlying her definition of Woman, issuing in a feminist critique of considerable subtlety. *Woman* ultimately shows that a feminist agency would have to depend on a radically revised reading strategy.

Indeed, in the face of the dangerous tendencies that the text discovers along the way, the efficacy of shifting perspectives as a type of reading strategy begins to emerge. And when prostitution becomes deployed in Fuller's text as the ultimate allegory for the conquest of women, it also serves as an allegory for the conquest of Native American nations. In this way the explosive discourse of race becomes aligned with the equally volatile discourse of gender in *Woman*. Whenever this type of double exposure occurs, whenever Fuller can highlight the two frames of reference simultaneously, her feminism gathers sophistication. What is reinforced in the process, moreover, is the need for critique cognizant of its own contested status.

The Liberty of Law: Choosing a Title

As in *Summer on the Lakes*, Fuller deliberately found herself relying on Fourier in order to counteract the fatalistic discourse of Western culture. The problem with turning to Fourier, as she well knew, was that his approach had led him to question the efficacy of the marriage bond. He found marriage and prostitution to be on a continuum in Western culture. Although she herself began to see the awful link between marriage and the shockingly fatalistic acceptance of prostitution in the discourse of civilization, she was not prepared to align with Fourier's radical advocacy of sexual promiscuity as a cure. Nor did she wish to align herself with those who did. George Sand, who drew support for her views on sexual practice from Fourier, proved most problematic for Fuller, who nevertheless admired the way in which certain aspects of Fourierism had proved enabling for Sand. Fuller's way of dealing with the conflicted nature of her own response toward Fourier and Sand was to return to the discourse of law. Even the title of her first essay, "The

---

[17] This bias is perhaps most evident in Appendix C, where Fuller completely ignores the racial implications of Lockhart's poem "The Wedding of Lady Theresa."

Great Lawsuit," revealed her hope that some sort of relationship between men and women could be legitimized and protected. But after
Summer on the Lakes, she also realized the need to reinterpret the law, for
it was clear that the juridical frame upon which the tenets of Western
culture had been hung had been too narrowly construed.

Thus in the preface to *Woman*, Fuller asks her female reader to "ascertain what is for them the liberty of law." She challenges her reader to
consider the value that the very phrase "liberty of law" might have by
adding, "It is for this [the liberty of law], and not for any, the largest,
extension of partial privileges that I seek" (WNC: vi). Although appear-
ing to stay within familiar legal boundaries, she actually moves well
beyond such boundaries with her syntax, implying that *any* "extension
of partial privileges" would be inadequate to her notion of the "liberty
of law." In so doing, she transvalues the words *liberty* and *law* in their
traditional bearing for women by using a phrase that demands an active
consideration of the tensions produced by their alliance in "liberty of
law."

In the same way, Fuller forces her reader to assume a complex response toward the two selected titles of her work by accepting the
efficacy of one title and then the other. Fuller first defends her original
choice of "The Great Lawsuit: Man versus Men. Woman versus Women"
only to accede to the change to *Woman in the Nineteenth Century* which
had been encouraged by her various readers.[18] Describing the way in
which her own desires had been thwarted, she insists that she preferred
the first title because it "require[d] some thought" and prepared the
reader to "meet" the author on her "own ground" (WNC: v) She subtly
implies, then, that her present reader will need to continue to do the
same work unaided. She writes that the new title should be considered
"expressive of the main purpose of the essay" (WNC: v), but there is an
irony in her assertion. Significantly, the title is culled from a prescriptive
phrase she places in the mouth of a nineteenth-century monk in Appendix E: "Woman in the 19th century should be a pure, chaste, holy being"
(WNC: 182).

But Fuller does not include the appendix merely to ironize her new
title. Mention of "Appendix E" occurs in her discussion of George Sand.
Fuller both praises Sand ("women, like Sand will speak now and cannot

[18] Fuller may have been willing to change her title because *Woman in the Nineteenth
Century* emphasized the issue of women inscribed in historical time. Having recently
traveled across the cultural boundary into the world of Native American cultures, she
attached a new value to the phrase "woman in the nineteenth century." The history with
which she was familiar had failed to prepare her for the condition of women in the alien
historical epoch of Native American life. History itself began to assume a new dimension
in her mind, and her new title allowed her to sustain a focus on that change.

be silenced") and qualifies that praise with the observation that Sand "shall not be the parent" of the new era (WNC: 65). She explains her judgment by observing that "those who would reform the world must show that they do not speak in the heat of wild impulse; their lives must be unstained by passionate error; they must be severe lawgivers to themselves" (WNC: 65).[19] In revising "The Great Lawsuit," Fuller adds a reference to Appendix E and the following: "They must be religious students of the divine purpose with regard to man. . . . Their liberty must be the liberty of law and knowledge" (WNC: 65).

These additional sentences, coupled with Fuller's new appendix, appear to blunt the radical edge of her feminism, but they do so only in part. The religious and legalistic piety that she summons is a rhetorical strategy to make palatable the incorporation of Fourier into the theoretical framework of the text.[20] As in *Summer on the Lakes*, she uses Fourier to help counteract the fatalistic language permeating discussions of women and their role in the nineteenth century as well as the discourses of fatality serving the dominant structures of power and control. But Sand, whose resistance to false institutions of society drew strength from Fourier's critique, also represented, through her unorthodox personal attachments, Fourier's most controversial theory about human sexuality. Thus, Fuller qualifies her appreciation of Sand in order to separate herself from the most dangerous aspect of Fourier's critique. The image proffered by the monk in Appendix E, with its emphasis on chastity, provides a counterexample to Sand and may be regarded less as a moralistic gesture than as an aid to Fuller's vision of feminist agency.

The phrase "liberty of law," with which Fuller criticizes Sand, deliberately echoes her wish expressed in the preface that women be given a chance to "ascertain what is for them the liberty of law." It would seem, of course, that she means to police Sand's activity by summoning the phrase "liberty of law." And, as we have seen, she means to do so in one very real sense. Although she only speaks euphemistically of Sand's

[19] For an excellent reading of Fuller's use of Sand in the two essays, see Julie Ellison, *Delicate Subjects*, chap. 8, "The Ethics of Feminist Discourse."

[20] Fuller's concern about her reader's reaction to the introduction of Fourier is particularly evident in another paragraph she inserts in the section on Sand. "The author, beginning like the man in assault upon bad institutions, and external ills, yet deepening the experience through comparative freedom, sees at last, that the only efficient remedy must come from individual character. These bad institutions, indeed, it may always be replied, prevent individuals from forming good character, therefore we must remove them. Agreed, yet keep steadily the higher aim in view. Could you clear away all the bad forms of society, it is vain, unless the individual begin to be ready for better. There must be a parallel movement in these two branches of life. And the rules left by Moses availed less to further the best life than the living example of one Messiah" (WNC: 64–65).

private life, implying that one must lead a life "unstained by passionate error" (WNC: 65), she cannot condone Sand's sexual promiscuity. But repeating "liberty of law" here also reveals how deftly she has prepared her reader for the larger concerns at issue in her critique of Sand. Sand's decision to smoke and to wear men's clothing and her insistence that she be addressed as "mon Frère" merely represented the largest extension of partial privileges and not something more fundamental and therefore radical. For Fuller, the "liberty of law" would be achieved only when such privileges were no longer gender-coded, enabling Sand to forget "whether she were brother or sister" (WNC: 63).

The Liberty of Chastity

Fuller's emphasis on chastity in Appendix E proves more complicated than it might at first appear. The focus of the monk's letter quoted there is important in that he continually emphasizes Woman's false dependency on men in society.

> So long as woman looks to man (or to society) for that which she needs, she will remain in an indigent state, for he himself is indigent of it, and as much needs it as she does.
> So long as this indigence continues, all unions or relations constructed between man and woman are constructed in indigence, and can produce only indigent results or unhappy consequences (WNC: 183).

The concept of chastity he endorses thus becomes a vehicle for breaking the familiar bonds of society. Fuller quotes from this letter in order to introduce the idea promoted by the monk that a radical change in all social bonds, and particularly in the marriage bond, is necessary. If his language has a conservative ring, it masks a deeper radicalism when he states, "It is not amended institutions, it is not improved education, it is not another selection of individuals for union, that can meliorate the sad result, but the *basis* of the union must be changed" (WNC: 183). In other words, the monk's feminism, his prescription for women in the nineteenth century, is drawn from a deep-seated belief that the most fundamental structure of relationships between people needed alteration. In this belief, he is clearly aligned with Sand, Fourier, *and* Fuller.

The paragraph Fuller next quotes from the monk's letter sounds like an endorsement of a position shared by Fourier and Sand: "If in the natural order Woman and Man would adhere strictly to physiological or natural laws, in physical chastity, a most beautiful amendment of the human race, and human condition, would in a few generations adorn the world" (WNC: 183). For both Fourier and Sand, the "natural laws" of men and women had been thwarted by society. According to their theory, allowing the natural passions to be expressed was crucial to the reorganization of society. What separates Fourier and Sand from the monk is the phrase "in physical chastity," a concept that in the view of Sand and Fourier had been a way of enforcing a powerful double standard demeaning to women. Fuller knew well enough how chastity could be used against women. In a letter to Georgiana Bruce she observed that, for the inmates at the Women's Prison in Sing Sing, New York, chastity was a "circumstance of condition" that "fallen" women apparently found meaningless.[21]

Yet it is clear from Fuller's treatment of these issues in her essay that she read "in physical chastity" in the monk's letter as an invitation to *reconsider* the prescriptions of society and not as an endorsement to return to them. She sees chastity as momentary protection against a host of ideological impositions upon men and women. Fuller does not believe that chastity will enable women to discover their essential attributes. Although she constantly asserts that the "electrical" and "intuitive" powers of women have been underdeveloped by society, she usually qualifies her assertions: "History jeers at the attempts of physiologists to bind great original laws by the forms which flow from them" (L: 43). She may invite an exploration of difference with this idea of chastity, but she also takes care to warn against the dangerous social restrictions that historically had developed from the rhetoric of difference.

By quoting from the monk's letter, in effect using it as a gloss for her new title, Fuller actively engages in a double strategy. The nineteenth-century woman may be a "pure, chaste, holy being" (WNC: 182) if given the opportunity to be chaste in the manner she implies: with the concept of "chastity" serving as a vehicle for the pursuit of the "liberty of law." Moreover, through Appendix E, she underscores her own focus on "celibacy as the great fact of the time" (L: 44). By using the idea of celibacy in this way, she attempts to redress the double standard that would assign chastity to a particular class of women while leaving men free to exploit one less fortunate. Her use of celibacy as the only fact, however provi-

---

[21] "You say few of these women have any feeling about chastity. Do you know how they regard that part of the sex, who are reputed chaste? Do they see any reality in it; or look on it merely as a circumstance of condition, like the possession of fine clothes? You know novelists are fond of representing them as if they looked up to their more protected sisters as saints and angels!" (LMF 3: 236).

sional, of the day promises an escape from the confusion set in motion by most discussions of woman's place in the culture.[22]

Conversational Sketches

Thus much of *Woman in the Nineteenth Century* is given over to clarifying both the difficulty and importance of establishing a viable feminist critique. Throughout the text, Fuller exhibits a powerful tendency toward a double strategy, shifting perspectives with nearly every theme she develops. Perhaps her most obvious example of this practice appears in the series of conversational sketches throughout the body of the text. Given her long interest in conversation, it is not surprising that the basic conversational structure around which she built "The Great Lawsuit" remains largely the same in *Woman*. And because the conversations invariably turn on the relationship of women with men, they consistently demonstrate the efficacy of her focus on celibacy.

"The Great Lawsuit" contains three conversational sketches, two between a man and a woman and one between two women. Fuller keeps these three sketches and adds a few more when she composes *Woman*. In the first sketch, which occurs early on in both versions, we are invited to listen in on a conversation between a husband and someone whose views are obviously similar to Fuller's.[23] The husband first tries to quell all discussion of feminist issues by insisting that he had contented his wife with "indulgences." His listener immediately inquires whether the man's wife "was satisfied with these indulgences" (WNC: 18). Pressed to admit that he had never asked his wife's opinion on the matter, the husband asserts that he would never consent to let his wife discuss such issues. Somewhat incredulous, his listener insists that it is not consent from the husband that is in question, but assent from the wife (WNC: 18). When the husband responds still more defensively by asserting his role as "head of the house," his interlocutor responds by challenging the efficacy of the paternalistic metaphors of "heart" and "head." The listener appears to have the last word in this conversational sketch, yet Fuller closes the account with the observation, "Thus vaguely are these

[22] Jeffrey Steele also sees something of the same quality in Fuller's emphasis on virginity. "Fuller begins to associate the image of virginity with . . . self-sufficiency." Of course, she goes on to show how complex the concept of self-sufficiency will be for women. See "Recovering the 'Idea of Woman': *Woman in the Nineteenth Century* and Its Mythological Background," chap. 5 in *The Representation of the Self*, p. 112.

[23] It is interesting to note that, of the three conversations, this is the only one Fuller refuses to call her own.

questions proposed and discussed at present" (WNC: 19). In other words, she refuses to endorse openly the position of the voice challenging patriarchy and "family union" (WNC: 18) even as she manages to show how each conversational turn between the two voices opens a potential site for critique.

Over the course of both "Lawsuit" and *Woman*, the reader learns just how completely Fuller endorses the position of the radical questioner in the first conversation. Certainly she has no difficulty showing her position in the second conversational sketch between a man and a woman which she uses in both versions.[24] Her willingness to expose her position in the second conversation derives in part from the way in which the doubts inscribed in the first are borne out by the rest of the essay. She tells her reader that she "overheard" a husband telling his wife that their daughter should not be educated because she would then be too smart to "find a husband" to "protect her" (L: 45). For the attentive reader, a terrible cycle presents itself: a woman is caught in a double bind, first through her father's "protection," which keeps her from developing her skills, and then through her future husband, who will likely refuse to consent to any deviation from her prescribed role as wife and mother. Unlike the first conversation, where Fuller attempts to show her reader that she will avoid taking sides, she makes clear her conviction that the father is misguided in attempting to protect his daughter. Thus she tells her women readers to "leave off asking" men to "look at both sides." She advises instead that women "retire within themselves" to "explore the groundwork of being till they find their peculiar secret" (WNC: 108).

The importance of Fuller's advice in both versions resides in the recognition that such a strategy is far more difficult than it might at first appear. This difficulty is wonderfully demonstrated in the conversational sketch placed close to the center of "The Great Lawsuit" and elaborated in *Woman*. Though only peripheral to the other conversations, Fuller is doubly central in this debate between a woman, whom she identifies as herself, and another thinly veiled autobiographical figure named Miranda. The initial version of the conversation in "The Great Lawsuit" has an air of debate. Yet the revised conversation in *Woman*

---

[24] In "The Great Lawsuit," Fuller uses this vignette toward the close, whereas in *Woman* she follows this sketch with a series of conversations, some drawn from historical contexts. Marie Urbanski points out that she probably borrowed historical examples from Lydia Maria Child's *History of the Condition of Women in Various Ages and Nations* (Boston: Otis, Broaders, 1838). See *Margaret Fuller's "Woman in the Nineteenth Century": A Literary Study of Form and Content, of Sources and Influence* (Westport, Conn.: Greenwood Press, 1980), 87. Fuller's decision not to credit Child may have reflected a desire to distance herself from the more conservative manner in which Child presented the history of women.

actually registers the various ideological frames through which one woman must shift in order to discover her "peculiar secret."

Fuller's character adopts something of a conservative posture and deliberately expresses surprise over some of the more radical claims put forth by Miranda. Yet her character, who also acts as a foil, enhances Miranda's position without seeming to adopt it. Miranda notes that her independence was fostered by her father's generous "bias" (L: 16) toward her, making independence a matter of good fortune, rather than— as the Fuller character suggests—of some inner resolution that "the restraints of the sex were insuperable only to those who think them so, or . . . noisily strive to break them" (L: 15).

The very fact that Fuller cannot rely on a stable and unified representation of her own experience to describe the benefits of self-reliance for women, that she relies instead on a fictional rendering of her selves, emphasizes not only the constructed nature of the self as a series of subject positions in debate, but also the peculiar agency dependent on an understanding of that construction.[25] Moreover, by inserting the dialogue into her text in such a way that the reader cannot really be sure when the conversation between Fuller and Miranda ends, the dialogue becomes coextensive with the larger text and argument of *Woman*. The double strategy embodied in Fuller's clever use of two versions of herself in conversation becomes the method she applies to the larger body of the essay.

The Cant of Culture

One of the most significant examples of this double method occurs in "Lawsuit," when Fuller addresses the "great moral law" that "All men

---

[25] It appears from Emerson's journals that Fuller had already engaged him in a conversation about the difficulty that the notion of self-reliance assumed when applied to women. He wrote, "In conversing with a lady it sometimes seems a bitterness & unnecessary wound to insist as I incline to, on this self sufficiency of man. There is no society, say I; there can be none. 'Very true but mournful,' replies my friend; we talk of . . . courses of action. But to women my paths are shut up and the fine women I think of who have had genius & cultivation who have not been wives but muses have something tragic in their lot & I shun to name them. Then I say Despondency bears no fruit. We do nothing whilst we distrust. It is ignoble . . . also to owe success to the coaxing & clapping of Society, to be told by the incapable, 'That's capital. Do some more.' That only is great that is thoroughly so from the egg, a god. Therefore I think a woman does herself an injustice who likens herself to any historical woman, who thinks that because Corinna or De Stael or M.M.E. do not satisfy the imagination and the serene Themis, none can, certainly not she. It needs that she feel that a new woman has a new as yet inviolate problem to solve" (JMN 5: 410).

are born free and equal" (L: 8). Even before her journey to the Midwest, she registered some concern about the possible corruption of this idea by writing, "We are tempted to implore these 'word-heroes' these word-Catos, word-Christs, to beware of cant above all things; to remember that hypocrisy is the most hopeless as well as the meanest of crimes" (L: 9). In so doing, she effectively locates American political rhetoric in a recognizable continuum, connecting it to Greek ("word-heroes"), Roman ("word-Catos"), and Christian ("word-Christs") doctrine. Nevertheless, she backs away from a wholesale condemnation of cant. For cant originally referred to the chant of beggars in Western civilization, the song of cultural outcasts whose ranks might well include women. With this in mind, the footnote she appends to this section is extremely suggestive: "Dr. Johnson's one piece of advice should be written on every door; 'Clear your mind of cant.' But Byron, to whom it was so acceptable, in clearing away the noxious vine, shook down the building too. Stirling's [sic] emendation is note-worthy, 'Realize your cant, not cast it off'" (L: 9). Through Sterling's insistence that we "realize [our] cant," Fuller advises her reader to be attentive to cant, not only as a defense against rhetoric, but also as a map for an important cultural dynamic. We must be wary of cant and seek its origin, read it as a poem gone bad, a political oration detached from its moral context. To "realize your cant," however, is to participate in a return to its source, to follow the chant of outcasts whose song Fuller celebrates. That women literally "can't" realize the world envisioned by the high rhetoric of the culture reveals how it is, indeed, always "cant" to them, even in its most robust formulation. Thus the imperative from Sterling recalls the imperative against Woman's participation in the social world. To conceive the pun is to send us back to a rhetorical meaning never intended, making the activity of return significant.

The conflation of cant and can't in "Lawsuit" had already sharpened Fuller's focus on the problematic if not duplicitous nature of the discourse of democracy. The cant of American culture, with its emphasis on progressive equality, had clearly created a conflict of powerful proportions. And after her trip to the Midwest, it was even more obvious to her that the inevitable aspect of "the great moral law" (L: 8) of America was leading to the inevitable demise of all those who did not fit its cultural expectation. So great was the sway of this cant that Fuller's autobiographical double in *Summer on the Lakes*, Mariana, actually finds herself succumbing to a fatal end. Because she is perceived by those around her as strange, or Other, Mariana, like the Native Americans Fuller sees around her, is doomed to perish in the narrative. But upon returning to the "Great Lawsuit" after her visit to the Midwest, Fuller embellishes the feminist conversation between her narrative self and her autobiographical double, Miranda, whose echo of Mariana is inescapable. Fuller adds certain specific statements to make the complaints of Miranda more apparent, particularly when describing how women are "overloaded with precepts by guardians, who think that nothing is so much to be dreaded for a woman as originality of thought or character" (WNC: 29). In other words, she emphasizes the dread of empowering those who are considered alien.

Another revision of this type involves the addition of a poem by Ben Jonson, whose phrase "manly soul" prompts a debate between the narrator and Miranda over its suitability in praise of women. Whereas the narrator, acting as one double for Fuller, suggests that Miranda may be "too fastidious in objecting to this," Miranda insists that *manly* is so invariably used "where a heroic quality is to be described" that she "would exchange these words for others of a larger sense" (WNC: 31). Although Fuller appears to let her reader choose sides in the debate, her decision to place Miranda's version of the poem on the frontispiece of the volume reveals her overall preference in this matter.[26]

Fuller also elaborates the little conversational scenario between Miranda and a well-meaning man, who in "The Great Lawsuit" tells Miranda that she "deserved in some star to be a man" (L: 16). In *Woman*, Fuller shows her friend's disbelief when Miranda responds that it is in fact "better now to be a woman" (W: 30): "He smiled incredulous. 'She makes the best she can of it,' thought he. 'Let Jews believe in the pride of Jewry, but I am of the better sort, and know better'" (WNC: 30). Fuller's decision to add the tinge of anti-Semitism to the man's response ("I am of the better sort") readily reflects how her trip to the Midwest enhanced her determination to explore the cant of culture. The man demonstrates how even sympathetic responses can depend on and promulgate hateful biases. And for Fuller the same difficulty is apparent in texts that hold themselves distinct from cant.

The additions to "The Great Lawsuit" made upon Fuller's return from the Midwest elaborate on the way in which the terms of valorization, words such as *manly* and *conquest*, are clues to the very structures entrapping women. In her effort to play this out, Fuller adds many more conversational sketches, sometimes borrowing them from legends and histories, and at other times drawing from her own personal experience. Most of the sketches tend to focus on the issue of marriage because—as her opening conversational sketch reveals—the relationship between

[26] That the same poem appears on the frontispiece of the *Memoirs of Margaret Fuller Ossoli*, with the original phrase "manly soul" restored, proves one of the productive ironies of Fuller's position.

husband and wife in marriage is the most obvious site of gender prescription. For her, as for Fourier, the discourse of marriage effectively
followed culture as a scene of overwhelming dominance. Yet she felt it
was imperative to avoid any alliance with those who were advocating a
dissolution of the bond. That she is drawn into a discussion of George
Sand in the middle of her section on marriage reveals how readily the
issue of marriage is nevertheless aligned in her mind with the prospect
of its disruption.

Fuller's sudden imposition of the issue of silence into her discussion
of marriage reveals a similar kind of recognition. In a passage that serves
as an important response to her opening conversational sketch between
the husband and the wife, she writes:

> I do not mean to imply that community of employment is essential to the
> union of husband and wife, more than to the union of friends. Harmony
> exists in difference, no less than in likeness, if only the same key-note
> govern both parts. Woman the poem, man the poet! Woman the heart, man
> the head! Such divisions are only important when they are never to be
> transcended. If nature is never bound down, nor the voice of inspiration
> stifled, that is enough. We are pleased that women should write and speak,
> if they feel need of it, from having something to tell; but silence for ages
> would be no misfortune, if that silence be from divine command, and not
> from man's tradition (WNC: 68).

Just as Fuller turns celibacy into a site of feminist resistance, a place from
which to critique the overwhelming forces moving women toward a
repressive and uncertain experience in marriage, she also transforms the
familiar attributes of silence. Of course, her focus on silence takes into
consideration the fears of her reader. An audience growing anxious over
the increased noise, or cant, of feminism might take comfort in her
appeals on behalf of silence. In the conversation with Miranda, the
Fuller character expresses concern over those who "noisily strive to
break" the restraints upon women. But in Fuller's deft handling, silence
is not strictly a vehicle for feminine oblivion; rather, it emerges as a form
of expression that escapes traditional channels of control. Because silence must be divinely inspired, the earlier phrase "Woman the poem,
man the poet!" takes on deeper political meaning. If Man insists on
being the poet, he is reduced in Fuller's reading to the noisy recorder of
poetry that has its counterpart in Woman's divine but silent revelation.
This formulation cuts to the most radical aspect of her treatment of
silence: it is not about creating more centuries of silence, but about the
generation of a reading of the silence already expressed. In this way, she

quietly appropriates silence for women and promotes it as a type of reading strategy.

Silence and Sirens

Fuller's practical application of this reading strategy occurs when she works to retrieve the silent history of women by recourse to classical myth. The full range of female characterization in ancient myth convinced her that "the Greeks knew more of real home intercourse, and more of woman than the Americans" (WNC: 199). Eurydice, who was reduced to oblivion by Orpheus when he attempted to retrieve her from Hades, functions as the most obvious symbol of silence and its retrievability in Fuller's work. Moreover, silence appears to take on ever more significance after the trip to the Midwest, as evidenced by the revisions in the various references to Orpheus and Eurydice. That the Native Americans lacked written histories probably accelerated Fuller's sense that unusual sources were needed in order to interpret the meaning of the lives of those outside the interpretive apparatus of civilization.

The initial rendering of Orpheus and Eurydice in "The Great Lawsuit" argues that previously unrecognized sources would answer the "needs of the age," and that a simple balancing of the old with the new sources was all that was needed. And Orpheus, accordingly, is described in glowing terms as a "lover" in "the highest sense" (L: 6). Though Fuller goes on to say that "not a few believe, and men themselves have expressed the opinion, that the time is come when Euridice is to call for an Orpheus, rather than Orpheus for Euridice . . . and that an improvement in the daughters will best aid the reformation of the sons of this age" (L: 7), the turn to Eurydice is nevertheless framed by her discussion of Orpheus. In her revisions for *Woman,* she alters her initial account of Orpheus, dropping the idea that he was a model lover and inserting in its place a narrative about Ulysses which works to deflate Orpheus as she originally conceived him.

The narrative Fuller adds is from Francis Bacon's interpretation of "the Syren coast" (WNC: 13), in which he compares the responses of Ulysses and Orpheus respectively in their passage by the famous Sirens. Described as a "wise" and "much experienced man," Ulysses is praised for his decision to listen to the song of the sirens in order to "understand its meaning" (WNC: 13). In recognition of his frailty, moreover, he orders himself bound as he passes. By contrast, Orpheus travels "unfettered, so absorbed in singing hymns to the gods that he could not even hear the sounds of degrading enchantment" (WNC: 13). In Fuller's view, then, the response of Ulysses is far more remarkable than that of Orpheus, for the responsiveness to the enchanting if "degrading" song of the sirens is no less than a realization of cant.[27] By contrast, Orpheus is oblivious to the voices of the sirens (the chant of beggars), and his self-absorption becomes a sign of his insensitivity. In the revised edition, therefore, the reference to Eurydice at this moment quietly condemns Orpheus for his failure to experience the voices. Just as turning back to Eurydice to see if she were following him becomes tantamount to turning his back on her forever, so silencing the voices of the sirens is tantamount to missing the voices of women in general. Ulysses then represents the positive response to culture and its cant; unlike most men, he listens to those who "can't," those who are outside the realm of the respectable and beyond the familiar domain of the law.

Fuller's revisions do more than reveal her conviction of the need for a feminist critique of culture; they also lay open to view a possible strategy for that activity. Both Eurydice and Ulysses become figures for a type of feminist reading, or agency, symbols of the route (or routes) that might be taken to recover "real home intercourse" (WNC: 199) or the value of concepts like silence and cant. In practical terms, the complex knot of Eurydice/Ulysses activates the aspect of Fuller's text which attempts to endorse more strongly than before the efficacy of a double strategy for feminism: one that seeks to enlarge the understanding of the culture by putting into question the very terms through which it is understood.

The figure of Ulysses listening to the song of "degrading enchantment" is also linked to the decision to include a more detailed discussion of prostitution in the revised essay. We know that Fuller began to work on her revisions around the same time that she began to receive a series of journals written by the inmates in the women's prison at Sing Sing. The reports came to her through her correspondence with the young Englishwoman, Georgina Bruce. Fuller appeared deeply moved by the reports from Bruce and sought to apply them to her revisions.[28] She entreated Bruce to send as much information as she could, explaining:

[27] Of course, Ulysses (Odysseus) is not only the master of rhetoric but also the complex figure of homecoming in Greek mythology. Fuller states her preference for the Ulysses of the *Odyssey* over Ulysses in the *Iliad* in a letter to William H. Channing. See LMF 3: 80.

[28] Fuller knew Bruce from Brook Farm and had introduced her to the matron of the women's prison, Eliza Farnham. In due time, Bruce found herself in Farnham's employ, an experience she eagerly shared with Fuller. See especially Fuller's response to some of the journals in her October 20, 1988, letter to Bruce (LMF 3: 235–36).

If you really think me capable of writing a Lehrjahre for women, (and I will confess that some such project hovers before me) nothing could aid me so much as the facts you are witnessing

For these women in their degradation express most powerfully the present wants of the sex at large. What blasphemes in them must fret and murmur in the perfumed boudoir, for a society beats with one great heart (LMF 3: 221–23).

The introduction of prostitution into Fuller's discussion results not only from her growing concern for a whole class of women whose misfortune she had become increasingly aware of (she visited Sing Sing in October 1844 before finishing her revisions on *Woman*), but also from her experience in the Midwest where a similar type of cultural fatality was at issue in the conflict between Anglo-American and Native American cultures. One of her most extended discussions of prostitution in *Woman* occurs in a reference to Mrs. Jameson, on whom she had depended in discussing marriage relations among Native Americans. Although she first describes Jameson as a sentimentalist, she emphasizes the boldness with which Jameson "speaks on the subject which refined women are usually afraid to approach, for fear of the insult and scurril jest they may encounter" (WNC: 118). Jameson represents an example of someone willing to stand up against the "daring with which the legislator and man of the world lifts his head beneath the heavens, and says [of prostitution] 'this must be; it cannot be helped; it is a necessary accompaniment of *civilization.*'" (WNC: 119).

The discourse, then, of the "legislator and man of the world," with its sense of inevitability, reiterates the discourse that had put into play the idea of the vanishing American. If Fuller could not bring herself to contend directly with that fatalistic way of framing things in *Summer on the Lakes*, she finds a means now to address the issue allegorically through prostitution. She heartily derides the claim that prostitution was the "necessary accompaniment of civilization" and summons examples from other cultures to make her point. Describing the polygamy of certain Asian cultures, an example that might inspire the Westerner to feel superior, she observes how the women in those relationships are at least respected, and therefore "not polluted in their own eyes" (WNC: 120). The same self-respect is emphasized in her description of the polygamous practices of Native American chiefs. Returning then to Western practice, where monogamy is stabilized by both a double standard and the inevitability of prostitution, she exposes the discourse at once racist and sexist on which the Anglo-American superiority depends.

"We are now in a transition state, and but few steps have yet been taken. From polygamy, Europe passed to the marriage *de convenance*. This was scarcely an improvement. An attempt was then made to substitute genuine marriage, (the mutual choice of souls inducing a permanent union), as yet baffled on every side by the haste, the ignorance, or the impurity of man" (WNC: 125).

Significantly, Fuller's reference to the "transition state" modifies her earlier statement in "The Great Lawsuit," which restricted this condition to Europe. The transition state now reflects a more general condition in Western culture. In making this change, she moves to endorse Fourier's position about the efficacy of crisis and transition as forms of cultural critique. Accordingly, she devotes considerable space to the "throng of symptoms" that "denote . . . a crisis" (WNC: 108) in the lives of women, in order to disclose the very material through which change must occur.

Not surprisingly, Fuller supports this focus on transition through references to Frederica Hauffe, the Seeress of Prevorst, on whom she had elaborated in *Summer*. She first referred to the Seeress in "Lawsuit," where she hinted that the Seeress could be used to show the important and undeveloped intuitive powers of women. She started in "Lawsuit" with the assumption that the Seeress could represent a site of subversion and critique because her "electrical" (L: 38) nature was prophetic, but that argument was soon complicated in *Summer* by the recognition that the Seeress represented a cultural bias alternately inimical to women and others. When viewed as an example of Western civilization *in extremis*, the condition to which the Seeress succumbs has virtually the same violent effect on her that the rhetoric of prophecy would have upon the alien Native American cultures. Fuller deals with this problem in her return to *Woman* by making a careful distinction between the undeveloped talent of the Seeress ("What might have been a gradual and gentle disclosure of remarkable powers" [WNC: 95]) and the social pressures that eventually marred and deformed her powers. In other words, she makes a point of separating the potential site of critique opened to view by the mesmeric qualities of the Seeress from the damaging influence of the dominating culture with which they are ultimately complicit. For Fuller, the disease that overcomes the Seeress is the direct result of an "unsuitable marriage" that is defined as the "inevitable destiny of woman" (WNC: 95). This argument shifts the focus a bit from the analysis in *Summer*, where the mesmeric trances of the Seeress are described as strategic responses to her unwanted marriage. In *Woman* Fuller emphasizes the active way in which the culture forces the Seeress to squander her gift. And to make her point she inserts the phrase "inevitable destiny of woman," (WNC: 95) suggesting the relationship between the hostile forces working against the Seeress and the forces transforming the lives of Native Americans.

In *Woman*, then, Fuller attempts to recover some of the efficacy of the electrical nature of woman (the site of crisis as noted by Mesmer, and the place of transition as understood by Fourier) by observing how the Seeress would sometimes "behold the true character of the person through the mask of his customary life. (Sometimes she saw a feminine form behind the man, sometimes the reverse)" (WNC: 104). In so doing, the Seeress is praised in *Woman* for her ability to see through the "masks" of "customary life" (WNC: 104). Her value as a critic lies in her ability to dismiss the familiar ideological frame through which human interaction takes place in Western culture.

Having thus distinguished the latent skills of the Seeress and the cultural imperatives that militate against their fulfillment, Fuller continues to reiterate her faith in a double strategy to address that problem. As we have seen, her terms for such doubling are multiple throughout *Woman*, including Eurydice and Ulysses, the narrator and Miranda, Sand and the monk, and the Muse and Minerva. The Muse represents the "unimpeded clearness of the intuitive powers" associated with the Seeress, and Minerva represents the power that can intervene against still stronger cultural barriers.

Although Fourier's understanding of the transition state enabled Fuller to develop her thoughts about the subversive powers of the Seeress, she had used only indirect references in *Summer* to make his influence clear. Her recognition that the power of critique represented by the Seeress is only latent in the culture compels her to acknowledge Fourier more directly. In a very real sense, Fourier functions as the Minerva element in Fuller's endorsement of the equally important idea that the material conditions of life can radically alter one's way of thinking about things, and indeed, one's radicalism. Certainly, the material conditions of the Seeress's life came to alter her way of viewing the world. The most important demonstration of this recognition on Fuller's part comes in the section of her text where she encodes another double strategy by contrasting Fourier with Goethe.

> Fourier says, As the institutions, so the men! All follies are excusable and natural under bad institutions.
> Goethe thinks, As the man, so the institutions! There is no excuse for ignorance and folly. A man can grow in any place, if he will.
> Ay! but Goethe, bad institutions are prison walls and impure air that make him stupid, so that he does not will.
> And thou, Fourier, do not expect to change mankind at once, or even "in

three generations" by arrangement of groups and series, or flourish of trumpets for attractive industry. If these attempts are made by unready men, they will fail.

Yet we prize the theory of Fourier no less than the profound suggestion of Goethe. Both are educating the age to a clearer consciousness of what man needs, what man can be, and a better life must ensue (WNC: 111–12).

In envisioning a correlation between Fourier and Goethe, Fuller continues her earlier mediation between liberty and law, Eurydice and Ulysses, Sand and the monk. Moreover, the important qualities she emphasized in her account of conversations between women, including the conversation between the narrator and Miranda, now become boldly refigured in her address to Fourier and Goethe. And much like the conversations between Miranda and Fuller (or, for that matter, those between Günderode and Arnim), no resolution between the two positions is intended. Instead a provisional relation is sought, one that embodies a type of double strategy rather than a dialectical sublation.

Fuller's discussion of Goethe's novel *Wilhelm Meister's Apprenticeship and Wandering Years* demonstrates something of this process. She notes that Goethe provided a variety of female characters who teach the reader how a new understanding of relation between men and women might be developed. The women are important for their diversity and for their ability to interact with Wilhelm without also being subsumed by him. Their contribution to the relationship resides in their ability to remain "unrelated" (WNC: 116). The large array of female characterization in this particular work leads Fuller to align Goethe's text with her feminist advocacy of the Muse, or Woman's underdeveloped nature. At the same time, she finds in Goethe's text a correspondence between this "model school" and the "plans of Fourier" (WNC: 117). Although she tells her reader that her elaboration of this idea will occur in "some other place" (WNC: 117), she hints at her understanding of the association when she refers to Fourier's plan to provide women with a "great variety of employments" (WNC: 160). Through such a material focus, she seems to suggest, a variety of female subject positions might flourish and inform an important transformation of Western culture. In the process, both Minerva and Muse are summoned to the account.

Emerson as Muse

In *Summer* Fuller's initial public support of Fourier appeared to represent an embellishment of her argument with Emerson about social reform, where the voice of self-poise clearly parodied his position. Her understanding of his response to Fourier, however, has now developed to the point where he no longer stands as counterpoint to Fourier. Her effort to show the relationship between Goethe and Fourier reveals her own growing understanding of the delicate but significant bond between writer and social critic which she had begun to find in Emerson's work and means here to portray. And reading *Second Series* appears to have encouraged this shift in her thinking.

Critics often comment on Fuller's letter to William H. Channing on November 17, 1844, shortly after finishing *Woman in the Nineteenth Century*, where she reports of the "delightful glow" she experienced and her sense that she had "put a good deal of [her] true life in it" (LMF 3: 241). They rarely note how on that same day she wrote a letter to Emerson in which she talks of completing the "never-sufficiently-to-be-talked-of pamphlet." Her second letter complicates our understanding of her sense of elation, since it also discloses that she had been reading *Second Series* carefully as she "spun [her] thread as long and many-colored as was pleasing." Although she writes that she found a few objections to his work ("Two or three cavils"), she also makes her admiration for the work clear by claiming that it would be a "companion" throughout her life (LMF 3: 243).

Emerson's famous hesitation in *Second Series*, which included a call for a radical reconsideration of the frame through which all social reform could be advanced, seems to have made more sense to Fuller after her visit to the Midwest. With her revisions of "The Great Lawsuit" underway, she began to see a powerful theoretical reason for some of Emerson's prudence, since his insistence on a self-questioning posture was scarcely heeded in the clash of Western and Native American cultures. Of course, her tolerance of his skepticism was based on the knowledge that he could act more directly on principle when he felt it necessary, as in his emancipation address, published independently of *Second Series*. She tried to unite both methods in *Woman*, advocating change based on a recognized understanding of the culture and, at the same time, promoting a radical inquiry into the very conditions and terms of that understanding.

Fuller was probably grateful, moreover, to see Emerson's address to Minerva in "Manners," which drew its power from the conversations they had been having, many of them around the reconsideration of Woman's role in Fourier's critique. (Indeed, she would not have been mistaken to interpret his use of Minerva as an acknowledgment of her representation of Minerva in "The Great Lawsuit.") *Second Series* made clear to Fuller that some fulfillment of Fourierism was itself inevitable, particularly since "Experience" had demonstrated Emerson's deep pre-occupation with Fourier. In any case, *Woman in the Nineteenth Century* suggests that she was developing a reading strategy that would eventually influence Emerson's position on Fourier. It was a strategy that, like the passage of Ulysses by the sirens, attempted to realize the cant of culture.

6
Reading before Marx:
Fuller and the *New-York Daily Tribune*

The Newspaper promises to become daily of more importance, and if the increase of size be managed with equal discretion, to draw within itself the [audience] of all other literature of the day.
—Margaret Fuller, *New-York Daily Tribune*, September 24, 1845

Fuller was well known in her lifetime as one of the most prodigious readers of her day. Perceiving the critical edge a knowledge of literature and history had given her, she regarded reading as an important site for significant social change. Yet her visit to the Midwest in 1843, where she saw the terrible effects of Western civilization on Native American cultures, rendered her faith in reading problematic until she found a way to incorporate the thinking of the popular but controversial Charles Fourier into her work. Of course, Fourier's vision of social change depended on the role given to women in society. Accordingly, much of Fuller's *Woman in the Nineteenth Century* explored what Alice Jardine has called the idea of Woman as "reading effect."[1] Still, it was only at the close of 1844, when she began to write for Horace Greeley's *New-York Daily Tribune*, that Fuller actually began to elaborate a theory of reading and social change—one that has been overlooked by even the most discerning of her critics.

Greeley's paper, which he founded in 1841 with the hope of raising the "masses," matched Fuller's interests beautifully. Determined from the beginning to avoid the sensationalism of the average New York newspaper (there were twenty-one at the time), he created a literary section for the front page.[2] Initially Henry Raymond, the future founder

[1] Here I refer to Jardine's description of the encounter between two "reading effects," found in her *Gynesis: Configurations of Woman and Modernity* (Ithaca: Cornell University Press, 1985), 31–49; see especially the chapter entitled "The Woman-in-Effect."
[2] The early editions of the *Tribune* were only four pages long, the last two pages covered with public notices and advertising. Political and national news filled the second page, until the Mexican war, when some of the dramatic headlines produced by the war suddenly shifted to the front page. For a good description of the newspaper see Catherine Casto Mitchell, "Horace Greeley's Star: Margaret Fuller's *New York Tribune* Journalism, 1844–1846," Ph.D. diss., University of Tennessee, Knoxville, 1987. See also Wilma [Robb] Ebbitt, "The Critical Essays of Margaret Fuller from the *New-York Tribune* with Introduction and Notes," Ph.D. diss., Brown University, 1943. Ebbitt's appendix lists the names and dates of all of Fuller's essays in the paper.

of the *New York Times,* handled the literary material but then moved on to a more lucrative position with the *Courier and Enquirer* in 1843. Greeley had encouraged Albert Brisbane to develop a column on the social vision of Charles Fourier for this same section of the paper, establishing a precedent for the mix of social and literary concerns that would soon distinguish Fuller's columns. Brisbane's dull translation of Fourier's satiric wit, however, brought more boredom than edification to the paper and his column eventually dropped from its pages. As a result, Greeley began looking for another writer who could assume responsibility for the work handled by Raymond and Brisbane. Molley Greeley, during an extended visit to New England, had been impressed with Fuller's ability, and she suggested to her husband that he give the job to Fuller. The critical and literary skills exhibited in *Summer on the Lakes,* including the provocative allusions to Fourier, made it easy for Horace Greeley to heed his wife's advice. Already familiar with her work as editor of the *Dial,* Greeley greatly admired Fuller's writing in *Summer,* calling it "unequaled" as "one of the clearest and most graphic delineations, ever given, of the Great Lakes, of the Prairies."[3]

Greeley expected a great deal from Fuller—she shared editing tasks with him and two other members of his fledgling staff—and she received fair compensation for her labor as one of the first women to work as a salaried newspaper writer. She apparently wrote some essays anonymously, but while in New York she signed nearly 250 with a large asterisk (or "star" as Greeley was fond of saying, often calling her "the 'star' of the *New-York Tribune*").[4] If Greeley occasionally complained about the time she spent in writing her columns, he greatly admired her work, and he insisted that she continue her affiliation with the paper as a foreign correspondent when she embarked on a trip to England and Europe in late 1846.

Without a doubt, Fuller's fascinating columns helped the paper achieve a respectable readership. By the end of the decade the *Tribune* had gone from being a competitive local newspaper to one of national and international status, so much so that when invited only a year after Fuller's death to write a column for the paper, Karl Marx welcomed the opportunity to do so, calling it the "foremost English language Ameri-

---

[3] Greeley's comment continues, "and of the receding barbarism, and the rapidly advancing, but rude, repulsive, semi-civilization, which were contending with most unequal forces for the possession of those rich lands." MMF, 2: 152–53.

[4] She signed with an asterisk to make it clear that someone other than Greeley was composing the literary section of the paper. In "Horace Greeley's Star," Mitchell argues that in her role as editor of the literary section Fuller may have authored a number of pieces without signing them (pp. 53–58).

can newspaper."[5] From December 1844 until August 1846, Fuller filled the pages of the *Tribune* with an enormous array of essays, including reviews of books, concerts, and operas; translations from foreign newspapers; and a generous range of social commentary. Later in 1846, after Fuller began her duties as foreign correspondent for the paper, her dispatches from England and France continued to provide commentary on social and cultural matters. From 1847, when she traveled to Italy, until 1850, her letters to the *Tribune* focused almost exclusively on that country's gathering national revival, the risorgimento.

Because scholars have assumed that the letters from Italy formed a rough outline of the lost manuscript of Fuller's history of the Italian Revolution, they have tended to overvalue them. According to Larry Reynolds, the most recent commentator on this material, the dispatches from Italy demonstrate "more artistry and power than any of her other writings," including her first *Tribune* letters from England and France, because they focus "upon the fate of the socialist republican cause in Europe" and are "polished, objective and elevated."[6]

Reynolds's admiration for the Italian correspondence rests most firmly on the consistency of Fuller's political position, which he describes as a "new ideological commitment." Had Reynolds addressed her earliest *Tribune* work, however, he would have seen more continuity in her thinking; at the very least, he would have found considerable evidence that her critique of the United States and her interest in socialism were already quite advanced while she was still in New York.[7] Bell

[5] Karl Marx, *On America and the Civil War*, vol. 2 of *The Karl Marx Library*, ed. and trans. Saul K. Padover (New York: McGraw-Hill, 1972), 2: xv. Because his English was not yet polished enough, Marx asked Engels to write the first set of articles for the *Tribune* (*Revolution and Counter-Revolution in Germany*), which he did under Marx's name. Marx's first article for the *Tribune*, "The Elections in England.—Tories and Whigs," appeared in August 1852, though Marx at first depended on Engels to translate his work. See *Karl Marx, Friedrich Engels: Collected Works*, 46 vols., ed. and trans. Richard Dixon et al. (London: Lawrence, 1975–88), 2: 629. See also Padover, "Introduction," in *On America and the Civil War*.

[6] Larry Reynolds, *European Revolutions and the American Literary Renaissance* (New Haven: Yale University Press, 1988), 61, 77.

[7] Ibid., 67. Reynolds cites Fuller's eighteenth letter, "written to appear in the United States on New Year's Day, 1848" (p. 65), where she "uses the European scene as the basis for a severe indictment of American society," as an example of her shifting ideological focus (p. 65). Yet she had chosen New Year's Day (and other notable holidays, including Christmas and the Fourth of July) to critique American society from the very first. See, for example, the following articles from the *Tribune*: "Thanksgiving," Dec. 12, 1844; "Christmas," Dec. 25, 1844; "New Year's Day," Jan. 1, 1845; "St. Valentine's Day—Bloomingdale Asylum for the Insane," Feb. 22, 1845; "The Fourth of July," July 4, 1845; "1st January, 1846," Jan. 1, 1846; "Colonel McKenney's New Book upon the Indians," July 4, 1846; "Memoirs, Official and Personal by T. L. McKenney," July 8, 1846. See especially "First of August, 1845" (the anniversary of the emancipation of slaves in the West Indies), where she mentions Emerson's address of the previous year.

Gale Chevigny does review some of Fuller's early *Tribune* writings, noting her habit of translating accounts of political and social events abroad from immigrant and foreign newspapers. In August 1845, for example, Fuller translated a column from the German immigrant newspaper *Deutsche Schnellpost*, entitled "The Social Movement in Europe," which called for an end to the conflicts between Marx and Ruge in Germany and included some passages from Engels's recently published *Condition of the Working Class in England*.[8] This column was one of the earliest English notices of Marx and Engels in the United States.

Although she acknowledges Fuller's radical disposition in these early pages of the *Tribune*, Chevigny finds troubling the unpredictable nature of Fuller's rhetorical position, calling her work "naive" and "condescending" as often as she calls it "moving or advanced." In this way, she dismisses the large bulk of Fuller's *Tribune* work as "apprentice exercises" for her later "more informed, critical, and independent role of foreign correspondent."[9] Like Reynolds, Chevigny is obviously in search of a unified political perspective in Fuller's writing, which, according to Chevigny, only begins to occur in the last Italian letters. Though she is somewhat more attentive to the earlier *Tribune* writing than Reynolds, Chevigny is no less impatient with the nature of that material. She agrees with Reynolds that Fuller's "new sociopolitical concerns" in her Italian letters resulted in "the best writing she ever did," but she slights the enormous range of Fuller's work in those early years.[10]

The position advanced by Chevigny and Reynolds is based on the conviction that the experience of Europe constituted an epistemological break in Fuller's thinking. In its crudest terms, Reynolds and Chevigny articulate that break as a departure from the aestheticism of Emerson and all that he came to represent in her thinking.[11] For Reynolds, the

[8] Bell Gale Chevigny, *The Woman and the Myth: Margaret Fuller's Life and Writings* (New York: Feminist Press, 1976), 294. Fuller translated the title of the article to "On the Situation of the Laboring Class in England" (*Tribune*, Aug. 5, 1845). *The Condition of the Working Class in England* was first published in German in March 1845 in Leipzig. In *Karl Marx, Friedrich Engels: Collected Works*, the *Schnellpost* is described by the editor in the index of periodicals as an "organ of the German moderate democratic emigres in the USA published twice weekly in New York from 1843 to 1851. In 1848 and 1851 its editor was Karl Heinzen; in 1851 Arnold Ruge was also on its editorial board" (2: 750). Marx mentions the *Schnellpost* often in his early writings, most notably in "The Great Men of Exile," where he argues that Karl Heinzen "very quickly manage[d] to ride the New York *Schnellpost* to death" (2: 279), suggesting that the earlier paper from which Fuller drew her material was more radical.
[9] Chevigny, *Woman and the Myth*, p. 292.
[10] Reynolds, *European Revolutions*, p. 61. Chevigny supplies brief selections from only ten essays written between 1844 and early 1847.
[11] Julie Ellison also finds a continuity of argument and insight in Fuller's early and later career. See her *Delicate Subjects: Romanticism, Gender, and the Ethics of Understanding* (Ithaca: Cornell University Press, 1990), 217–98.

European tour convinced Fuller to reject Emerson's belief in the "primacy of individualism" and the "ineffectiveness of cooperative reform." Such an argument necessarily restricts the range and scope of her extended conversation with Emerson, reducing their thinking to a type of caricature. To say that Emerson advances the "primacy of individualism" in his work overlooks his struggle with the same concept.[12] And to argue that Fuller resisted the promise of association held out by advocates of Fourier in North America greatly diminishes her fascination with socialism and the part that interest played in Emerson's thinking about these issues. Emerson's ambivalence toward reform was genuine, on the evidence of *Second Series*, particularly as he understood the similarities between the unique attributes of his relationship with Fuller and those at the center of Fourierism. Nor should we forget that her first column for the *Tribune* was a review of the *Second Series* and an ambiguous one at that. Yet it would be wrong to read this review as her parting gesture to New England and Emerson's influence. He plays a much more interesting role in her *Tribune* writing. Indeed, that she would fill Brisbane's old column with a review of the *Second Series* highlights her sense of the way in which the discourse of Fourier had permeated Emerson's text as well. In fact, she so internalizes Emerson's account of the "strange alternation of attraction and repulsion" (CW 3: 61) in the relationship he offers in his essay "Character" that she uses it as a model of social interaction in her *Tribune* articles, noting at one point that the "game of society" is the most "fascinating where the attractions and repulsions, shocks and balances alternate through a sufficient number of peers."[13]

Like Reynolds, Chevigny contends that Fuller's experience in Europe gave her what she needed to repudiate Emerson. According to Chevigny, her change entails a rejection of the "specialness and autonomy of American destiny" in favor of a "multiple and morally dialectic" sense of the culture which acknowledges how "nations change under the pressure of challenges posed them by other societies."[14] But as we have seen on more than one occasion, the idea of "multiple and morally dialectic" change is evident long before Fuller's trip to Europe: it begins with her

[12] Reynolds, *European Revolutions*, p. 57. The recent work of Sacvan Bercovitch would seem to support Reynolds in this emphasis on Emerson's slow movement toward an "antipathy to socialism." Bercovitch largely bases his argument on random quotes selected from Emerson's journals. But an equal number of quotes from the same journals demonstrate that Emerson remains far more ambiguous in his relationship to socialism. Moreover, as I show in Chapter 4, his references to Fourier become far more positive in tone. See Bercovitch, "Emerson, Individualism, and the Ambiguities of Dissent," *The South Atlantic Quarterly* 89 (Summer 1990): 623–62.

[13] "Items of Foreign Gossip," *Tribune*, Aug. 27, 1845.

[14] Chevigny, *Woman and the Myth*, p. 376.

early interest in translation and the study of comparative literature and develops steadily from the moment she encounters the clash of Anglo- and Native American cultures during her trip to the Midwest. Although her influence over Emerson on this issue was never as strong as she might have liked, it was considerably stronger than she sometimes imagined it to be.[15] At the same time, she never wholly relinquished her faith in the unique destiny of the United States, a faith she shared with Emerson, even as disappointments with the culture abounded.

The unfortunate result of the criticism that seeks to establish Fuller's political credentials has been a crude thematization of her writing in New York and her early dispatches from England and France. In the process, the real contribution of these writings, their elaboration of a radical theory of reading in those pages, has remained obscure. Conceding that she did in fact write about such controversial matters as prostitutes, Native Americans, slavery, insanity, prison reform, poverty, and growing class conflict, Chevigny and Reynolds manage to dismiss the manner in which she wrote, attributing her style to her old preoccupation with aesthetic concerns. In effect, both critics are impatient with the enormous range of book and cultural reviews that fill her early column. Yet her aesthetic concerns are precisely what lend complexity to her approach to social issues in the early *Tribune* work; her skill as a reader, particularly her interest in literary discourse and the problematic of translation, gives her an enlarged sense of the vast network of ideological discourse through which we all function. These concerns help her to elaborate a radical theory of reading for the culture, one meant to develop a form of political agency that would include a more diverse group of people than those who traditionally hold power.

Clearly, we have discovered another way to frame our understanding of Fuller's *Tribune* work. Instead of viewing the material written early in New York as her transition period (a position that reinforces the idea that she would require the liberating factors of Europe to gain true political insight), we should see them as essays dedicated to the transitional state of the culture. What in Reynolds' opinion constitutes a structural weakness in Fuller's writing, her tendency to cover a "multitude of topics related only by the fact that they happen to engage her interest at the time,"[16] may instead be seen to comprise a more sophisticated political strategy, one designed to observe the multiple fronts through which real social change must be negotiated. As we will see, this strategy

---

[15] Emerson's decision to translate Dante's *Vita Nuova* merits serious consideration on this score. His relationship with Fuller is very much tied up with this decision. See JMN 8: 369.

[16] Reynolds, *European Revolutions*, p. 63.

becomes articulated through Fuller's constant return in her writing to the political efficacy of a certain type of reading.

My interpretation of Fuller's early *Tribune* writing is aided by the distinction between political hegemony and domination developed by the Italian theorist Antonio Gramsci, one of the first political theorists to move away from the limited understanding of ideology as false consciousness.[17] Against the strain in Marxist thinking that emphasizes inexorable economic forces, Gramsci emphasizes the importance of cultural and intellectual factors. In a move anticipating Althusser, he defines ideology as the horizon "on which men move, acquire consciousness of their position, [and] struggle."[18] This idea allows him to posit that an ideological consensus, aptly described as hegemonic activity, may be reached among various classes. He believes that the success of any revolutionary idea depends on such hegemonic activity. This complex process of consent, a process working through a variety of intellectual and educational channels, distinguishes hegemonic power from the power of domination essentially realized through the "coercive machinery of the state."[19] At the same time, the concept of "hegemony" also helps to explain the success of certain counterrevolutionary forces. Gramsci's analysis shows how an uneven consensual process can result in a "passive revolution" and the ascendancy to power of political reactionaries. Chantal Mouffe supplies a useful description of the two methods of hegemony that Gramsci develops:

[17] Gramsci's thinking has recently received considerable attention, particularly in its relation to Louis Althusser's work on ideology. Both Gramsci and Althusser viewed ideology as the inevitable medium through which all social organization occurred. Unlike Gramsci, who believed that some form of agency could emerge through ideological formations, Althusser insisted that agency could only occur through the development of a theory of ideology, which he called "science" (See his "On the Materialist Dialectic" and "Marxism and Humanism," in *For Marx*, trans. Ben Brewster [London: New Left/Verso, 1986], 161–247). Still, Althusser's equivocal view of art as somehow outside the realm of ideology yet in a tandem relationship with both ideology and science bears an important affinity to Gramsci's notion of hegemony. At this provisional intersection I situate my reading of Fuller. For more on Gramsci and ideology see Chantal Mouffe, "Hegemony and Ideology in Gramsci," in *Gramsci and Marxist Theory*, ed. Chantal Mouffe (London: Routledge, 1979). For an interesting reading of Althusser's position on science and art see Michael Sprinker, *Imaginary Relations: Aesthetics and Ideology in the Theory of Historical Materialism* (London: Verso, 1987).

[18] Gramsci did not reverse the classic Marxist axiom that base determines consciousness by returning to the idealist notion that consciousness determines everything, as some have averred; rather, he made a subtle analysis of the way in which a material and economic base might determine "what forms of consciousness are possible." See Joseph V. Femia, *Gramsci's Political Thought: Hegemony, Consciousness, and the Revolutionary Process* (London: Oxford University Press, 1981), 121. Quote from Gramsci is from *Prison Notebooks*, quoted in Chantal Mouffe, "Hegemony and Ideology in Gramsci," p. 185.

[19] Femia, *Gramsci's Political Thought* p. 24.

If hegemony is defined as the ability of one class to articulate the interest of other social groups to its own, it is now possible to see that this can be . . . articulated so as to neutralise them and hence to prevent the development of their own specific demands, or else they can be articulated in such a way as to promote their full development leading to the final resolution of the contradictions which they express.[20]

Rather intriguingly, much of Gramsci's theory of hegemony develops through his analysis of the risorgimento, the historical event Fuller analyzes in her late *Tribune* dispatches. Her assessment of the political transformations in Italy tends to support Gramsci's later evaluation. For Gramsci, the movement begun in 1848 by Joseph Mazzini (and what would become the Action Party) failed to displace the more dangerous Moderate Party because it was too restricted in its approach. Confined largely to the upper and middle classes, the hegemonic activity eventually advanced by the Moderate Party "became merely an aspect of the function of domination."[21] For her part, Fuller is also suspicious of Vincenzo Gioberti and the members who would make up the so-called Moderate Party criticized by Gramsci. And although her support for Mazzini is strong, she understands what Gramsci later fully elaborates when she criticizes Mazzini's failure to pay attention to a host of social issues. "Mazzini sees not all: he aims at political emancipation; but he sees not, perhaps would deny, the bearing of some events, which even now begin to work their way. Of this more anon, but not to-day nor in the small print of *The Tribune*. Suffice it to say, I allude to that of which the cry of Communism, the systems of Fourier, etc. are but forerunners."[22]

This parallel between Fuller and Gramsci's thinking about the Italian Revolution also serves to confirm Chevigny's analysis of her later *Tribune* writing. But Fuller's analysis drew its sophistication from the fact that she had long been developing contact between various sectors of her society, including its subaltern constituents. Though her work in this area is uneven, all of her *Tribune* activity worked to construct a new consensus for an expansive hegemony. The terms Mouffe uses to describe Gramsci's notion of hegemonic transformation fit the method that

[20] Chantal Mouffe, "Hegemony and Ideology in Gramsci," p. 183.

[21] Antonio Gramsci, *Selections from the Prison Notebooks*, trans. and edited Q. Hoare and G. Nowell Smith (New York: International Publishers, 1971), 60, 76. See also Walter L. Adamson, *Hegemony and Revolution: A Study of Antonio Gramsci's Political and Cultural Theory* (Berkeley: University of California Press, 1980), 185–96. Gramsci quoted in Femia, *Gramsci's Political Thought*, p. 48.

[22] Letter 24, *At Home and Abroad, or, Things and Thoughts in America and Europe by Margaret Fuller Ossoli*, ed. Arthur B. Fuller (1856; rpt. Port Washington: Kennikat, 1971), 320. This letter appeared in the *Tribune* on June 15, 1848.

Fuller herself defines in the *Tribune*: "The objective of ideological struggle is not to reject the system and all its elements but to rearticulate it, to break it down to its basic elements and then to sift through past conceptions to see which ones, with some changes of content, can serve to express the new situation. Once this is done the chosen elements are finally rearticulated into another system."[23] In her *Tribune* work, Fuller develops a theory of reading that follows this same pattern. Moreover, she adopted within her columns what Gramsci would later call a "war of position" rather than a "frontal attack" in order to accomplish this transformation in her audience.[24] Aware that the issues with which she deals are often highly volatile, she chooses to engage in a protracted trench warfare. The consistency of her goal may be obscured by the enormous variety of her approach, yet the efficacy of such a strategy has gained considerable support among cultural critics who have begun to observe the radical dispersion of power in the variety of discourses through which we make our daily negotiations. Fuller's critical writings reveal an awareness of the complex overlay of ideological frames through which we are forced to read our lives, as well as a willingness to shift those frames in order to make some conversation or translation between them possible.

Realize Your Cant

Two years after Fuller's death in 1850, Marx began to write his own column for the *Tribune*. This provocative coincidence was undoubtedly

[23] Mouffe, "Hegemony and Ideology in Gramsci," p. 192. This type of strategy is everywhere apparent in Fuller's *Tribune* work. Her opening paragraphs of "The Rich Man—An Ideal Sketch" (Feb. 6, 1846) provide just one example:

"All benevolent persons, whether deeply thinking on, or only deeply feeling, the woes, difficulties and dangers of our present social system, are agreed either that great improvements are needed, or a thorough reform.

"Those who desire the latter, include the majority of thinkers. And we ourselves, both from personal observation and the testimony of others, are convinced that a radical reform is needed. Not a reform that rejects the instruction of the past, or asserts that God and man have made mistakes till now. We believe that all past developments have taken place under natural and necessary laws, and that the Paternal Spirit has at no period forgot his children, but granted to all ages and generations their chances of good to balance inevitable ills. —We prize the Past; we recognize it as our parent, our nurse and our teacher, and we know that for a time the new wine required the old bottles to prevent its being spilled upon the ground.

"Still we feel that the time is come which not only permits, but demands, a wider statement, and a nobler action. The aspect of society presents mighty problems, which must be solved by the soul of Man 'divinely intending' itself to the task, or all will become worse instead of better, and ere long the social fabric totter to decay."

[24] See Mouffe, "Hegemony and Ideology in Gramsci."

behind Chevigny's traditional Marxist approach to Fuller, with its emphasis on Fuller's growing interest in material and economic concerns. But such a focus also reduces the elaborate complexity of her early *Tribune* writing and its unusual anticipation of the theoretical revisions now in play in social theory. In looking over the enormous range of writing she produced from 1844 until her death, one could argue that she prepared a space for Marx even as she exceeded him in framing certain reading formations that he would find difficult to pursue. Such an argument must consider both the problematic split between aesthetic and political concerns besetting much of our reading and the way that feminism can supply an important conversation between the two.

Hired in 1844 to review books and artistic public performances, Fuller immediately extended the review format to include her reading of the culture. And, as with her other work, she came to invest the reader with enormous significance. Because it was now the space where those who had been denied access to the dominant forms of power could reassert themselves, reading became the privileged site of cultural change. The fact that she was a woman, then, certainly enhanced her interest in reading. Moreover her rigorous training in several classical languages— unusual for most American women of the day—had widened her access to history. Yet the clash of historical sensibilities that she experienced in the Midwest had the stronger effect of setting into motion a transvaluation of the historical itself. For Fuller, the historical became radically enmeshed in reading, and her *Tribune* articles were the proving ground for this thesis.

Fuller began her work for the *Tribune* just after completing *Woman in the Nineteenth Century*, and naturally she sustained an interest in issues relating to women, though it is interesting to see the subtle way in which she incorporated a feminist critique into her developing theory of reading. Two projects were uppermost in her mind during her tenure in New York: the "importance of promoting National Education by hightening and deepening the cultivation of individual minds, and the part which is assigned to Woman in the next stage of human progress in this country."[25] Fuller's way of articulating her goal reveals the complex double strategy she had learned to adopt in her other work. One aspect of this strategy, the promotion of "National Education" through the "cultivation of individual minds" appears to echo the familiar strategy of the transcendentalists: the education of the country into a better state by turning each citizen into a cultivated reader. Yet her additional comment

[25] "Farewell," *Tribune*, Aug. 1, 1846.

about the part to be assigned to "Woman" (not "women") in this project alters that familiar individualistic frame by invoking what would have been recognized as a Fourieristic strain. Fourier had made it quite clear that the place of Woman in culture formed the "pivot" of all cultural reform. And by 1844 Fuller had certainly found in his work an important counterbalance to the developing trends of the day, as her references to him in both *Summer on the Lakes* and *Woman in the Nineteenth Century* indicate. In effect, she problematizes the project of national education with her reference to the role of Woman in the "next stage of human progress." In so doing, she alters the normative cultural understanding of the reader.

I do not argue that Fuller aspired to turn the nation into a nation of women readers. Rather, her concern for the place of Woman is the result of her recognition that cultivation as such had been a vehicle of dominance and control. She was well aware that women were often trained to read uncritically and therefore were badly prepared as readers. Yet she also believed that the *position* of Woman in culture, at once inside and outside its dominant discourses of power, could be instrumental in changing the act of reading itself. By 1844, in other words, she understood all too well the strange alterity of woman's place; she saw how, in the words of Biddy Martin, "Women are faced . . . with the challenge of refusing to be the Other of male discourse and an equally important refusal to be integrated as Same."[26] Introducing the idea of Woman, as she did here, was Fuller's way of transforming the project of cultivation to include the project of social change. For her, Woman represented the irruption of difference into the project of national education.

Fuller had always been comfortable with this type of double strategy. In her earliest translations, she had been determined to show that both cultures benefited in the process of converting one language into another. By translating works by Goethe and Bettina von Arnim, for example, her ambition was not to appropriate knowledge from Germany but to put the German and North American way of knowing into conversation. The same goal manifested itself in her Conversations and throughout the writing of "The Great Lawsuit." In both, she wanted to circulate the idea that social change could have shared goals with different origins. Her confidence in the power of such exchanges, however, was put to test by the conflict of European and Native American cultures she witnessed during her trip to the Midwest. The idea that reading was itself a West-

[26] Biddy Martin, "Feminism, Criticism, and Foucault," *New German Critique* 27 (Fall 1982): 2.

ern tool or standard gave her pause, chiefly because she had seen how the theory of progress itself had been used to destroy entire cultures.[27] As a result, she began to seek a theory of reading that could engage the various constituents of a culture or cultures without appropriation and domination. She drew from Fourier's critique of Western civilization where transitional formations were crucial to establishing a social critique and the idea of Woman represented its most significant transitional formation. Fourier's idea of the universal subjection of women (or the transhistorical nature of that subjection) became Fuller's way of identifying a space outside the local effects of cultural bias. In this way, she came to view reading from the position of the strangely excluded and those who, like women, were not always part of the Western way of viewing the world. Conceived in this way, reading became for her another way of interpreting, one which, if put in conversation with traditional ways of interpreting, might alter the way the world was read and understood.

When Fuller writes that one of her goals is to discover "the part which is assigned to Woman in the next stage of human progress in the country," she is less interested in having women participate in the progress of North America as it has already begun (indeed, after viewing the cruel path of progress on the frontier, where the demise of Native American cultures becomes inevitable, she comes to loath the very notion) than she is concerned to find ways in which the idea of Woman—offering an insight into alterity—might help to transvalue the meaning of progress.

In this way, the idea of Woman supplies Fuller with a sense of the importance of ideological positioning. Paying attention to gender now becomes one way of signaling the range of subject positions available in any social cluster or conflict of cultures.[28] Thus, in an important way, her

---

[27] She readily found herself in agreement with Henry R. Schoolcraft, who wrote that "books, and the readers of books, [had] done much to bewilder and perplex the study of the Indian character." See her essay "*Oneota, or the Red Race of America* by Henry R. Schoolcraft," *Tribune*, Feb. 12, 1845.

[28] In a review of Mrs. Jameson's *Memoirs and Essays*, for example, Fuller justly praised Jameson's critique of "the unthinking, willfully unseeing million, who are in the habit of talking of 'Woman's sphere' as if it really was, at present, for the majority, one of protection and the gentle offices of home." Fuller made clear her admiration for the way that Jameson exposed how "rhetorical gentlemen and silken dames" forgot "their washerwomen, their seamstresses, and the poor hirelings for the sensual pleasures of man that jostle them daily in the streets" in order to "talk as if Woman need be fitted for no other chance than that of growing like a cherished flower in the garden of domestic love." At the same time, she found fault with Jameson's essay "On the Relative Social Position of Mothers and Governesses." For Fuller, Jameson's advice "to the governesses reads like a piece of irony, but we believe it was not meant as such—Advise them to be burnt at the stake at once rather than to this slow process of petrifaction. She is as bad as the reports of the 'Society for the relief of distressed and dilapidated Governesses.' We have no more patience. We must go to England ourselves and see these victims under the water torture." See "Mrs. Jameson's *Memoirs and Essays, Tribune*, July 24, 1845.

feminist focus is enlarged throughout her *Tribune* columns. Whereas she continues to refer to specific conditions relating to women in her writing, notably in her discussion of prostitution and the working conditions of the poor, her interest also turns to the variety of social effects that a consideration of gender yields.[29] Gender offers the most visible sign of the efficacy of what Fourier had called transition and shifting frames of reference, offering in turn a new model of reading and cultivation.

This relationship between gender and a changing model of reading is neatly demonstrated in one of Fuller's more innovative columns entitled "Some Items of Foreign Gossip." In this column she inserted assorted news items she had translated from European newspapers. Of course, all of her *Tribune* reviews extol the benefits of translation and language skills, emphasizing that we must "learn from all nations."[30] She continually encourages her audience to read foreign newspapers and, as an incentive, she occasionally translates directly from the French and German newspapers that she recommends to her readers, notably *Deutsche Schnellpost*, *Review Française*, and *Courrier des Estats Unis*. The items she culls from foreign and immigrant newspapers tend to be more overt in their political commentary, concerned as many of them are with the developing interest in communism and socialism throughout Europe.[31] In making these translations, she demonstrates a far more sympathetic and advanced sense of the European struggle for social and political transformation than many of her North American contemporaries. Yet her decision to segregate one segment of these translations under the title "Items of Foreign Gossip" bears our immediate attention, for

[29] Fuller's concern for the Other perspective of the workingwoman, though general, was genuine; she tended to focus on domestic servants, washerwomen, and prostitutes, in part because in the 1840s no visible organization among other female laborers existed in New York City. Christine Stansell, *City of Women: Sex and Class in New York, 1789–1860* (New York: Alfred A. Knopf, 1986), notes that in March 1845 a "major organizational effort, the Ladies' Industrial Association" was launched by a cross section of New York women "from all ranks of trade," including "shirt sewers, plain sewers, tailoresses and dressmakers, fringe and lace makers, straw workers, the comparatively prosperous book folders and stitchers and the lowly cap makers and shoe crimpers" (p. 145). According to Stansell, however, the organization fell apart by late spring and nothing more was heard of it. Fuller, who was visiting a variety of city charities at the time, including the Bellevue Alms House, the Farm School for Children, the Asylum for the Insane, and the Penitentiary on Blackwell's Island (see her review on March 19, 1845), did not take note of the event. Stansell writes that the "short-lived, fragile tradition of female labor organization was buried in reformers' well-intentioned efforts and in workingmen's rhetoric of the working-class home" (p. 152).

[30] "French Gayety," *Tribune*, July 9, 1845. Fuller sometimes dropped the word *Some* from the title of this column, as will become apparent in later references.

[31] See especially the following issues of the *Tribune*: Dec. 16, 1844; Jan. 6, 1845; Jan. 11, 1845; Jan. 25, 1845; Jan. 27, 1845; Feb. 4, 1845; Feb. 24, 1845; March 12, 1845; June 7, 1845; July 9, 1845; July 25, 1845; Aug. 5, 1845; Jan. 8, 1846; April 1, 1846; April 25, 1846.

within these columns gender intersects politics in some very provocative ways.

One particular column under that heading begins with a description of three cases of transgendered behavior, or what Fuller called an "exchange of parts between the two sexes."[32] In her account Fuller first describes a man in France who had both dressed and acted the part of a woman in order to be in the company of men. As she tells the story, this person had held the attention of "many admirers" until "denounced by the Police as a man and a notorious offender against justice." Her next example involves the case of a woman who had played the part of a man throughout her life. According to Fuller's account, the woman—who went by the name of Mr. Douglass—had received a great deal of praise for "his" generosity as well as his "mildness of disposition" (an attribute noted particularly when he had allowed his "wife" to desert him for another man without prosecution). The third case concerns a woman named Maria Schellynk, who had served actively for seventeen years in the French Army under Napoleon. These three examples were listed in order of their "success." The first instance of gender shifting had been discovered very early and openly scorned, whereas the sex of the second person had only been discovered by the larger public at her death, with little or no public criticism. Finally, Fuller shows how the third person's sex was discovered yet made irrelevant by the honors Napoleon and her fellow soldiers bestowed upon her. Thus, in the process of telling her reader about these three unusual lives, she enacts an important transformation of focus. If the reader would be inclined to echo the disdainful response that greeted the first case (and she had every reason to expect that her reader would be so inclined), Fuller is able by the end to cultivate a different response. In other words, she shows her reader not only alternative modes of behavior, but, more importantly, alternative modes of interpreting that behavior. As usual, her focus on gender becomes the most efficient way to demonstrate the shifting ideological constraints binding her audience.

Yet gender was merely the most obvious reminder of a whole range of subject positions Fuller wanted her reader to understand and explore. For central to her concern was the development of a broadly based cultural critique. Thus, it follows quite naturally that she would end this particular column with a description of the value of newspapers, for she

---

[32] "Items of Foreign Gossip," *Tribune*, Sept. 24, 1845. Even the heading under which Fuller places this account has a transformative value, since it is in this "gossip" column (a site heavily coded as "effeminate") that traditional gender expectations end up being thwarted. I use *transgendering* for lack of a better term.

sees the newspaper as the site of an important cultural transition, the meeting of high and low culture and the place where conversation among various constituencies can begin.[33] Fuller's opening story from "Items of Foreign Gossip" on the "exchange of parts" made by men and women allegorizes her sense of the need for an active exchange of parts among the constituents of a society at large.

One of Fuller's earliest columns gives a clear indication of her ambition to mix the project of national cultivation with cultural critique in this way. In an 1844 essay commemorating Thanksgiving, she admonishes her readers to remember those less fortunate who are still subject to the vagaries of "ignorance, corruption and wo[e]." Although this type of charge is not particularly unusual, it *is* remarkable for its affiliation of political and artistic change. Fuller describes a "movement of contrition and love" which had called "the King from his throne of gold, and the Poet from his throne of Mind to lie with the beggar in the kennel, or raise him from it." According to her, this movement had said to the Poet, " 'You must reform rather than create a world,' and to him of the golden crown, 'You cannot long remain a King unless you are also a Man.' "[34] She makes it plain from the start, in other words, that she is determined to establish a relationship between the political and literary changes she sees everywhere around her. For her, the political transitions of Europe, particularly those involving the shift away from monarchies to some form of representative government, were being matched by a transition in the idea of genius and artistic achievement. Evidence of this transformation occurs relatively early in her *Tribune* writing, marking the most interesting development of her thinking during her tenure with the paper. Not only does it show her growing sympathy for the implicit critique of individualism embedded in European socialist thought, it also demonstrates her increasing desire to assign the role of reading a central part in that critique.

Fuller is helped in this project by her reading of Emerson's work. Her opening review of the *Second Series* attests to the challenge she sets before herself with her columns. The review has been analyzed as both adulatory and dismissive, in part because critics have been attempting to fit it into a larger narrative about her break from New England: either it is adulatory because she is still in Emerson's thrall, or dismissive

[33] Fuller's faith in the newspaper no doubt drew its power from her own memory of her very first publication, a letter to the editor of the *Boston Daily Advertiser* ("Brutus," Nov. 27, 1834). There she had made a bold and provocative start to her publishing career by criticizing the historical method of the historian George Bancroft.

[34] "Thanksgiving," *Tribune*, Dec. 2, 1844.

because she has begun to advance her own critical perspective. But, in fact, the review testifies to the continued usefulness of her conversations with Emerson.

Fuller's review of Emerson is striking in its anticipation of a review she wrote two years later when she went abroad. While she was in England, the spirited controversy over the abstract nature of painter J. M. W. Turner's late work drew her interest. She wrote that "something real and vital [was] going on" when she observed "the fervor of feeling on either side" of the debate. Fascinated by the "mysterious looking things," Fuller clearly prefered Turner's later paintings, emphasizing as she did how these works transform the viewer. Nothing fascinated her more than the way issues of representation become secondary to "certain primitive and leading effects of light and shadow, or lines and contours" (AHA, 199–200). Yet she also refrained from calling the later paintings "fine works of art" because they too readily evince a "transition state" as "hieroglyphics of picture, rather than picture itself."[35] Because she referred so often in her *Tribune* writing to the "transition state" of society, her disclaimers give a clue to her understanding of the more radical significance of Turner's painting.[36]

Similarly, Fuller makes much of the controversial response generated by Emerson's work. Though willing to concede that posterity will grant him "the honors of greatness," she again refrains from calling his writing "masterly."[37] In both reviews, however, withholding the highest aesthetic praise in no way diminishes her obvious admiration. In reading Emerson, she spends several lengthy paragraphs describing how his unusual and provocative style motivates his readers to question their way of perceiving the world around them. Although she concedes that his writing is "sometimes obstructed or chilled by the critical intellect," she locates the source of his power in his ability to enable his reader to become a kind of "liberating God."[38] Thus she ends her article by claiming that his essays would ultimately "lead to great and complete poems—somewhere."

Fuller's assessment, in other words, lays emphasis on Emerson's ability to work changes on his readers, which she affiliates with social and historical change. "History will inscribe his name as a father of the

[35] Letter 11, *At Home and Abroad*, pp. 199–200.
[36] See "Story Books for the Hot Weather," *Tribune*, June 20, 1845; and "Thom's Poems," *Tribune*, Aug. 22, 1845.
[37] *Tribune*, Dec. 7, 1844.
[38] When Fuller writes that some people had criticized Emerson's work for its "underdevelopment," she summons the phrase of a mesmerist who came up with this assessment when given a poem of Emerson's to read through magnetic channels. Fuller reported this event to Emerson in one of her letters: LMF 3: 177.

country, for he is one who pleads her cause against herself." In the same way, she describes his lectures as "grave didactic poems, theogonies, perhaps, adorned by odes when some Power was in question whom the poet had best learned to serve."[39] As in her Turner review, her focus remains on the moment of discernment provoked by Emerson's language.

Genius and Practical Power

Throughout her *Tribune* writing Fuller seems to have taken to heart Emerson's paradoxical claim that the "true romance which the world exists to realize, will be the transformation of genius into practical power" (CW 3: 49). We see her struggling most visibly with this complex double strategy in her musical reviews. One of her favorite tasks while in New York was to review orchestral performances, particularly performances of Beethoven's symphonies. She admired Beethoven well before her arrival in New York, and her assessments were often more technical than theoretical. Our discussion, however, concerns her rhetorical use of the concept of Beethoven's genius, a subject she developed most fully in reviewing a biography of his life in February 1845.

For Fuller, the biographer's understanding of the life of Beethoven is only of marginal importance because, as she puts it, the "life of a Beethoven is written in his works." She uses the occasion of her review to write more generally about the value of music for "open[ing] new realms to thought. . . . It is dynamics that interest us now, and from electricity and music we borrow the best illustrations of what we know."[40] Her focus not only reveals her sustained belief in the transforming potential of all great art, but suggests as well her internalization of Fourier's social criticism that had developed around an idiosyncratic understanding of musical, electrical, and mathematical principles.[41]

This sense of music's powerful influence appears in Fuller's review of an address given before the Harvard Musical Association by Christopher Cranch. She quotes generously from the lecture, emphasizing Cranch's belief that "Music is the . . . voice of struggling humanity pleading with the crushing discords of social evil, the voice of infinite

[39] *Tribune*, Dec. 7, 1844.

[40] "The Life of Beethoven edited by Ignace Moscheles," *Tribune*, Feb. 7, 1845.

[41] For more on the interrelationship between music, electrical, and mathematical principles in Fourier's theory, see "The Mathematical Poem," in *The Utopian Vision of Charles Fourier*, ed. Jonathan Beecher and Richard Bienvenu (Columbia: University of Missouri Press, 1983), 398–99. See also Roland Barthes, "Fourier," in *Sade, Fourier, Loyola*, trans. Richard Miller (New York: Hill and Wang, 1976), 76–120, esp. 102–6.

love itself, which is the imprisoned soul of the universe." Her support of this position is made clear by her decision to discuss in this same article the series of concerts available to workingmen in Liverpool, England. In making the connection, she suggests some practical effects of Cranch's manifest idealism.[42]

Fuller's discussion of the Liverpool meetings (which she learned about from the *Liverpool Mercury*) is worth pausing over, for it reveals how subtle her rhetorical shifts can be. For example, she ends her essay with this statement: "The benefits of such meetings must be very great— no less to those who give than those who receive. Come we and do likewise, and we shall think more and love more in our country, and the Capitalist and Laborer may yet be bound in a harmony cheerful as the music of Haydn, prophetic as that of Beethoven." A reader intent on thematizing Fuller's thinking might easily conclude from this paragraph that she is hopelessly naive about the conflict between classes in the developing capitalist world. Yet she is less interested in promoting a discussion of the errors of the capitalist system in this piece (whose title, after all, is "Music") than in promoting a form of hegemonic discourse that would enable various segments of society to interact and form some basis for building a political consensus. For her, music provides the model for such an interaction.

This abstract concept, which Fuller draws from Cranch's own idealistic speech, is refined through her discussion of the concerts at Liverpool. Though attracted to the idea of the concerts, she explores how a project undertaken in all good faith for the "instruction and refinement of the laboring classes" can prove problematic. She examines a record of one of the dinners given in celebration of the concerts and observes that one of the members of the committee in charge, a Mr. Smith, had confused "pleasure" of the concerts with "idleness" and insisted that the men "go a step further" and assemble on a weekly basis to hear lectures. By subtly juxtaposing the issues in her essay, she suggests a connection between Smith's work ethic and the fact that the "working classes suffer and are degraded beyond what tongue can tell or pen set down." She observes that Mr. Smith, "the best intentioned man in the world and as liberal as he thinks it prudent," is actually depriving the workingmen of their pleasure and the other advantages that might accrue from a more open-ended assembly. Even as she approves of the development of the concerts for the benefit of the workingmen, she objects to the way in which their subversive potential, symbolized by the music, is being managed by the liberal and all-too-prudent middle-class organizers of

---

[42] "Music," *Tribune*, Jan. 31, 1846.

the affair. Her closing comment about the "benefits . . . to those who give . . . [and] . . . those who receive" thus takes on a new value, for she means by this statement to critique the haphazard idealism she would otherwise seem to be promoting.

The Great Mutual System of Interpretation

As the traditional hierarchies of political structures are questioned, so, for Fuller, must the traditional hierarchy of elite and popular literature come under scrutiny. Without a doubt, the articles she translated from European and immigrant newspapers encouraged her to pursue this line of inquiry. One of the most influential of these essays was written by Gottfried Kinkel, "Popular Literature in Germany," which she found in the *Deutsche Schnellpost* and published in full in the *Tribune* in January 1845. According to Kinkel, all literature depends on "the spiritual tendencies of its time." Thus, the social and political transformations of Europe, including "the Communist" and socialist "tendency" generate "a new interest in the life of the common people." By Kinkel's account, it was imperative, therefore, to promote an interest in what he called "popular literature" because "the writer, educated among the cultivated, [can] rarely translate his thoughts to the mind and manners of the peasant and burgher."[43] Though Kinkel's idea of popular literature and social change remains largely circumscribed by an elitism in which ideas can flow in only one direction, his articulation of the imbrication of political and literary concerns proves immensely valuable for Fuller. She seems to have been particularly taken by his argument that "belles lettres, . . . once the property of these educated classes, have condescended a step to those whom we designate by the strange name of the people, as if we ourselves were no part of the people.—In this sense is rising among us a popular literature that may easily begin a revolution in the literary world."[44]

More than anything else, the affiliation of social and political change with literary transformation complicates Fuller's way of addressing artistic Genius. Although she continues throughout her criticism to distinguish between two types of writing, "high" and "low," the relationship

[43] "Popular Literature in Germany by Gottfried Kinkel," *Tribune*, Jan. 25, 1845. A German poet and journalist, Kinkel participated in the Baden-Palatinate uprising in 1849 and was imprisoned by a Prussian court for his role in the uprising. He later escaped and emigrated to London, where he soon came out against Marx and Engels. As a result, Marx and Engels subjected him to severe mockery in "The Great Men of Exile," *Karl Marx, Friedrich Engels: Collected Works*, 2: 227–326.
[44] "Popular Literature in Germany," Jan. 27, 1845.

between the two becomes increasingly volatile. For example, in March 1845, she introduced her column "English Writers Little Known Here," with the declaration that

> the office of Literature is two-fold. It preserves through ages the flowers of life which came to perfect bloom in minds of genius. . . . A small part of literature has a permanent value. But the office of the larger part is temporary, as affording the means of interpreting contemporary minds to each other on a larger scale than actual conversation in words or deeds furnishes. . . . The common and daily purposes of literature are the most important. It cannot, and will not, dispense with the prophecies of genius, but the healthy discharge of its functions must not be disparaged to exalt these.[45]

Fuller's growing desire to turn reading into the site of social agency makes it increasingly difficult for her to separate her understanding of the "common and daily purposes of literature" from the offices of prophecy. She never completely relinquishes her faith in works of genius, believing that they may generate an important type of cultural agency. Perhaps her most succinct sense of that agency appears in a review of Plato in May 1845, where she writes that "it is impossible to read or repeat him with absolute servility. It is impossible to get at the outmost sense of his speech without some action of one's own intelligence."[46] Indeed, she struggles to support two conflicting types of agency: that which the great work of literature could yield to the reader by the intellectual challenge it offered and that which popular literature might supply by providing another significant perspective on the culture.

Fuller's way of avoiding this conflict is to shift her attention from the author to the reader. This shift coincides nicely with her interest in transitional modes spawned by the social criticism of Fourier, for whom "transitions [are] to passionate equilibrium what bolts and joints [are] to a framework."[47] Roland Barthes nicely describes the centrality of transition in Fourier when he writes:

> In Harmony, Transitions have a beneficent role; for example, they prevent monotony in love, despotism in politics: the distributive passions (composite, cabalistic, and butterfly) have a transitional role (they "mesh": ensure changes of "objects"); Fourier always reasoned contrariwise, what is beneficent in Harmony necessarily proceeds from what is discredited or rejected

[45] "English Writers Little Known Here," *Tribune*, March 4, 1845.
[46] "Plato against the Atheists by Taylor Lewis," *Tribune*, May 14, 1845.
[47] Quoted in Barthes, "Fourier," in *Sade, Fourier, Loyola*, trans. Miller, p. 107.

in Civilization: thus Transitions are "trivialities," ignored by civilized scholars as unworthy subjects: the bat, the albino, ugly ambiguous race, the taste for feathered fowl. The prime example of Trivial Transition is Death: transition ascending between Harmonian life and the happiness of the other life (sensual happiness), it "will shed all its odiousness when philosophy deigns to consent to study the transitions it proscribes as trivial."[48]

As Fuller came to believe in the importance of a hegemonic discourse in culture, she also came to believe in the efficacy of what she called "transitional" texts. Her interest in literary and artistic works began to focus, then, on the way in which any work can generate a new dynamic relationship between disparate groups. She finds in works of genius a more accomplished and immediate sense of empowerment, but it is an empowerment that works through the reader, the most important agent of social transition.

Fuller's focus on reading expanded in the summer of 1845 when she reviewed the poems of the British laborer, William Thom. Once again she begins with an attempt to designate two types of literature. Her description of literature, however, turns out to be more a description of the critical method used to *read* literature.

> There are two ways of considering Poems, or the products of literature in general. We may tolerate only what is excellent, and demand that whatever is consigned to print for the benefit of the human race should exhibit fruits perfect in shape, . . . enclosing kernels of permanent value. . . . [or] *literature may be regarded as the great mutual system of interpretation between all kinds and classes of men. It is an epistolary correspondence between brethren of one family, subject to many and wide separations, and anxious to remain in spiritual presence one of another.*[49]

In her analysis, Fuller goes on to suggest that both schools of criticism have their "dangers": the first being "hypercriticism" and "pedantry" and the second an "indiscriminate indulgence and a leveling of the beautiful with what is merely tolerable." And although she expresses the hope that "these two tendencies" can "be harmonized," she makes obvious her support for the second excess. Once again, her preference carries a political value: "The spirit of the time, which is certainly seeking, though by many and strange ways, the greatest happiness for the greatest number . . . declares that the genial and generous tendency

---

[48] Barthes, *Sade, Fourier, Loyola*, p. 108. Barthes is quoting Fourier here.

[49] "Thom's Poems," *Tribune*, Aug. 22, 1845. She thought highly enough of this piece to republish it as "Poets of the People" in *Papers on Literature and Art*, 2 vols. (New York: Wiley and Putnam, 1846), 2: 1–21.

shall have the lead."[50] There is no question that her understanding of the "spirit of the time" has been strongly influenced by the transitional modes of socialism and communism. Nor is it a coincidence that her review of Thom's poems came out just two weeks after her translation of "The Social Movement in Europe," the article from the *Deutsche Schnell-post* which included an excerpt from "The Condition of the Working Class" by Engels. With these developing social concerns, Fuller's literary criticism became heavily focused on the social agency of reading.[51]

Fuller's address for New Year's Day 1846 tells a great deal about how completely she internalized this way of viewing things. As was routine for her, she takes the occasion of the first of the year to critique the state of the union; she was particularly disappointed with the events of 1846:

> What a year it has been with us! Texas annexed, and more annexations in store; Slavery perpetuated, as the most striking new feature of these movements. Such are the fruits of American love of liberty! Mormons murdered and driven out, as an expression of American freedom of conscience. Cassius Clay's paper expelled from Kentucky; that is American freedom of the press. And all these deeds defended on the true Russian grounds: "We (the stronger) know what you (the weaker) ought to do and be, and it *shall* be so."[52]

Although Fuller glumly reports that another "sign of the times" was that "there are left on the earth none of the last dynasty of geniuses," her choice of the word *dynasty*, with its negative political connotations, is deliberate, because she sees a positive side to the eclipse of genius. Earlier in the essay she endorsed "Associative" and communist principles as useful antidotes to the dangerous individualism of American culture. Thus she ends her discussion of genius arguing that "the time of prophets is over, and the era they prophesied must be at hand; in its conduct a larger proportion of the human race shall take part than ever before."[53]

By the summer of 1845, Fuller had essentially outlined the theory of reading which would guide her thinking for the remainder of her *Tribune* writing. Her description of literature as "the great mutual system of

---

[50] "Thom's Poems," *Tribune*, Aug. 22, 1845.

[51] "The Social Movement in Europe," *Tribune*, Aug. 5, 1845. Thus, the second mode of criticism she described in her review of Thom was shown in her argument to be superior for its method, which, rather than "crushing to earth without mercy all the humble buds of Phantasy," instead "enters into the natural history of every thing that breathes and lives, . . . believes no impulse to be entirely in vain, which scrutinizes circumstances, motive and object before it condemns, and believes there is a beauty in each natural form, if its law and purpose be understood." "Thom's Poems," *Tribune*, Aug. 22, 1845.

[52] "First of January 1846," *Tribune*, Jan 1, 1846.

[53] Ibid.

interpretation between all kinds and classes of men" is less a theory of literature than a theory of cultural interaction anticipating Gramsci's notion of hegemonic transformation. She emphasizes the wide separations that the offices of reading are expected to cross and bring into communication. For her, a certain type of reading can foster an interaction among people who are manifestly different by developing some form of equality between them. As her columns amply show, such differences can be of gender, race, or class.

This formulation helps to explain why in the same summer in which she reviewed Thom's work and translated the piece "The Social Movement in Europe," Fuller was also happy to review Thomas Arnold's *Introductory Lectures on Modern History*. For Fuller, Arnold's tolerance of "other men" and their way of life raises him above a host of other thinkers. Clearly, she reviews his book for the sole purpose of emphasizing his maxim that one should keep one's "view of men and things extensive. . . . He who reads deeply in one class of writers only, gets views which are almost sure to be perverted."[54]

In other words, Fuller makes a direct correlation between the activity of reading and the process of social change, for reading can offer a way to disrupt certain ideological assumptions. Throughout her columns, she is always working to open a space of negotiation and communication between cultural and social differences. Her columns on care for the insane, prison reform, prostitutes, the repression of the Jews, and even certain health issues, reflect her continued effort to establish a hegemonic discourse that would replace some of the more repressive forms of dominance and control throughout society. She argues that a subaltern position could offer an important new perspective on life. She frequently emphasizes the idea that the poor are in a unique position to "read" the cruelties of class differences.[55] Her excellent series "The Irish Character" clearly promotes this position, harshly criticizing the spurious notion that the Irish were "ungrateful" for the help being extended to them by their employers.[56] In one of these columns she gives a particularly vivid example of the failure to consider the perspective of the employee.

> Only a day or two since, we saw, what we see so often, a nursery maid, with the family to which she belonged, in a public conveyance. They were having a pleasant time, but in it she had not part, except to hold a hot,

---

[54] *"Introductory Lectures in Modern History* by Thomas Arnold," *Tribune*, Aug. 28, 1845.
[55] See, for example, her essay "Asylum for Discharged Female Convicts," *Tribune*, June 19, 1845, in which she writes that the poor are "usually, the most generous. Not that they are, originally, better than the rich, but circumstances have fitted them to appreciate the misfortunes, the trials, the wrongs, that beset those a little lower down than themselves."
[56] "The Irish Character," *Tribune*, July 15, 1845.

heavy baby and receive frequent admonitions to keep it comfortable. No inquiry was made as to *her* comfort—no entertaining remark, no information as to the places of interest we passed was addressed to her. Had she been in that way with that family ten years, she might have known *them* well enough, for their characters lay only too bare to a careless scrutiny, but her joys, her sorrows, her few thoughts, her almost buried capacities, would have been as unknown to them and they as little likely to benefit her, as the Emperor of China.[57]

For Fuller, the need to translate from class to class, an idea first summoned in Kinkel's essay, is no less imperative than the need to translate across cultural differences. America proves this point most strikingly, for the crisis of urban and frontier living almost always reflects the lack of understanding among various cultural differences. Accordingly, in her review of Commander Wilke's expedition to the South Seas, she focuses on the confused contact between explorer and native and quickly draws a parallel to contact between Anglo- and Native Americans at home:

> Not only those who come with fire and sword, crying "Believe or die," "understand or we will scourge you"—"understand *and* we will only plunder and tyrannize over you"; not only these ignorant despots, self-deceiving robbers, have failed to benefit the people they dared esteem more savage than themselves, but the good and generous have failed from want of patience and an expanded intelligence. —Would you speak to a man, first learn his language![58]

Thus by the time she went to England in the latter half of 1846 and began to observe the oppressive nature of industrialization, Fuller was already well prepared to describe her reaction to the Castle of Stirling:

> We were shown its dungeons and its Court of Lions, where, says tradition, wild animals, kept in the grated cells adjacent, were brought out on festival occasions to furnish entertainment for the court. So, while lords and ladies gay danced and sang above, prisoners pined and wild beasts starved below. This, at first blush, looks like a very barbarous state of things, but, on reflection, one does not find that we have outgrown it in our present so-called state of refined civilization, only the present way of expressing the same facts is a little different. Still lords and ladies dance and sing, unknowing or uncaring that the laborers who minister to their luxuries starve or are turned into wild beasts. Man need not boast his condition, methinks, till he can weave his costly tapestry without the side that is kept under looking thus sadly.[59]

[57] Ibid.
[58] "United States Exploring Expedition," *Tribune*, June 28, 1845.
[59] Letter 6, *At Home and Abroad*, p. 161.

The Difference of Reading

It would be a mistake to assume that Fuller always reduced the aesthetic to the political in her *Tribune* writing, or that she drained all meaning to one simple ideological reading. Her dual focus on cultivation and social change, working as it does through her easy affiliation of literature, translation, and social commentary, provides us with a deeper sense of the way we are all framed by a bewildering grid of ideological formations. The value of her position on reading is not simply that we are encouraged to read *about* different things, but that we must read *in a different way*. We should not simply read *more* in order to accumulate knowledge, but we should also read in order to transform *how* we know. This task proves to be the most rigorous and complex aspect of Fuller's project, and, sometimes, the most confusing.

Fuller published many of her most fascinating articles in the summer of 1845, including "Irish Character," "Asylum for Discharged Female Convicts," "The Social Movement in Europe," and two scathing critiques of the United States.[60] As we have seen, however, her social criticism in these articles is not restricted to political or social issues; her most subtle critical assessments of important cultural problems often occur in her reviews of literary texts, including works by Frederick Douglass, Bela Marsh, Mrs. Norton, Thomas Hood, P. J. Beranger, John Critchley Prince, Eugene Sue, and Benjamin Disraeli.[61] One of her most provocative essays is entitled "Story Books for the Hot Weather." Her stock of hot-weather reading includes Disraeli's *Sybil; Or, The Two Worlds of the Rich and the Poor*; Eugene Sue's *De Rohan*; *Self* by an unnamed author; and *Dashes at Life* by the American writer N. P. Willis. Because her column is more about the unsettling nature of reading and what might be called the productive work of reading than about the novels themselves, her "Story Books for the Hot Weather" essay naturally becomes more an allegory about social crisis than a story about passing the summer days in leisure. The essay confronts and brackets the idea of leisure in its odd affiliation with the work of reading.

The complex paragraphs with which Fuller opens her review provide a strong sense of how quickly she directs herself to the problematic of reading and its cultural significance:

[60] *Tribune*, "The Irish Character," July 15, 1845, and July 24, 1845; "The Fourth of July," July 4, 1845; "The First of August, 1845," Aug. 1, 1845.

[61] See, for example, *Tribune*, "Narrative of the Life of Fredrick Douglass," June 10, 1845; "The Nubian Slave," June 24, 1845; "The Child of the Islands by the Hon. Mrs. Norton," July 26, 1845; "Thomas Hood," July 18, 1845; "Prose and Verse of Thomas Hood," Aug. 9, 1845; "Prince's Poems," Aug. 13, 1845; "Thom's Poems," Aug. 22, 1845.

Does any shame still haunt the age of bronze—a shame, the lingering blush of a heroic age, at being caught in doing anything merely for amusement? Is there a public still extant which needs to excuse its delinquencies by the one story of a man who liked to lie on the sofa all day and read novels, though he could, at times of need, write the gravest didactics! Live they still, those reverend signiors, the object of secret smiles to our childish years, who were obliged to apologize for midnight oil spent in conning story books, by the "historic bearing" of the novel, or the "correct and admirable descriptions of certain countries, with climate, scenery and manners therein contained," wheat for which they, industrious students, were willing to winnow bushels of frivolous love-adventures? We know not— but incline to think the world is now given over to frivolity so far as to replace by the novel the minstrel's ballad, the drama, and worse still, the games of agility and strength in which it once sought pastime, for indeed, *mere* past-time is sometimes needed. The nursery legend comprised a primitive truth of the understanding and the wisdom of nations in the lines—

> "All play and no work makes Jack a mere toy;
> *But,* all work and no play makes Jack a dull boy."

We having reversed the order of arrangement to suit our present purpose. For we, O useful reader, being ourselves so far of the useful class as to be always wanted somewhere, have also to fight a good fight for our amusements, either with the foils of excuse, like the reverend signiors above mentioned, or with the sharp weapons of argument, or maintenance of a view of our own without argument, which we take to be the sharpest weapon of all.[62]

Fuller's writing is difficult to read here precisely because of the burden it takes upon itself. The column enacts a cunning play on fading protocols of reading. Fuller creates a reader in her own image in order to provide an analysis of the paradoxical impossibility and necessity of "past-time." Ending her column with the statement "God has time to remember the design with which he made this world also," she takes the redundancy of value in the familiar narrative of creation to focus on reading, showing that it is not merely the initial moment of inscription (in the beginning there was the Word) that we must value, but also the consequences of that inscription. God needed his leisure or "past-time" in order to "remember the design" with which he made the world. In the end, it is important for God to take the time to read and imitate us in the process.

The extremely transitional nature of Fuller's argument highlights her interest in the complexities of reading. The emphasis on transition is her

[62] "Story Books for the Hot Weather," *Tribune*, June 20, 1845.

way of highlighting the complex ideological formations we all negotiate. Consider for a moment the "reverend signior" in her introductory comments. Is he the representative reader of leisure? If so, it is interesting that the words *reverend* and *signior* traverse several discourses—crossbreeding the clergy with jaded aristocracy—and that the behavior of this hybrid male is made an "object of secret smiles" by children. Through these shifts the reader is forced to ask a number of important questions. For example, who is really watching this troubled male figure of reading in their early childhood? Fuller avoids reference to women of leisure, because the essay is far to the left of that prescription (indeed, a reference to the transformation of Englishwomen into "work tools" in British factories occurs toward the end of the essay). For Fuller there is no leisure in reading if the slow perusal of texts must be apologized for with the idea that "didactics of writing" are the official work of the reverend signior. Yet there is pleasure, somehow, in the smiles of childhood, the auxiliary space of reading, which fosters a special insight into the codes of the didactic, the "correct and admirable." Even as the reader settles on this position from which to interpret her view of the "reverend signior," however, that reader is forced by the very structure of Fuller's complex sentence into a new position, that of the "industrious students" grateful for the historical information interspersed among love stories. We know, and the reader of her daily column would know, that Fuller was herself such a student of history, but she is not casting blame on the reader of love stories. She finds a way instead to critique the division between the two forms. Indeed, when she reviews the books that she selected for her "hot weather," she demonstrates the interdependence of the historic with the love story.

The point is that Fuller's readers are given no stable subject position in the opening paragraphs. Instead they slide along a shifting series of positions, places from which they might read. This shifting is affected by the tension within phrases that would find a more complacent reading if they were allowed to flow back to their usual oppositional valences, particularly the oppositional valence based on gender that tends to subsume all others.

Fuller's inclusion of the phrase "nursery legend" works just this way. Once again, she mixes discourses, that of the nursery rhyme with that of legend, bringing the domain of women and children (understood but not stated by the absence of the phrase *nursery rhyme*) into the domain of history or legend.

As usual, Fuller does not take the "leisure" to describe her method and materials; instead she industriously puts them to use, without apology. Hence, there is an inevitable compounding and confounding of meaning in her work. She goes on to use the nursery legend to gloss the "primitive truth of the understanding and the wisdom of nations" (a truth left intentionally vague) and in so doing again challenges (without the "leisure" of argument) the idea that primitive truth should be held in opposition to understanding. Instead, the nursery legend works to make primitive sense, following the smirks of childhood, out of the leisure of the reverend signior.

Of course there is more to this, for if the nursery rhyme reporting Jack's dullness has become a legend, it has become so by reversing the usual order of enunciation. The reversal does far more than exchange one hierarchical formation for another. If, initially the emphasis was on keeping Jack sharp (ending with "all play and no work makes Jack a mere toy"), warning him against easy manipulation through stupefying and lazy behavior, so Fuller's transformation of the legend (ending now with "all work and no play makes Jack a dull boy"), emphasizes the terrible accomplishment of that manipulation. Jack has become a drone to the forces earlier warned against. Turning the legend around, she transforms the nursery rhyme into the legend, or the history of industrialization to which she refers in her reading of Disraeli, Sue, and Willis in the remainder of her piece.

Fuller, however, inserts that history as a legend for her work of reviewing: Jack becomes a potential reference for both the reverend signior and Fuller. This double association does not mean that she and the signior merge as one figure through Jack. Quite the contrary. She remains divided from the signior by her method. For the signior, the foil of history is an excuse for his leisure, and Jack is the labored figure of that excuse. For Fuller, by contrast, the "absence of argument" is precisely her tool for reading history, and Jack is the playful vehicle of that reading.

The essay's opening thus brings into play the ideas of amusement, work, and "past-time." In one sense Fuller means to show how pastime could be productive leisure, allowing time for reflection and memory, thoughts of times past and time passing. Leisure is work in this sense, but useful work that can make her readers members of the "useful class." They can be inducted into this class if they are useful readers, though by doing so they are also condemning themselves to a struggle, which consists in learning how to uncoil the argument, as she tells her audience, from a "view of your own" in order to battle the forces changing the face of Jack's world encoded in her reading of the nursery legend.

Fuller's opening paragraphs are unsettling in the extreme, and meant to be. Our position as readers is radically destabilized by her conscious denial of argument, allowing a form of unconscious writing to take control. Her sharpest weapon is thus an intense invitation to the unconscious, manifested in the movement toward such complexities of the phrase "*mere* past-time," which test, through the word *mere*, concepts as remote and connected as "boundary," "purity," "limitation," and "mother." After all, what is "mere past-time" for the culture determined to make pastime both effeminate and impossible? Fuller's division between the conscious intention of the word *pastime* and its unconscious play of possibility in the hyphenated version of that word exposes a crucial division in her work, a division marking the division or gap in reading that she uses with such facility. This division is intended to show her reader how very complex an analysis of culture must be.

Fuller's review of four books in her column reflects this same division. She praises Disraeli for attempting to "do justice to the claims of the laboring classes," in his *Sybil*, yet she finds fault with the limits of his perspective, writing that "D'Israeli shows the stain of old prejudice in the necessity he felt to marry the daughter of the People to one not of the People."[63] Yet her review of Disraeli does not call for a simple ideological rendering of the growing class conflict in England. Rather, her review of Sue suggests something of the complexity that she was seeking. Although she admires Sue, observing that he holds "clearer notions of what he wants" than Disraeli, she criticizes his narrow rendering of the character of Louis XIV in his novel *De Rohan*. Agreeing with Sue that the "Great Marnarque was really brutally selfish and ignorant," she nevertheless cautions that the "illusion" the king "diffused" is worth considerably more artistic investment than that which Sue supplied. Her critique is astute: "It is not by an inventory of facts or traits that what is most vital in a character and which makes its due impression on contemporaries can be apprehended or depicted."[64] The same resistance to such reductive renderings informs Fuller's review of a work entitled "Self, by the author of Cecil," whose focus remains "the very dregs, in a social life, now at its lowest ebb." She also finds fault with the work of N. P. Willis, claiming that his novel *Dashes at Life* falls short of the goal she had set for American writers—to be "rooted to the soil." Yet she hesitates to dismiss Willis altogether as she does the author of *Self*, supposing that his work may well be viewed as one of the "mongrel products" from the "transitive state we are in now."[65]

In reviewing these books together, Fuller subtly makes the point that a simplistic rendering of the venality of the aristocracy is no more effective

[63] Ibid.
[64] Ibid.
[65] Ibid.

than cheap sensationalism in descriptions of poverty. According to her, the purpose of literature—whether depicting a character of the highest aristocracy or looking instead at the lowest ranks of the social scale—is to assist in "unlearning the False, in order to arrive at the True." Such a project requires a variety of skills, and all of the works she reviews require an active yet leisurely reader, one now enlisted in a larger social project, as suggested by the close of the "Story Books" essay: "All these story books show even to the languor of the hottest day the solemn signs of revolution. Life has become too factitious; it has no longer a leg left to stand upon, and cannot be carried much farther in this way."[66] The column ends with a provocative statement: "God has time to remember the design with which he made this world also."

The Efficacy of Reading

Over time, Fuller obviously began to feel a certain confidence in the efficacy of her focus on reading. We see this attitude most strikingly in the way that she finally attempts in her writing about Native Americans to change the rhetoric of the vanishing American. Upon her arrival in New York, the memories of the Midwest still fresh in her mind, she makes a point of recalling the Native American crisis to her reader in a number of reviews, including her New Year's Day critique ("We are not fitted to emulate the savages in preparation for the new fire. The Indians knew how to reverence the old and the wise."[67]) One of her early *Tribune* articles even sustains the fatal view that it was already too late to change the terrible course of events.[68] But through her increasing aware-

---

[66] In the end, Fuller's particular focus remains England. She writes, "England must glide, or totter or fall into revolution—there is not room for such selfish Selves, and unique young Dukes in a country so crowded with men and with those who ought to be women, and are turned into work-tools." Yet because she also reviews works by French and American writers (Sue and Willis), Fuller's focus also includes the insight into the "difficulty of the era" provided by such eclectic leisure reading.

[67] *Tribune*, "New Year's Day," Jan. 1, 1845.

[68] In *"Oneota, or the Red Race of America, by Henry R. Schoolcraft," Tribune*, Feb. 12, 1845, she writes, "Mr. Schoolcraft says, 'The old idea that the Indian mind is not susceptible of a high, or an advantageous cultivation, rests upon very questionable data.' He might have added, that the experiment has never been tried. For ourselves, brought up, like others, in the vulgar notion that the Indian obstinately refused to be civilized, and long ignorant that the white man had no desire to make the red owner of the land his fellow citizen there, but to intoxicate, plunder, and then destroy or exile him, we have been amazed, on looking into such experiments as have been made, at the degree of success that has attended them. In every instance where any fidelity was shown to the duty of reconciling two races opposed to one another in every characteristic of organization and manners, surprising success has ensued. We mention this merely to do justice in word and thought; it is too late

ness of the extraordinary potential of both the newspaper's extraordinary ability to affect public opinion and the *Tribune*'s success in developing a faithful and growing readership, she begins to think that some hope might remain for a change in Native American policy. Hence, a month before her departure for England, she reviewed T. L. McKenney's *Memoirs*.[69] Claiming that she deliberately read McKenney's book on Independence Day, she uses her review to critique the enormous range of wrongs troubling the country, from slavery to the war in Mexico. Yet, for Fuller, the "conduct of this nation toward the Indians" is the most egregious sign that the United States has failed to live up to its "fundamental idea" of equality. Her review becomes less an endorsement of McKenney's "civilizing" project than an appeal for her readers to take the Indian crisis to heart and act on it. Indeed, she subtley critiques McKenney's idea of "civic life"—particularly as it relates to his personal dealings with several Native American children and men.[70] Breaking from the discourse of the vanishing American demonstrates her own faith (however qualified by her distress over the state of the country at the time of her article) in the possibility of significant social exchange. And it is a faith, I argue, based on hegemonic activity rather than the sheer acts of dominance that had characterized the U.S. policy toward Native Americans until that time. Fuller's faith was not rewarded, of course. Yet this shared cultural failure should not diminish our appreciation of her early effort to produce a theory of reading that, if taken seriously, might have made possible such a break from the old rhetoric of progress.

Ironically, Fuller's new confidence is based on her gathering observation of the trials and limitations around her. Her dispatches from Europe

---

for act; the time is gone by when the possessors of the soil might have been united as one family with their invaders; nothing remains but to write their epitaph with some respect to truth."

[69] Fuller made a symbolic gesture by discussing T. L. McKenney's "New Book on the Indians" on the Fourth of July: "Colonel McKenney's New Book on the Indians," *Tribune*, July 4, 1846. Her review occurred four days later: "Memoirs, Official and Personal," *Tribune*, July 8, 1846.

[70] In "Memoirs, Official and Personal," *Tribune*, July 8, 1846, she writes, "Col. M'Kenney, in showing the mistakes that have been made, and the precious opportunities lost of doing right and good to the Indians, shows also that, at this very moment, another such opportunity is presented, probably the last. We bespeak attention to this plan. We do not restate it here, preferring the public should be led to it by gradual steps, through his own book, which we hope to see in general circulation. We shall content ourselves with repeating that the time to attend the subject, get information and act, is NOW, or never. A very short time and it will be too late to release ourselves, in any measure, from the weight of ill doing, or preserve any vestiges of a race, one large portion of the creation of God, and whose life and capacities ought by all enlightened and honest, not to say religious, minds to be held infinitely precious."

continue to work this dangerous double vision, enhancing her sense that change is forthcoming, albeit with a sense of urgency. By 1850, as she is forced to leave Italy following the collapse of the early stages of the revolution, her faith takes on a strident character:

> It will be an uncompromising revolution. England cannot reason nor ratify nor criticize it—France cannot betray it—Germany cannot bungle it—Italy cannot babble it away—Russia cannot stamp it down nor hide it in Siberia. The New Era is no longer an embryo, it is born; it begins to walk—this very year sees its first giant steps, and can no longer mistake its features. Men have long been talking of a transition state—it is over—the power of positive, determinate effort is begun.[71]

These late dispatches, in which Fuller clearly gives her support to "what is called Socialism, as the inevitable sequence to the tendencies and wants of the era,"[72] are less demonstrative of a radical change in her position than they are reinforcements of the position she had developed in the course of her career. The language of her last dispatch, quoted above, reveals most readily the odd continuity of her thought. If she appears to be casting aside her interest in the transition state, a conceptual frame so important to her social and political insight, her dismissal is rhetorical, and aimed rather at the loss Italy had just encountered. The transition state is cast out as that language that had denied the New Era its legitimate status, yet Fuller is well aware that what she advocates (and has always advocated) is transition itself.

[71] *Tribune*, Feb. 13, 1850.
[72] *Tribune*, Jan. 9, 1850.

7

Representative Others: Uses of Fuller and Fourier in *Representative Men*

And thou shalt not be able to rehearse the names of thy friends in
thy verse, for an old shame before the holy ideal.
—Emerson, "The Poet," CW 3: 24

All the notable Americans, except Webster . . . , are female minds.
—Emerson, JMN 9: 452

In a real as well as subtle way, Emerson's *Representative Men* forms a
conversational response to Margaret Fuller's double advocacy of Goethe
and Fourier in *Woman in the Nineteenth Century*. Although not published
until January 1850, much of *Representative Men* was composed from
lectures given in 1846, after *Woman in the Nineteenth Century* appeared,
and during Fuller's early tenure with the *New-York Daily Tribune*. Of
course, the issues bound up in her advancement of Goethe and Fourier
continued to play an important part in her later *Tribune* work, particularly the reading strategy developed through her twin endorsement of
national education and the idea of woman. And because of the odd
delay between the composition and publication of the volume, *Representative Men* demonstrates how the reading strategy she developed from
the tension between Goethe and Fourier exerted an influence over Emerson's thinking long after her departure for England and Europe, an
influence that became even more significant after her death.[1]

In *S/Z* Roland Barthes makes a distinction between "readerly" and
"writerly" texts that can help us to understand the nature of Emerson's
engagement with Fuller's reading strategy during this period. "The goal
of the literary work," writes Barthes, "is to make the reader no longer a
consumer, but a producer of the text." As we have seen, Fuller's theory

[1] With his choice of title, Emerson seemingly displays a new confidence in the political
process of representation and democracy. Yet the body of the book displays the familiar
polarities of the *Second Series* and shows him vacillating between a faith in the efficacy of
representation and skepticism concerning its disruptive qualities. With the notable exception of Napoleon, his subjects are men who in one way or another engaged in a study and
critique of representation: the philosopher, the mystic, the skeptic, the poet and, finally, the
writer. The choice of Napoleon as the representative "Man of the World" (W 4: 223) served
to expose the materialistic excess abroad in modern society. The crisis in political representation suggested by Napoleon merely signaled Emerson's deeper concern for the crisis in
linguistic representation. Thus the idea that political and linguistic representation are *both*
important determinants in the conduct of life subsumes the structure of the volume.

of reading was inspired by a similar ambition: her goal was to turn the reader into an active agent in the interpretive field created by literary works. According to Barthes, a writerly text enables a reader to open the work to the plurality of value through which it is constructed, and a readerly text produces meaning that arrests the "infinite play of the world."[2] Though for Barthes the distinction is never strict and often fraught with inconsistencies, the separation makes it easier to specify the attributes necessary for the development of a cultural critique. As always, he is attentive to the ideological pressures through which we define ourselves: we are at once torn between the laws of representation as they have been codified in a readerly fashion and the chaotic but often liberating promise of their disruption in the writerly sense. Or, as Paul Smith explains in his telling analysis of Barthes' work, the readerly text "relies upon the fixity of the 'subject' within the codes and conventions it inhabits," whereas the writerly text enables a "transgressive" reading in which the reader can observe "the symbolic codes which attempt to keep us in place."[3]

I have argued that Fuller saw a tension between writerly and readerly tendencies in Emerson's work. She believed that the habitual inclination of his thinking toward the writerly held significant consequences for the conduct of life. Bringing together the lessons of Fourier and Goethe enabled her to elaborate how a successful cultural critique could depend on the properties of language most fully at work in literary texts. But, as we have seen, Emerson found the popular use of Fourier in North America to be far too threatening. Because some proponents of Fourier were espousing radical doctrines about marriage and the family without consulting women, Emerson often retreated into a readerly posture on certain issues pertaining to Fourier. Like Emerson, Fuller recognized the need for the readerly text; her concern for women and other marginalized groups led her to see how the opinion and experience of women could disappear through the total release of meaning into the "infinite play of the world." Yet she felt that Fourier could be used differently, and showing the relationship of his vision to the subtle nuances of Goethe's world became her way of demonstrating that use.[4]

As we saw in Chapter 6, Fuller's double strategy is most fully devel-

---

[2] Roland Barthes, *S/Z*, trans. Richard Miller (New York: Hill and Wang, 1974), 4, 5 ("what plural constitutes it").

[3] Paul Smith, *Discerning the Subject* (Minneapolis: University of Minnesota Press, 1988), 17. Smith uses this description to elaborate on the distinction between *jouissance* and *plaisir* in Barthes's work.

[4] For Fuller, the disruptive or writerly aspect of Fourier's approach to culture was dominant. Yet he manifested significant readerly qualities as well. His focus on Woman could be seen as a move toward an important new faith *in* representation, giving women a place in the new grammar of social codes.

oped in her *Tribune* writing, with its simultaneous focus on national education and Woman. But we can easily see how the terms of this double strategy would emerge most sharply for Emerson in her attempt to balance the thinking of Goethe and Fourier. Goethe represents the shifting powers of pedagogy and education, whereas Fourier represents the efficacy of a new social order. Although Fuller recognizes that education is an important source of agency and development, she also recognizes how education reinforces the prescriptive codes of society. For her, therefore, the position of Woman (both inside and outside of society) acts as a writerly agent on those codes, revealing ways, not to dismantle meaning into chaos, but to open meaning to the plurality of its construction. Because Goethe as well as Fourier recognized the provisional place of woman in culture, Fuller sees a useful bond between the two.

Clearly taken with Fuller's attempt to bring together the work of Goethe and Fourier, Emerson alludes to both thinkers in *Representative Men*. In fact, he was still struggling with the representative status of Fourier; an early listing of the table of contents in one of his notebooks shows that he considered ending his book with a chapter on Fourier.[5] Ultimately, however, no section on Fourier appeared; instead, a chapter on Goethe, who plays the part of the "representative" writer of the age, ends the work. Nevertheless, Fourier figures significantly throughout the text, both by direct references, notably the essays on Montaigne and Napoleon, and in a more figurative and allegorical way in Emerson's treatment of Swedenborg and Goethe. In the literal references, the figure of Fourier poses as the agent of human desire, passion, and, ultimately, skepticism, whereas in the more figurative allusions, he begins to command a representative status closer to Fuller's conception of him. That status becomes most vivid in Emerson's introductory essay entitled "Uses of Great Men," in which many of Fuller's ideas developed through her reading of Fourier are internalized and rearticulated. Indeed, Fuller herself makes a figurative appearance in "Uses" and the use to which she is put discloses Emerson's growing acceptance of a subtle double strategy of his own.

Uses of Great Men

From Emerson's journals we know that shortly after the publication of *Representative Men* in 1850 he expressed dissatisfaction with the work. He was particularly concerned that he had allowed himself to "continue

---

[5] JMN 12: 580. The order is only slightly changed from his final arrangement: "1 [blank] 2 Plato 3 Swedenborg 4 Montaigne 5 Shakespear Saadi 6 Goethe 7 Napoleon 8 Fourier."

the parrot echoes of the names of literary notabilities & mediocrities" while ignoring the "unexpressed greatness of the common farmer & laborer" (JMN 11: 192). His self-critique certainly echoes the idea of "unexpressed greatness" in men and women as Fuller had begun to elaborate it in her *Tribune* writing. Yet his writing in *Representative Men*, particularly in his essay "Uses of Great Men," is even more Fullerian (and, by association, Fourieristic) in its obvious attention to the theoretical problem of greatness and its bearing on the social fabric of the day.

Fuller's emphasis on the significance of changing political hierarchies enters directly into the structure of Emerson's first chapter. His description of the uses of great men echoes the language of her *Tribune* columns on genius: "He is a monarch who gives a constitution to his people, . . . an emperor who can spare his empire" (W 4: 23). Few readers have noticed how Emerson deliberately attempts to praise those men who can "abolish [themselves] and all heroes . . . destroying individualism" (W 4: 23). Apparently he had begun to concur with Fuller—and Fourier—that "we shall cease to look in men for completeness, and shall content ourselves with their social and delegated quality" (W 4: 34). In adopting this position Emerson sets out to explore two radically different but related ideas: the prospect of "destroying individualism" (W 4: 23) and the hope of maintaining the "law of individuality" (W 4: 28).[6] The first reflects his effort to "see other people and their works" (W 4: 25) without succumbing to the totalizing tendencies of individualism; the second represents the desire to lend hope to subaltern constituents of society by discouraging those "impos[ing] . . . [their] being on every other creature" (W 4: 28). Thus a subtle double strategy informs the opening structure of *Representative Men*. To destroy individualism is to disrupt the codes of humanism which mask certain ideological dangers and constraints. At the same time, maintaining the law of individuality serves to protect the integrity of those others who are often the first victims of those constraints.

Emerson also shares Fuller's central concern for the "possibility of interpretation," which, as he argues, "lies in the identification of the observer with the observed" (W 4: 11), and in so doing directly addresses the skepticism sometimes generating a mood of crisis and isolation in the *Second Series*. The title of the essay, with its utilitarian resonance, forms a playful reference to the "true romance" of the *Second Series*. The idea that "great men" could be "useful" makes teasing reference to his paradoxical call in "Experience" for the "transformation of

---

[6] This complex engagement with the problems of individualism is overlooked by Sacvan Bercovitch in his essay "Emerson, Individualism, and the Ambiguities of Dissent," *The South Atlantic Quarterly* 89 (Summer 1990): 623–62.

genius into practical power." Unlike the diffident voice in "Experience" ("let us treat the men and women well: treat them as if they were real, perhaps they are,") the voice in "Uses" is forthright: "We must not contend against love, or deny the substantial existence of other people" (W 4: 5). No longer quarreling with those would would ask Why not realize your world? Emerson actively attends to the power of personal intercourse. According to him, "Each man seeks those of different quality from his own, and such as are good of their kind; that is, he seeks other men, and the *otherest*" (W 4: 5).[7]

We know from Emerson's letters that Fuller often provided him with his most vivid vision of the Other in his explorations of identity. She is also his model for the representative man of the text, if only in the way that she is a model of human agency for him. We recall how his early description of the "delicious sense of indeterminate size" (W 4: 17) wrought by "intellectual feats of all kinds" (W 4: 16) matches his description of the excitement stimulated by her intellectual prowess during her first visit to Concord.[8] And when in *Representative Men* he describes the power of certain people to "divine another's destiny better than that other can," (W 4: 14–15), he is describing the power he often attributed to Fuller, first privately in his letters to her and later publicly in his discussion of her after her death.[9] Nor is it a coincidence that his

[7] For John Michael, this engagement with the Other merely helps Emerson to refine his developing theory of skepticism. According to Michael (*Emerson and Skepticism: The Cipher of the World* [Baltimore: Johns Hopkins University Press, 1988]), Emerson's focus on the Other was the inevitable outcome of his reading of Hume and Montaigne, both of whom believed in their own way that the "question of relation [was] the question of identity" (p. 46). In his analysis, Michael correctly observes how Emerson became increasingly intrigued by the play of identity in the process of interpretation. Yet a curious determination to sustain a sense of crisis in Emerson's thinking prohibits Michael from seeing the insights that develop for Emerson through his recognition that the self can exist "only in relation to [an] other" (p. xii). Michael focuses much of his attention on Emerson's essay "Montaigne" and ignores the earlier "Experience." Through this oversight he fails to see how Emerson's engagement with Fuller and the discourse of Fourier slowly altered his ability to absorb without crisis the idea that "personal identity is a public matter" (p. 57).

[8] Writing to his brother William, Emerson described Fuller's visit to his house and added, "It is always a great refreshment to see a very intelligent person. it is like being set in a large place. You stretch your limbs and dilate to your utmost size" (EL 2: 32).

[9] When Emerson recalls Fuller's initial visit to his house in *Memoirs of Margaret Fuller Ossoli*, he paraphrases the passage on destiny: "The auditor jumped for joy, and thirsted for unlimited draughts. What! is this the dame, who, I heard, was sneering and critical? this the blue-stocking, of whom I stood in terror and dislike? this wondrous woman, full of counsel, full of tenderness, before whom every mean thing is ashamed, and hides itself; this new Corinne, more variously gifted, wise, sportive, eloquent, who seems to have learned all languages, Heaven knows when or how,—I should think she was born to them,—magnificent, prophetic, reading my life at her will, and puzzling me with riddles like this, 'Yours is an example of destiny springing from 'character:' and, again, 'I see your destiny hovering before you, but it always escapes you'" (MMF 1: 215).

earlier journal entry entitled "Margaret" resembles his description of
great men. One recalls his claim that "in her presence all were apprised
of their fettered estate & longed for liberation, of ugliness & longed for
their beauty; of meanness, & panted for grandeur" (JMN 8: 368–69). The
same type of agency is attributed to great men in his opening essay.

Fuller is, of course, representative in a figurative rather than a literal
way in these essays. The decision not to credit the relationship with her
appears to be Emerson's way of protecting himself (and her) from what
he took to be the prurient interest of his audience. It is as if he believed
that by concealing her identity, his "use" of her would be free of the
instrumentalism that had so worried him about Fourier and the Fourier-
ists.[10]

The tension between the titles *Representative Men* and *Woman in the
Nineteenth Century* is suggestive in itself. The more carefully one reads
Representative Men, in fact, the more Emerson's decision to use the title
appears to reflect his continuing engagement with issues made prominent by Fuller in her writing. His reference to the double significance of
"human education and agency" (W 4: 35) at the close of his introductory
essay resembles her articulation of her double focus on national education and Woman in the *Tribune*. Like her, he feels the need to modify the
concept of education by separating out the idea of agency. Thus he
makes an argument about education that sounds very much like her
own understanding of its dynamic. "Society," he writes, "is a
Pestalozzian school: all are teachers and pupils in turn" (W 4: 31). Because Fuller aligns the concept of agency with the place of Woman in
culture, she advances a feminist position more directly than he does,
despite the fact that her simultaneous focus on education and a type of
feminist agency does not restrict itself to questions of gender. As is clear
from her *Tribune* articles, her feminism enables her to construct a theory
of reading that in turn engages her in a larger critique of the ideological
formations of culture. That larger critique is what appealed to Emerson,
but, ironically, it remained elusive throughout *Representative Men* precisely because he could not accept what he understood to be its particular Fourieristic dimension. Indeed, flashes of the same skepticism that
threatened to subsume the reading of *Essays: Second Series*, a skepticism
regarding the instrumental threat of Fourieristic reform, continually appear in the later work.

At the same time, however, the "Minerva" side of Emerson's thinking

[10] Yet it is impossible to imagine that all of Emerson's readers missed the provocative
tension between the very titles *Representative Men* and *Woman in the Nineteenth Century*.
And more than likely, his closest friends, those with whom he had shared letters and
journal entries, recognized Fuller's "use" in his opening essay.

continues to gain force in this work. Fuller's focus on the unique and problematic position of women in culture and the way in which an understanding of that position could provide a site of critique enabled her to emphasize the efficacy of a provisional space—what I call the space of paraphernalia. In many ways her feminist theory had begun through her focus on conversation as the site provisionally given to women by the culture; after all, conversation had enabled her to bring Goethe and Fourier together. Her earliest translations focused on Goethe's investment in the unique conversational space culture gives to women, which was virtually the same transitional space so important to Fourier. Though Emerson had already acknowledged in his journals that the "conversation of a woman will be the solidest pledge of truth and power" (JMN 7: 515), *Representative Men* marks the first stage in his slow but steady endorsement of the reading strategy figured by the provisional space of conversation. Glimmers of a confidence in the agency of conversation are apparent throughout, particularly in the opening essay in which he emphasizes how a particular type of conversation can redistribute power itself.

> The imbecility of men is always inviting the impudence of power. It is the delight of the vulgar talent to dazzle and to blind the beholder. But true genius seeks to defend us from itself. True genius will not impoverish, but will liberate, and add new sense. If a wise man should appear in our village he would create, in those who conversed with him, a new consciousness of wealth, by opening their eyes to unobserved advantages; he would establish a sense of immovable equality, calm us with assurances that we could not be cheated (W 4: 18).

Even here, the tensions in his thinking are readily apparent. The "vulgar talent" he assigns to the "impudence of power" makes veiled reference to the "secret doctrines" of Fourier so disturbing to Emerson. At the same time, the conversation that opens "eyes to unobserved advantages" draws directly from Emerson's experience with Fuller.

Uses of Fourier

Emerson's decision not to include a chapter on Fourier suggests that he continued to have serious reservations about the efficacy of Fourier's work. Nevertheless, he adverts to Fourier throughout the volume, and his chapter "Swedenborg; Or, The Mystic" can even be said to form an allegorical commentary on Fourier. (In his *Dial* essay on Fourier, he had earlier remarked upon the "strange coincidences" between the two men.[11]) His reading of Swedenborg mounts the same complaint earlier put forth concerning Fourier's elaborate plan: Swedenborg's system of correspondences lacks the vital element of "spontaneity," and shows little evidence of the spark of energy necessary "to generate life" (W 4: 133).

The strange affinities between Swedenborg and Fourier also prompt Emerson to espouse in his analysis of Swedenborg what he had sought to deny in his article on Fourier. Because the object of Swedenborg's vision is theological, Emerson freely enlists the radical theory of language that he had found problematic in his analysis of Fourier. The problem with Swedenborg's theory of correspondences, according to Emerson, is that it "fastens each natural object to a theologic notion" (W 4: 121) and that it misinterprets the fluid nature of signs. For Emerson, Swedenborg fails in his work to recognize how in "nature, each individual symbol plays innumerable parts, as each particle of matter circulates in turn through every system" (W 4: 121). Thus Emerson's earlier alarm over Fourier's assumption that man and his social life could be changed through a plastic view of language was based on affinity rather than difference, or the recognition that Fourier differed from Emerson only in his focus on the institution of marriage instead of the institution of religion.

The shadowy parallels between Swedenborg and Fourier become still more prominent when Emerson turns to an analysis of Swedenborg's treatise on marriage entitled "Conjugal Love." According to Emerson, Swedenborg makes a direct correspondence between earthly marriage and its heavenly counterpart. And because he advances the argument in "Conjugal Love" that "sex is universal, and not local; virility in the male qualifying every organ, act, and thought; and the feminine in woman" (W 4: 127), Swedenborg also claims that "in the real or spiritual world the nuptial union is not momentary, but incessant and total" (W 4: 127). Emerson thus contends that Swedenborg's treatise on marriage "fail[s] of success" (W 4: 127) because he makes the mistake of "pinning" his theory "to a temporary form"—in this case, the form of earthly marriage and the role of man and wife in that marriage (W 4: 128). This critique resembles Fuller's analysis of Emerson's thinking when he first attempted to come to terms with Fourier's critique of marriage. At the time, his restraint came from his concern for the instrumental and self-serving potential of Fourier's critique, a concern shared by Fuller. But as we see from his journals, Emerson found it difficult to dismiss the paral-

---

[11] "Fourierism and the Socialists," *Dial* 3 (July 1842): 87.

lels between his argument against organized religion and Fourier's critique of marriage. Perhaps more frightening, Emerson's theoretical thinking about marriage had even anticipated some of Fourier's critique. Interestingly, he returns in the Swedenborg essay to elaborate on a journal passage he had written shortly after he made his decision not to participate in the Brook Farm experiment (JMN 7: 532–33). In the revised version he writes:

> God is the bride or bridegroom of the soul. Heaven is not the pairing of two, but the communion of all souls. We meet, and dwell an instant under the temple of one thought, and part, as though we parted not, to join another thought in other fellowships of joy. So far from there being anything divine in the low and proprietary sense of Do you love me? it is only when you leave me and lose me by casting yourself on a sentiment which is higher than both of us, that I draw near and find myself at your side; and I am repelled if you fix your eye on me and demand love. In fact, in the spiritual world we change sexes every moment. You love the worth in me; then I am your husband: but it is not me, but the worth, that fixes the love; and that worth is a drop of the ocean of worth that is beyond me. Meantime I adore the greater worth in another, and so become his wife (W 4: 128–29).

Because a substantial part of the original passage remains unchanged, it shows that in 1840 Emerson had already begun to experiment with a critique of marriage and gender relations not unlike Fourier's. His preference for the "communion of all souls" over the "pairing of two" parallels Fourier's critique of the isolated household. Even so, his argument remains tainted by the literal world from which he draws his metaphors and therefore appears pinned to a temporary form—the hierarchical model of husband and wife in the traditional concept of marriage.

Emerson's confusion on this issue is local and momentary, particularly since his description of God as "the bride or bridegroom of the soul" marshals gender as an arbitrary sign of power. (He adds this phrase when he incorporates the journal entry into the essay for *Representative Men*.) The confusion in his use of gender at the end of the passage, moreover, would appear to reflect his uneasiness with Fuller's suggestion that he apply the radical (or writerly) view of language he had found so useful in his dismissal of traditional forms of religion to the "literal" limits of marriage. Although Fuller never intended her challenge as a literal assault on Emerson's marriage, we know from the reaction recorded in letters and journals that he took it that way. As always, the problem for him was that he could see how readily his own thinking could be aligned with the social plans of Fourier.

Emerson continues to remain divided and somewhat defensive on the issue of marriage, as another addition to the journal passage he developed for the essay on Swedenborg makes evident. He speculates that "perhaps the true subject of the 'Conjugal Love' is *Conversation*, whose laws are profoundly set forth. It is false, if literally applied to marriage" (W 4: 128).[12] At first he seems to suggest that Swedenborg's essay provides a figural analysis of the structure of conversation. Yet from what he says elsewhere about the nature of conversation—notably in "Uses of Great Men"—he more likely is suggesting that the "true subject" of marriage *should* be conversation.[13] In so doing, he turns the discussion of marriage into a linguistic issue, all of which explains why he quickly adds, "It is false, if literally applied to marriage." Throughout the 1840s he continued to separate the literal world of domestic life from his writerly sense of signs and their play in a sociolinguistic system. His insistence on the separation here suggests that he recognizes the risk he has taken with his analysis by introducing the concept of conversation.

Emerson seems to have understood that by 1850 such a separation of issues could not have been sustained in an essay on Fourier. For this reason, perhaps, he did not include a separate essay on Fourier, a notable omission given Fourier's influence in the United States at this time. Turning to the literal world, and to the men making the strongest impact there, he instead chose Napoleon as his representative "man of the world." (Napoleon and Fourier were often mentioned together in American letters in the nineteenth century, offering as they did radically alternate models for the materialistic development of the country.) We cannot fault Emerson for this choice, but his chapter on Napoleon introduces Fourier in his analysis—and simultaneously excludes him from the book.

> Every experiment, by multitudes or by individuals, that has a sensual and selfish aim, will fail. The pacific Fourier will be as inefficient as the pernicious Napoleon. As long as our civilization is essentially one of property,

[12] The statement is compellingly obscure, particularly in its different versions. Compare the 1904 Riverside Press edition, as quoted, to another version (American Authors in Prose and Poetry [New York: P. F. Collier & Son, 1903]), which reads: "Perhaps the true subject of 'Conjugal Love' is *Conversation*, whose laws are profoundly eliminated" (p. 118).

[13] See his description of conversation in his essay "Circles," written in 1840, at the height of his intimacy with Fuller: "In common hours, society sits cold and statuesque. We all stand waiting, empty,—knowing, possibly, that we can be full, surrounded by mighty symbols which are not symbols to us, but prose and trivial toys. Then cometh the god and converts the statues into fiery men, and by a flash of his eye burns up the veil which shrouded all things, and the meaning of the very furniture, of cup and saucer, of chair and clock and tester, is manifest. The facts which loomed so large in the fogs of yesterday,— property, climate, breeding, personal beauty, and the like, have strangely changed their proportions. All that was settled, shakes and rattles; and literatures, cities, climates, religions, leave their foundations, and dance before our eyes" (CW 2: 184).

of fences, of exclusiveness, it will be mocked by delusions. Our riches will leave us sick; there will be bitterness in our laughter; and our wine will burn our mouth. Only that good profits which we can taste with all doors open, and which serves all men (W 4: 258).

Such an analysis provides an extraordinary finish to the essay on Napoleon. It comes to closure by demeaning Fourier and Napoleon alike, but it also ends by promoting the socialistic rhetoric of Fourier against all that has just preceded it.

Although Fourier appears only briefly or by indirection in the other sections of *Representative Men* to which I have referred, he receives considerable attention in the closing section of "Montaigne, Or, the Skeptic." There, Emerson's use of Fourier echoes his use in the Napoleon essay. Again, Fourier serves both to provoke and unhinge Emerson's argument about skepticism and faith. He quotes one of the three credos etched into Fourier's actual gravestone: "The attractions of man are proportioned to his destinies" (CW 4: 183). He paraphrases this credo as "every desire predicts its own satisfaction" (CW 4: 184). His interpretation of Fourier enables him to thematize the inevitable development of a skeptical perspective. If, as Emerson argues, "all experience exhibits the reverse of this"—namely the incommensurability between "the ambition of man" and "his power of performance" (W 4: 183)—then disappointment over the "yawning gulf" between the two is the actual source of skepticism. This odd paragraph brings us back, then, to a familiar pass in Emerson's work, the "crack" (EL 2: 52) in his world that now finds its sharpest allegorization in the words of Fourier.

This radical compression of Fourier's theoretical world into one credo highlights Emerson's sense of the seductive nature of Fourier's theory, for reduced in this way, Fourier's polyphonic text becomes a veritable "syren." But Fourier can also function as a tool for reversing and disrupting this reading. His double function is apparent in the paragraph mentioning Fourier; it reads like a series of novel plots all strung together, all sharing an emplotment of desire and disappointment.

It has shown the heaven and earth to every child and filled him with a desire for the whole; a desire raging, infinite; a hunger, as of space to be filled with planets; a cry of famine, as of devils for souls. Then for the satisfaction—to each man is administered a single drop, a bead of dew of vital power, *per day*,—a cup as large as space, and one drop of water of life in it. Each man woke in the morning with an appetite that could eat the solar system like a cake; a spirit for action and passion without bounds; he could lay his hand on the morning star; he could try conclusions with gravitation or chemistry; but, on the first motion to prove his strength,—

hands, feet, senses, gave way and would not serve him. He was an emperor deserted by his states, and left to whistle by himself, or thrust into a mob of emperors, all whistling: and still the sirens sang, "The attractions are proportioned to the destinies." In every house, in the heart of each maiden and of each boy, in the soul of the soaring saint, this chasm is found,—between the largest promise of ideal power, and the shabby experience (W 4: 184).

Emerson does not settle on the idea that man's desire is the sponsor of skepticism. Rather, he closes with the idea that such skepticism can be transvalued, as can this emplotment of desire.[14] The two paragraphs with which he ends his essay on Montaigne posit a kind of hope that will become doubly important to him in his later essay "Fate." In view of the "events forced on us which seem to retard or retrograde the civility of ages," we are advised to remember that "the world-spirit is a good swimmer, and storms and waves cannot drown him. He snaps his finger at laws" (W 4: 185). Emerson does not literally return to Fourier to transform his argument about skepticism, but he does invoke a sense of the writerly or plastic approach to life, advising, "Let a man learn to look for the permanent in the mutable and the fleeting" (W 4: 186). Moreover, he follows this section on the skeptic with two sections on important *writers*, Shakespeare and Goethe.

Although both Shakespeare and Goethe are described in terms borrowed from Fourier, the former receives the highest valorization as the poet, capable of "perfect representation" (W 4: 214). The decision here to distinguish between the poet and the writer represents what I take to be Emerson's growing acceptance of the changing cultural role of contemporary writers. For him, the offices of the writer reflect the larger cultural move toward a cooperative social order, not unlike the move toward socialism described in the theories of Fourier. Fourier's influence, therefore, is most readily seen in Emerson's closing chapter on Goethe, whose books contain plot lines very much like the ones Emerson gathers together in his argument for "Montaigne." As the title "Goethe; or the Writer" suggests, he elaborates here on two separate but interrelated ideas: the idea of writing in a changing cultural climate and the exemplary nature of Goethe's writing.

Emerson begins by theorizing the world as text—"Nature will be reported. All things are engaged in writing their history" (W 4: 262)— which leads to a provocative sentence: "In nature, this self-registration is incessant, and the narrative is the print of the seal." Here he experiments

[14] Here Emerson toys with what Fredric Jameson has called Lacan's "zero degree of the psychic"—that which gives up the "myth of total satisfaction, analogous to the myth of total presence denounced by Derrida" (*The Prison House of Language* [Princeton: Princeton University Press, 1972], 173).

with a locution that will become still more important in his essay "Fate." (Indeed, *Representative Men* appears to function as a trial for many ideas reappearing in "Fate," a fact that will make more sense when we see how Fuller's death influenced that essay.) In the later essay, as we shall see, he contends with the way in which nature prescribes our destiny ("the event is the print of your form" [W 6: 140]), whereas, in "Goethe; Or, the Writer" he empties the value of nature's "self-registration" (W 4: 262). Trapped by the circular referentiality of the "print of the seal," the narrative of nature becomes legible only as a trace. He makes it clear that a human author is necessary to transform the incessant and natural process of inscription into something important and useful. "It makes a great difference," he writes, "to the force of any sentence whether there be a man behind it or no" (W 4: 282). Nature is constantly signing itself, and the writer gives special value to that process. Thus, "in man, the report is something more than print of the seal" (W 4: 262). Although Emerson insists on the signature, the mark of the authorial presence in a sentence, his position nevertheless disturbs the familiar platonic view of writing. No longer simply a technology with which to copy some original presence, writing actually becomes that which produces "a new and finer form of the original" (W 4: 262). To establish this finer form, the writer does not bind signs to one meaning as the mystic might, nor does she find the elusive nature of language problematic, as the skeptic does. Rather she revels in the plastic attributes of language and meaning production, for in that plasticity lies the route to escape from seemingly overwhelming cultural forces.

Emerson's description of the writer therefore employs several key phrases from Fourieristic discourse, most notably the idea of cooperation. "In man, the memory is a kind of looking-glass, which, having received the images of surrounding objects, is touched with life, and disposes them in a new order. The facts do not lie in it inert; but some subside and others shine; so that we soon have a new picture, composed of the eminent experiences. The man coöperates" (W 4: 262). Emerson's elaboration demonstrates the writer's role as cultural critic. She is an "organic agent" (W 4: 264) with "adequate powers of expression to hold up each object of monomania in its right relations" (W 4: 265). Throughout, Emerson's emphasis remains the writer's ability to discern the "knitting and contexture of things" (W 4: 264). Whereas contemporaries commend the "practical man," the writer instead reveals the invisible ideological forces operating behind actions of those claiming to be above them. Emerson momentarily assumes the role of the writer to make this point, demonstrating how a knowledge of linguistic signification can open to view hidden but important chains in social and political activity.

Our people are of Bonaparte's opinion concerning ideologists. Ideas are subversive of social order and comfort, and at last make a fool of the possessor. It is believed, the ordering a cargo of goods from New York to Smyrna, or the running up and down to procure a company of subscribers to set a-going five or ten thousand spindles, or the negotiations of a caucus and the practising on the prejudices and facility of country-people to secure their votes in November,—is practical and commendable (W 4: 266).

The writer, finally, performs not as the advocate of individualism, but as the overseer and facilitator of a type of cooperative individuality. Significantly then, Goethe becomes the representative writer for transformation along the lines that Fuller had been advancing in her newspaper writing. Indeed, Emerson's initial description of Goethe reads as if it emerged directly from one of Fuller's *Tribune* columns.

He appears at a time when a general culture has spread itself and has smoothed down all sharp individual traits; when, in the absence of heroic characters, a social comfort and cooperation have come in. There is no poet, but scores of poetic writers; no Columbus, but hundreds of post-captains, with transit-telescope, barometer and concentrated soup and pemmican; no Demosthenes, no Chatham, but any number of clever parliamentary and forensic debaters; no prophet or saint, but colleges of divinity; no learned man, but learned societies, a cheap press, reading-rooms and book-clubs without number. There was never such a miscellany of facts. . . . Goethe was the philosopher of this multiplicity; hundred-handed, Argus-eyed, able and happy to cope with this rolling miscellany of facts and sciences, and by his own versatility to dispose of them with ease (W 4: 270–71).

As described, Goethe is the writer who fathoms the plastic nature of language, or what Emerson earlier called the circulation of "each particle of matter . . . through every system" (W 4: 121). Goethe understands the fluid nature of life in its relationship to language, and this understanding gives him the ability to recognize how "the dulness and prose we ascribe to the age" is only another mask of "the old cunning Proteus" (W 4: 273). For Emerson, his significance as a writer lies in his ability to make the familiar strange by "tracing the pedigree of every usage and practice, every institution, utensil and means, home to its origin in the structure of man" (W 4: 274). Forcing his readers to adopt a new relationship to the world around them, Goethe becomes a writerly author.

Emerson appears to have absorbed and internalized Fuller's sense of the necessary relationship between Goethe and Fourier. He represents Goethe as the figure of education—"*What can you teach me?*" (W 4: 284)—*and* agency. Emerson's understanding of Fuller's double strategy remains incomplete, however, because the "Minerva" or feminist component of that double strategy remains obscure (save, perhaps, for those who remembered Fuller's association of Goethe with "Minerva" in her *Dial* essay on the writer[15]). Emerson acknowledges this problem when he decides to interrupt his discussion of Goethe to praise George Sand's novel *Consuelo*, which had been received as a type of Fourieristic novel in America. In reviewing the first English translation, Fuller expressed the hope that Sand's novel would encourage "prejudiced men" to "elevate and enlarge their hopes as to 'woman's sphere' and 'woman's mission.'"[16] Although Emerson refrains from making direct reference to the feminist issues involved, the mere mention of Sand's novel introduces a strong Fourieristic note. He finds Sand's book superior to Goethe's *Wilhelm Meister* because the main characters live up to their socialistic ambitions, or to ambitions consonant with a feminist agenda. Unlike Goethe's hero, with his "many weaknesses and impurities" (W 4: 279), the protagonists of Sand's novel "expand at a rate that shivers the porcelain chess-table of aristocratic convention: they quit the society and habits of their rank, they lose their wealth, they become the servants of great ideas and of the most generous social ends" (W 4: 279).

Thus Emerson allows Sand to play the same corrective role to Goethe as does Fourier in *Woman*. The allegiance to Fuller's method is still stronger when we realize how Emerson also uses Sand to *sustain* his positive reading of Goethe. Fuller, we recall, envisioned a conversation between the theoretical positions of Goethe and Fourier rather than a cancellation of one by the other. Thus, although Emerson interrupts his discussion of Goethe's *Wilhelm Meister* to praise Sand's *Consuelo*, he nevertheless closes his reading of Goethe's novel by noting how it "ha[d] only begun its office" for "millions of readers" (W 4: 279). Presumably the "office" of Goethe's text will be enhanced by a Fourieristic reading.

Indeed, the very decision to pause over *Wilhelm Meister* no doubt reflects Fuller's earlier promise that she would supply a Fourieristic reading of the text. In *Woman* she observes the correspondence "between

[15] "Goethe always represents the highest principle in the feminine form. Woman is the Minerva, man the Mars," in "Goethe," *Dial* 2 (July 1841), reprinted in *Life Without and Life Within; Or, Reviews, Narratives, Essays, and Poems by Margaret Fuller Ossoli*, ed. Arthur B. Fuller (1859; Boston: Roberts Brothers, 1895), 41.

[16] The first English translation of *Consuelo* was published in the Brook Farm journal, *The Harbinger*, and Fuller wrote not one but two favorable reviews in the *New-York Daily Tribune*. In the first she discussed the French edition, and in the second, a year later, she addressed issues involved in the American translation: "Jenny Lind—The Consuelo of George Sand," *Tribune*, Sept. 19, 1845; "*Consuelo* by George Sand," *Tribune*, June 24, 1846. The quote is from the later review.

[Goethe's] hopes and those of Fourier," but she also expresses her intention one day to "point out similar coincidences between Goethe's model school [as expressed in *Wilhelm Meister*] and the plans of Fourier" (WNC: 117). She suggests, moreover, how the coincidences between the two thinkers would "cast light upon the page of prophecy" (WNC: 117). Though she never finds time to write her essay on this topic, she hints at her method in her *Dial* essay on Goethe: "Wilhelm is a master when he can command his actions, yet keep his mind always open to new means of knowledge; when he has looked at various ways of living, various forms of religion and of character, till he has learned to be tolerant of all, discerning of good in all."[17] Not surprisingly, her description anticipates Emerson's more general comment about the novel: "No book of this century can compare with it in its delicious sweetness, so new, so provoking to the mind, gratifying it with so many and so solid thoughts, just insights into life, and manners and character; so many good hints for the conduct of life, so many unexpected glimpses into a higher sphere, and never a trace of rhetoric or dulness" (W 4: 278). Emerson apparently borrows from Fuller's earlier defense of Goethe to complete his discussion of *Wilhelm Meister*. To those who see Goethe as "debauchee" or an "epicurian sage" (Emerson had once done so), Fuller answers that Goethe's focus on the present is "not for the Epicurian aim of pleasure, but for use."[18] By the end of the essay in *Representative Men*, Goethe emerges as Emerson's figurative rather than literal agent for change because he is attuned at the most profound level to the "*morgue* of conventions" (W 4: 289) permeating society. And because Goethe is a writer, in Barthes's sense of writerly, he serves this position well, allowing Emerson to end his text on the "Uses of Great Men" with the hope that Goethe will help him to "honor every truth by use" (W 4: 290).

Representative Men does not mark Emerson's complete acceptance of the double strategy or the writerly text. That acceptance will emerge only through his elaborate mourning for Fuller after her tragic death. If, as I argue, Fuller became the embodying sign of Fourier and the problems his theory posed in Emerson's thought, her death held an oddly

---

[17] "Goethe," in *Life Without and Life Within*, ed. Arthur Fuller, p. 39.

[18] "Menzel's View of Goethe," in ibid., p. 20. Emerson also drew a great deal from Fuller's essay "Goethe," which she also published in the *Dial*. If he reviewed her work on Goethe (which he probably did) before he completed his own essay, this line about "use" would have assumed a new value for him: her defense of Goethe anticipated her later support of Fourier. Fourier's use of "pleasure" was exactly what Emerson found so disturbing about him. Yet Fuller's transvaluation of pleasure into something positive seems to have held appeal for Emerson. Certainly his final defense of *Wilhelm Meister* can be read as a sign of his own growing transvaluation of "use."

liberating effect. By losing the literal sign, the body that complicated his theoretical position by threatening to expose his literal response, he is better able to accept the feminist tendencies of his thought, which he does through a series of essays, beginning in *Memoirs of Margaret Fuller Ossoli*.

Even in her absence, then, Fuller's challenge to Emerson's work and life continued to bind him to her as the "Bright foreigner, the foreign self" (JMN 11: 148). Indeed, this influence may underlie his characterization of the writer's best audience as the "unknown friend" (JMN 11: 98), when Fuller was in Europe. Emerson pretended to ignore her immersion in the politics of the Italian Revolution, particularly her passionate attachment to its leaders (Mazzini among them), but her absence made him increasingly impatient with the intellectual climate of the United States and the political passivity of his own literary production. Thus, when he went to Europe in 1848, he wrote to Fuller in his old seductive tones, hoping to lure her home to serve as "sibyl" to the culture.[19] These entreaties were politely refused. When, following the collapse of the revolution, Fuller's attempt to return to the United States with her lover and their infant son ended in a shipwreck off the coast of Long Island, Emerson was forced to examine his behavior and to confront the various hard realities of his friend's life. In so doing, he discovered that her insistence that he apply himself to life ("You are intellect, I am life" [LMF 3: 209]) was her strongest theoretical gesture, one returning him to the provisional space of conversation in the double advocacy of Goethe and Fourier. Her career, viewed as a whole, seemed to embody that provisional space, demonstrating as nothing else could the efficacy of her reading strategy.

---

[19] EL 4: 27. See also EL 3: 446. Emerson remembered well Fuller's argument that the "Muses only sang the praises of Apollo; the Sibyls interpreted his will" (MMF 1: 190).

8

Emerson's Scene before the Women:
Memoirs of Margaret Fuller Ossoli and "Woman"

I have lost in her my audience.
> —Ralph Waldo Emerson, upon hearing the news
> of Margaret Fuller's death, JMN 11: 258

It is a bitter satire on our social order. . . . such is the expansiveness
of America, that, the best use to put a fine woman to, is, to drown
her to save her board!!
> —Emerson, JMN 13: 139

If nature availed in America to give birth to many such as she,
freedom & honour & letters & art too were safe in this new
world. . . . The timorous said, What shall we do? how shall she be
received, now that she brings a husband & child home?
But . . . she had only to open her mouth, & a triumphant success
awaited her. She would fast enough have disposed of the circumstances & the bystanders.
> —Emerson, JMN 11: 256–57

When the Italian Revolution collapsed, Margaret Fuller, Angelo Ossoli, and their young son Angelino needed to leave the country and find a
new home. Hopeful of finding an American publisher for her history of
the revolution, Fuller and her family sailed in 1850 from Europe on a
small merchantman vessel loaded with a shipment of Italian marble.
Unfortunately, it was not long before the captain contracted smallpox
and died. The illness then fell upon young Angelino, and Fuller and
Ossoli spent several agonizing days nursing their child through the
disease. The journey continued under the guidance of the first mate,
Captain Bangs, who navigated the long sail across the ocean but proved
unready for the tempest that rocked the ship against the shoals of Long
Island. The force of the storm shifted the cargo of marble through the
hull and the boat wrecked four hundred yards from the U.S. shore. (The
short distance was a painful detail for Emerson, who in his journals
repeated the distance in two different measures—"400 yards, 60 rods"
(JMN 11: 256)—as if to shorten it.)

The passengers could see shadows on shore, but they were shadows
of wreckers inured to the human struggle on board. Whether as a matter

of expedience or safety, no lifeboat was launched. Fuller might have saved her own life, as others did, by diving into the sea with the aid of a sailor, but she refused to divide her family. In that decision, the legend goes, all were drowned. Her son's body washed ashore, still warm, only minutes after his death. The bodies of Fuller and Ossoli were never recovered. The only object found was a small trunk filled with love letters exchanged between Fuller and Ossoli.[1]

Devastated by the news of Fuller's death, Emerson began to fill his notebooks with thoughts about her and the stir caused by her death. Enlisted by family and friends to write a memoir, he worried about proceeding too quickly. " 'Margaret & her Friends' must be written," he wrote in one journal entry, "but not post haste. It is an essential line of American history" (JMN 11: 258). The redoubtable task of collecting and sorting the remains of a career at the moment of its greatest power (Fuller was forty years old when she died) was made more difficult by the loss of what many have thought would have been its greatest document—the history of the Italian Revolution. "Chaos of ruins, are of no account without result," Emerson wrote in despair at one point, " 'tis all mere nightmare" (JMN 11: 431).

Emerson's journals show him so conflicted about the best way to proceed with the history of Fuller's life that he essentially wrote three versions of it. His contribution to the *Memoirs of Margaret Fuller Ossoli* was written quickly and published in 1851 to quell the tide of gossip about her. He made another attempt to deal with Fuller's loss in "Woman," a lecture he gave before the Boston Woman's Rights Convention in 1855. And he wrote the essay "Fate" simultaneously with his work on *Memoirs*, only to publish it years later in *The Conduct of Life* (1860). The difference between the works relates directly to his shifting perceptions of his audience and may best be characterized by the Barthean distinction between "embarrassed" and "playful" figuration.[2] In the *Memoirs*,

---

[1] Apparently the trunk also contained some letters written in Italian from Constanza Arconati. See EL 4: 296–97. Elizabeth Hoar translated some of the love letters between Fuller and Ossoli; Thomas Wentworth Higginson used these in his biography *Margaret Fuller Ossoli* (Boston: Houghton Mifflin, 1887). Hoar's decision to make that translation is a provocative one, part of the ever-increasing interest in the narrative of Fuller's love life. For more on that interest, see my essay "Womanizing Margaret Fuller: Theorizing a Lover's Discourse," *Cultural Critique* 16 (Fall 1990): 161–91.

[2] Roland Barthes makes an important distinction between "figuration" and "representation" in *The Pleasure of the Text*, trans. Richard Miller (New York: Hill and Wang, 1975), 55–56. "Figuration is the way in which the erotic body appears (to whatever degree and in whatever form that may be) in the profile of the text. For example: the author may appear in his text (Genet, Proust), but not in the guise of direct biography (which would exceed the body, give a meaning to life, forge a destiny). Or again: one can feel desire for a character in a novel (in fleeting impulses). Or finally: the text itself, a diagrammatic and not an imitative structure, can reveal itself in the form of a body, split into fetish objects,

Fuller's oddly represented life is the product of Emerson's hostility toward—and embarrassment over—the frigid account he feels compelled to provide. In "Woman" and "Fate," however, he eradicates his hostility by taking Fuller's mimetic profile out of the work and replacing it with what amounts to her feminist agency. In this way, her life becomes integral to the figurative play and historical intervention of his work.

At least three separate notebooks record the nature of Emerson's struggle. In the first (which he called "AZ"), his thoughts on a lecture series, The Conduct of Life, and his musings over the omissions of his most recent publication, *Representative Men*, are interrupted by the news of Fuller's death. In the second, ("MO"), devoted specifically to the projected memoirs of Fuller's life, his public and private considerations collide. And in the third ("BO"), his anger over the barren nature of American culture, an anger stimulated by the fall of Webster as a model of eloquence in American politics, is intensified by his anger over the loss of Fuller as an alternative model of eloquence or agency for the culture.

What Emerson says about Fuller in his journals depends entirely on the context in which she variously appears. In the first journal, his surprise and horror over her death is compounded by his surprise and horror over the way some people were using the occasion to give vent to the anxieties they harbored about her remarkable life. "To the last her country proves inhospitable to her," he writes (JMN 11: 256). One woman, for example "had the superiority" to proclaim Fuller's shipwreck "a fit & good conclusion to the life" because it ended all discussion of her relationship with Ossoli, which had been generally characterized as a Fourieristic affair (JMN 11: 259).

Emerson discovered that the audience for his projected *Memoirs* was rather suspicious of Fuller's liberation in Italy and grateful that she failed to liberate the United States in the same fashion. The recovery of her liberating powers, which Emerson believed in, given his sense of the intellectual crisis in America, was complicated by the culture's reading of those powers as merely erotic, echoing in a vulgar way his own sense of their potential efficacy. Thus the notebook that he uses for the *Memoirs* assumes a familiar pattern. In one moment he exalts in the freedom of her power, writing, "How can you describe a Force? How can you write the life of Margaret? Well, the question itself is some description of her"

---

into erotic sites. All these movements attest to a figure of the text, necessary to the bliss of reading. . . . Representation . . . is embarrassed figuration, encumbered with other meanings than that of desire: a space of alibis (reality, morality, likelihood, readability, truth, etc.)."

(JMN 11: 488).[3] In the next moment he finds something fatal and frightening about it, admitting that "the unlooked for trait in all these journals . . . is the Woman, poor woman. . . . She is bewailing her virginity and languishing for a husband" (JMN 11: 500).

To be sure, some of Emerson's circumspection came from guilt and confusion over the nature of his own relationship with Fuller. The trunk of love letters that drifted onto the Fire Island beach symbolized her erotic life exposed. But it also functioned as a symbol of his confused love for her, and for this reason, he pauses several times over the detail of the trunk of letters. When he mistakenly believes the trunk to contain letters from a variety of her correspondents (in the last year of her life she corresponded with over a hundred people), he broods about the discovery of *his* letters to her, observing the "panic [that] would strike all her friends, . . . as if a clever reporter had got underneath a confessional & agreed to report all that transpired there on Wall street" (JMN 11: 258). In fact, Emerson's letters to her were neither lost at sea nor washed ashore and exposed (placing his writing in an embarrassing context). She had taken care to leave them with various friends. Because of her amazing, protective, and ennobling gesture (suggesting to him that the letters had a larger context than the private one between them), Emerson had time to reconsider his panic ("You look as if you had locked your trunk & lost the key" [JMN 11: 262]) and fairly assess his method in them as natural and powerfully related to Fuller's worthy force.

Emerson as Mythologist

In his essay "Myth Today," Roland Barthes defines the mythologist as an intervening reader of culture, one particularly alert to the function of myth in "bourgeois ideology."[4] In his later work, including his work on Fourier, Barthes revises this oddly reductive view of ideology in ways more consistent with Althusser's important and more productive argument that ideology is pervasive and "eternal, exactly like the unconscious."[5] Barthes's changing position reflects the inevitable outcome of

---

[3] Emerson here repeats Sam Ward's question to Emerson, a question with which Ward withdrew his help for the projected *Memoirs*. For Fuller's complicated relationship with Sam Ward, see Charles Capper, *Margaret Fuller: An American Romantic Life*, vol. 1 (New York: Oxford University Press, 1992), 276–79.

[4] Barthes, *Mythologies*, trans. Annette Lavers (New York: Hill and Wang, 1984), 141.

[5] "Ideology and Ideological State Apparatuses (Notes toward an Investigation)," in *Lenin and Philosophy and Other Essays*, trans. Ben Brewster (New York: Monthly Review Press, 1971), 161. Althusser writes that we can only "outline a discourse which tries to break with ideology" "while speaking in" and "from within ideology" (p. 173). This sense

his movement from a structuralist to a poststructuralist perspective; Althusser's reformulation of the concept of ideology with its "absolute rejection of the notion of historical totalization" has been described as a poststructuralist move.[6] Yet because Barthes, like Althusser, never focused on the feminist implications of this revision in his later work, the earlier, more humanistic form of Barthes's thought is more helpful in our discussion of Emerson. Barthes's earlier formulation of the problem tends to match more exactly the formulation to which Emerson initially returns in his own struggle with a humanism that proves vital to his developing feminism.[7]

Certainly Barthes's pronouncement that the mythologist is "condemned to live in a theoretical sociality"[8] conforms to the traditional reading of Emerson as a man whose theoretical orientation makes him somewhat aloof and suspicious of both the convivial tendency of his friends and the rhetoric of cooperation associated with Fourier. Emerson's determination to read and critique the signs of his culture means that he often appears trapped in the peculiar isolation to which Barthes condemns the mythologist: Emerson's work is marked everywhere by a critical alternation between a reality "entirely permeable to history" and a reality that is "ultimately impenetrable, irreducible," and poetic.[9] The marking of this alternation situates him firmly within the humanistic tradition out of which we hail him as the father of American literature. But as we have already seen, his writing also moves beyond this alternation through his engagement of a writerly strategy, wherein we locate his nascent feminism. By writerly I mean those moments when Emerson is comfortable with a double strategy that leaves everything in a transitional or provisional stage rather than seeking a more familiar dialectical

---

of ideology enables Andrew Parker to align Althusser's work with Derrida, for it is Derrida's belief that we must begin the project of deconstruction from within the discourse of Western civilization. See Parker, "Futures for Marxism: An Appreciation of Althusser," *Diacritics* 15: 4 (Winter 1985): 69–70.

[6] Michael Sprinker, *Imaginary Relations: Aesthetics and Ideology in the Theory of Historical Materialism* (London: Verso, 1987), 185; see esp. chaps. 7 and 8. See also Parker, "Futures for Marxism." That Althusser's argument about "hailing" has been criticized as a recuperation of the unified subject is less problematic than suggestive for our concerns, because the tension between what is conceptualized as humanistic and what is conceptualized as poststructural inevitably opens the terrain for the double strategy of a feminist critique. See Paul Q. Hirst, *On Law and Ideology* (Atlantic Highlands, N.J.: Humanities Press, 1979), 6. For a persuasive rebuttal, see Michael Sprinker, *Imaginary Relations*, pp. 197–203. See also Warren Montag, "Marxism and Psychoanalysis: The Impossible Encounter," *minnesota review*, n.s. 23 (Fall 1984).

[7] Barthes's humanistic oppositions—descriptions vs. explanation, object vs. knowledge, poetry vs. ideology—are familiar ones, yet their displacement into the pleasure of the text is of little value if that displacement rushes too quickly beyond the issue of gender.

[8] Barthes, *Mythologies*, p. 157.

[9] Ibid., p. 158.

resolution. This kind of writerly approach to life is always evident in his work, particularly in his critique of religious orthodoxy. Yet Emerson remains uneasy with his approach when he sees how it might be abused by those who were advocating an equally radical reform of the conduct of life. Only through an assessment of Fuller's writerly sense of agency can he begin to accept the efficacy of the same double strategy in his work. Fuller's feminism, then, which develops through her reading of Goethe, Emerson, and Fourier, effectively convinces him that the radical tendencies of his thought are in fact *necessary* for the successful conduct of life.

Emerson's contribution to the *Memoirs*, where he attempts to stage the complexities of his relationship with Fuller, provides a useful tour of his gathering awareness of the radical method she had already encouraged in his thinking. Through this staging of his relationship with her—one attentive to the suspicious, sometimes stridently antifeminist, temper of his culture[10]—he creates one of the most unique documents of his career. He effectively scripts a play for two characters, one male and one female, both sharing and then yielding the part of interpreter to the other. In the end, the key humanistic opposition—the hailing of male and female in the individual—is firmly placed before our view in roles played by Emerson and Fuller. His feminist production is drawn from his conflicting understanding of the consequences of that opposition, a conflict figured in his struggle to envision a world *beyond* the traditional humanistic dialectic. In a sense, the characters Fuller and Emerson also stand in as figures for national education and Woman as Fuller defined them in her *Tribune* writing. Emerson sometimes represents a traditional view of education, but she more often represents the important writerly disruption of that view.

Emerson shared the responsibility for the structure of the *Memoirs* with two of Fuller's friends—James Freeman Clarke and William Henry Channing. It is an odd document, to be sure. The three use large blocks of Fuller's writing to construct a choppy narrative of her life, and they think nothing of editing and modifying her words to suit the occasion. This willingness to write over the words of an important feminist critic has been at the center of the critical dissatisfaction with the work.[11] Yet

---

[10] Emerson's journals during this period are filled with angry references to and anecdotes about the misogyny of the culture, references that sometimes become self-reflexive, forcing him to reframe his thoughts about gender. "Fenimore Cooper said to a lady in conversation, 'I can make any woman blush.' The lady blushed with natural resentment. 'I can lay it on deeper than that, madam,' said the pitiless talker. Out of vexation at her own selfdistrust the lady crimsoned again to her neck & shoulder—the power of impudence" (JMN 11: 446).

[11] See Bell Gale Chevigny, "Introduction," in *The Woman and the Myth: Margaret Fuller's Life and Writings* (New York: The Feminist Press, 1976), 9–10.

the embarrassed figuration of the text provides a valuable clue to the complex motivations behind this mutant *Memoir*. Although all three men are deeply sympathetic with Fuller, Emerson is the most attuned to the ideological riot of the moment. His contribution to the *Memoirs* provides an uncanny insight not only into his writerly method but also into the vital way that her life strengthened that method by revealing to him its important feminist potential.

The Role of Force in History

Fuller's friends knew that some form of literary response to her death was imperative, but the task seemed redoubtable. Emerson knew how the rumor and gossip about her life had inflamed public reaction. She was a woman of high energy, and the prurient interests of the public were harder to deter because of her sex. Her Fourieristic marriage to Ossoli and their illegitimate child, therefore, caused considerable stir. The men writing the *Memoirs* sought to show her historical value, but they also wanted to protect her reputation as a woman. How could a woman with the force of Margaret Fuller, they asked, enter into the text of history without offending and being martyred in the process?

One strategy the three devised to defuse the radical nature of Fuller's life was to break it down into a series of geographical boundaries. The title headings of each section in the *Memoirs* create a kind of map of her life. The reader is expected to view her geographical peregrinations as a sign of her historical value. This approach borrows directly from a tendency in American intellectual history: reading geography as history. What is cunning about this approach is the relative tameness of Fuller's geographical wanderings. Following the chapter headings of her *Memoirs*, we are given an edited view of her travels, watching her move from Cambridge to Groton and Providence, then on to Concord and Boston, next to Jamaica Plain, New York, Europe, and, finally, "Homeward." In the process, all of her movements toward the frontier either in the United States or in the Old World—where she skirted the borders of revolution—are elided. The narrative constructed by these locations brings to mind, if anything, the cosmopolitan character of a figure such as Ben Franklin.

Fuller's geographical movement resembles Franklin's in its nearly turnstile alternation from village to city and back with the final arrival in Europe. But even when the geographical profile is forgotten, Franklin provides a useful model for the authors of the *Memoirs*, beginning with the initial chapter's subtitle, "Autobiography." The legitimizing quality of this heading is forthright: a woman is expected to be personal, auto-biographical. But, of course, Fuller's death keeps her from writing and rendering her life for public consumption. Because men compose the autobiographical fragments of her youth, they lend credence to the work by shaping it into the received form of autobiography as their nineteenth-century readers understood it through Franklin's text.

Another way to defuse the threatening aspects of Fuller's historical value was to measure it through her interaction with friends. Emerson reports that the initial project was conceived under the title "Margaret and Her Friends." Yet he also explains, "On trial, that form proved impossible," adding that "it only remained that the narrative, like a Greek tragedy, should suppose the chorus always on the stage, sympa-thizing and sympathized with by the queen of the scene" (MMF 1: 205). If Greek tragedy becomes the model for the text, Emerson alters it as Fuller herself did in order to release the woman from martyrdom. He is convinced, in fact, that "Margaret and Her Friends" must be written, because the story provides "an essential line of American history," but he is not interested in conceiving of American history in tragic, nor, for that matter, epic terms (JMN 11: 258). His interest lies in conceiving of a new form of historical narrative.

If history is biography, as his friend Carlyle proposed, then Emerson set out to write a biography of Fuller. He describes himself as a biogra-pher in the first chapter, thus shifting the narrative away from its ersatz autobiographical format. Yet because he also recognized that Carlyle's sense of history is insufficient for Fuller (when mulling over the task ahead of him, he felt that the life of Fuller should be written with the "coolest ignoring" of "Mr. Carlyle and Boston and London" [EL 4: 222]), his biographical form is also a bit of a parody.[12] Certainly his notion of what he calls "another . . . sort of biography" reveals Fuller's influence when he remarks in his journals on the inspirational "advan-tages . . . [of] meditative conversation" for creating a "bold, experimen-tal, [and] varied" biography (JMN 11: 285). As a result, his text is an odd medley of biography and autobiography, a story of both Fuller and Emerson. It is this conflation and alternation of the two modes— sometimes Emerson writes "Fuller," sometimes Fuller writes "Emerson" —that gives the work its value for us today.

As biographer, Emerson immediately concedes the difficulty of his task, noting that the unique alternation between a feminine "tempera-

---

[12] Emerson constantly cross-examines the nature of biography and history in his jour-nals during this period, as when he writes "Biography & history make us gape. But the true biography & history is that which is heard over the tavern stove, & overheard in the railroad train" (JMN 11: 328).

ment" and philosophical (and masculine) "good sense" in Fuller's character "perplexes the biographer," forcing him to change his "impressions of her" and to "contradict on the second page" what he "affirms on the first" (MMF 1: 227). To know Fuller is not to know in the traditional sense (to have impressions of her is to have a feminine sense of her), which is what he most values about his role as her biographer. It is a challenge to the traditional sense of history and to the sense of knowledge as history. In many ways his contribution to her *Memoirs* reads as a final chapter to *Representative Men*, with Emerson as the ironic representative man. The importance of this representation lies in its complete exploitation of the myth of Emerson and the average way of knowing him then and now. To match the biographer's unknowingness with the uncertainties of knowing Fuller is finally to expose the patriarchal bias hidden in some of the most familiar values of the Western world, including those sometimes adopted by Emerson in reading himself.

Visits to Concord

In taking over the narration of the *Memoirs*, Emerson sabotages the geographical way of knowing, not only with his titles (changing Concord to "Visits to Concord" and Boston to "Conversations in Boston") but also with his subtitles, which again tap into the reader's expectations about Emerson. We no longer expect to read about Fuller in geographical terms; we now expect to read about her through his familiar abstractions: Arcana, Daemonology, Temperament, Self-Esteem, Books, Criticism, Art, Letters, Friendship, Problems of Life, Heroism, Truth, Ecstasy, and Conversation. But like the overall title of the work, whose authorship is immediately cast into question, titles of Emerson's section are similarly misleading. The heading "Visits to Concord" situates the reader in a false position from the start by suggesting that the narrative will describe Fuller's visits to Emerson's Concord home, the site of his writing. Although it is the plot line of the first and largest part of his contribution (the second will include Emerson's visits to Fuller's famous "Conversations in Boston"—the site of her "writing"), a careful reading shows that the first part of the text works around the problematic pun of the word *concord* in the title. As I have suggested, this punning follows a normal pattern in Emerson's work; his titles invariably place his reader in a false position. What we get in the *Memoirs*, though, is a clue to the ideological constructions hidden behind this epistemological sleight of hand.

Emerson consistently attempts here to put discord between Fuller and himself, although it is superficial, part of what I have earlier called, after Barthes, the embarrassed figuration of the text. Emerson's audience was curious, indeed, *too* curious, about the nature of their "intercourse, as such." He deflected their curiosity by highlighting the "war of temperaments" between them, even by insisting at one point that she was "unattractive in person" (MMF 1: 280). Such deflections enable him to pass beyond the simple complications of difference at work in the "intercourse" between a man and a woman—describing Fuller as "unattractive" temporarily suspends that problem for his intended reader—and to make the more important and seemingly gender-free idea that she had more "personal influence" than anyone he ever knew. Such deflections are also crucial to the deeper and more important work of the essay, since they purposefully negotiate traditional gender roles in order to transgress them and open them up. Emerson persistently identifies the difference in sex between himself and Fuller as the source of the conflict between them; but this difference in turn becomes the vehicle for the more important attributes of her character to which he as a writer aspires.

Emerson knew that few of his readers could agree about Fuller. Men and women feared her, he wrote, because of her "overweening sense of power." Men "thought she carried too many guns," and women "did not like one who despised them" (MMF 1: 202). But he also knew that the image of a woman with "too many guns" was a projection of the negative use of masculine power, just as the description of a woman who hates women was a projection of the negative use of humility, a feminine self-hatred projected out of self-denial. For him, the task of the *Memoirs* was not to strip Fuller of her power but the opposite, the transvaluation of power for men and women as revealed in the force of Fuller's life. To do this he employs her power and his own in a strange alternating fashion, acting out a dramatic presentation of the conflicts of their interaction. The attentive reader discovers that Emerson is creating a fable within a fable to address the issue of "concord" and the problems that a man and a woman have in their efforts to "visit" there. Working this out not only entails the development of a fictive character named Fuller but also the elaboration of a character named Emerson who happens to be the rather unreliable narrator of the work. To simplify my discussion I call this character and narrator "Waldo."

Emerson's narrative play is subtly revealed in the decision to place all quotes by Fuller within single quotation marks, whereas all other citations are given the standard double marks. When she speaks in the text, she speaks through the already present quotation of Waldo's text. This sly procedure reveals Emerson's strong sense of the fictive presence of both characters. If we are to read Fuller through Waldo, we must also read *Emerson* through Waldo, and sometimes we are even allowed to read Emerson through Fuller, as in this account of his early response to her:

> The auditor jumped for joy, and thirsted for unlimited draughts. What! is this the dame, who, I heard, was sneering and critical? this the blue-stocking, of whom I stood in terror and dislike? this wondrous woman, full of counsel, full of tenderness, before whom every mean thing is ashamed, and hides itself; this new Corinne, more variously gifted, wise, sportive, eloquent, who seems to have learned all languages, Heaven knows when or how,—I should think she was born to them,—magnificent, prophetic, reading my life at her will, and puzzling me with riddles like this "Yours is an example of a destiny springing from 'character:' and, again, "I see your destiny hovering before you, but it always escapes you" (MMF 1: 215).

Sifting through the tiers of Emerson's narration is not a simple task, nor did he want it to be. When we encounter his familiar subtitles, we begin to understand that they too are enclosed in invisible quotation marks and that we are reading the narrative of a character whose destiny is always already eluding him. The reader familiar with *Representative Men*, for example, will notice how in the above quote, Waldo espouses bewilderment over a position that Emerson adopts with relative ease and certainty in "The Uses of Great Men." There, we recall, Emerson describes the power of certain people "to divine another's destiny" and "hold him to his task" (CW 4: 14–15). Including this paragraph about Fuller's reading of Emerson's destiny discloses the source of his insight, even as it shows how that insight could be resisted by the representative or common man.

As readers we watch Waldo employ familiar title headings such as "Nature," "Daemonology," and "Friendship" in an attempt to show how Fuller embodies a threat to the usual reading of these themes. Once we understand how the text has been built up, layering one "hailing" of the subject upon another, we begin to see how Fuller always encourages the cross-reading of these subjects in Emerson's work. Waldo is consistently forced to interrupt his way of describing each concept in order to accommodate Fuller's perspective. This pattern of interruption reinscribes a pattern visible throughout Emerson's work, from *Nature* to the *Conduct of Life*. For the first time, however, the gender roles influencing Emerson's strange hailing procedure begin to emerge.

Nature

When the subject heading is "Nature," for example, the reader imme-diately learns that Fuller's "imperfect vision" and "bad health" were "serious impediments to intimacy with woods and rivers." Moreover, she did not view nature with an eye toward "natural sciences," because she "neither botanized, nor geologized, nor dissected" (MMF 1: 263). When Waldo insinuates that her physical and emotional perspective gave her a limited view of nature, insisting that her "descrip-tions . . . must appear sickly and superficial," Emerson provides the reader with material from her writing that contradicts that verdict. She is given the last word in a series of quotes that supply an effective re-sponse to Waldo:

> You say that nature does not keep her promise; but surely, she satisfies us now and then for the time. . . . Here and there she speaks out a sentence, full in its cadence, complete in its structure; it occupies, for the time, the sense and the thought. We have no care for promises. Will you say it is the superficialness of my life, that I have known hours with men and nature, that bore their proper fruit,—all present ate and were filled, and there were taken up of the fragments twelve baskets full? Is it because of the superfi-cial mind, or the believing heart, that I can say this?
> Only through emotion do we know thee Nature! . . . Thought will never reach it (MMF 1: 264–65).

Waldo's absurd reference to Fuller's eyesight, moreover, supplies a kind of parody of Emerson's transparent eyeball passage in his earlier essay *Nature*, where the only threat to his vision is the literal threat to his eyes. Waldo's reference stubbornly ignores Emerson's displacement of that argument in "Prospects," in which the "ruin or blank, that we see when we look at nature" is said to be "in our own eye."[13] Certainly, though Fuller cannot take a literal view of nature, her theoretical posi-tion, enhanced by the "blank" in her eye, challenges Waldo's theoretical position and recalls Emerson's crucial transvaluation of theory at the end of "Prospects." If, as Waldo argues, Fuller's response to nature situates her in the feminine realm of emotion, it also recalls the manly standards delineated by Emerson at the end of *Nature*, where "empirical

[13] *Nature* is found in *Nature, Addresses, and Lectures*, ed. Robert E. Spiller and Alfred R. Ferguson (Cambridge: Belknap Press, Harvard University Press, 1979), 10. "There I feel that nothing can befal me in life,—no disgrace, no calamity, (leaving me my eyes,) which nature cannot repair. Standing on the bare ground,—my head bathed by the blithe air, and uplifted into infinite space,—all mean egotism vanishes. I become a transparent eye-ball. I am nothing. I see all."

science" is said to "cloud the sight . . . and bereave the student of the manly contemplation of the whole." Emerson's manly sense is born from qualities that cannot be associated with the geologist, the botanist, or the naturalist until "he satisfies all the demands of the spirit. Love is as much its demand, as perception."[14]

In fact, Fuller may well have discussed Emerson's problematic valorization of the eye in the earlier section of *Nature* when she first stayed with him at his Concord home, as he completed "Prospects" just after her departure.[15] As we have seen, her tendency to supply him with "undiscovered regions of thought" is inscribed throughout his work (CW 1: 41). The section "Nature" in the *Memoirs* merely hints how the conversation that first began in Concord in 1836 became an inevitable part of that inscription.

Fate

The feminist dimension of Fuller's inclusion in Emerson's work is only nominally present in this section of the *Memoirs*, but it becomes far more obvious in "Daemonology." There Waldo introduces the chapter with a statement heavily marked by the masculine gender:

> This catching at straws of coincidence, where all is geometrical, seems the necessity of certain natures. It is true, that, in every good work, the particulars are right, and, that every spot of light on the ground, under the trees, is a perfect image of the sun. Yet, for astronomical purposes, an observatory is better than an orchard; and in a universe which is nothing but generations, or an unbroken suite of cause and effect, to infer Providence, because a man happens to find a shilling on the pavement just when he wants one to spend, is puerile, and much as if each of us should date his letters and notes of hand from his own birthday, instead of from Christ's or the king's reign, or the current Congress. These, to be sure, are also, at first, petty and private beginnings, but, by the world of men, clothed with a social and cosmical character (MMF 1: 221–22).

Out of context, this passage reads as a flat dismissal of the "puerile" (feminine) fatalism used by some against the providential (masculine) patterns of cause and effect governing the universe. In context, however, the passage explains the striking feminist text beneath Fuller's argument that "this remote seeking for the decrees of fate . . . is the most beautiful species of idealism in our day" (MMF 1: 222). Waldo's grudging defense

---

[14] *Nature* is found in *Nature, Addresses, and Lectures*, pp. 39, 43.
[15] See Emerson's letter to his brother William, EL 2: 32.

of the "propensity" Fuller "held with certain tenets of fate" is in fact the beginning of Emerson's paradigmatic revision of the "unbroken suite of cause and effect" he will make in his essay "Fate." After Fuller's death, as we shall see in Chapter 9, Emerson slowly began to identify her feminism and her reading strategy with the concept of fate. It is no coincidence that he began "Fate" just after completing the *Memoirs*, for his renewed interest in what he calls the "negative method of spirit" emerges from the curious juxtaposition of Fuller's experience as a woman, which "seemed strangely to justify" (MMF 1: 222) her fatalism, and Waldo's strong rhetoric of dismissal, which depended entirely on a rigid, patriarchal, view of the world). As in the chapter "Nature," Waldo's narration does not close this section of the *Memoirs*; the chapter is subsumed by testimony from Fuller, all of it working directly against Waldo's opening statement. Such transitions in Emerson's work are common, but here the feminist dress of that transition is suggestive. We see the way in which Emerson's writing tracks out of orbit whenever he considers Fuller's feminist reading of it.

Woman, or Artist

This exorbitant pattern repeats itself throughout the text, indicating that Fuller's resistances to Waldo's way of knowing are virtues that Emerson absorbs and structures into the pattern of his work from "Nature" to "Fate." Fuller's reading of Waldo proves active in this sense, continuously providing a feminist transvaluation of his terms. Emerson explains Fuller's skill as a reader of men by providing a survey of her own enormous reading of texts, which Waldo attempts here to enumerate, focusing heavily on Fuller's reading of Goethe; he claims, "Nowhere did Goethe find a braver, more intelligent, more sympathetic reader" (MMF 1: 243). The gradual success of Fuller's reading is disclosed through the emergence of subtitles that break out of Emerson's familiar abstractions: "George Sand, Again," "Alfred de Vigny," "Beranger," and "Woman, or Artist." Through these, he shows the character and quality of some of her most interesting writing, especially her criticism of French literature. Waldo, following Emerson's lead, keeps references to Fourier to a minimum, remarking only on Fuller's keen interest in "French socialism, especially as it concerned women" (MMF 1: 218). The impediments to displaying the full array of Fuller's critical reading, the most immediate being the ludicrous lack of space, allow Emerson to show instead how Fuller's plight as a female critic was not only filled with difficulty, but also, in the paradoxical movement of the work, filled with a difficulty much like his own.

This odd similarity is most apparent in the section whose very title, "Woman, or Artist," plays with this association. Here Waldo makes his most famous comment about Fuller's writing, claiming that her "pen was a nonconductor" (MMF 1: 294). Ironically, Emerson uses a quotation from Fuller's pen to reinforce Waldo's idea: "'My verses,—I am ashamed when I think there is scarce a line of poetry in them,—all rhetorical and impassioned, as Goethe said of de Stael'" (MMF 1: 295). By using Fuller to support Waldo's account of her writing, he shows that Waldo's position has more to do with gender than with textual power: the comments of Goethe on Madame de Stael to which she alludes reinscribes the social hierarchy between Waldo and Fuller. Yet with his quote from Fuller, Emerson does more than delineate the power structure at work in Waldo's comment. On another level, he uses Fuller to account for the failing that he himself felt about his own writing. Her way of expressing skepticism about her work and her role in society closely resembled his, and he could easily ventriloquize his frustrations through her voice. He selects innumerable quotations that operate this way. Inevitably, the activity of doublespeak leads him to a twin correspondence between himself and Fuller, woman and artist: when she complains of the cultural resistance to her feminism, it conforms to the same resistance he often felt and expressed as a poet. This association is abetted by her constant use of the terms of the poetic crisis to describe her feminist dilemma.

> For all the tides that flow within me, I am dumb and ineffectual, when it comes to casting my thought into form. No old one suits me. If I could invent one, it seems to me that the pleasure of creation would make it possible for me to write. What shall I do, dear friend? I want force to be either a genius or a character. One should be either private or public. I love best to be a woman; but womanhood is at present too straightly-bounded to give me scope. At hours I live truly as a woman; at others, I should stifle; as, on the other hand, I should palsy, when I would play the artist (MMF 1: 297).

If Fuller has difficulty choosing between being a woman, a role too narrowly defined, and being an artist, too unrealistic and unattached to the problems of life made apparent by the restricted role of women, Emerson feels the same divided loyalty. Being a man is too charged with the negative weight of "guns"; at the same time, being a poet is ineffectual, falling short of the reconciliation of object and knowledge, description and explanation that he desires. Fortunately, frustration is not the only quality that Emerson can express by sharing a subjectivity with Fuller. She also has confidence in the unmeasured power of her voice, a power literally attached to its conversational success. Conversation emerges as the figural vehicle for the important double strategy she employed to displace the traditional opposition of public and private roles. Her sense of conversation transvalues the categories of "woman, or artist" by intervening with a transformed sense of her role as a reader or critic of culture—an identity very much shared by Emerson.

At the beginning of the *Memoirs*, Waldo calls himself an "eager scholar of ethics," the phrase he uses to describe himself during his first meeting with Fuller. But, as Emerson shows, it is an interpellation immediately put to test by Fuller's insistence on calling him a philosopher (MMF 1: 202). With her help, Waldo slowly finds a way to celebrate and accept the confluence of those terms, a confluence born out of their shared sense of themselves as critics. The false dichotomies of "woman, or artist," and "man, or artist" become displaced by conversation and the concord created by the term. If anything, conversation enables Emerson to recover a sense of himself as a student of ethics and philosophy because conversation allows for the irruption of the ethical into the codes of representation.[16]

Emerson's focus on conversation does not constitute a retreat to the old humanistic hierarchy of voice over writing, though he first alludes to that hierarchy in order to move beyond it. Waldo begins to account for Fuller's conversational power by citing the argument of an ancient philosopher that "Mind must be *in the air*" (MMF 1: 216). The sign that something other than the old philosophical emphasis on presence is at stake in Fuller's conversation is Waldo's immediate insistence that there could be no "mind in the air" at all without language and his further insistence that language itself is the best philosopher (MMF 1: 217). Only through languages, according to Waldo, can we recognize "superior or purer sense as *common* sense." This common sense is at the base of Fuller's conversational skill, giving her the ability to "speak to Jew and Greek, free and bond, to each in his own tongue" (MMF 1: 217). Conceding this, Waldo also notes the limitations, and strictures operating against Fuller, both as a woman and as a philosopher in the "common sense."

In looking over Fuller's papers, Waldo is compelled to recognize her distance from the intellectual and literary tradition leading back to

---

[16] Alice Jardine, in *Gynesis: Configurations of Woman and Modernity* (Ithaca, N.Y.: Cornell University Press, 1985), 47, articulates this position for the twentieth-century American feminist: "The (American) feminist in dialogue with (French) contemporary theory may be in a special position to approach this problem by remediating and rethinking the feminist insistence on personal experience as practice with the movement of these theoretical fictions as experience and practice—thus working, potentially, toward a new disposition of the ethical grounded in symbolic process."

Homer. The fact that she did not produce the epic of America even as she lived it through a series of stunning intellectual and personal feats causes him to examine the awesome and annihilating power of patriarchy. With this conflation, literal and figurative meaning collide and her feminism offers an uncanny insight into his own literary crisis and success. Subsumed by the trappings of patriarchy and its tradition, his work consistently frustrates his expectations. Her promise and success, by contrast, resides in her feminist skills of conversation, which liberates her genius from the artifice of artistic character by negotiating a new understanding of the relationship between public and private worlds, indeed by negotiating a shift away from the unsatisfactory categories of artist and genius altogether.

This realization accounts for the dramatic change in Waldo's treatment of the subtitles with which he closes "Visits to Concord." Although early in the narrative Fuller embodies what for him remain the problematic values of "Temperament" and "Daemonology," she now embodies the positive but elusive values of "Truth" and "Heroism." By the odd logic of the text, of course, truth and heroism are usable, thanks to her transvaluation of these terms.[17] In the chapter "Heroism," for example, we are told that Fuller had an "extraordinary degree" of "influence"—indeed, as Waldo concedes, "more than any person I have known." Yet whereas Waldo attempts to speak "strictly" and remove all of the usual trappings of gender in the hailing of influence (i.e., the "effects of power, wealth, fashion, beauty, or literary fame"), an account of the deeper structure of gender at work in the culture appears through the order of his narrative. Fuller's heroic influence works literally from the margins, a point driven home at the end of the chapter by Waldo's offhand account of the young artist in Florence who, upon reading a statement scribbled by Fuller in the margin of a book, received sufficient inspiration to "revive resolutions long fallen away" and "set" his "face like a flint" (MMF 1: 298).

Fuller's influence on truth is no less radical than her influence on heroism. Waldo begins his chapter by describing her "love of truth, and the power to speak it" (MMF 1: 303), a comment that must be understood as a radical transformation of truth's meaning for Waldo. If, as Waldo continues, a "soul is now and then incarnated" in someone such as the Athenian Themistocles, who "can speak the right word at the right moment" (MMF 1: 305), Fuller emerges as an odd yet similar

[17] The term *hero* is simultaneously undergoing transvaluation in the pages of Emerson's journals: "*Hero.* How much Language thinks for us, witness the word Hero. What has Carlyle, what has Charles Newcomb added to the bare word, which has been the inspiration of them both, & will be of all the generous" (JMN 11: 267).

incarnation, particularly since she has also been described in earlier sections, namely "Temperament" and "Daemonology," as one afflicted with "cramp and frost" (MMF 1: 305). Though Waldo argues that most people "want the organ to speak" the truth "adequately" (MMF 1: 305), Fuller finds that organ by transforming it through an acceptance of terms like *temperament* and *fatalism*. The elaboration of these terms and Fuller's heroic and truthful affiliation with them forces Waldo to return to the ultimate site of her transvaluation: conversation.

Waldo thus emerges from this conflict at concord as the ironic representative man, having gained this knowledge only after first espousing and confounding himself with the binary verities of humanism. Fuller, by contrast, emerges as the real and paleonymous representative man, who is both removed from and engaged with those crippling oppositions. Because her conversation allows her to escape without leaving, Emerson has to move his narrative out of the oppositional configuration of "Visits to Concord" in order to define the site out of which those oppositions must be read. This he does in a separate section titled "Conversations in Boston."

Conversations in Boston

"Visits to Concord" is about Waldo's rocky attempt to receive Fuller into his manly way of knowing. In contrast, "Conversations in Boston" is about Fuller's smoother reception of Waldo into a feminist way of knowing. In this section the character of Fuller grows in stature while the character of Waldo loses credibility. The eyewitness account of her class quoted by the narrator Waldo, for example, includes a negative description of Emerson's behavior there.

> Mr. E. only served to display her powers. With his sturdy reiteration of his uncompromising idealism, his absolute denial of the fact of human nature, he gave her opportunity and excitement to unfold and illustrate her realism and acceptance of conditions. What is so noble is, that her realism is transparent with idea. . . . She proceeds in her search after the unity of things . . . not by exclusion, as Mr. E. does, but by comprehension (MMF 1: 349–50).

But Emerson is also being clever; by placing the reading of his own behavior at Fuller's seminar in the mouth of a third party, he opens the possibility that this is in fact a misreading. At one level, this reading reinforces the reading of the opposition between Fuller and Waldo of the earlier section, a reading that Emerson himself is at pains to promulgate. Yet neither Emerson nor Fuller ultimately shares this reading, but both use it to advantage by displacing it in their conversation with one another. The site of that displacement, then, becomes the site of their strongest critical judgment. For Fuller it is the site of literal conversation, the place where women in particular are given a chance to read, mutate, and decanonize the texts of humanism. For Emerson, the site is transposed through the conversational profile of his writing, where the old dead forms of humanism are put to test by the sailing of his language around them. Emerson's behavior, as described here, is the humanistic text, and Fuller's movement beyond becomes the body of the feminist text. Yet because her response is also described by a third party, her response and the body of that feminist text is necessarily misread so that, in the end, Fuller and Emerson are misread *together*.

If this misreading is deeply narrativized and endorsed by the conflict staged between them in "Visits to Concord", the feminist components of that misreading emerge in a rather straightforward manner in the section on Fuller's Boston seminar. Waldo makes very clear the feminist argument not only behind her decision to hold the Conversations, but also behind his decision to write about them:

> A woman in our society finds her safety and happiness in exclusions and privacies. She congratulates herself when she is not called to the market, to the courts, to the polls, to the stage, or to the orchestra. Only the most extraordinary genius can make the career of an artist secure and agreeable to her. Prescriptions almost invincible the female lecturer or professor of any science must encounter; and, except on points where the charities which are left to women as their legitimate province interpose against the ferocity of laws, with us a female politician is unknown (MMF 1: 321–22).

In fact, the feminist argument Waldo makes is more overt than the one he attributes to Margaret Fuller. When he lists some of her important publications to explain the boldness of her decision to hold the Conversations, he makes no mention of the text that emerged from the experience, *Woman in the Nineteenth Century*. This muting of her feminism in the narrative remains a protective gesture and part of the embarrassed figuration of the *Memoirs*, yet through that muting Emerson also manages to connect the activity of the women in the seminar with the activity of his work in general, and, in so doing, he enlarges the domain of feminism beyond the usual reductive reading of the term.

Fuller argues that the seminars are necessary as sites of "reproduction," not display (MMF 1: 329). Because women rarely reproduce what they have learned, she argues, the Conversations are intended to encourage women to do so. Although her seminars begin with material and subject matter that appears to be more appropriate to women than men, over time they begin to explore topics resembling those in one of Emerson's lecture series: "Faith," "Creeds," "Influence," "Culture," "Influence," "Prudence," "War," "Bonaparte," and "Goethe" (MMF 1: 351). The narrative leads us to believe that her success with these topics is even stronger than Emerson's. Indeed, her sense of conversation as reproduction is essentially a description of criticism. Conversation, for Fuller, depends entirely on texts: her idea of conversation is not about escaping the limits of the written word so much as it is about escaping the limits of the reading encouraged by the hierarchy between men and women in culture. It is the place where women best engage the texts of history and literature as critics because conversation is the uncontested site already given to them by the culture. The power of the method she employs, the strategic potential of conversation with its focus on transition and the provisional production of meaning, is what Emerson admires and advocates. As we saw in Chapter 6, Fuller's use of a radicalized conversational strategy enabled her to develop her theory of reading. By 1851 it is Emerson's desire to show how that theory of reading matches his own.

Emerson's Scene before the Women

Nowhere is this interest in Fuller's method better revealed than in the speech Emerson delivered before the Woman's Rights Convention held in Boston in 1855.[18] By the time of Fuller's death in 1850, such conventions were periodically held throughout New England. Because the woman's movement did not get under way until 1848, Fuller never had the opportunity to participate in any of the activities, though her writing for the *Tribune* continued to be an inspiration to women. Emerson's relationship with her no doubt encouraged Paulina Wright Davis and Lucy Stone to invite him to attend the meetings of the New England Woman's Rights Organization. Although he excused himself in response to their first entreaties, he lent his name in support. In 1855 he accepted the invitation to speak in Boston.[19] Even though his was one of the first

[18] "Woman," in W 11.
[19] EL 4: 230, 261. Emerson's first letter refusing Paulina Davis was written before he began to write the *Memoirs* and the hesitation over the "mode of obtaining redress, namely, a public convention called by women" has been seen as representative of his position toward the goals of feminism in general. His growing support of the woman's movement can be said to be directly related to the composition of *Memoirs*. He continued to support the movement, lecturing again at one of their conventions as late as 1869.

lectures in support of the woman's movement by a major literary figure, it remains largely obscure. Ironically, those who have read the lecture have attacked it for its failure to supply a strong foundational feminism.[20] But it is precisely a foundational feminism that he attacks. Like Fuller's most famous treatise, *Woman in the Nineteenth Century* (1845), Emerson's 1855 lecture (its title is "Woman") challenges the critical assumptions underlying the dominant trends of literary history, including the first strains of feminist criticism emerging from that history. In fact, the theoretical sophistication of his lecture compares favorably with the theoretical sophistication of Fuller's "scene before [the] women."[21]

The very title of Emerson's lecture reflects his desire to explore the important notion of feminist agency that Fuller had explored in her *Tribune* writing. Once again, direct mention of Fourier is absent from the presentation, but Fourier's use is implicit in the very structure of the lecture, particularly his focus on "woman's place" which Fuller had found so important. (Emerson may well have known that the organizer of the meeting, Paulina Davis, was also a proponent of Fourier.[22]) Fourier believed that by focusing on the paradoxical position from which women viewed the culture, at once inside and outside its concerns, a provisional space for social change could be found. Emerson endorses this belief by following Fuller's example. The difficulty for him, as for Fuller, resides in acknowledging two versions of "woman's place": one that focuses on the important difference of men and women, and one that eliminates all differences and establishes a type of equality of experience among the sexes in the home and elsewhere. Like Fuller, he supports the new claims for women by providing a reading of the cant of culture, all of which entails a new understanding of the paradoxical terms upon which any discussion of women needed to rely. Not surprisingly, conversation becomes the allegorical figure for his interpretation of "woman's place" in culture, and Fuller is the exemplary agent of the double strategy implicit in the term.

[20] See, for example, the reaction of Margaret Vanderhaar Allen, *The Achievement of Margaret Fuller* (University Park: Penn State University Press, 1979). A more recent negative response is found in Amy Schrager Lang's interesting study *Prophetic Woman: Anne Hutchinson and the Problem of Dissent in the Literature of New England* (Berkeley: University of California Press, 1987), 137–145.

[21] Jacques Derrida and Christie McDonald, "Choreographies," in *The Ear of the Other: Texts and Discussions with Jacques Derrida*, ed. Christie McDonald, trans. Peggy Kamuf (Lincoln: University of Nebraska Press, 1985), 169.

[22] Davis wrote an article for *The Una* in 1855 calling for an "appeal to Fourier's principle of 'oneness of the race.'" Quoted in Dolores Hayden, "Two Utopian Feminists and Their Campaign for Kitchenless Houses," *Signs* 4 (Winter 1978): 203. Emerson also appears to have been influenced by the chapter "Women in the Phalanstery" in *The Phalanstery; Or, Attractive Industry and Moral Harmony*, trans. from the French text of Madame Gatti de Gamond by an English Lady (London: Whittaker and Company, 1841).

As with the treatment of Waldo, Emerson's lecture should probably be cast in quotation marks, since he stands before the women only because Fuller cannot. In thus addressing the convention, he does not presume to say what Fuller would have said; he does, however, often say what it is she has prompted him to think. As Derrida has observed of the quotation mark, the value of the quotation resides in the way that "the hermeneutic project which postulates a true sense of the text is disqualified." Emerson's lecture, though, is not filled with what Derrida calls the "tenter-hooks" of the familiar quotation mark: "the screeching machinations of a hooker or crane . . . its flight and clapping claws."[23] Instead the activity of citation is internalized by his representation of himself as part of the dominant text that had made a woman's movement necessary. Emerson's speech, like his early letters refusing Stone and Davis, are filled with reminders that he is at the center of the very tradition that he seeks now to displace. And with this in mind, he no longer hesitates to return to the idea of the home and explore its value for women. Indeed, he even acknowledges how his exploration will remain empty without a return to the home and without the paraphernalia of self particular to women in his culture.

The Lecture as Homing Device

Historians have often noted the influence of the abolitionist cause on the development of the woman's movement in America, a connection that Emerson promotes in the middle of his lecture. "The Antagonism to Slavery," he tells his audience, "turned out to be . . . a terrible metaphysician," giving women "self respect" and urging "[their] rights . . . to one half of the world" (W 11: 416). He foregrounds the interaction between the two major reform movements because he believes the evils of Woman's role in society are, like the evils of slavery, "real and great"; the plight of women, he believes, is "piteous to think of" (JMN 11: 444). He also makes the connection between abolition and the woman's movement a double challenge to the politicians, notably Daniel Webster, who exploited it to condemn the "sickly sentimentalism" (JMN 11: 321) of the abolitionist cause.[24] (Webster's part in the passage of the Fugitive Slave Law was well known to Emerson's audience.) Though Emerson himself had once criticized the effeminate nature of the church, the

[23] Jacques Derrida, *Spurs* (Chicago: University of Chicago Press, 1979), 107, 57.
[24] Emerson's journals are filled with rancor over the way in which the accusation of sentimentalism was used by politicians against those who objected to slavery. See esp. JMN 11: 321, 347, 359.

terrible events of his times made him reconsider the gender distinctions upon which political decisions, including his own, were being made. Indeed, he began to ask whether the feminization of culture was not precisely what was needed. This frustration, mixed with his new conviction, undoubtedly underlies his confession before the assembled supporters of the woman's movement that "all my points would sooner be carried in the State if Women voted" (W 11: 420).

But Emerson understands that one does not liberate the slave by giving him or her the freedom of the master, if only because the mechanism for slavery is perpetuated by the master's freedom. For the same reason, he believes that one does not liberate women by giving them the freedom of men. He does not labor, as Nietzsche later did, to describe the woman's movement as the inevitable byproduct of Western civilization, making it the handmaiden to yet another form of servility. Instead, he works to show how an active feminism is always threatened by reactive forces of the culture. This position is apparent from the beginning of the lecture, where he notes that "in the race that now predominates over all races of men," women are said to have "an oracular nature." By conceding that "[he] share[s] this belief," Emerson situates himself at the center of a dilemma, because from his description the belief in woman's oracular nature depends on an hierarchical and colonizing social contract. But he soon extricates himself from this problem by borrowing from Fourier to show how woman's oracular nature had persisted as an idea outside of history. This transition proves both typical and imperative; only when the feminine assumes a value outside the development of Western culture can Emerson sustain the argument that women are the "best index of the coming hour" (W 11: 405).

Of course, Emerson's task is made more difficult by the progressive view of history saturating the rhetoric of American democracy. Even in its early days of organized protest, the vote was a central concern of the woman's movement, in part because representation was the punning metaphor for the most important aspect of culture hitherto withheld. Certainly, the progressive view of history depended on an entry into language; barbarians—the people assumed to be illiterate because their speech could not be understood—were conquered by a language. Emerson understood from his relationship with Fuller that the quarantine from representation at all levels made the condition of women piteous. "If you do refuse them a vote," he warned the resistors in his audience "you will also refuse to tax them—according to our Teutonic principle, No representation, no tax" (W 11: 424). Yet both Fuller and Emerson knew that the progressive view of history dominated the world by conquering the "barbarians" and making provision for slavery. Poised between a desire to give women representative status and a recognition that representation itself might be the trap of some taxing Teutonic principle, he employs Fuller's double strategy to make his point.

At one level, Emerson does not hesitate to use progressive rhetoric on Woman's behalf. Early on he exploits the claim that the political arena is too debased for women to enter (the argument being that the "uneducated emigrant" (W 11: 422) vote gave it the atmosphere of a "dance-cellar" (W 11: 423) in order to demonstrate the need for a feminizing influence. "If the wants, the passions, the vices, are allowed a full vote through the hands of a half-brutal intemperate population, I think it but fair that the virtues, the aspirations should be allowed a full vote, as an offset, through the purest part of the people" (W 11: 423). This argument appealed to reformers who used it with increasing effect against the swelling immigrant population. But Emerson understands its racist bias; his willingness to cross rhetoric with rhetoric is provisional because he understands how the move from a masculine to a feminine morality can become a recuperative gesture, a dialectic whereby one discourse of dominance is replaced with another. Thus he immediately problematizes the argument for a feminizing influence by showing how it fails in being too closely aligned with the progressive rhetoric of the culture:

The fairest names in this country in literature, in law, have gone into Congress and come out dishonored. And when I read the list of men of intellect, of refined pursuits, giants in law, or eminent scholars, or of social distinction, leading men of wealth and enterprise in the commercial community, and see what they have voted for and suffered to be voted for, I think no community was ever so politely and elegantly betrayed (W 11: 423).

When he adds "I do not think it yet appears that women wish this equal share in public affairs," Emerson shows that he is less interested (though by no means uninterested) in clearing the route to equality between men and women than in finding the positive, rather than this negative, source of their difference. Though his discussion of the political rights of women always returns to the argument that they must not be refused, his discussion is everywhere cross-biased by his theoretical investigation of the rhetoric of those rights. Thus when he is at pains to show how a woman out of context is "disfranchised" (W 11: 410), he is not mounting an argument against her entry into the political arena, as some readers of the essay have feared, but reinvesting her context in order to displace the rhetoric of rights altogether. The unique value of his lecture resides in his unpresumptuous speculation that there remains an untapped feminine place that could assist in the displacement of that rhetoric. This hope helps to explain why he returns to the question of the home in his lecture, since he writes toward the acquisition of what I have earlier called the "paraphernalia" of the home.

Emerson enters the home by constructing his lecture around several stanzas from Coventry Patmore's poem "The Angel in the House." Patmore's work perpetuates the standard mystification of the home as the seat of the self and sanctuary for identity, a home ruled by the Victorian woman. Like everything else in the lecture, however, Emerson's allusion is treacherous; he employs a double strategy, at once sabotaging *and* salvaging the version of the home that he cites. Oddly, though not uncharacteristic of his work, a fragment of another poem placed at the front of the lecture as an epigraph prefigures the nature of his method.[25]

---

[25] It is unclear who placed the fragment before the lecture, as the lecture was never published during Emerson's lifetime. In his preface to the posthumous edition of essays that included the lecture, Emerson's son Edward claimed that he had placed "mottoes" drawn from Emerson's papers before each essay. Edward likely found the fragment with Emerson's lecture, since the poem is itself a highly edited version of a longer poem Fuller used in a *Tribune* article on prostitutes and other female convicts, published shortly before Emerson's visit to her in 1845. He seems to have been intrigued by the poem; certainly the shortened version of the poem (the entire first stanza and four lines from the last half of the second and third stanzas have been removed) is suggestive of the method he follows in his lecture, forming a striking counterstatement to Patmore's "Angel of the House." (The words *Angel* and *woman* are capitalized in the edited version.) See Fuller's article, "Asylum for Discharged Female Convicts," *Tribune*, June 19, 1845. The poem, to which Fuller attributes no author, reads:

> Cities of proud hotels,
>   Houses of rich and great,
> A stack of smoking chimeys,
>   A roof of frozen slate.
> It cannot conquer folly,
>   Time and space conquering steam,
> And the light-outspeeding telegraph
>   Bears nothing on its beam.
> The politics are base,
>   The letters do not cheer,
> And 't is far in the deeps of history
>   The voice that speaketh clear;
> Trade and the streets ensnare us,
>   Our bodies are weak and worn,
> We plot and corrupt each other,
>   And we despoil the unborn.
> Yet there in the parlour sits
>   Some figure of noble guise,
> Our angel in a stranger's form,
>   Or woman's pleading eyes;
> Or only a flashing sunbeam
>   in at the window pane,
> Or music pours on mortals
>   its beautiful disdain.

The politics are base
The letters do not cheer,
And 't is far in the deeps of history,
The voice that speaketh clear.

Yet there in the parlour sits
Some figure in noble guise,—
Our Angel in a stranger's form;
Or Woman's pleading eyes.

The opening lines read like a familiar complaint. Politics and writing are disparaged so that a voice or metaphysical presence can be praised. The feminine connotations in the phrase "deeps of history" prepare the reader for the suggestion in the second stanza that the "parlour" is now the site of that voice. If the parlor is indeed the site, however, its proficiency is immediately put into question by the conjunction "yet," which calls attention to the marginal situation of women. This marginality does not mean that the parlor is eliminated as the site of the "voice that speaketh clear," since Woman's marginality has often been inflated (as in Patmore's poem) as a salvific center. But such a reading generates a tidy circularity: the utopian valuation of the world of women sets an unattainable standard that effectively allows the pragmatic and flawed world of men to endure. Throughout his lecture, Emerson works to discredit this circularity, but he does so *without* eliminating feminism (or the home) altogether. Because we can also interpret "yet" as an adverb, suggesting the odd temporality of "now" or "still," the parlor, as the haunt of women, begins to supply another kind of alternative. The poem subverts the view of the parlor as the utopian vehicle of politics and letters, the borrowed dwelling, by transforming it into a ghostly dwelling and filling it with a phantom presence. The parlor, after all, is occupied by "some figure in noble guise." Nobility itself is cast into question by its adjectival activity; we cannot ascertain if the figure is falsely represented as noble or what its nobility implies. The suggestion that such nobility identifies "our Angel" brings into focus the alignment between the narrator, or voice, of the second stanza and the reader. The alignment becomes problematic because the revelation that "our Angel" (Patmore's angel, the angel created by the implicit theology of the first stanza and the hierarchical reading it sets in motion) assumes a "stranger's form" because we are uncertain whether it is strange to the narrator, the reader, the angel, or whether it is the stranger made to appear as an angel. To return to the home thus described is to return to uncertainty.

This uncertainty becomes still more problematic for the reader through the rather precise alternative of the last line, "Or Woman's pleading eyes," because the language of pleading keeps the reader from attempting to escape or evade that uncertainty. The sudden reversal of the motion of the poem—the reader, once entering into the parlor, is now confronted by a cloying glance issuing from it—implies that a movement away from the parlor, and, by association, a movement out of the poem, would be a movement back into the crisis of the initial stanza. For Emerson, the site of transvaluation hovers in the realm of paraphernalia, the undefinable yet imperative context that is the haunt of the attentive reader. It is the space that cannot be escaped once the activity of reading (the culture, the poem, the parlor) has begun.

What Emerson begins to establish with his lecture is that the "woman question" (as the "question of woman") extends well beyond (without excluding) certain pragmatic issues related to women into questions of style and the conduct of life that have been central to his intellectual career. Through the "woman question," he directly confronts the clash of meaning and nonmeaning that had characterized his intellectual orientation since his departure from the church, and perhaps before. One could say that his desire for meaning and belief ultimately led him to the belief in a world where no style or poetics could be found to achieve it. ("God is a reality, & his method is illusion" [JMN 11: 95].) This negative theology enabled him to detach himself from meaning altogether. The system of delay and deferral that characterized his writing as a result has led some twentieth-century critics to label his work deconstructive. But his faith in this method was incomplete because of its detachment; it was Fuller's influence as a feminist reader of his work that helped him to see how his movement away from the traditional rendering of meaning could be revalued as a movement toward a new style of meaning. With meaning salvaged but disencumbered from the traditional sense of the term, his work begins to express a type of feminist agency.[26]

The developing lines of Emerson's feminism are apparent in the early stages of the lecture when he argues that "Men remark figure: women always catch the expression" (W 11: 406). In one sense, of course, he flatters by extending the hyperbolic tenor of the Nordic myth he paraphrases: "All Wisdoms Woman knows: though she takes them for granted, and does not explain them as discoveries, like the understanding of man" (W 11: 406). But he does more than invent another chorus to feminine intuition. He endorses the myth in order to explore its complex

---

[26] Again, Alice Jardine nicely characterizes the oxymoronic nature of such a poetics when she talks about "working, potentially, toward a new disposition of the ethical grounded in symbolic process" (*Gynesis*, p. 47).

political and cultural matrix. After all, in his essay on the poet, he wrote, "man was only half himself, the other half is his expression" (CW 2: 4). His reference to expression in his lecture on Woman is not arbitrary, since he intends to align women with poetry without invoking the traditional notion of the muse. By this construction, women no longer inspire; rather, they receive poetic expression. As such, women are associated with the "receptive" quality that Stanley Cavell identifies as crucial to Emerson's reversal of Kantian notions of representation, the quality of thinking as "the receiving or letting be of something, as opposed to the positing or putting together of something."[27] By contrast, men are distanced from this form of poetic expression. That "men remark figure" suggests a masculine circularity, emptying their speech of content.

Yet even as Emerson embellishes feminine power as a privileged form of cognition, he neither simplifies nor ignores the complications of such an assertion. Men remark *upon* figure as well, with women most assuredly catching the expression, twisting the act of reception into an act of violation. If the muse exists, in this reading, it remains concealed in the punctuation separating the two acts of the sentence. Emerson's formulation of the Nordic myth about the oracular nature of women, therefore, becomes reflexive, in effect a poem whose reading dramatizes the mathematical rape of the poetic sensibility, itself made vulnerable, sentimental, and devious ("catch" can also suggest "ensnare") by its isolation. In one quick stroke he provides a feminist analysis of the dangerous cultural division between social and domestic spheres. Such political sensitivity permits him to end the same paragraph, glittering with toppled stereotypes, with intimations of political disruption: "Any remarkable opinion or movement shared by woman will be the first sign of revolution" (W 11: 406). If trifles and delays are part of Woman's oracular power, Emerson argues that they constitute the only remaining and unfulfilled power of value, since women "finish society, manners, language" (W 11: 499). "Finish" at once suggests an embellishment, a polishing, and an apocalyptic entry into the sublime. To say that women "finish" society is finally to argue that women have the potential to transmute it.

Emerson invests the woman's movement with just such a supremacy, telling his audience that there is "none more seriously interesting to every healthful and thoughtful mind." Because for him the value of the movement lay in its power to transform value, including the value of supremacy itself, he argues that the concern for the position of women is

[27] Stanley Cavell, "Thinking of Emerson," *The Senses of Walden*, exp. ed. (San Francisco: North Point Press, 1981), 132.

not the "single inspiration of one mind," setting it back into a patriarchal structure, but a movement that is "sporadic in the public mind" (W 11: 405), making it a kind of Derridean project of dissemination.

Not surprisingly, Emerson's argument about the promise of the movement draws on the example of Margaret Fuller. He was aware that her conversational power was well known, particularly to members of this audience. We have few ways of reconstructing that power, but through a patchwork of her writing and testimony from Emerson, who described her conversation as rhythmic and improvisational, we can easily imagine men and women pulling their chairs closer and realigning their feet to match her unexpected cadences.[28] Fuller apparently gathered her insights promiscuously, slipping ancient verities in with the gossip and fictions of the present, shading her topic with a marvelous array of wit and good humor. Nearly everyone, Fuller included, agreed that this power never was transcribed to the page, but the unfinished nature of this transition Emerson finds especially useful.[29] Her conversational prowess had a distinctly feminist dimension; conversation, like the house, was the site of Woman's intellectual world, the place given to her by the culture. Fuller's elaborate development of that site, however, exceeded traditional expectations for the Angel of the House, not only because of the intellectual rigor of her success, but also because of her persistent desire to transfer that power to the written text and to the texts of history and politics. Emerson seizes her desire and uses it retroactively in a critique of traditional representation. Already paying homage to her by delivering the lecture before the Woman's Rights Convention, he caps his tribute by elevating her conversational genius as the finishing function of Woman in general.

Appropriately, when Emerson transforms this historical trait into a theoretical one, he brings Plato back into his argument. He agrees with Plato that women never achieved a mastery equal to the mastery of men, but he mocks the notion that they should do so and displaces Plato's argument altogether with a tribute to conversation: "There is an art which is better than painting, poetry, music, or architecture,—better

[28] "Margaret Fuller had rhythm in her speech. And her speech was improvisation" (JMN 13: 437).

[29] Emerson cites Fuller in his section of the *Memoirs*: "'When I look at my papers, I feel as if I had never had a thought that was worthy the attention of any but myself: and 'tis only when, on talking with people, I find I tell them what they did not know, that my confidence all returns. . . .

These gentlemen are surprised that I write no better, because I talk so well. But I have served a long apprenticeship to the one, none to the other. I shall write better, but never, I think, so well as I talk. . . . I shall not be discouraged, nor take for final what they say, but sift from it the truth, and use it'" (MMF 1: 295–96).

than botany, geology, or any science; namely Conversation. Wise, cultivated, genial conversation is the last flower of civilization and the best
result which life has to offer us,—a cup for gods, which has no repen-
tance" (W 11: 408). At first, he seems to be returning Woman to the
"presence" of the spoken word. But he has already warned us of the
culture's duplicity toward women concerning this place. In her exclusion from writing and the world of politics, Woman occupies a place
theoretically closer to that of Socrates than Plato. Historically, however,
she did not have a Plato, as did Socrates, to confirm that place through
writing. Emerson generates the concept of conversation as the product
of the house that is not the borrowed dwelling of metaphor or philosophy but the necessary dwelling of uncertainty (or paraphernalia) upon
which women are forced to rely. He does not pretend to achieve Being
with conversation. He does not speak in elegiac tones of a quality lost,
but in the manner of uncertainty and promise, of a quality yet to be
found. Moreover, he emphasizes the reproductive aspects of conversation. "Conversation is our account of ourselves," he tells his audience.
"All we have, all we can, all we know, is brought into play, and as the
reproduction, in finer form, of all our havings" (W 11: 408–9). Nor is it
any accident that this description recalls Emerson's earlier description of
writing in his essay on Goethe: "[The report] is a new and finer form of
the original" (W 4: 262). His purpose is to avoid privileging the voice
over the written word by showing how conversation performs a writerly task. Yet he also discloses a subtle shift of place for his scene of
writing by making conversation analogous to the activity of reading.
Because, as he would argue, this activity is the especial province of
Woman, her paraphernalia, it escapes the violent tendencies of the written word historically mastered (and read) by men.

Emerson is in a perilous position, to be sure, writing and reading as
Plato to his Socrates, in this case, Fuller. But his lecture does not focus on
its falling away from her presence as a woman; rather it engages in a
rather gleeful reunion with the work she produced both on and as a
woman. This concession to Fuller and her feminism is what distinguishes his lecture. His interaction with her and his genuine concern for
the condition of women conspire to generate a plenary feminist poetics.
If he had, in the course of his work, found reason to believe the limit of
Man's poetics to repair or even report cultural experience, he now expects the "terrible metaphysics" (W 11: 416) of Woman's experience to
work in reverse, adopting faith in a lopsided dynamic between base and
superstructure. In effect, he argues that the tragic social condition of
Woman will be diminished to the degree that Fuller's conversational
mode is transcribed into written form. This change is not a total appro-

priation of the social issue into the literary crisis, for it is Emerson's conviction, as it was Fuller's before him, that the cures of both history and writing are integral to each other. Incorporating women into the culture will improve the text insofar as language and culture are reciprocal.

When Emerson addresses conversation, he truly means an oracular voice among us—neither a chorus of common voices at one extreme nor the tightly controlled dialectic of the philosopher at the other. Women are finally "poets who believe their own poetry" (W 11: 412), and their conversational realm of the home, released from the false seductions of "truth" yet cognizant of an undecidable responsibility toward it, he finds attractive. Moreover, to argue that conversation embodies a privileged artistic medium is to exalt moods and temperament, challenging the vertigo of moods and temperament of his earlier essay "Experience."[30] In this way, the temperamental and conversational profile of his writing emerges as the formal correlative to Fuller's conversational strategy. It is possible, of course, that he began to hope that the shape of his own work would become the model for the reforming literary text. But in his "scene" before the women of Boston, he openly confronts what he earlier evaded by making the home the site of the reforming text. He proffers neither the sentimental nor isolated home as text, but the home buttressed by a feminist poetics of paraphernalia.

[30] See Emerson's essay "Experience" (CW 3: 25–49). See Cavell's comment in "Thinking of Emerson," p. 126, that "experience is about the epistemology, or say the logic, of moods." Throughout his mature life, Emerson's model for spontaneity and surprise was Margaret Fuller.

9
Reading Fate

In conversation, in calamity, he finds new materials.
—Ralph Waldo Emerson, W 4: 263

Why is a kiss like a sermon?
two heads and an application.
—Emerson, JMN 11: 301

In *The Twilight of the Idols*, Friedrich Nietzsche draws a fascinating comparison between Thomas Carlyle and Emerson. Carlyle's "craving" for a "strong faith" and "his incapacity" to sustain that faith mark the radical oscillation of a "typical romantic." In striking contrast, Emerson is seen as "roving, . . . subtler" and "above all happier" than Carlyle. Nietzsche's elaboration of Emerson's escape from the romantic dialectic of skepticism and faith proves as provocative as it is revealing: Emerson is likened to an old man who takes pleasure in an "amorous rendezvous" long after he has the physical power to consummate his ardor. Despite this ridiculous analogy, Nietzsche's levity of tone indicates a deep sympathy with Emerson's "clever cheerfulness." And, indeed, Emerson's complex response to Fuller's death endows Nietzsche's image with a compelling authenticity.[1]

After Fuller's death, Emerson's notebooks reveal a greater acceptance of Fourier and his theory of passionate attraction.[2] The epitome of this

---

[1] Nietzsche makes the analogy in Latin: "At times he touches on the cheerful transcendency of the worthy gentleman who returned from an amorous rendezvous, *tamquam re bene gesta*. '*Ut desint vires*,' he said gratefully, '*tamen est laudanda voluptas*'" (*The Portable Nietzsche*, trans. Walter Kaufmann [New York: Viking Press, 1954; rpt. 1969], 522).

[2] Emerson was encouraged, perhaps, by the realization that his poetry was being used to promulgate the doctrines of Fourier. See Marx Edgeworth Lazarus, *Passional Hygiene and Natural Medicine: Embracing the Harmonics of Man with His Planet* (New York: Fowlers and Wells, 1852), and *Love vs. Marriage* (New York: Fowlers and Wells, 1852). Lazarus begins *Passional Hygiene* with a quote from Emerson's "Experience" and later calls "Woodnotes" a "great Hygienic poem" (pp. 94–102). In the controversial *Love vs. Marriage*, he quotes Emerson throughout. Emerson's notebooks (JMN 13: 210–11) show him reading a number of works written by American followers of Fourier, including these two works as well as a third by Lazarus, *The Solar Ray* (New York: Fowlers and Wells, 1851); and three by Stephen Pearl Andrews: *Love, Marriage, and Divorce* (Boston: Benjamin R. Tucker, 1889), *The Sovereignty of the Individual* (Boston: Benjamin R. Tucker, 1889), and *The Science of Society* (Boston: Benjamin R. Tucker, 1853). He also looked at the translation by Henry James, Sr., of Victor Henniquin, *Love in the Phalanstery* (New York: Dewitt and Davenport, 1849); Charles Bray, *Philosophy of Necessity* (London: Longmares, Green, 1841); and "Position of Women in Harmony," chapter 10 of *The Phalanstery; Or, Attractive Industry and Moral Harmony*, trans. from the French Madame Gattie de Gamond by an English Lady (London: Wittaker and Company, 1841).

shift is Emerson's simple equation "Fate = Passion" (JMN 12: 584). Although much of his writing exhibits the radical and romantic alternation between Carlyle's "dyspeptic states," his consideration of Fuller's loss clearly evokes his "Minerva" side.[3] Emerson's response both in his journal entries and in the essay "Fate" recalls the tone displayed in his letters to Fuller, where his skepticism is transvalued into an acceptance of the feminist poetics of paraphernalia, the provisional site at once inside and outside the codes of culture. This transformation includes an acceptance of the ridiculous as a critical tool for reexamining the conduct of life. A steadfast reader of Emerson, Nietzsche loved the essay "Fate," and his understanding of Emerson's potent glee no doubt drew on that work. In "Fate" Emerson most forcefully addresses the tangle of issues central to his feminist conversations with Fuller. That he deliberately eschews the style of "Carlyle and Boston and London" to address those issues makes Nietzsche's comparison between Emerson and Carlyle all the more intriguing.[4]

Nietzsche is hardly the only commentator to appreciate Emerson's "Fate." Even more than "Nature" or the powerful essays of the *Second Series*, "Fate" is the essay upon which many of his critics seem to fix their understanding of his career. There is something aggressively satisfying about taking the measure of an author—and one's critical theory—in a work with so dramatic and adamantine a title. In the past thirty years, a number of important critiques have used the essay to address the fate of American Romanticism and, more recently, the fate of reading itself. Stephen Whicher, whose deep research in Emerson's journals and notebooks furnished him with a particularly effective critical base, employed the terms *freedom* and *fate* as the chronological and artistic poles in Emerson's career. By Whicher's account, the essay "Fate" demonstrates a quest for Power, which in turn marks a retreat from Emerson's transcendental struggle for artistic Freedom.[5] Harold Bloom would later alter without radically changing Whicher's constants by describing Emerson's attachment to Power as the apocalyptic outcome of a dialectic of Freedom and fate occurring throughout his career.[6] According to Bloom, "Emerson's most frequent triad was the famous Fate, Freedom

[3] Nietzsche, *Twilight of the Idols*, in *The Portable Nietzche*, p. 521.

[4] In a letter to Sam Ward concerning the proposed "Life of Margaret," Emerson writes, "I think it could really be done, if one would heroically devote himself, and a most vivacious book written, but it must be done tête exaltée, & in the tone of Spiridion, or even of Bettine, with the coolest ignoring of Mr Willis Mr Carlyle and Boston & London" (EL 4: 222).

[5] Stephen Whicher, *Freedom and Fate: An Inner Life of Ralph Waldo Emerson* (Philadelphia: University of Pennsylvania Press, 1963).

[6] See JMN 11: 295: "A Journal is to the author a book of constants, each mind requiring, as I have so often said, to write the whole of literature and science for itself."

and Power. . . . [He] wanted Freedom, reconciled himself to Fate, but loved only Power, from first to last."[7] More recently, Eric Cheyfitz has transformed Bloom's dialectic by arguing that Emerson's ambiguous understanding of Power constitutes the basis for an ironic feminist critique. Although conceding that Emerson sustained a masculine perspective, Cheyfitz contends that he deploys a consistently feminine subversion of the masculine in his work. Cheyfitz reconstitutes Bloom's thesis in this manner: "Emerson wanted manliness [Freedom], reconciled himself to motherliness [Fate], but from the first to last he loved only the dream of manliness [Power], a dream expressed, ironically, in feminine form."[8]

Julie Ellison has shown how the apparent dialectic of Emerson's thought is more accurately defined as an unresolved antithesis, one particularly suited to the figure of allegory.[9] By eschewing the dialectic of skepticism and hope prevalent in other romantic accounts of Emerson's work, Ellison's reading moves closer to Nietzsche's. According to her, Emerson didn't write allegories; he merely used "allegory as a tactic in the composition of a stylistically and generically miscellaneous prose"—that is, as a strategy for theorizing itself. Like Nietzsche, Ellison also observes the "demented cheerfulness" of Emerson's essay, noting that his recognition of allegory's "violent displacement" of man and nature cannot mute his pleasure in the "productive aggressiveness" of allegory's theoretical power.[10] Despite her astute theoretical reading, Ellison's argument is equally remarkable for its dismissal of contemporary critical practice. For her, Paul de Man's insistence that allegory functions as a play of *différance* rather than force is as inapplicable to Emerson's vision as Cheyfitz's imposition of a social, feminist perspective on his textual use of power. Her simultaneous dismissal of deconstruction and feminism makes her a "strong" reader in the Bloomian sense, yet it forces her to miss the developing feminist theory at work in Emerson's allegorical method.

As Emerson's response to Fourier suggests, no one worried more about the type of theoretical aggression that Ellison describes than he did. His continued anxiety about the Fourieristic critique of the isolated household and the marriage bond reflected his concern that men would use Fourier's theory to take advantage of women. Not until he understood the feminist potential of allegory as Fuller began to work with it—

[7] Harold Bloom, *Wallace Stevens: The Poems of Our Climate* (Ithaca: Cornell University Press, 1976), 8.

[8] Eric Cheyfitz, *The Trans-Parent: Sexual Politics in the Language of Emerson* (Baltimore: Johns Hopkins University Press, 1981), 95.

[9] Julie Ellison, "Aggressive Allegory," *Raritan* 3 (Winter 1984): 100–115, and *Emerson's Romantic Style* (Princeton: Princeton University Press, 1984).

[10] Ellison, "Aggressive Allegory," pp. 102, 108, 110.

one offering the advantages of a provisional rather than prescriptive site—did his own fascination with the process become a source of his "clever cheerfulness." In other words, Fuller helped Emerson accept the writerly nature of his own thinking.

Fuller's double strategy was itself an endorsement of a type of allegorical process, one meant to transform the theoretical aggression Ellison finds so problematic by endorsing many of the same principles later recognized by Paul de Man. She saw that the concept of the home needed to be opened to the fluidity of allegory in order to disrupt the traditional symbolic process where roles for men and women became fixed in a hierarchical system of value. The idea of Woman held a very different meaning when viewed allegorically and symbolically. A symbolic view tended to freeze and constrain value by fitting the idea of Woman into some preexisting cultural expectation, whereas, taken allegorically—which is what Fuller did when she proposed the work of Goethe and Fourier as supplemental agents for the culture—the idea of Woman could be productive of a new type of meaning precisely because it was willing to engage shifting frames of reference.

Emerson slowly began to see the value of Fuller's constant resort to this type of double strategy. *Representative Men* marks the beginning of his effort to embrace what we have elsewhere described as her writerly understanding of the shifting cultural frames through which meaning must be established. His work in *Memoirs* and "Woman" amply demonstrates his recognition of her method, yet in "Fate" his embrace of that method is complete.

"Playing Dido to His Aeneas"

A conflicted suspicion of the feminist theory at work in Emerson's writing hovers at the center of another recent reading by Stanley Cavell, one of Emerson's most astute modern interpreters. He argues that Emerson's miscellaneous prose takes us to the vital question of Emerson's audience. Why, asks Cavell, if we can make intense theoretical claims for Emerson (and, like Fuller, Cavell is most interested in "stuffing out" [MMF 1: 202] the philosopher in Emerson), is his work unknown to his American audience in a way that would be unthinkable for European theorists to be unknown to theirs?[11] Cavell's question is grudgingly

[11] Stanley Cavell, "Genteel Responses to Kant? in Emerson's 'Fate' and in Coleridge's *Biographia Literaria*," *Raritan* 3 (Fall 1983): 34–51. Here I make reference to Emerson's comment about Fuller (MMF 1: 202), who was equally engaged in the process of "stuffing out" the philosopher in Emerson.

rhetorical. Emerson is not known as a traditional theorist because he cannot be read like one. This idea sometimes troubles Cavell even though he knows that nothing would have pleased Emerson more. Yet changing the expectations of his reader, reformulating his audience is part of the radical project of "Fate." Cavell inadvertently makes this point by showing how Emerson's engagement with "Kantian complexities," particularly the "two worlds" of "Freedom" and "Fate,"[12] is deliberately obscured by the fractious, genteel surface of his prose. Again, Cavell is sometimes troubled by that gentility, and when he attempts to argue that the essay displays a theoretical engagement with certain issues being generated by the slavery crisis, he feels pressed to explain Emerson's roundabout method. All founding fathers teach us to repress something, Cavell tells us, but why, he asks, does Emerson manage to repress the thinking culture he helped to originate? Why does Emerson act as "Dido to [his] own Aeneas"?[13]

Cavell's question frames the answer he cannot quite supply, particularly as the allegory of Dido is not strictly a narrative of self-sacrifice. Emerson's alignment with Dido rather than Aeneas can also be read as an endorsement of a feminist position. Cheyfitz in fact makes this argument, but he feels compelled to stress the irony of Emerson's feminism. Nevertheless, once we recognize the part that Fuller plays in the composition of "Fate," his feminism appears far less ironic than the determination on the part of critics to shun it. Cavell is not wrong to posit the association between "Fate" and the slavery question, for Emerson's journals also show that he was deeply troubled by the passage of the Fugitive Slave Law in 1850 and the "fall" of Daniel Webster, whose support of the bill forced Emerson to seek a new model of eloquence and agency for the culture.[14] Indeed, the close of "Fate," with its panegyric to "Beautiful Necessity," recalls the "blessed necessity" (W 11: 147) from Emerson's 1844 speech on emancipation in the West Indies. But what Cavell cannot quite see (in part because Emerson deliberately obscures all direct reference) is how powerfully Fuller functions as the new model of eloquence and agency for the culture in Emerson's later essay. "Fate" became his tribute to the provisional space occupied by this powerful American Dido, and as such signals a feminist poetics far bolder than even Cheyfitz can allow.

Certainly, by the time Emerson had decided to publish "Fate" as the

---

[12] Cavell, "Genteel Responses," p. 39.

[13] Ibid., p. 36.

[14] Robert Hudspeth offers a particularly acute reading of the interaction of the Webster issue and Fuller's death in his essay "Emerson's Anger: The Context of 'Fate.'" I am very grateful to Hudspeth for his willingness to show me his early draft of this essay.

lead essay in his collection *The Conduct of Life*, tradition was preparing to erupt into a bloody Civil War. The housewife's proverb that "there are a thousand things to everything" (JMN 11: 441), recorded by Emerson in one of his journals during this period, more aptly tells the critical possibilities of the essay. Kantian complexities and the association of allegory and theory are at issue in the work, as both Cavell and Ellison so deftly show. Yet these issues are implicated in a far larger, more complex, allegory about America's most prominent feminist, Margaret Fuller. In his 1851 journals, where he oscillated between his dismay over Webster's fall and Fuller's death, Emerson recorded his growing despair over the country's political climate with the following passage: "Thirty Years's War . . . made Germany a nation. What Calamity will make us one?" (JMN 11: 409). "Fate" marks his attempt to make the calamity of Fuller's death serve that office. In it, he hopes to forestall the impending Civil War and the national conflict of meaning it foretold by changing the reading habits of his culture.

Feminism: The Ridiculous and the Fatal

At a very basic level, Fuller's death brought to mind at least two earlier and important calamities: the death of Emerson's brother Charles and the loss of his son Waldo. When his brother died, Emerson had also attempted to assemble a memoir, but the task proved too difficult and never came to fruition. When faced with the same task after Fuller's death, he displayed a similar sense of hopelessness and confusion. Finding a way to express his debt to her, as he finally did through the complex composition of *Memoirs* and "Fate," was in the end both gratifying and therapeutic.[15] Moreover, by returning once more to address some of the Fourieristic questions so important to the composition of "Experience," the work of mourning accomplished in "Fate" also enabled him to revalue the terms he had used in his response to Waldo's death. Once again, then, a consideration of Fuller's life enabled him to reconstitute the theory through which he had experienced his own.

Emerson set a high value on that type of recollection, for it is integral to the writer's task. He writes in a journal entry: "Never was truer fable than the Sibyl's writing on leaves which the wind scatters. . . . The difference between man & man is, that, in one, the memory with inconceivable swiftness flies after & *re-collects* these leaves;—flies on wing as fast

---

[15] Fuller's part in the work of mourning for Charles cannot be underestimated. We know, for example, that she copied the letter Emerson wrote to his aunt, Mary Moody Emerson, eulogizing Charles. See EL 7: 259–60.

as that mysterious whirlwind; & the envious Fate is baffled" (JMN 11: 390 Emerson's emphasis). The process of reading Fuller's death enables him to return to himself in certain key moments of his career. Most notable, perhaps, is the way he returns to the spirit of his essay "Circles." Because he composed "Circles" at the height of his intimacy with Fuller, his description of conversation in that essay matches what he later says about her conversational skill. In *Memoirs*, he described her power this way:

> With the firmest tact she led the discourse into the midst of their daily living and working, recognizing the good-will and sincerity which each man has in his aims, and treating so playfully and intellectually all the points, that one seemed to see his life *en beau*, and was flattered by beholding what he had found so tedious in its workday weeds, shining in glorious costume. Each of his friends passed before him in the new light; hope seemed to spring under his feet, and life was worth living. The auditor jumped for joy, and thirsted for unlimited draughts (MMF 1: 215).

In "Circles" we can see in Emerson's description of the "game of circles" a reflection of Fuller's transforming use of conversation:

> In common hours, society sits cold and statuesque. We all stand waiting, empty,—knowing, possibly that we can be full, surrounded by mighty symbols which are not symbols to us, but prose and trivial toys. Then cometh the god and converts the statues into fiery men, and by a flash of his eye burns up the veil which shrouded all things, and the meaning of the very furniture, of cup and saucer, of chair and clock and tester, is manifest. The facts which loomed so large in the fogs of yesterday,—property, climate, breeding, personal beauty and the like, have strangely changed their proportions. All that we reckoned settled shakes and rattles; and literatures, cities, climates, religions, leave their foundations, and dance before our eyes (CW 2: 184).

What is striking about this quote is the way it anticipates the description of the hero in "Fate." There, "a personal influence towers up in memory" and "we gladly forget numbers, money, climate, gravitation, and the rest of Fate" (W 6: 34). Emerson's ecstatic tone throughout "Fate" reveals his sense that he has discovered a method that will help to "re-collect" the disparate goals of his career and "baffle" the "envious Fate" (JMN 11: 390).

But reading Fuller's death also encourages Emerson to consider the broader implications of her reading strategy as well. After extensively reviewing her life for the *Memoirs*, he came to believe that her power resided in her cunning inversion of the context in which she found herself and with it her reading of the ideological forces at work in the concept of the ridiculous. As a woman in a patriarchal culture, her strategy for success was her vital transformation of the fatal position of Woman into a site of critique and social change. Thus in "Fate" Emerson endorses her feminist strategy, particularly her desire to work from a provisional space or "limit" marked by the culture. Although he endorses her theory of reading, like her he did not use the term *feminism* to describe this theory, as the word did not yet have the meaning it has today. And instead of using the term *Fourierism*—which in Fuller's absence did not carry the distinctly feminist value she had given it— *fatalism* became his expression for the method she employed. Indeed, *fatalism* nicely consolidates his understanding of the reading strategy implied in her double advocacy of Fourier and Goethe. Consequently, the term becomes his way of describing the writerly method that provokes and enables an ethical agency in the reader, since it lends a unique perspective on the codes framing our sense of ourselves and the conduct of life.

The association between Fuller and fate is made easier by Emerson's recollection of her argument that "this remote seeking for the decrees of Fate, this feeling of a destiny . . . is the most beautiful species of idealism in our day" (MMF 1: 222). In a letter he wrote to their close mutual friend, Carrie Sturgis, the link between fate and Fuller is again strongly implied. Stephen Whicher included the letter in his well-known *Selections from Ralph Waldo Emerson*,[16] and many critics have noted its obvious relevance to "Fate," though few have seen the thinly veiled description there of Emerson's indebtedness to Fuller. Beginning with an apology, perhaps for the "generalizings" of the *Memoirs*, Emerson employs the idea of fatalism to describe his new theory. Sturgis would have easily recognized Fuller as the "intelligent soul" whose method was "now tragically, now tenderly" being "illustrated":

> I believe my slowness to write letters has grown from the experience that some of my friends have been very impatient of my generalizings. . . . Friends are few, thoughts are few, facts few—only one . . . now tragically, now tenderly, now exaltingly illustrated. . . . The universe is all chemistry, with a certain hint of a magnificent *Whence* or *Whereto* gilding or opalizing every angle of the old salt-acid acid-salt, endlessly reiterated & masqueraded thro' all time & space & form. The addition of that hint everywhere,

[16] *Selections from Ralph Waldo Emerson*, ed. Stephen Whicher (Boston: Houghton Mifflin, 1951).

saves things. . . . Fatalism, foolish & flippant, is as bad as unitarianism or Mormonism. But Fatalism held by an intelligent soul who knows how to humor & obey the infinitesimal pulses of spontaneity, is by much the greatest theory in use. All the great would call their thought fatalism, or concede that ninetynine parts are nature & one part power, tho' that hundredth is elastic, miraculous, &, whenever it is in energy, dissolving all the rest (EL 4: 376).

This famous passage resembles a letter Emerson wrote to Fuller in May 1841:

If our incarnations here could manage to acquire some little increments, if we could play at dice as Hermes did with the moon for intercalary lunations . . . We could afford then to try experiments & obey all beautiful motions. We could live alone & *if that did not serve*, we could associate. We could enjoy *and* abstain, *and* read *and* burn our books *and* labor *and* dream. But fie on this Half this Untried, this take-it-or-leave-it, this flash-of- lightning life. In my next migration, O Indra! I bespeak an ampler circle, the "vast year of Mizar & Alcor," an orb, a whole! Come, o my friend with your earliest convenience, I pray you, & let us seize the void betwixt two atoms of air the vacation between two moments of time to decide how we will steer on this torrent which is called Today Instantaneously yours, Waldo E. (EL 2: 399–400).[17]

Indeed, because Fuller's death was so fraught with significance for Emerson's writing, constructing a monument to her memory was not unlike publishing his letters to her. Such a display is effectively what happens in "Fate." His oddly elated tone in "Fate," his "clever" and "demented" cheerfulness so baffling to Ellison and Cavell probably did not surprise Sturgis, who had been privy to the Emerson-Fuller correspondence on numerous occasions. She may even have remembered the day she and Fuller reviewed all of the letters Emerson had sent to them in the summer of 1840. Fuller later reported the experience to William H. Channing, noting how the letters "make a volume . . . finer than any thing he has published" (LMF 2: 183). Certainly his enthusiasm over "Fate" grew when he saw for himself that he had already experimented with a kind of fatalism in his letters to Fuller. "I have, I think, in my letter to Margaret Fuller, an account of the negative method of spirit" (JMN 11: 268). The excitement he conveys in his letter to Sturgis emerges in part from his realization that Fuller provided both a model and a site for

[17] See the footnotes to this letter for the interesting connection between the letter and his essays "Illusions" and "Experience."

the recovery of an important type of agency. The model was her reading strategy, and the site was recoverable for him in his writing whenever he returned to the experimental tone of his letters to her.

Recognizing that he experienced great dissatisfaction whenever he yielded to the conservatism of his reader, Emerson began to prize the feminist reading that Fuller had always supplied for his work. Indeed, when she died, he recorded the loss by observing, "I have lost in her my audience" (JMN 11: 258). As we discovered in Chapter 1, writing to her encouraged a feminist conversation, a provisional site for him; their unorthodox relationship became a useful writerly field and a haven for experiment. Understanding the importance of that provisional space marked a revolution in his thinking, a Fourieristic shift in his view of the conduct of life. Where once he felt the need to impose a conservative reading of domestic life to project the theoretical limits of power, he now appears ready to consider a radical allegory of domestic life, drawn from Fuller and her use of Fourier, to move beyond those theoretical limits back to life.

Emerson's journals repeatedly demonstrate this transition. One entry in particular exhibits its relevance to his thinking about fate:

> It is with religion as marriage. A youth marries in . . . haste before the years of discretion, and at thirty, when his mind is opened to the entertainment & discussion of the conduct of life, he is asked, what he thinks of . . . the institution of marriage, & the right relations of the sexes. . . . "Too late," he says, "too late, I should have much to say if the question were open. I have a wife & five children & . . . all question is closed to me." So with religion, in the youth of a nation in its barbarous days, some *cultus*, is fastened up on it, altars are built, tithes are imposed, a hierarchy organized. The education & expenditure of the country take that direction, and when wealth, refinement, great men & ties to the whole world, supervene, its wise men say, "Why fight against fate, or lift those absurdities which are now of mountainous size? Better pick out some cave or crevice in the mountain wherein you may bestow yourself & find shelter than attempt anything ridiculously and dangerously above your strength" (JMN 13: 257–58).

Although Emerson uses the socialist critique of marriage to expatiate on the limits of organized religion (and indeed, this journal entry finds its way into an essay entitled "Religion"), he also employs the radical critique of organized religion—upon which he based his career—to test the strength of the socialist critique.

The significance of Emerson's effort to make the two issues of religion and the conduct of life interact in this way cannot be overstated, since they constitute the major semiotic (or allegorical) fields for his life, neatly encompassing the attributes of freedom and fate that continually run through his work. Until Fuller's death, his view of freedom was often based on an exploration of the scandal of organized religion. Tearing down the false structure of religion, synonymous in many ways with the mordant structures of literary history, gave him enormous pleasure. His interaction with Fuller had made clear to him that his view of the poetic spirit was also loosely based on an erotic metaphor ("The religions of the world are the ejaculations of a few imaginative men" [CW 3: 20]), and he therefore became skeptical about applying this radical allegory of spirit to the conduct of life.

This skepticism meant that the freedom of spirit embodied in his view of religion was destined to remain "something ridiculously and dangerously above his strength" (JMN 13: 258). Yet, as the journal entry shows, he also was beginning to accept the idea that the conduct of life was as much an allegorical or writerly field in Fuller's sense as the field of religion was. That is, both were fluid and not fixed to immutable symbols. The argument of the young man that it is too late to consider the conduct of life represents Emerson's memory of the restraint he had once placed at the center of his interaction with Fuller.[18] By acknowledging the equivalent figural value of religion and the conduct of life as theoretical fields, by viewing his resistance to the socialist critique of the conduct of life as comparable to the resistance of the "wise men" of religion who refuse to question the dangerous and fraudulent trappings of their faith, he redresses the largest limitation of his career.

The specific feminist application of this reversal is most explicit in Emerson's 1855 lecture before the Woman's Rights Convention. There he deliberately inverts the familiar complaint that it is too late to alter the way things are by showing how many women had no choice but to insist on change. It is no accident that he introduces the idea of providence in order to make his point, since his thoughts on fate are already working behind this transformation.

> Providence is always surprising us with new and unlikely instruments. But perhaps it is because these people have been deprived of education, fine companions, opportunities, such as they wished,—because they feel the same rudeness and disadvantage which offends you,—that they have been stung to say, "It is too late for us to be polished and fashioned into beauty, but, at least, we will see that the whole race of women shall not suffer as we have suffered" (W 11: 419).

[18] As F. O. Matthiessen has already surmised, the poem "Days" provides his most vivid account of this restraint. See Matthiessen, "A Few Herbs and Apples," in *American Renaissance: Art and Expression in the Age of Emerson and Whitman* (London: Oxford University Press, 1941), 55–61.

As with Fuller, Emerson's feminism is not coincident with the secular program of the woman's movement. Armed with his new understanding of Fuller's fatalism, her emphasis on a double strategy emphasizing the provisional space given to women, he begins here to explore the many benefits that will accrue from his new willingness to consider the conduct of life as a fluid reservoir of value. The "Conduct of Life" now becomes a writerly project, one that would open up a new field for critique.

Even the descriptions of Fourier in his journals begin to anticipate the character of Emerson's argument throughout "Fate." "Fourier is immensely rich and joyous in his ranges and gradations of power," he wrote. "It suffices him to say, Nature had made it; so I know there is a turnpike way out. Is the thing desireable? Then there is a way to it" (JMN 11: 391). More important, Fourier becomes inextricably entwined with the project of writing itself: "When the Socialistic Idea stirs in the mind, it causes writing, with efforts of all kinds" (JMN 11: 372). Emerson's acceptance of Fuller's double strategy now appears complete: he has combined his reading of Goethe the writer with Fourier the social critic.

Emerson's conversion to this position is all the more remarkable when we consider the growing tendency toward "free love" among various proponents of Fourierism in North America and his own fear of a scandalous association.[19] Discussions became particularly heated in 1852 with the publication of *Love vs. Marriage* by Marx Edgeworth Lazarus, a work that heartily endorsed Fourier's "passional liberty."[20] Indeed, the publication embroiled Stephen Pearl Andrews, Horace Greeley, and Henry James Sr. in a debate about Fourier and marriage in the pages of the *New-York Daily Tribune*. The controversial and strangely reductive nature of this debate encouraged Emerson to keep his new Fourierism general.[21] Yet he could not have ignored the obvious relationship between the terms of his thinking and the issues at stake in the heated discussion over *Love vs. Marriage*, particularly when Lazarus supported his thesis with liberal quotes from Emerson's poetry. Only the writer Bettina von Arnim appears to have received more attention than Emerson in *Love vs. Marriage*, all of which lends still more authority to Fuller's prophetic role in the new social order being so hotly contested.

[19] See Carl Guarneri, *The Utopian Alternative: Fourierism in Nineteenth-Century America* (Ithaca: Cornell University Press, 1991), 348–67.

[20] Lazarus, *Love vs. Marriage*, p. 346.

[21] The debate began with the publication of Lazarus's *Love in a Phalanstery*. The *Tribune* debate ran from September until the close of 1852. See the discussion of this episode in Guarneri, *The Utopian Alternative*, 358–59.

Lazarus may well have appeared far less controversial (and "ridicu-lous") to Emerson than other proponents of Fourier. His journal entries during this period show that he closely read Lazarus's many works published in the early part of the 1850s. Unlike other American apostles, Lazarus remained closely engaged with the whole of Fourier's social theories, and his wide range in the fields of science, biology, agriculture, and industry also appealed to Emerson. While he was writing the *Memoirs* and composing the early lecture on "Fate," he carefully culled the translation of *Passional Zoology* by Alphonse Toussenel, which Lazarus had published, copying into his journals many passages that bear direct-ly on the issue of fate (JMN 13: 210). His interest in Lazarus may have been strengthened by his reaction against Stephen Pearl Andrews, who took advantage of the growing interest in Fourier to advance a theory of free love that ultimately had little to do with Fourier's sense of associa-tion. The anarchistic tendencies of Andrews, who was influenced more by Josiah Warren than Fourier, must have appalled Emerson. Andrews soon became an active proponent of "Individual Sovereignty," which in his handling became a terrible parody of Emerson's earlier defense of the individual against the world. By contrast, Lazarus held the principle of association to be central to the new social order.[22]

"The Event Is the Print of Your Form"

The task Emerson sets for himself in "Fate" is enormous. His general goal is to change the reading strategy of his culture, to empower his reader with a new type of agency. Because his goal entails an endorse-ment of Fuller's reading strategy, it also entails the radical reshaping of the historical consciousness of his audience. In reshaping this conscious-ness, the events of history are no longer placed into a narrative accord-ing to the dominant codes of the culture; rather, they are chosen as signs

[22] Though Lazarus was tolerant of the anarchistic movement, he maintained his faith in association. See Guarneri, *The Utopian Alternative*, 353–67. Again, we can hear Emerson gathering support for his fatalism in the language Lazarus employed to defend Fourier in *Passional Hygiene*: "To act or not to act is determined by the passions which arise in us without our bidding. Only through experience and observation, as on other natural forces, can we calculate their seasons and organic laws. Passion is the fountain of will. Science and intellect may guide the will to its object, but can neither create nor suppress it. Hence the partizans of fatalism and those of free-will, have shown no remarkable discrepancy in their energy of action. Human wills and actions are the partial and temporary aspects and manifestations of forms of the Divine will, which is fate or destiny. The action and senti-ment of the creature, which has nothing but what is given it, can be only the creative action and sentiment under the limitations of time, space, and circumstance. . . . We need not fear to acknowledge and define these collective influences" (p. 237).

for a potential disruption of these codes. Accordingly, Emerson uses the event of Fuller's death, the shipwreck, as the most potent sign that will lead to a new way of viewing things. Unhappy with the way in which the culture has read her death, he exploits the allegorical potential of shipwreck to provide his reader with an alternative way of reading.

Divided into four sections, Emerson's essay bears an uncanny resemblance to the structure of old Puritan sermons. After formulating the problem and situating himself and his audience at its center, he shifts in part two to a brief and general description of a theory that might be used to dispel this crisis. In the third section, he presents a portrait of the hero capable of using that theory; here Fuller makes her boldest figural appearance. Finally, he closes his essay with an application of his theory, one meant to return himself and his audience back to the conduct of life. Once again, however, this application is not prescriptive or descriptive, but speculative and aesthetic.

Emerson's contemporary reader would have understood how his opening reference to the lecture, journal, and pamphleteering activity of citizens in New York, Boston, and London was a specific allusion to the growing popularity of this activity around the theories of Fourier. Those "cities bent on discussing" the "spirit of the times" were mainly, in Emerson's view, "bent on discussing" various interpretations of Fourier's work (W 6: 9). (Indeed, many would have known of William Channing's Fourieristic journal entitled *The Spirit of the Age.* Channing, of course, was one of Emerson's collaborators in *Memoirs*.) Emerson's audience would have been so familiar with this activity that his *failure* to mention Fourier's name reveals how powerfully it had become a symbolic register for the "theory of the age" (W 6: 9), as well as the potent symbol for Emerson's own private negotiations with his culture.

Emerson's response to Fourier even merits a confession: "To me, however, the question of the times resolved itself into a practical question of the conduct of life. How shall I live?" (W 6: 9). Of course, his confession is little more than a rhetorical invocation to his reader, which is clarified by his immediate return to the inclusive pronoun "we": "We are incompetent to solve the times. Our geometry cannot span the huge orbits of the prevailing ideas, behold their return and reconcile their opposition" (W 6: 10). Again his journals show us that the initial version of this idea is made with specific reference to Fourier: "I affirm the sacredness of the individual. . . . I see also the benefits of cities, and the plausibility of phalansteries. But I cannot reconcile these oppositions" (JMN 11: 210). In effect, he turns his private dilemma into a general, cultural one. By using "we," he presents a double history; the rhetorical promise is that the history of his response will provide a useful model for the history of his listeners.

As in his journal entry about religion and the conduct of life, Emerson willingly aligns these various histories—once construed as warring temperaments—in order to describe them as interdependent allegorical perspectives. "By the same obedience to other thoughts we learn theirs, and then comes some reasonable hope of harmonizing them" (W 6: 4). By advocating this method he endorses a type of double strategy easily affiliated with Fourier and Fuller. *Harmony* was a key word associated with Fourier, and Emerson uses the word here and throughout the essay in recognition of that association. Certainly his assertion in the final pages of his essay that "the central intention of Nature [is] harmony and joy" (W 6: 48) aligns completely with Fourier's doctrine.

Thus the horizon of controversy set by Fourier becomes the general historical context of the essay. Moreover, the problem that Emerson addresses in "Fate" is drawn from his personal response to Fuller and Fourier. Simply stated in the opening paragraph, the problem concerns the conflicting imperatives of the "spirit of the times" and the "theory of the age," the practical question, as he puts it, of the "conduct of life." At the same time, Fuller's life informs the topography of the essay because the problem being addressed by the essay is initially presented through a complex allegory of shipwreck, one that becomes, by turns, a demonstration of the difficulties attached to the composition of a secular history.

Even though shipwreck was a common trope of disaster in the nineteenth century, few among Emerson's initial audience would have failed to make the connection between Emerson's allegory and Fuller's untimely death. Indeed, he began delivering the lecture "Fate" at roughly the same time that he was lecturing on Fuller to various groups around New England. The allegorization of her death, however, becomes the basis of a problematic or theorizing activity in the essay, one that opens the story of shipwreck to multiple interpretations. Emerson continually summons the idea of shipwreck in the first section, but he refuses to develop one coherent narrative around it. Instead, the presentation of the terror of life (the facts of fate) develops the figural *potential* of shipwreck. He intersperses literal descriptions of various stages of shipwreck with lists and fragmentary scenes from the world of politics, domestic life, history, geography, chemistry, and religion. These scenes function as interchangeable moments from the zodiac of meaning simultaneously produced and shattered by shipwreck itself.

This unconventional and self-reflexive use of allegory is actually a strategic hedge against what Julie Ellison calls the violence or aggression of allegory.[23] Emerson's protracted horror over the symbolic process

23 Ellison, "Aggressive Allegory," p. 100.

that transformed the facts of Fuller's shipwreck into a reductive and fatal history of her life turns his writing in "Fate" into the most self-reflexive example of this strategy at work.[24] His obvious preference is to read the signs of her shipwreck as she would have: that is, for their *transformative* potential.[25]

When Emerson first introduces shipwreck into the essay, he again interrupts a normal grammatical pattern in an effort to manipulate his reader. This time he begins with the inclusive pronoun "we," shifting mid-sentence into the possessive pronoun "your": "We must see that the world is rough and surly, and will not mind drowning a man or a woman, but swallows your ship like a grain of dust" (W 6: 16). With his cool transition to "your" in the middle of the sentence, he arrests the attention of those readers distancing themselves from calamity. At the same time, the shift allows him to sustain his temporary theoretical target, the play of hypocrisy and duplicity in life, by superimposing a fragment from a different allegory on it: "You have just dined, and however scrupulously the slaughterhouse is concealed in the graceful distance of miles, there is complicity" (W 6: 7). He is purposefully inclusive, perhaps to show how seductive and potentially violent such allegories can be. Because we nearly all forget the slaughterhouse when surrounded by the fineries of the table, we all participate in the extended allegory of shipwreck, and Emerson's task now is to explain the difficult implication of our complicity.

Emerson emphasizes the polysemous value of shipwreck. Even when he writes that "the forms of the shark, the *labrus*, the jaw of the sea-wolf paved with crushing teeth, the weapons of the grampus, and other warriors hidden in the sea, are hints of the ferocity in the interiors of nature" (W 6: 8), the reader moves from a graphic account of the conditions of shipwreck to a recognition of the strangely dull reading of fate they signify. As mere hints of the ferocious condition at the center of nature, these fearful experiences are proof only of the uncertainty of nature's most horrific signs.

Still, the power of Emerson's multivalent exploitation of shipwreck resides in the way it reveals his own complicity in the same dull reading.

[24] Emerson's journals are filled with unhappy revelations of this sort. "Mrs. Barlow has the superiority to say of Margaret, that the death seems to her a fit & good conclusion to the life. Her life was romantic & exceptional: So let her death be; it sets the seal on her marriage, avoids all questions of Society, all of employment, poverty, old age, and besides was undoubtedly predetermined when the world was created" (JMN 11: 259).

[25] Here Emerson adopts a position not unlike Kant's determination to read the signs of history, not the facts. For an interesting description of Jean-François Lyotard's use of this important Kantian notion, see David Carroll, "Rephrasing the Political with Kant and Lyotard: From Aesthetic to Political Judgments," *Diacritics* 14 (Fall 1984): 74–88.

Because he believes that the average conservative response to shipwreck (now an allegory of fate) is synonymous with the conservatism of his early response to the conduct of life, he closes the same paragraph with a denigrating autobiographical reference. It is "of no use," he argues, to "dress up that terrific benefactor in a clean shirt and white neckcloth of a student of divinity" (W 6: 8).

This figurative allusion criticizes more than Emerson's youthful attempt to dispatch fate with the formalities of organized religion. It opens the way for an attack on the violent principle of sacrifice, dependent on a traditional use of symbol, at the center of the history-making process, whether sacred or secular. His impatience with the argument that Fuller's death—like Dido's—was somehow necessary is an impatience as well with his earlier sacrifice of her ideas. He now understands, as he did in his journal entry comparing religion and marriage, that he did not eliminate the violence of sacrifice in his movement away from organized religion; he merely shifted it from the sacred to the secular world with his conservative and stable reading of the conduct of life. The public reaction to Fuller's death merely highlighted Fourier's argument that women were the sacrificial force at the center of that symbolic procedure.

Emerson emphasizes his complicity in this process when he ends the first section of the essay with a description of the agonizing last moments of a shipwreck. His description effectively allows the facts of Fuller's death and his own life to converge. Part of the legend of Fuller's death had been her refusal to separate her family at the moment of shipwreck; her decision to sustain the traditional family unit had cost them their lives. Emerson exploits this reading of the event even as he revises it. In one sense, his revision is therapeutic: he places himself at the center of a tempest to relieve some of the horror resulting from it. Yet he is not uncritical of the role he allows himself to play. Presumably if a woman were included, the expectation generated by the scene would change considerably. Emerson appears to seek an unproblematic connection between the helpless glances of the men toward one another and his own toward them: "I seemed in the height of a tempest to see men overboard struggling in the waves, and driven about here and there. They glanced intelligently at each other, but 't was little they could do for one another; 't was much if each could keep afloat alone. Well, they had a right to their eye-beams, and all the rest was Fate" (W 6: 19). Finally Emerson's account of the shipwreck is itself an allegorical rendering of his passive response to Fuller. And because it uses the theater of shipwreck as the representative allegory of fate, he strengthens the bond he is trying to build between his history and the history-making process of his audience. The first section aims, then, to establish this problem in the histories of Emerson and his audience and to prepare the way for a different, less sacrificial, view of history.

The clue that Emerson will continue to reverse this reading of shipwreck (and the clue that Fuller will be implicated in that reversal), is adumbrated by his reference to the ridiculous in the opening lines of the same paragraph: "The force with which we resist these torrents of tendency looks so ridiculously inadequate that it amounts to little more than a criticism or protest made by a minority of one under compulsion of millions" (W 6: 19). Through his earlier effort to give an account of Fuller's life, he discovered that her Fourierism deconstructed the ridiculous as nothing more than a radical loss of context. Fear of the ridiculous registered a fear of being tossed, like the men in his imaginary shipwreck, into an unfamiliar or heterogeneous environment. For a woman like Fuller, encounters with the ridiculous were routine. Her strategic success suggested to Emerson that all texts, including his own, could be rewritten away from the ridiculous if supplied with a better understanding of the conditions of their production.

Emerson's excitement over this discovery is in essence an excitement over the writerly possibilities of the ridiculous. A trace of the sublime is lodged within the image of the minority of one against millions that he projects. Fear of the ridiculous often figured in his work, yet, as we know from the journal about marriage and religion, he no longer has sympathy for a defeated retreat from that fear. Rather than arguing against attempting "anything ridiculously and dangerously above your strength," he now condones the "comic poet" (W 6: 18) who, like the Hindus, makes "a poetic attempt to lift this mountain of Fate" (W 6: 12).[26]

Thus Emerson's earlier statement in this section that "the book of Nature is the Book of Fate" (W 6: 15) is the clue to the revised, rewritten history of himself that he will provide in "Fate." Whereas in his first essay Nature he concedes that there is something ridiculous about nature until out of the sight of man (CW 1: 39), he now insists on a person's presence, in all the ridiculous details of living. In this way he is able to eliminate the traditional rendering of "Fate." In the end, "Fate" has less to do with the "shocks and ruins" of shipwreck, than with the "stealthy

[26] Emerson often aligned Asia with the idea of Woman; so it is not surprising that his alignment with a poetic and Eastern sensibility coincides with his appropriation of Fuller's Fourierism. But here the word *appropriate* is inadequate, since his use of Fourierism involves a concession: Fuller's Fourierism does not force a disjunction from his past so much as it gains access to certain of its unread continuities. With Fuller's help, the ridiculous becomes a mode of transition, a way of recovering displaced voices from the past, including his own.

power of other laws that act on us daily" (W 6: 8), the very context of our lives. When he writes that "every spirit makes its house; but afterwards the house confines the spirit" (W 6: 9), he concedes that the most dangerous site of sacrifice is not in nature, but the home, the simultaneous seat of language and the conduct of life.[27]

Although shipwreck is the initial allegorical figure, leading in the direction of his past, the fragmented trope of the house supersedes it as the figure of the future, leading back to the conduct of life. The figure of the house is at once pragmatic and philosophical, social and linguistic, covering a broad range suggestive of Emerson's central activity in the essay. In his early work the house or the private sphere was constantly defined in opposition to society and a variety of social formations in the public sphere, including Fourier's socialism. He often thought that the home had a fixed representational value based on natural attributes and that the Fourieristic critique of the conduct of life posed a serious threat. Now he accepts a concept of home based on the figurative play of both the natural and the conduct of life. Thus, in "Fate" the world and the house become "suppletory" figures, each heavily implicated in the other's production.[28]

In Emerson's writing the concept of the house also stood for individual consciousness. In this formulation, words are the predetermined unit of consciousness. Thus, "each word is like a work of nature, determined a thousand years ago" (JMN 11: 232). Yet after Fuller's death, Emerson balanced this belief that words are "not alterable" against his larger understanding of language: "Language is a quite wonderful city, which we all help to build" (JMN 11: 232). Because words are useless in isolation, and, in fact, impossible to conceive without an idea of language, the home also becomes inconceivable without some conception of society or the world. Such is Emerson's thinking as he equates a certain type of Fourierism with writing ("*Phalanstery* means, the use which a wise man makes of a large city" [JMN 11: 242].) Thus in "Fate" Emerson makes a distinction between language as it has been "determined a thousand years ago" and the language of writers. Words, when used in a field of figuration, a "phalanstery" of expression, release themselves from the "irresistible dictation" of representation (W 6: 4). Both consciousness and the world are impossible without the city of language, and hence they meet at the matrix of a continuous, exploratory figuration, a fiesta

[27] Again, Emerson returns to his idea in "Nature" that "every spirit builds itself a house, and beyond its house, a world; and beyond its world, a heaven" (CW 1: 44).

[28] "Every man is a new method, & distributes all things anew. If he could attain complete development, he would take up first or last atom by atom all the world into a new crystal hitherto undescribed. . . . Characters & talents are complemental & suppletory, & the house & the world stand by balanced antagonisms" (JMN 11: 374).

of allegory. With the figure of writing, therefore, Emerson dismisses the figure of shipwreck.

The substitution of the home for shipwreck takes place in the last section of the essay, the "application" section, where the image of shipwreck is itself dissolved, transformed into a process where vulnerabilities are mobilized as assets: "But every jet of chaos which threatens to exterminate us is convertible by intellect into wholesome force. Fate is unpenetrated causes. The water drowns ship and sailor like a grain of dust. But learn to swim, trim your bark, and the wave which drowned it will be cloven by it and carry it like its own foam, a plume and a power" (W 6: 32).[29] Moreover, the fragmented allegory of the house that weaves in and out of this part of the essay, effectively displacing shipwreck, slowly subverts the rhetoric of homecoming as a trailing back to a cause. The issue of penetration is not rape and adventure, the familiar historical byproducts of theoretical aggression, but a Fourieristic coupling and harmony. True heroism resides in penetrating the sacrificial force at the center of the home from which we all depart, representation.

For Emerson, the issue is not so much mastery and control, those values most often associated with the masculine act of penetration; rather, the issue for him is the possibility that penetration could be revalued as a "wholesome force." Here his revised opinion of Fourier's theory of "passionate attraction" greatly assists him. Where once he understood the "ejaculations of a few imaginative men" to be a masculine and potentially dangerous method of troping, he now accepts the possibility that the "passions and retarding forces" of man might be converted to "wings" (W 6: 30).

The most obvious example of this transformation occurs at the opening of the last section, where Emerson describes the agonistic struggle of father and son. "We stand against Fate, as children stand up against the wall in their father's house and notch their height from year to year. But when the boy grows to man, and is master of the house, he pulls down that wall and builds a new and bigger" (W 6: 30). The destruction basic to this notion of the home is reinforced later in the essay when he portrays another typical domestic scene as the prevailing model of history: "History is the action and reaction of these two,—Nature and Thought; two boys pushing each other on the curbstone of the pave-

---

[29] Emerson may actually be alluding to the fact that Fuller was not a swimmer. A historical consideration of those people who literally "learned to swim" and those who did not would be of immense interest, since issues of gender and class obtained. I thank Richard Slotkin for a discussion of this issue as we considered together Fuller's terrible death by drowning.

ment. Everything is pusher or pushed; and matter and mind are in perpetual tilt and balance" (W 6: 43). Fourier saw the world's history as a sorry account of war, a barbaric system of confrontation much like the struggle between father and son that Emerson portrays here. Fourier's cunning resided in founding a system upon the thwarted passion generating the conflict. By continually identifying with the "pushed," Emerson employs a "Fullerized" Fourierism to transform this sacrificial model of history. In his allegory, thought is initially passive, a feminine force acted upon by a harsh, violent nature. His solution is not to make thought (that is, the son, or any initially passive agent) respond in kind; "Fate against Fate is only parrying and defence" (W 6: 25). Instead, like Fuller, he shows that we can all participate in something that disdains the foolish, repetitive conflict of individual personalities. To do this he summons an idea from Anaximenes used earlier in *Memoirs*, the idea that "Mind" is "in the air." His purpose there was twofold: to find what he calls a "sufficiently diffusive source" in order to show that "when all men breathed, they were filled with one intelligence," and to convince his readers that Fuller "had . . . these larger lungs" (MMF 1: 216). Now, in "Fate," he argues that "truth" is "in the air" and that "the most impressionable brain will announce it first" (W 6: 44). This demonstration enables him to end his paragraph about history with the argument he used in his lecture before the Woman's Rights Convention in Boston, namely that "women . . . are the best index of the coming hour" (W 6: 44). The vulnerability and negative power usually associated with women thus assumes a central position in his elaboration of history, as it did for Fourier. Where once he ruefully reported that temperament was "the iron wire on which the beads [were] strung" (CW 3: 30), he now celebrates temperament as a type of model for power. Temperament, like a certain paradigm of the home, reveals the texture and structure with which we work, providing the given of our lives, the text through which a provisional meaning must and can be negotiated.

Understanding all too well the difficulties of his argument about the "web of relation" (W 6: 37) between power and temperament, Emerson demonstrates how the old historical struggle between nature and thought, spirit and house, has been hypostatized in culture itself, with its division between public and private worlds.

> The bulk of mankind believe in two gods. They are under one dominion here in the house, as friend and parent, in social circles, in letters, in art, in love, in religion; but in mechanics, in dealing with steam and climate, in trade, in politics, they think they come under another; and that it would be a practical blunder to transform the method and way of working of one

sphere into the other. What good, honest, generous men at home, will be wolves and foxes on "Change" (W 6: 31).

The division is something like the division he earlier tried to impose on his own life between a religious freedom (once seen as aggressive as the marketplace) and domestic pieties, ruled by the tropes of traditional family life. His earlier argument that it would be a blunder to cross the operating principles of the two worlds here becomes impractical. Following Fuller's example, he makes a feminist argument for a genuine exchange between the two spheres of influence. He now looks upon both as allegorical fields, each acting as a type of supplement to the other.[30]

Like Fourier, Emerson uses a rather amusing if not ridiculous image to describe the method he means to promote:

> One key, one solution to the mysteries of human condition, one solution to the old knots of fate, freedom and foreknowledge, exists: the propounding, namely, of the double consciousness. A man must ride alternately on the horses of his private and public nature, as the equestrians in the circus throw themselves nimbly from horse to horse, or plant one foot on the back of one and the other foot on the back of the other (W 6: 47).

His call for a "double consciousness" (also described as a "cunning co-presence") (W 6: 47) is a rhetorical concession to allegory as a necessary process, rhetorical because he seeks to disrupt the traditional hierarchical movement of the symbol-making process reified in the divisions of culture. The humorous element of his call for a double consciousness is vital to its transformational power; like his conception of the right use of allegory, the humorous image of the circus rider works to release meaning from its grasp even when it invests that release with a type of value. The entire essay exploits this double consciousness about itself, particularly in the last section where the allegory of shipwreck is dissolved into the heterogeneous allegories of the home.

Fuller plays a substantial part in this formation. Indeed, Emerson's double consciousness resembles her double strategy and serves as an

---

[30] What is interesting in Emerson's revision of the dichotomy is how religion has now been subsumed under the feminine, domestic sphere; earlier, he had affiliated it with the masculine world of commerce. Here the world of commerce is narrated almost solely on the principles of aggressive troping, whereas the domestic world seems to be a haven for spirit. Still more impressive is the way that he understands the traps of both; spirit is no less violated in the troping of the home than it is in the release of commercial exchange, where it takes on the property of a commodity changing character with the vagaries of exchange.

endorsement of the conversation he shared with her.[31] Her relationship to this double consciousness becomes manifest in his statement that "the secret of the world is in the tie between person and event. Person makes event and event person" (W 6: 39). With this statement, he echoes the earlier crisis between house and spirit, where "the spirit made the house" and "afterward" the house "confined" the spirit (W 6: 9). In his attempt to link the concepts of person and event, the problem of the spirit and the house earlier presented itself as the useful substitute for the fragmented allegory of shipwreck, but now the concepts of person and event are recognizable as familiar historical terms substituting for the earlier figure of the house.

Emerson's transition to person and event plays on the fatal flow of cause and effect even as it attempts to skew it. If *cause* and *effect* are the terms used in empirical narratives, *person* and *event* are their substitutes in traditional historical narratives. Emerson seeks to interrupt the tidy narrative flow of cause and effect usually affiliated with a fatalistic history by putting them into a kind of disturbance or turbulence with each other. Fuller's shipwreck was the primary example of the facile infiltration of the principles of cause and effect into an understanding of history, person and event. He does not argue that Fuller was the cause of her shipwreck, though this was the common reading of her experience. Rather he wishes to show how cause and effect, person and event, and ultimately freedom and fate are on a different kind of continuum, one that unsettles the ties between them usually worked out by culture.

The problematic of the house and spirit, person and event, meets its most powerful reformulation and resolution in the form of a question that Emerson inserts along the way: "But where shall we find the first atom in this house of man which is all consent, inosculation, and balance of parts?" (W 6: 36–37). The answer resides in the question itself, with his punning inversion of the primal scene of the Bible (swerving as he does from "Adam" to "atom"). He disrupts the traditional operation of cause and effect by revealing how that which has priority, the Brownian movement of life, destroys the system of priority it appears to establish by manifesting a "cunning co-presence" within itself.

He repeats the process when he writes "the event is the print of your form" (W 6: 40). This locution recalls Emerson's discussion of writing in "Goethe," where he made a distinction between nature and the writer. If in nature "the narrative is the print of the seal," Emerson asserted that in

---

[31] Even the idea of a "cunning co-presence" can be said to emerge from a letter to Fuller. After reviewing her portfolio of letters, journals, and poems which she had lent to him, he requested to "see it again and again as it grows" because it would enable him to "have presence in two places" (EL 2: 142).

the writing of man "the report is something more than the print of the seal" (W 4: 262). In "Fate" he makes a similar attempt to show how the "irresistible dictation" (W 6: 4) of nature can be thwarted, moving in effect from natural disaster (shipwreck) to human creation (the home). Although he seems to give priority to experience over writing, his phrasing ("the event is the print of your form") disrupts "common sense" by revealing that the experience of an event is itself also a text or sign. Thus, that which is presumed to be anterior is already part of that which it becomes.

Because Emerson's method for the resolution of spirit and house, person and event assumes an elemental configuration, his most provocative demonstration of it occurs when he introduces the concept of steam in order to show the "cunning co-presence" of natural and allegorical properties. According to him, steam was once considered a "devil," but was transvalued into a "god" by the "Marquis of Worcester, Watt and Fulton" (W 6: 33). Here the movement from devil to god follows the traditional path of revolution, a reversal that destroys one hierarchical structure in deference to another. But when he goes on to use the terms of this revolution (terms borrowed not coincidentally from the field of religion) in a fable about society, the nature of the revolution goes through a significant transformation closely aligned with a Fourieristic construction.[32]

According to Emerson, the "opinion of million" was once perceived to be as dangerous as steam, accordingly controlled by "pil[ing] it over with strata of society,—a layer of soldiers, over that a layer of lords, and a king on top; with clamps and hoops of castles, garrisons and police." But when "believing in unity," the "Fultons and Watts of politics" "decided to form an "energetic" state, they grouped it "on a level" "instead of piling it into a mountain" (W 6: 34). Emerson effectively transforms the fabulous potential of steam: the "opinion of million" now permeates society, being neither a controlling nor controlled property. Although he shows how nature can provide a dangerous metaphor for society (the

[32] Here Emerson could have received support for his argument from Lazarus in his *Solar Ray* (New York: Fowlers and Wells, 1851), part 1: "Man remains inferior to the Lion or the Eagle, the Deer or the Thrush, in vigor, fleetness, independence, sanity, health, and happiness, so long as he seeks only a simple individual destiny, such as suffices to the inferior animals in awaiting their connection with the Harmonic Man. . . . It is in ratio as he associates and combines his forces that he rises in the scale of beings and of societies through the grades of the patriarchate and civilization; and all the great works of spherical unity, railroads, steam navigation, magnetic telegraphs, and even of local unity, such as gas works, steam mills, and the like, pivot upon the combinations of forces and the serial hierarchy of functions, whose theory now explained to us in the works of Fourier, enable us forthwith to advance with gigantic strides in the career of progress, by combining the development of the producer with that of the thing produced" (pp. 11–12).

"mountain" of society, with its "strata," upon "strata" is shown to need "clamps and hoops and castles, garrisons and police" to keep it in its "natural" state), he does not destroy the possibility that a useful metaphor can be drawn from natural properties, since the new model of society is decidedly based on a principle of energy. More important, perhaps, he makes the "energetic form of a State" a projection of the future and not an established historical fact. The "Fultons and Watts of politics" are no longer specific in time and place but playful tropes for the architects of social transformation.

In many ways this passage returns us to Cavell's argument that Emerson made a "realistic" resolution of Kant's two worlds of freedom and fate as "perspectives, aligning him with the reformulations of both Freud and Marx."[33] This is a vexed theoretical issue, to be sure, since there is considerable debate about the positive and negative results of such resolutions. Emerson's resolutions are far more indirect, precisely what Cavell finds so frustrating. Still, Cavell is correct to locate the power of the essay with Emerson's articulation of a continuous supplementation of ethical and cognitive fields.

The interaction of the two fields is most visibly portrayed in the third section of his essay, where Fuller makes her boldest appearance as the heroine of the essay. Emerson begins the section with his famous claim that "Fate has its lord; limitation its limits" (W 6: 22). His description of the power that forms that limit borrows once again from Fourieristic discourse. Fourier argued that man was part of a "stupendous Cosmogony," and Emerson agreed, offering "Man is not order of nature, sack and sack, belly and members, link in a chain, nor any ignominious baggage; but a stupendous antagonism, a dragging together of the poles of the Universe" (W 6: 22).[34] Those "poles" are transformed into two essential attributes of the human condition: thought and moral sentiment. In Emerson's account, both are important for the construction of agency. Thought alone, which "dissolves the material universe by carrying the mind up into a sphere where all is plastic" (W 6: 28), is not sufficient for that agency. It needs an ethical perspective driven by desire, or what Emerson calls "affection" (W 6: 28). Here we see the full development of his acceptance of Fuller's Fourierism. Agency comes not from the plastic attribute of writing alone, which has the ability to unset-

[33] Cavell, "Genteel Responses to Kant", p. 45.

[34] Emerson may have adopted this vocabulary from any number of sources, but among the most intriguing was Victor Henniquin, *Love in the Phalanstery*, trans. Henry James Sr. (New York: Dewitt and Davenport, 1849). Henniquin outlines three aspects to the theories of Fourier: industrial organization, "a Poetic and stupendous Cosmogony," and a "plan of organization for the minor relations, or those of the sexes" (p. 2).

tle all things; rather, it emerges from someone who can provide that disruption with an effective if provisional grounding.

Once again, Fuller's feminist conversation is the model for this type of grounding. Earlier in "Circles," Emerson distrusted his feeling about the ability to shake and rattle "all that we reckoned settled" (CW 2: 184), but now, given the provisional ethical position supplied by the idea of Woman, he can accept those moments when "literatures, cities, climates, religions leave their foundations and dance before our eyes" (CW 2: 184). Thus Fuller appears in the end of "Fate" as the model for this type of agency. In line with his revision of history and the usual formulation of cause and effect, her name is elided from the actual essay, even when it clearly manifests itself in his original journal entry. There he writes:

> A personal influence towers up in memory the only worthy force when we would gladly forget numbers or money or climate, gravitation & the rest of Fate. Margaret, wherever she came, fused people into society, & a glowing company was the result. When I think how few persons can do that feat for the intellectual class, I feel our squalid poverty (JMN 11: 449).

From this "feat" Emerson constructs his text of heroism for his reader, as "Margaret" now enters into the text as the "hero." "One way is right to go; the hero sees it, and moves on that aim, and has the world under him for root and support. He is to others as the world. . . . A personal influence towers up in memory only worthy, and we gladly forget numbers, money, climate, gravitation, and the rest of Fate" (W 6: 30).

Aware at last that the "personal influence tower[ing] up in memory" is Fuller, many readers will probably find the ascription of a masculine gender to the "hero" somewhat troubling.[35] But Emerson suspends the gender in his final sentence where the "personal influence towers up" in ambiguous form. Given the gathering hostility toward Fourier's theories in the culture, he must have felt that Fuller's release from the false claims of history could only occur in this simultaneous veiling and exposure. The veiling came in the submergence of her name, but the larger and more productive exposure came in his radical advocacy of her method, a procedure lending renewed power to his thought.

---

[35] Emerson obviously felt it would have been counterproductive to make Fuller's identity known, though here it is interesting to consider how many of his readers caught the reference. I suspect that there were more knowing readers than one might initially assume, particularly given Emerson's confession in the *Memoirs* that her "personal influence" was the strongest he had ever experienced. See MMF 1: 298: "Of personal influence, speaking strictly,—an efflux, that is, purely of mind and character, excluding all effects of power, wealth, fashion, beauty, or literary fame,—she had an extraordinary degree; I think more than any person I have known."

Index

Emerson (*cont.*)

25–27, 30, 42–43, 46, 48, 50, 53–57, 91, 118, 127, 131, 145, 148–54, 159, 183, 187–88, 222, 227–37, 251, 258, 260, 269, 271, 280–89, 293; friendship of, with Fuller, 1, 14–17, 24, 29–30, 32–58, 61, 66–67, 78–79, 81, 85–86, 91, 158, 165, 192–93, 237; Fuller's influence on, 4, 8, 29, 34, 39, 44, 48, 79, 128, 131–39, 144–60, 194, 221–37, 269–94; on Fuller's life, 43, 239–68; influence of, on Fuller, 24, 115–18, 124, 203–5, 243; and organized religion, 32, 41, 52, 53, 55, 228, 278–79, 285; skepticism of, 44, 46, 52, 53, 55, 91–92, 117–18, 126–60, 187, 221n, 225n, 226, 231–32, 252, 269, 270, 279; titles of works by, 246; writing style of, 15, 41, 56–57, 131, 142–43, 267. *See also* journals; letters (Emerson's); marriage; *names of specific works*

Emerson, Waldo (son), 42–43, 49–50, 127, 143, 145, 146, 148, 274

Emerson, William (brother), 39, 45

Engels, Friedrich, 6, 192, 207n, 210

"English Writers Little Known Here" (Fuller), 208

Essays, First Series (Emerson), 30, 85

Essays, Second Series (Emerson), 42, 55, 85, 187, 221n, 270; Fuller's influence on, 117n, 125–60; Fuller's review of, 193; influence of, on Fuller, 161, 203–4; and reform, 16n, 193; and romance, 30, 129–30, 148, 154–55, 160, 224. *See also names of specific essays*

Eurydice (mythological figure), 181–82, 185, 186

"Experience" (Emerson), 17, 18, 188, 224–25, 274; on reform movement, 127, 144–45; romance in, 130, 131, 148, 154–55; voice in, 143, 149–55, 268

Farnham, Eliza, 182n

fatalism, 276–77

fate, 43, 45, 46. *See also* "Fate" (Emerson)

"Fate" (Emerson), 16n, 30, 43, 58, 135, 232, 233, 239–40, 251, 269–94

Felman, Shoshana, 8, 9

Feminine Soul (Novalis), 165–66

feminism: and deconstruction, 8, 17–24, 54, 62–66, 125, 128–30, 271–72; definition of, 2–3; double strategy of, 17, 128–30, 144, 145; and Emerson, 3, 15–18, 24, 30, 32–58, 127–28, 140–41, 155, 159–60, 237, 242–43, 250–51, 257–89; and Fourierism, 25–26, 37–39, 85, 128, 129; and Fuller's theory of reading,

159–60, 162–63, 198–200; and Native American plight, 97–125, 162, 167–70; and translation, 59–61. *See also* agency; double strategy; women

Fetterley, Judith, 9, 21n

Fiedler, Leslie, 20n

Fish, Stanley, 78n

Foucault, Michel, 40n, 44

Fourier, Charles: critiques of Western culture by, 25, 52–57, 98, 114–19, 162, 170, 200–201; and feminism, 25–26, 37–39, 85, 128, 129; influence of, on Emerson, 25–27, 30, 42–43, 46, 48, 50, 53–57, 91, 118, 127, 131, 145, 148–54, 159, 187–88, 193, 222, 227–37, 251, 258, 260, 269, 271, 280–89, 293; influence of, on Fuller, 13, 25–27, 30, 36, 48, 50, 52–55, 98, 114–16, 120, 124–25, 162–63, 170, 172, 184–85, 189, 199, 243, 244, 278; influences of Goethe and, on Fuller, 40, 54–55, 185–87, 221–23, 227, 272, 276; theories of, 25–26, 37–39, 116–18, 137–40, 142, 146, 155, 172–74, 199, 205, 285; views of, in *Tribune*, 190, 221. *See also* marriage; transition

"Fourierism and the Socialists" (Emerson), 53, 148, 227–28

Franklin, Benjamin, 244–45

freedom, 43, 45, 270–71, 273, 279, 293

free love, 170–73, 280–81

Freud, Sigmund, 119, 293

Frothingham, O. B., 127, 140

Fugitive Slave Law, 259, 273

Fuller, Arthur, 74

Fuller, Margaret: apparent absence of, from Emerson's works, 39, 294; Conversations in Boston of, 30, 78, 154n, 163–67, 199, 255–57; critical response to, 1, 4–5, 7–8, 10–11; death of, 29–30, 43, 57, 85, 237, 240, 269, 274–75, 279, 282–92; education of, 6, 10, 60, 78, 96; Emerson's assistance to, 79; Emerson's influence on, 24, 115–18, 124, 203–5, 243; feminism of, 2–4, 10, 24, 243, 251–57; forms of writing favored by, 2, 13–14; Fourier's influence on, 13, 25–27, 30, 36, 48, 50, 52–55, 98, 114–16, 120, 124–25, 162–63, 170, 172, 184–85, 189, 199, 243, 244, 278; friendship of, with Emerson, 1, 14–17, 24, 29–30, 32–58, 61, 66–67, 78–79, 81, 85–86, 91, 158, 192–93, 237; influence of, on Emerson, 4, 8, 29, 34, 39, 44, 48, 79, 128, 131–39, 144–60, 194, 221–37, 254–55, 269–94; journalism of, 6–7, 9, 10, 23, 189–220; Midwestern trip of, 52, 97–124, 126,

Reading Women Writing

A SERIES EDITED BY

Shari Benstock and Celeste Schenck

Woman and Modernity: The (Life)Styles of Lou Andreas-Salomé
by Biddy Martin
In the Name of Love: Women, Masochism, and the Gothic
by Michelle A. Massé
Outside the Pale: Cultural Exclusion, Gender Difference, and
the Victorian Woman Writer
by Elsie B. Michie
Reading Gertrude Stein: Body, Text, Gnosis
by Lisa Ruddick
Conceived by Liberty: Maternal Figures and Nineteenth-Century American Literature
by Stephanie A. Smith
Feminist Conversations: Fuller, Emerson, and the Play of Reading
by Christina Zwarg